CW00811114

THE NINE YEA:
AND THE BRITISH ARMY
1688-1697

IN MEMORY OF
THOMAS CONDRON THOMPSON

THE NINE YEARS' WAR AND THE BRITISH ARMY 1688–1697:
The operations in the Low Countries

JOHN CHILDS

MANCHESTER
UNIVERSITY PRESS
Manchester and New York

distributed exclusively in the USA and Canada by St. Martin's Press

Published by Manchester University Press
Oxford Road, Manchester M13 9NR, UK
and Room 400, 175 Fifth Avenue, New York, NY 10010, USA
www.manchesteruniversitypress.co.uk

Distributed in the United States exclusively by
Palgrave Macmillan, 175 Fifth Avenue,
New York, NY 10010, USA

Distributed in Canada exclusively by
UBC Press, University of British Columbia, 2029 West Mall,
Vancouver, BC, Canada V6T 1Z2

British Library Cataloguing-in-Publication Data is available

Library of Congress Cataloging-in-Publication Data is available

ISBN 978 0 7190 8996 1 paperback

First published by Manchester University Press in hardback 1991

This paperback edition first published 2013

The publisher has no responsibility for the persistence or accuracy of URLs for any external or third-
party internet websites referred to in this book, and does not guarantee that any content on such
websites is, or will remain, accurate or appropriate.

Printed by Lightning Source

Contents

Abbreviations

The following abbreviations have been used in the notes.

Add. MSS.   Additional Manuscript
ARA   Algemeen Rijksarchief, The Hague
Archives d'Orange-Nassau *Archives ou Correspondence inédite de la Maison
   d'Orange-Nassau*, 3rd series, ed. F. J. L. Kramer (Leiden, 1907–9)
BCRO   Berkshire County Record Office, Reading
BL   British Library
BNB   Biographie Nationale de Belgique (Brussels, 1866–1944)
Bod. Lib.   Bodleian Library, Oxford
Childs, *Nobles, Gentlemen*   John Childs, *Nobles, Gentlemen and the Profession
   of Arms in Restoration Britain, 1660 to 1688* (London, 1987)
CJ   Journals of the House of Commons
CMC   Cumberland Map Collection, Royal Library, Windsor Castle
CSPC   Calendar of State Papers Colonial: America and the West Indies
CSPD   Calendar of State Papers Domestic
CTP   Calendar of Treasury Papers
DBF   Dictionnaire de Biographie Française (Paris, 1933 cont.)
DCRO   Dorset County Record Office, Dorchester
DNB   Dictionary of National Biography
DNF   Dictionnaire de la Noblesse de la France, ed. A. de la Chenaye-Desbois et
   Badier (Paris, 1863–73, 3rd ed.), 19 vols.
GAA   Gemeentearchief, Amsterdam
Harl. MSS.   Harleian Manuscripts, British Library
HMC   Reports of the Royal Commission on Historical Manuscripts
HSL   Het Staatsche Leger, 1568–1795, eds. F. J. G. Ten Raa, F. De Bas & F. W.
   Wijn (Breda, 1911 cont.), 8 vols.
IESCRO   Ipswich & East Suffolk County Record Office, Ipswich
Japikse (Welbeck)   *Correspondentie van Willem III en van Hans Willem Bentinck*,
   ed. N. Japikse (The Hague, 1927–8), 2 vols.
Japikse   *Correspondentie van Willem III en van Hans Willem Bentinck*, ed. N.
   Japikse (The Hague, 1932–7), 3 vols.
LG   London Gazette
LJ   Journals of the House of Lords
LUL   Brotherton Library, University of Leeds
Luttrell, *Historical Relation*   Narcissus Luttrell, *A Brief Historical Relation of State
   Affairs, 1678–1714* (Oxford, 1857), 6 vols.
MS.   Manuscript
MSS.   Manuscript
NCMH   New Cambridge Modern History
NLI   National Library of Ireland, Dublin

NNBW *Nieuw Nederlandsch Biografisch Woordenboek*, eds. P. C. Molkhuysen,
  P. J. Blok & Fr. K. H. Kossman (Leiden, 1911–33), 10 vols.
n.s. new series
OED *Oxford English Dictionary*
o.s. old series
PRO Public Record Office, London
SP State Papers, Public Record Office
Walton Clifford Walton, *A History of the British Standing Army, 1660–1700*
  (London, 1894)
WO War Office Papers, Public Record Office

Dates, spelling and punctuation

The theatre of war in the Low Countries was separated from the British
Isles by a mere 150 kilometres of the North Sea but on each side of the
water a different system of dating was in operation. For easier reference
between events in Europe and in England, all dates in the text have been
given in dual form with the English Old Style (Julian) date preceding the
Continental New Style (Gregorian) date. In the seventeenth century, the
Julian Calendar was ten days behind the Gregorian. The new year has been
taken to begin on 1 January and not on Lady Day, 25 March.

Spellings in quotations from manuscripts and printed sources have been
modernised. The punctuation has been altered in those instances where the
meaning of the original was not immediately apparent when it was read
for the first time at normal speed.

Maps and place-names

Many of the towns, villages and districts in modern Belgium and Luxembourg have place-names which can be rendered in either French or Flemish. To achieve some consistency in the text, the form most commonly used in English has been adopted though this is sometimes in one language and sometimes in the other. The following list presents the French and Flemish renderings of those places mentioned in the text which suffer from dual spellings. The form adopted in the text has been italicised.

As few readers will have ready access to seventeenth century maps, all place-name spellings conform to those found in the following modern maps on which the campaigns can best be traced:

Belgien-Luxemburg, 1:300,000 (Kümmerly & Frey, Bern, 1987).
Belgique-Luxembourg, 1:350,000 (Michelin, Brussels, 1987), Sheet 409.
France: Champagne-Ardennes, 1:200,000 (Michelin, Paris, 1988), Sheet 241.

FRENCH	FLEMISH/DUTCH/GERMAN	FRENCH	FLEMISH/DUTCH/GERMAN
Aix-la-Chapelle	*Aachen*	*Liège*	Luik
Alost	Aalst	*Lierre*	Lier
Anvers	*Antwerp*	*Lincent*	Lijsem
Ath	Aat	*Louvain*	Leuven
Audenarde	*Oudenarde*	*Malines*	Mechelen
Bethlehem Abbey	Bertem	*Menin*	Menen
Bois-le-Duc	*'s-Hertogenbosch*	*Mons*	Bergen
Braine-le-Comte	's-Gravenbrakel	*Namur*	Namen
Bruges	Brugge	*Nieuport*	Nieuwpoort
Courtrai	Kortrijk	*Nivelles*	Nijvel
Deinse	*Deynze*	*Ostend*	Oostende
Dixmude	*Dixmuyde*	*Perwez*	Perwijs
Enghien	Edingen	*Renaix*	Ronse
Furnes	Veurne	Roulers	*Roeselare*
Gammerages	Galmaarden	St. Trond	*St. Truiden*
Gand	*Ghent* (Gent)	*Soignies*	Zinnik
Grammont	Geraadsbergen	Termonde	*Dendermonde*
Halle	Hal	*Tirlemont*	Tienen
Helchin	Helkijn	*Tongres*	Tongeren
Huy	Hoei	*Tournai*	Doornik
Jodoigne	Geldenaken	*Tubise*	Tubeke
Kenoque, Fort	*Knokke, Fort*	*Visé*	Wezet
Leau	Zoutleeuw	*Waremme*	Borgworm
Lessines	Lessen	Waver	*Wavre*
		Ypres	Ieper

Contemporary maps used

In addition to the three modern maps listed on p. viii, the following contemporary maps have been employed frequently whilst composing the text.

Petrus Mortier, *Téatre de la Guerre en Flandre et Brabant, Cleve, Cologne et le Bas-Rhein* (Amsterdam, 1690)

Guillame Del Lisle, *Le Cours du Rhin depuis Worms jusqua Bonne et les Pays Adjacé* (Paris, 1704)

BL, Add. MSS. 64,108–9, The Louvois Atlas.

PRO, MPH 16/Parts 1 & 2, 'Camps et Ordres de Marches de l'Armée du Roy en Flandres commandé par Monseigneur le Maréchal de Luxembourg en l'année 1690', by S^r. Pennier, Ingénieur et Géographe du Roy.

PRO, MPH 17/Parts 1 & 2, 'Camps et Ordres de Marches de l'Armée du Roy en Flandres commandé par Monseigneur le Maréchal Duc de Luxembourg, en l'année 1691', by S^r. Pennier.

PRO, MPH 18/Parts 1 & 2, 'Camps et Ordres de Marches de l'Armée du Roy en Flandres commandé par Monseigneur le Maréchal Duc de Luxembourg, en l'année 1692', by S^r. Pennier.

PRO, MPH 19/Parts 1 & 2, 'Camps et Ordres de Marches de l'Armée du Roy en Flandres commandé par Monseigneur le Maréchal Duc de Luxembourg, en l'année 1693', by S^r. Pennier.

PRO, MPH 20/Parts 1 & 2, 'Camps et Ordres de Marches de l'Armée du Roy en Flandres commandé par Monseigneur le Maréchal Duc de Luxembourg, en l'année 1694', by S^r. Pennier.

Jean de Beaurain, *Histoire Militaire de Flandre depuis l'année 1690 jusqu'en 1694 inclusivement* (Paris, 1755), 2 vols. Beaurain's maps are printed copies of those by Pennier (PRO, MPH 16–20).

Other contemporary maps are cited in the footnotes to each chapter.

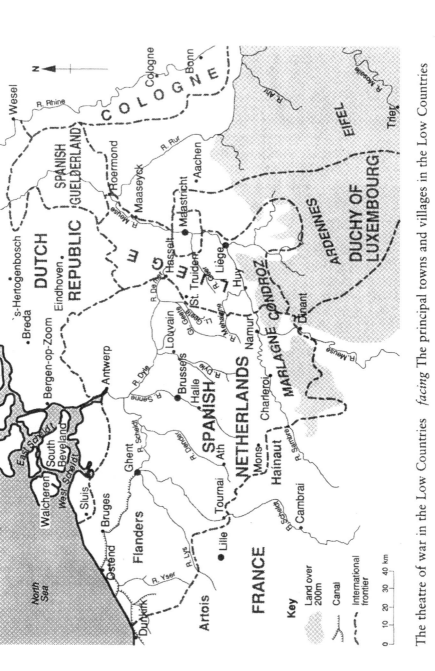

The theatre of war in the Low Countries   *facing* The principal towns and villages in the Low Countries

Key

Land over 200m

Canal

International frontier

0 10 20 30 40 km

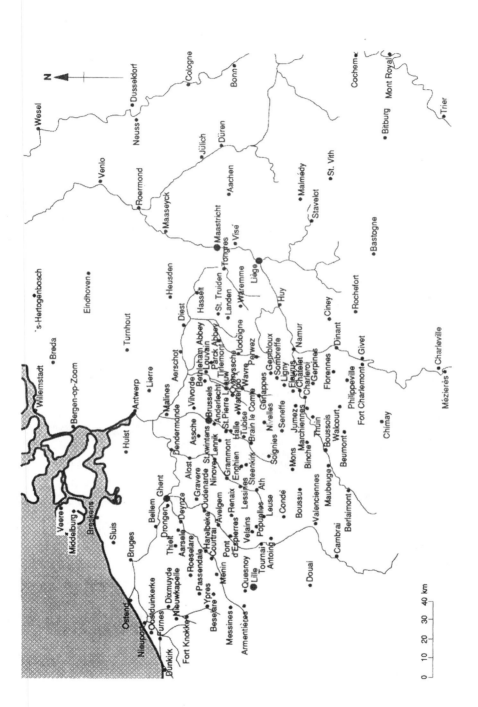

N

Willebroek

MALINES

R. Demer

Willebroek Canal

R. Senne

ALOST

Vilvorde ● Perk

● Asse

Diegem

● Bethlehem Abbey

LOUVAIN

Zellik

● Parck Abbey

Dilbeek ●

Anderlecht

BRUSSELS

TIRLEMONT

NINOVE

St.Pieters Leeuw

Forest of Soignes

Meerdaal Wood

R. Great Geete

● St.Kwintens Lennik

● Gammerages

Overyssche

● Jodoigne

HALLE

Wavre

Little Geete

● Enghien

Tubise

Ottignies

Brain-le-Chatau

R. Dyle

Steenkirk ●

Brain-le-Comte

Bois St.Isaac

Promelles

Genappes

R. Mehaigne

● Soignies

NIVELLES

GEMBLOUX ●

Sombreffe

R. Piéton

Pont-à-Celles

Ligny

Fleurus ● Mazy

MONS ●

Trazegnies

Jemeppes

NAMUR

● St. Ghislain

Gosselies

Auvelais

Floreffe

Piéton

Farciennes

Marchiennes

Montignies-sur-Sambre

Fontain l'Evêque

Chatelet

Binche

CHARLEROI

Merbes St. Marie

Gerpines

Merbes-le-Chateau

THUIN

Ham-sur-Heure

R. Heure

DINANT

R. Sambre

Thy-le-Chateau

MAUBEUGE

WALCOURT

FLORENNES

BEAUMONT

● Boussu

● PHILIPPEVILLE

● Cerfontaine

FORT CHARLEMONT

GIVET

R. Meuse

0   10   20 km

Southern Brabant

Introduction

Participating countries put maximum effort into the Nine Years' War. Eighty per cent of England's revenues were devoured by the conflict and one in seven of her adult males served in the army. The level of commitment was restricted by the bluntness of the armies and navies, the inefficiency of government and the enormous problems of supplying the forces with food and forage. France, England, the United Provinces and Austria maintained massive military establishments during the war, usually recruited by varieties of conscription, from economic and bureaucratic resources which predated the Industrial Revolution by a century. National establishments, the total number of military personnel employed by the state, were to remain high throughout the eighteenth century but the size of field armies grew out of control in the course of the Nine Years' War. From an average of around 25,000 during the Thirty Years' War, field armies had waxed to nearly 100,000 by 1695. They had become too large too soon. The strain of paying and feeding huge concentrations of soldiers reduced England to a fiscal crisis whilst France stumbled to peace under the weight of a shattered economy. After 1697, the mean size of European field armies diminished to about 60,000 men until the French Revolutionary Wars brought new and enduring growth. Revolutions in industry, government and transport were required before mass field armies could be adequately supported. The Nine Years' War represented a premature and unsustainable peak in the size of field armies. This was a consequence of the broad coalition of catholic and protestant states which opposed France, each willing to contribute troops to a confederate army maintained by the combined financial power of England and the Dutch Republic. Faced with numerous enemies, France reciprocated by raising large numbers of soldiers concentrated into sizeable field armies.

These lumbering monsters could only engage in slow and methodical operations, reflecting both the physical constriction of massive bodies of men packing into the small geographical region of the Spanish Netherlands and the ensuing logistic nightmares. The French had so many troops that they were able to build a series of field fortifications, or 'lines', along the length of their frontier with the Spanish Netherlands and the Bishopric of Liège creating an almost continuous front. However, despite their limitations, armies did not lack the will to win. William III, Boufflers and Luxembourg were all aggressive commanders but their methods were seriously hampered by numbers, supply and communications. In order to overcome some of these handicaps, the French practised a vigorous economic warfare. The Spanish Netherlands and Liège were sucked dry through forced contributions and requisitions whilst, at sea, French privateers from Dunkirk and the Channel ports sought to sever the jugular of British and Dutch foreign trade. Slow martial results in the Low Countries encouraged the combatants to seek indirect strategies. The British and Dutch, the 'Maritime Powers', raided the coasts of France and Louis XIV showed great interest in trying to subvert the English political regime by invasion and exploitation of the Jacobite movement. For the first time in a major European war, the colonies in the West Indies and North America played a significant role in the broadening of strategic choice.

The fact that all the armies fought with similar weaponry and none possessed a technological advantage further emphasised the importance of numbers. More than training, drill or the quality of the troops, it was numbers that mattered. The majority of infantrymen never fired their muskets in anger; their task was to march and counter-march. Even if it had been desirable, the turn-over rate from sickness and desertion was of such enormity that it would probably have been impossible to achieve a high level of proficiency amongst the wartime levies. Battlefield formations were adapted accordingly. Infantry fought in battalions five or six lines deep giving safety in numbers plus ample time to reload the cumbersome firearms. Equally important, only about twenty per cent of a battalion was in contact with the enemy at any one time, a factor which tended to bolster confidence and morale whilst diminishing combat effectiveness and efficiency. The two and three-rank battalions of the mid-eighteenth century demanded a much superior standard of drill, training, competence and leadership. The foot soldiers of the Nine Years' War were better suited to fighting from trenches, ramparts and fortifications rather than in the open field. The armies were consciously geared towards the dominant forms of warfare: manoeuvre and the siege.

The 'new military history' has principally been concerned with the study of military institutions and their interaction with social, political and economic forces. Campaign history has been deliberately eschewed as representative of the 'old military history', a form too often practised by 'amateur' historians and retired service officers. Expressed crudely, the 'new military history' has been adopted by 'professional' historians at universities to bring academic respectability to a branch of their discipline which has long been the poor relation of its political, religious, social and economic brothers. A modus vivendi between the two varieties is slowly emerging, especially in the military history of the twentieth century, but divergence remains strong in the early modern period. It is, of course, an artificial division. Armies were raised, at great expense, to conduct legalised violence against both the internal and external enemies of the state. Their campaigns, actions and methods are as historically vital and relevant as their institutions and personnel. To study armies without investigating their wars and battles makes as much sense as learning to write but not to read. After completing a trilogy devoted to the social and political history of the British army between 1660 and 1702 – 'new military history' – the time has come to complete the job by donning the coat of the 'old military historian' and observing that army in action during the Nine Years' War.

This book has evolved from the author's *British Army of William III, 1689–1702* (Manchester University Press, 1987) in which Chapter 10 was designed as a bridge into a projected military history of the Nine Years' War in the Low Countries. Some additional material relating to Flanders has been extracted from that book as well as from *Armies and Warfare in Europe, 1648–1789* (Manchester University Press, 1982). In both cases, the information has been substantially revised and expanded. Although the British army fought in Ireland, Scotland, the colonies and on the French coast, these campaigns have been excluded. Sufficient coverage exists although new accounts are planned. The Low Countries were the seat of war, the theatre in which the main armies of the Grand Alliance opposed the principal forces of France. The opening chapter considers the political origins of the war whilst the next two discuss its conduct and the organisation of the armies. The remainder is concerned with the military history of land operations in the Low Countries although international politics and diplomacy continue to have their place in order to set the context for the campaigns. Of necessity, the approach is narrative and chronological. The sources do not permit an overt concentration on the British corps, a development which would be undesirable as it only formed a part of the cosmopolitan army of the Grand Alliance, but the British contribution has been highlighted wherever possible and relevant. There is a dearth of personal memoirs and information relating to the British in Flanders: Sergeant Milner, Peter Drake and John Deane served in the next war.

Most of the sources describe the grand operations of the armies but omit the humdrum everyday lives of the officers and soldiers.

Maps have been extensively employed. Although contemporary cartographers were notorious for plagiarising one another, their sheets have proved invaluable in assessing camp sites, visualising the topography and vegetation, tracing communications, illustrating the details of fortifications and in calculating distances and routes of march. Long hours have been spent poring over manuscripts maps in the British Library, the Public Record Office, Windsor Castle and The Hague. The resultant information has often been impressionistic and not easy to footnote or attribute but it has been immensely useful. Sketch maps have been provided but the campaigns involved such a plethora of remote villages and hamlets that it might be easier to follow the narrative on the three modern sheets mentioned on page viii. As far as possible, on its first appearance in the text, each smaller settlement has been located by a rough compass bearing and an approximate distance from a major town. This should enable readers to make sense of the campaigns from the sketch maps.

Colonel Clifford Walton marched over this ground ninety-six years ago. The debt to him is huge. However, as this is supposedly history and not fiction, Uncle Toby and Corporal Trim have no place even though their creator, Laurence Sterne, almost certainly used the books of Edward d'Auvergne as one of his principal sources.

I

THE NINE YEARS' WAR

The Nine Years' War, which occupied much of western Europe between 1688 and 1697, has at least five different names.[1] The title, War of the Grand Alliance, infers responsibility for causing the conflict on the coalition of catholic and protestant states which opposed the ambitions of Louis XIV of France. French historians, perhaps, tend to employ this nomenclature. A close neighbour, but different in one vital respect, is the term, the War of the League of Augsburg. Again, culpability rests firmly at the door of the Dutch and the Germans, and indeed Spain and Sweden, but whereas England signed the Grand Alliance she was never a member of the League of Augsburg. This usage suits British 'Tory' historians wishing to depict the struggle as a dispute between continental powers into which England was drawn as a consequence of the invasion of William of Orange in 1688. In North America and the West Indies, it is usually known as King William's War, suggesting that the colonial hostilities spilled over from the confrontation between England, France and the Dutch Republic in mainland Europe. John B. Wolf has gone so far as to see this international war as but a single stage in the 'world war' which commenced with the Turkish invasion of Hungary and Austria in 1683 and ended at Carlowitz in 1699.[2] The only neutral and generally satisfactory solution is to revert to chronology and refer to the Nine Years' War.

The period from the outbreak of the War of Devolution between France and Spain in 1667, through the Franco-Dutch War (1672–8), the Nine Years' War and concluding with the War of the Spanish Succession from 1702 to 1714, was dominated by the foreign policy of Louis XIV. By collecting these events under the phrase, the Wars of Louis XIV, blame for the instability of late seventeenth century Europe is placed squarely upon the shoulders of the French monarch. To historians, particularly the French and North Americans who dominate the investigations of both the foreign and domestic affairs of Louis, his motivations remain uncertain.[3] His foreign policy has been variously described. He may have been concerned with the rise to economic dominance of the United Provinces of the Dutch Republic and felt the need to repress and control these conspicuously successful rebels. The quest for 'natural frontiers' to secure the territorial integrity of France has been put forward as a prime motive. Louis needed to block the 'gates' through which France had been invaded from Germany and the Spanish Netherlands during the sixteenth and early seventeenth centuries. Much of this reasoning assumes too great a degree of sophistication in a basically crude age. Policy is not a word which ought to be applied to seventeenth century governments without considerable caution. It carries too many connotations derived from the twentieth century in which governments have been made responsible and responsive to broad electorates through the process of democracy. Seventeenth century government was, more often than not, simply reactive, government by the seat of the pants. Some recent historians have been applying this more primitive view to Louis XIV.[4] Rather than being some visionary, he was a sovereign deeply rooted in the processes and attitudes of his own times. His foreign dealings were not all part of a giant masterplan aimed at the creation of a stronger and economically more powerful France. Louis hovered and havered, compromised and altered, and was rarely consistent in anything apart from misjudgements. He was impatient, regal and overbearing with an unsubtle mind which failed to appreciate the more delicate points of diplomacy and international relations. Above all, he lacked patience. He seemed unable to wait upon events and frequently forced the pace in an effort to ripen unripe time. In an epoch where communications were extremely slow and unwieldy, this constituted a perilous weakness of character.

If Louis's foreign policy was controlled by any single issue, then it was the seemingly juvenile but entirely acceptable contemporary notion of 'La Gloire'. As the personification of France, Louis needed to flex his martial muscles and acquire glory and honour for himself, his dynasty and, indirectly, for France as well. In effect, this boiled down to one objective: the limitation and suppression of France's principal enemy, Spain. By the time of Louis's reign, this traditional rivalry between the Bourbons and the Spanish Habsburgs was already out-of-date, a fact which Cardinal Mazarin had realised, but Louis reverted to the attitudes of Richelieu and the previous century and pursued Spanish power wherever it could be encountered. In reality, by the second half of the seventeenth century Spain was a spent force and no danger to France. The position had been reversed and France was now the principal political and military power in western Europe. Louis's foreign policy had surprisingly little contact with the actualities of the political situation. Spain was no more than the medium through which Louis aimed to achieve personal glory. Because of this gratuitous aggression towards Spain and her allies, France became isolated and was obliged to fight the majority of her wars without substantial assistance. Apart from some small, client states in Germany, only during the War of Devolution did France enjoy the alliance of the Dutch whilst England half-heartedly supported her during the opening two years of the Franco-Dutch War between 1672 and 1678. Not until the War of the Spanish Succession, with the Spanish crown now safely in the Bourbon grasp, did France enter a major conflict in conjunction with another power. Up to this point, France had faced and fought coalitions of great and small powers mainly from her own resources. It is possible that Louis's motives altered in the decade between the Peace of Nijmegen in 1678 and the commencement of the Nine Years' War in 1688. Initially he was youthful and bellicose, anxious to prove himself; the more mature man wished to preserve his conquests and his strategic offensives masked a more defensive political stance.

Louis did not even have a consistent policy towards the French frontiers. There is no convincing evidence that Louis adopted Vauban's scheme for the creation of a systematic border between France and the Spanish Netherlands to establish a pré carré, or duelling field, to protect the hinterland from invasion and depredation. Towns and fortresses were captured and their fortifications improved but not according to any pre-ordained plan. The French north-eastern frontier became more readily defensible during Louis's reign simply because France seized many of the important towns and cities during the War of Devolution and the Franco-Dutch struggle. Vauban and his engineers consolidated French territorial gains.[5] Yet, the majority of French historians agree that, whatever his demerits, Louis XIV was the founder of modern France. Whether by design or accident, he formulated the borders which have remained largely unchanged to the present day and made those frontiers difficult to violate. His absolutist rule did much to bring internal unity to France by breaking down some of the religious and provincial boundaries within the state and through the provision of a centralised and effective administration. Above all, he exploited the conditions which allowed France to realise her considerable potential and become the principal European power of the later seventeenth and eighteenth centuries.

Despite Louis XIV's obsession with the Spain of Carlos II, his main opponent after 1672 was William III, Prince of Orange-Nassau and Stadholder of the United Provinces of the Dutch Republic. Although Louis harboured a deep loathing for the Dutch on account of their Calvinist faith, their economic hegemony and the fact that they were rebels who had succeeded in overthrowing their legitimate sovereign, the United Provinces were not the sole object of Louis's aggression. In the War of Devolution, France had assisted the Dutch in their simultaneous conflict with England, known as the Second Anglo-Dutch War, 1665–1667, in order to further her own ambitions in the Spanish Netherlands. Even in 1672, when the French assault on the United Provinces brought the Dutch Republic to its knees and French cavalry to the gates of Amsterdam, the target of Louis's armies was not just the humiliation of the Dutch but also the creation of an expedient with which to draw Spain into a war with France.[6] However, the subtleties of Machiavellianism on this grand scale were entirely lost upon the States-General. The danger and then the actuality of the French attack were sufficient for the traditional offices of the Captain-Generalcy of the Dutch armed forces and the Stadholderate of the United Provinces to be restored to the House of Orange in the person of Prince William. He immediately repaid the States-General for their trust by halting the French advance behind the flooded polders of the 'Water Line'. Thereafter, William regarded Louis as a personal enemy, an attitude which was exacerbated by the French occupation of Orange in 1680 and Louis's increasing antipathy towards the Huguenots. Until his death in 1702, William pursued his vendetta against Louis XIV whom he viewed as a menace to the physical safety of the United Provinces.

The intentions of Louis XIV towards the United Netherlands were masked by the question of the Spanish Netherlands. This remnant of nine of the original seventeen provinces of the Burgundian, and later Spanish Netherlands, stood as a buffer zone between the Dutch Republic and north-eastern France. After eighty years of fighting for their independence from Spain, the Dutch well understood that the southern frontier of the Spanish Netherlands effectively formed the southern border of the United Provinces themselves. This conquest was expressed both politically and manifestly in the form of Dutch troops garrisoning Spanish fortresses. By the treaty of 9 April 1668, Dutch troops were allowed to occupy a number of towns in the Southern Netherlands, whilst another agreement, on 30 August 1673 in the heat of the Franco-Dutch War, extended the concept. These arrangements were the forerunners of the Dutch Barrier, created in 1697 at the Peace of Rijswijk, which gave the Dutch the right to garrison Mons, Charleroi, Namur, Luxembourg, Oudenarde and Nieuport.[7] This principle of garrisoning the fortresses of a neighbouring, friendly power was extended by the States-General to the line of the Lower Rhine. The towns and forts belonging to the Elector of Brandenburg's Rhenish provinces — Wesel, Büderich, Orsoy and Rheinberg — were also occupied by Dutch troops between 1648 and 1714. Maastricht, captured in 1632 and perhaps the most important fortress of the United Provinces, was an enclave within the Bishopric of Liège. In modern parlance, the Dutch practiced forward defence and sought to defend their country by fighting the principal invader and predator, France, in the Spanish Netherlands.

Naturally, this policy of 'scheidingszone' required an absolute guarantee of good relations with Spain. When this condition failed to apply, as in 1701 when France occupied the whole of the Spanish Netherlands after Louis XIV had accepted the terms of the will of Carlos II of Spain concerning the succession to the Spanish crown, the States-General found the French on their own southern border and their forward garrisons in the Barrier Fortresses isolated and forced to surrender. Luckily for the Dutch, French policy usually played directly into their hands. Spain was extraordinarily difficult for France to reach. Direct invasion across the Pyrenees was not feasible and the imagined danger to France from Spain could not develop from that direction. Similarly, the Spanish possessions in Northern Italy, especially Milan, did not pose even an imaginary threat to France. The sole feasible route by which Spain could endanger France lay through the Spanish Netherlands and the Duchy of Luxembourg. In response, Louis's vendetta against the Spanish Habsburgs was principally expressed by campaigns of extension into these regions. The reciprocity was rendered easier by geography. No natural boundary existed between France and the Spanish Netherlands just as no dividing line separated the Spanish Netherlands from the Generality of the United Provinces. In Luxembourg as well, the hills and forests of the Ardennes stretched from the Grand Duchy into north-eastern France. The decision of the Dutch to seek a buffer state between themselves and France was a decision to which there was no alternative. French attitudes towards Spain made the Southern Netherlands into that buffer state. It was an international Hobson's Choice.

The Treaty of Nijmegen, which brought the Franco-Dutch War to an end in 1678, slightly favoured the United Provinces. By this means, Louis XIV hoped to distance the Dutch Republic from Spain and some of the Germanic states of the Holy Roman Empire. The King of Spain lost much of Franche-Comté to France and the frontier between France and the Spanish Netherlands was rationalised to the benefit of Louis. Vauban and his engineers were immediately set to work fortifying the new posts and towns. Lorraine, except for its capital Nancy, was returned to Duke Charles V, but as he refused to take possession of his duchy without Nancy and Longwy, French troops remained in occupation of the entire territory effecting a *de facto* annexation. This gave France a reasonably logical frontier with the Rhenish states of the Holy Roman Empire but in Alsace the situation remained confused with the Emperor retaining the important fortress of Philippsburg and the French acquiring Freiburg with a right of passage to and from Breisach. Finally, the Elector of Brandenburg was required to return Pomerania to Sweden, France's sole, although less than effective ally during the Franco-Dutch War.[8] Louis emerged from the war as the leader of the most powerful nation in Western Europe, the new arbiter of continental affairs. During the next decade of 'peace', France retained a standing army of 140,000 men, supported by a substantial population and a relatively buoyant economy, the creation of Colbert. Unfortunately for both France and Europe, this was insufficient for the vainglorious Louis. Conscious that his partial success had been gleaned from a war in which France had failed to achieve decisive results, Louis set about consolidating his gains and attempted to elevate France to an unassailable international position. This ambition was sought through two policies which were to become closely related: the continuation of the search for defensible frontiers in the Rhineland and Alsace, and the creation of a unified kingdom cemented by universal adherence to the catholic religion.

Through the medium of the Parlements at Besançon and Metz and the Superior Court at Breisach, Louis pressed his claims to the remainder of Franche-Comté, Alsace, the entirety of Lorraine and the three bishoprics of Toul, Metz and Verdun. By 1680, the County of Montbéliard, to the west of Basel, had been separated from the Duchy of Württemberg, and the noblemen of Alsace had been obliged to swear an oath of allegiance to Louis XIV. During August 1680, all of Alsace, with the exception of the key city and fortress of Strasbourg, had been transferred from the suzerainty of the Holy Roman Emperor, Leopold I, to Louis XIV. Whilst the court at Besançon extended Louis's kingdom to the banks of the Rhine, the Chamber of Reunion in the Parlement of Metz looked to the tangle of feudal principalities and territories which made up the French boundary with the Duchy of Luxembourg. This court moved with indecent haste, claiming and seizing lands from the

Holy Roman Emperor, the King of Spain, the King of Sweden, the
Electors of Trier and Mainz and many other smaller German princes.
Even the peninsula of Mont Royal on the Moselle near Traben-Trarbach
was taken and fortified in order to control traffic on the river and
communications with the Rhine. Nearly all of the Duchy of Luxembourg had been occupied by French troops by the beginning of September 1680 who quietly established a blockade of Luxembourg City.
When the Governor of the Spanish Netherlands refused to cede territories claimed by Louis, French soldiers invaded Flanders and ruined the
countryside in retaliation. Not all of these annexations enjoyed the
cloak of contrived legality. The principality of Orange on the River
Rhône was seized in 1680 for no better reason than the fact that the
Prince of Orange was an enemy of Louis XIV and the fief had become
a haven for Huguenot refugees. On 30 September, Louvois entered
Strasbourg with a French army and Marshal Nicolas Catinat took
possession of Casale on the upper reaches of the River Po in the Duchy
of Montferrat. Strasbourg was the victim of naked force whilst Casale
cost Louis one million livres and an annual rental of 60,000 livres
payable to the Duke of Mantua.[9]

This mixture of bullying diplomacy and armed force during a period
of supposed peace, rang alarm bells across much of catholic and protestant Europe but concerted action against France still lay in the future.
Emperor Leopold I was distracted from affairs in Western Europe by
a serious revolt in Hungary and then, in 1683, the Turks invaded
Hungary and Austria along the line of the Danube Valley and laid siege
to Vienna. In the face of this Islamic incursion, Louis XIV withdrew his
soldiers from the blockade of Luxembourg City in order to demonstrate
Christian solidarity. In reality, the Turks attacked Austria with French
connivance and Louis had little doubt that Leopold would succumb to
the superior forces of Sultan Mehmet IV. With the Emperor defeated
in the east, reasoned Louis, Germany would be unable to resist further
French depredations along the Rhine. His calculations went hopelessly
awry. Whilst von Stahremberg's resolute defence prevented the Turks
from taking Vienna, King John Sobieski of Poland and Duke Charles
V of Lorraine assembled a relief army of Germans, Austrians and Poles
and launched a hugely successful assault on the Turkish encampment.
The Turks abandoned the siege and fled down the Danube into Hungary
with the Imperial troops in pursuit.[10] Cynically, within a few days of
hearing of the Turkish humiliation, Louis ordered his troops to resume
the blockade of Luxembourg City. In desperation, Spain, the major loser
at the Peace of Nijmegen, declared war on France. It was hopelessly one-

sided. Spain had no allies and was unprepared for war. France invaded the Spanish Netherlands, bombarding cities and instituting a full-scale investment and siege of Luxembourg City. Louis's next victim was the free city of Genoa. Its politics were anti-French, largely because it was the port through which Habsburg troops and supplies passed *en route* from Spain to Milan and Austria, and in the short Hispano-French War of 1683–4 she had allowed Spain to recruit soldiers within her territories and had provided ships for the Spanish fleet. As Europe's attention focussed on the Siege of Luxembourg, the French Mediterranean fleet appeared before Genoa and the resulting bombardment left well over half the city in smoking ruins.

Now at the height of his power, Louis magnanimously proposed a truce between Austria, Spain and France which would guarantee the new frontiers of France for a period of twenty years. French gold cowed the Orangists and the War Party in the United Provinces; Spain had been reduced to impotence in Flanders and Luxembourg and desperately needed peace; Austria preferred to exploit her new-found opportunities in Hungary rather than contain France in the west; the Elector of Brandenburg was of the opinion that France was so strong that a compromise had to be sought; and England undertook to guarantee the truce. No power could stand against France. An additional attraction of the truce which was signed at Regensburg, or Ratisbon, in 1684 was that it did not concede a legal right to France's ill-gotten gains. It was only a truce for twenty years, not a treaty or a permanent settlement and, as such, it was compatible with the interests of all parties. The victims of Louis's aggression, actual or prospective, gained a breathing space, and Louis hoped that French diplomacy could convert the truce into an international treaty within the alloted span of twenty years. Yet, although the Truce of Regensburg marked the high-water mark of Louis XIV's territorial expansion, it also established his reputation as an over-mighty monarch who threatened Europe's stability through a mixture of illegality, terror and violence. This was exacerbated by the campaign against the Huguenots.

The Edict of Nantes of 1598 had given the Huguenots the right to enjoy public worship and permission to garrison and fortify certain towns in the south and west of France. In an age which believed that confessional unity was one of the principal bonds which held a state together, the Edict was tantamount to the creation of two separate French polities. Richelieu clawed back some of the lost ground for the catholic majority, ending with the siege and capture of the Huguenot stronghold of La Rochelle in 1628, but the onset of the Thirty Years'

War and the Frondes distracted the French monarchy from solving the Huguenot question. Louis, at the beginning of his reign, exuded a simple tolerance towards his protestant subjects, who now possessed no more than a freedom of worship and education. As he became increasingly aware of his growing absolutism, both nationally and internationally, tolerance metamorphosed into bigotry and pressure on the Huguenot communities commenced. From the termination of the Franco-Dutch War in 1678, the under-employed army was used to terrorise the Huguenots into converting to the Catholic faith. With the penalty for refusing to embrace Rome taking the form of 'dragonades', the enforced free-billetting of deliberately ill-disciplined soldiers, the majority rapidly changed religion but sufficient held to their beliefs for a series of horror-stories, many of them grossly exaggerated, to flood across protestant Europe. The Revocation of the Edict of Nantes by the Edict of Fontaine-bleu in 1685 was the final act in the seven-year campaign against the French protestants. Thousands of Huguenot refugees left France to settle in Holland, Brandenburg, Switzerland and England, living witnesses to the religious intolerance of Louis XIV. When England, Germany, the Netherlands and other European protestant states were slowly coming to terms with the concept of religious toleration, Louis was visibly moving in the opposite direction. To the brutality and immorality of his international dealings was added the label of violent and intolerant Catholic extremist. The supreme arrogance of the French king was about to be tested.[11]

The four years following the signature of the Truce of Regensburg were marked by the gradual coalescing of an alliance to oppose Louis and an alteration in the international climate which was disadvantageous to France. The initial consequence of the Revocation of the Edict of Nantes was to convince many protestant German states that France was not going to act as their protector against the intolerant catholic practices of Emperor Leopold I. Although Leopold was busy reconquering Hungary and imposing Catholicism as he progressed, he was not on the verge of trying to overthrow the Religious Peace of Augsburg or the Peace of Westphalia, nor was he a foreign aggressor seizing territory along the Rhine Valley on the most specious of pretexts. Based on the decision of the Diet of Regensburg in 1681 to raise 40,000 German troops from the Circles of the Empire, a German army had come into existence under the command of Count George Frederick von Waldeck and this force had been hardened in the campaigns against the Turks. The majority of these troops had been raised in Swabia and Franconia under the terms of the Luxembourg Alliance of 1682. Count

Hohenlohe, the Imperial envoy in Franconia, intended to use this alliance as the basis for a more general, German league aimed at the protection of Teutonic lands from French aggression and incursion. In 1685, a number of German states, of which the largest was Bavaria, formed the League of Augsburg to defend German soil. Spain, Sweden and the Emperor joined the League in the following year. In July 1686, William of Orange and the Great Elector of Brandenburg, met at Cleves and although no formal alliance resulted the Elector appeared to be making a statement to the effect that he was about to abandon his policy of adopting a cautious neutrality towards France. This change in direction was also detectable in his enthusiastic welcome of Huguenot refugees to Berlin.[12] Brandenburg was well on the way to providing the troops which were to enable William of Orange to invade England in 1688.

An alteration in the political balance was also noticeable in the United Provinces after 1684. The Republican Party, whose principal base was the province of Holland and its capital city of Amsterdam, tended to favour a policy of peaceful compromise towards France. They argued that the Dutch Republic lived from the fruits of seaborne trade and France, with its long coastline along the English Channel, the Atlantic and the Mediterranean, was in a strong position to interrupt Dutch commerce. Besides, much Dutch trade, especially in foodstuffs, ran directly into France. The Republican interest also believed strongly in the importance of the buffer-state in the Spanish Netherlands and tried to prevent Franco-Spanish hostilities from overflowing into a war which might endanger the security of the Spanish Netherlands. To this end, the Republicans strongly supported the Truce of Regensburg as it halted a conflict between France and Spain which threatened the safety of the Southern Netherlands. Louis's aggressive diplomacy and his persecution of the Huguenots did much to convince the Republican Party in Holland that France was not to be trusted, particularly as the accession of the catholic James II to the throne of England in 1685 presaged an alliance between England and France which might well ring the death-knells for Dutch maritime enterprise.

The balance of power was also shifting in central Europe. The Imperial forces besieged and captured Budapest in 1686 and Belgrade in the following year. Further to the south, Venice was enjoying marked success against the Turks with the capture of Athens in 1687 and much of the Morea in 1688. It was now quite feasible for Leopold to reduce the weight of his military effort against the Turks and turn some of his forces, especially the German Army of the Circles, towards the Rhine

Valley to resist further French attempts at territorial acquisition. Whereas Louis had offered and agreed to the Truce of Regensburg on the assumption that twenty years was a very long time in international politics and that he would have ample opportunity to translate his seizures into permanent accretions through formal treaties, the rapid collapse of the Turkish war effort threw these plans into chaos. Instead of being coerced into confirming the terms of Regensburg, Leopold would soon be in a position to head a coalition of German princes with the aim of limiting French advances and recapturing lost lands. Desperately, an attempt was made through Pope Innocent XI and directly to the Diet at Regensburg to force the Emperor and the German princes to transfer the terms of the truce into a lasting peace settlement. All parties declined although Leopold saved French face by stating that he would 'respect' the truce of 1684 'even though a peace might be made with the Turks'.

With his calculations having proved inaccurate and many of his infantry dying or deserting as they laboured to bring water to the fountains and canals of Versailles, Louis witnessed affairs coming to a head in the Electorate of Cologne. Maximilian Heinrich, the Archbishop-Elector, had been an ally and client of France since 1671 when his Rhenish fortresses had proved vital staging posts for the French attack on the United Provinces. As the old Elector approached the end of his life in 1688 two main contenders for his throne emerged. The first was Cardinal Wilhelm von Fürstenberg, a French agent who had been one of Louis's advisers and negotiators in German politics for well over twenty years. Fürstenberg was accepted by the cathedral chapter as coadjutor in January 1688 and when Maximilian Heinrich expired on 3 June 1688 there seemed little obstacle to Fürstenberg's succession. The second candidate was the young Prince Joseph Clement of Bavaria, a nephew of Maximilian II Emmanuel, the Elector of Bavaria, and a brother of Maximilian Heinrich of Cologne. At the election, neither Joseph Clement nor Fürstenberg received the necessary two-thirds majority and the impasse was referred to Pope Innocent XI for adjudication. There was no prospect of Innocent, who had been insulted and ill-treated by Louis, finding in favour of the French candidate and Joseph Clement was duly installed as Archbishop-Elector on 26 August 1688. In itself, the Cologne affair need not have led to a general European war. Certainly, the League of Augsburg and the Imperial successes in Hungary had greatly altered the balance of military and political force in western and central Europe in the four years since the Truce of Regensburg, and the high-handed French treatment of states

from Rome to Brandenburg had shifted many rulers from neutrality
into positive antipathy towards France, yet Cologne was no Sword of
Damocles hanging over Versailles. It was a small, Rhenish principality,
important because it gave France access, via Luxembourg, to the Rhine
and formed one of her spheres of influence in Germany. However,
rather than sitting back and waiting for the dust to settle in order to
assess the real impact of his defeat at Cologne, Louis, urged on by
Louvois, decided upon a pre-emptive strike against the Holy Roman
Empire. He was persuaded into this course of action because of the
mounting power of his opponents beyond the Rhine. Since 1686, William of Orange had done much to improve and enlarge the army and
navy of the United Provinces, and the League of Augsburg, with Spanish
and Imperial support, promised to provide the basis for a German army
much larger than that derived from the organisation of the Circles.
Above all, after their defeats of the Turk, Leopold and the Imperial
army were in a position to intervene along the Rhine at any time.[13]

On 14/24 September 1688, a French army under the Dauphin and
the Duke de Duras with Vauban and his engineers in attendance,
invaded the Rhineland and laid siege to the Imperial fortress of Philippsburg. This fort covered Alsace from attack from the north and defended
an important bridge across the Rhine. Built to counter-balance Landau,
Philippsburg stood one mile to the east of the Rhine on the River Saltza,
but a very large crownwork, then a hornwork and finally a ravelin took
the fortifications up to the banks of the Rhine. A bridge traversed the
river from the ravelin and landed in another crownwork which formed
a bridgehead on the Rhine's west bank.[14] The possession of Philippsburg
would have greatly strengthened the French frontier along the Rhine
and was the key post between Luxembourg, which had been annexed
in 1684, and Strasbourg which had been seized in 1681. Louis probably
hoped for a short, sharp war. Oddly enough, for a monarch who prized
military glory and endeavour so highly, his greatest successes had not
come through war but during the period of the reunions and the international bullying between 1679 and 1684. The attenuated and utterly
decisive war against Spain in 1683–4 was probably the model upon
which Louvois based his scheme to assault Philippsburg in 1688. He
intended to capture the fortress before Leopold and the German armies
could intervene and then present Europe with a *fait accompli*. It might
even have provided sufficient pressure for translating the Truce of
Regensburg into a permanent peace settlement. If the worse came to
the very worse, and there is no indication that Louis was so pessimistic,
the annexation of the fortress of Philippsburg would at least give France

a solid eastern frontier. The siege of Philippsburg took two months, the defence aided by heavy rains. As the prospect of a quick war receded, Louis and Louvois decided to accept the advice of Chamlay and force the German princes to come to terms by the 'ravaging of the Palatinate', a systematic destruction of the villages, towns, fortresses, supplies and livestock in the Palatinate, Trier and Württemberg to create a *cordon sanitaire* through which the German armies could not march in order to relieve Philippsburg or interfere in French manoeuvres. The policy of terror and maximum violence was extended from diplomacy and politics into the conduct of warfare itself. The eastern and north-eastern frontiers of France had become a gigantic fortress and just as the opening move in any siege was the razing of buildings outside the glacis within the defenders' field of fire, so Louvois wanted to clear away the German fortresses and fortified towns along the central and southern sections of the Rhine Valley. Tübingen, Heilbronn, Heidelberg, Worms, Mainz, Mannheim, Eslingen, Oppenheim, Pforzheim, Kaiserslauten, Spiers, Coblenz and Cochem were all partially or totally destroyed. French raiding parties stretched as far into Germany as Nuremberg and Würzburg.[15] The diplomatic defeat in Cologne had led to the siege of Philippsburg. The vigorous defence of this post had led to the ravaging of the Palatinate. That act was sufficient to unite many German princes in a resolve to resist Louis XIV. Louis's invasion of Germany also created sufficient time for William of Orange to put into place the final piece in the puzzle – England.

Since the restoration of Charles II in 1660, English foreign policy had been vacillating and uncertain. Although he frequently tried to pursue two contradictory directions in overseas relations, Charles was basically pro-French but needed to hide his francophile sympathies from a suspicious and protestant House of Commons. As a result, Charles's dealings with foreign governments tended to be reactive and inconsistent. Until 1670, or perhaps as late as 1672, the power and aggression of Louis XIV's France were not readily apparent to English politicians. There had been the warning scare of the War of Devolution between 1667 and 1668 but it had been settled relatively rapidly although at some cost to Spain and to the physical security of the United Provinces. England had concentrated on her own ancient disputes with the Dutch over trade, colonies and fisheries, culminating in the Second Anglo-Dutch War between 1665 and 1667.[16] After this defeat, Charles reluctantly acquiesced in the Triple Alliance of 1668 in which England, the United Provinces and Sweden guaranteed the Treaty of Aix-la-Chapelle and England and the Dutch Republic additionally agreed to support one another if they were attacked by France. Charles was restless in this contrived position. He liked France and all things French having spent many of his formative years in that country and he was, after all, the son of a French princess. However, Charles realised one central fact which escaped the attention of most of his contemporaries and has evaded subsequent historians.

France was not a physical danger to England during the seventeenth century. There was no risk or threat of a French invasion of the British Isles and this enabled Charles to treat with France in a relatively detached manner. After Colbert's economic and naval reforms during the decade of the 1660s, the French had become more substantial rivals on the high seas and in the American and West Indian colonies but their efforts were still below the scale of those of the English and the Dutch. In economic terms, the United Provinces remained the principal opponents of England's major international interests throughout the reigns of Charles II and James II leaving France as a convenience, a diplomatic tool which Charles could turn to his advantage in domestic politics without embroiling England in gambles and enterprises which he could not control. The Secret Treaty of Dover of 1670 recognised this simple truth and set the seal for the remainder of Charles II's tenure of the throne. Even though Parliament grew increasingly alarmed at the intentions of the French, especially after their attack on the United Provinces in 1672, and worried incessantly at the brutal and religiously-inspired foreign policy of Louis XIV after that date, Charles could only be pulled away from his pro-French stance temporarily. The decision to enter the Franco-Dutch War on the side of the protestant angels in 1678 too late to commit any British troops to actual combat was Charles's response to six years of parliamentary pressure. Once the Popish Plot and the Exclusion Crisis had been successfully weathered, Charles reverted to his clandestine alliance with France and was happy to spend his last years taking French subsidies in order to keep England neutral within Europe. The reality was that France needed England's help and alliance far more than England needed international assistance from France. England was a naval power with little or no interest in territorial expansion into Europe. France was essentially a land-based state which possessed definite territorial objectives but with the additional need to balance the Dutch and the Spanish at sea. England's ships were of great concern and potential value to France. Charles II cynically exploited and used Louis XIV for his domestic aims of religious toleration and the extension of royal authority and the central-isation of government. The fact that members of the Country Party in

Parliament during the 1670s were also content to receive French bribes on occasion, indicates that perhaps the fear of France which fuelled so much of the politics of Charles's reign was less than genuine. France was no more than a pawn within the context of the internal political struggles between Charles II and the Country interest.

Yet, the place of England within the European context was shifting. At the beginning of the seventeenth century, England had been an offshore island of some importance in continental politics. By the Treaty of Westminster in 1604, where she ended her war with Spain, England entered a long period when she was of little or no account, distracted from Europe by internal political crises which resulted in two civil wars. There followed a decade of political experimentation that made her a pariah amongst the monarchical states across the narrow seas. Some movements back towards a higher international profile occurred during the Commonwealth with the initial Anglo-Dutch War between 1652 and 1654 and Cromwell's war with Spain which led to the Western Design in 1654 and participation in the capture of Dunkirk and Mardyke in 1657 and 1658. Gradually, under the restoration monarchy, England rose in importance in the western world. This was partly because of her strategic geography, lying between France, the United Provinces and the Spanish Netherlands. More significantly, England developed rapidly during the second half of the seventeenth century. Her colonies in North America and in the West Indies increased in number, waxed in population and contributed to the economy of the mother country. England's military and mercantile fleets expanded massively under the protection of the Navigation Acts, whilst her agriculture and manufactures moved steadily forwards. The standing army became a permanent fixture and numbered around 40,000 men by 1688. On top of all this was the commencement of the 'Financial Revolution', that maturation of the system of government borrowing which had begun with the introduction of the excise in 1643, had taken account of the need for war finance during the Civil Wars, had maintained the Cromwellian military machine during the years of the Commonwealth and had developed through the reform of the Treasury after 1667. By 1688, the English financial and banking system was sufficiently sophisticated and flexible to support the insatiable demands of war. No longer was England an offshore island of no account in the affairs of Europe. On the contrary, her participation in continental politics had become vital for whichever state or group of states was to be blessed with her alliance.

When the catholic James II ascended the English throne in February

1685, there seemed a possibility that England might end her period of biased neutrality in Europe. From the very beginning of his brief sojourn on the throne, James's relations with his nephew and son-in-law, William of Orange, deteriorated through a series of relatively minor disagreements. Trade, the harbouring of religious and political dissidents in the United Provinces and the control of the six British regiments in the Dutch service all contributed to the souring of Anglo-Dutch friendship. Over the questions of religion and the succession to the English throne, these trivial disputes grew into a major diplomatic impasse. William, who as a nephew of James II had a remote claim to the throne in his own right, had married James's eldest daughter, Mary, in 1677. As James and his Italian queen, Mary of Modena, were childless, William's wife was the heir apparent. William surmised that James, as a catholic, was more likely to side with France during any international confrontation than with the protestant United Provinces or the League of Augsburg. As the tension in Europe mounted during 1687 and early 1688, the neutrality of England became an increasingly urgent matter for the Prince of Orange. England's financial, military and naval power was so considerable that whichever state secured the alliance of King James might well prove successful in any forthcoming general European conflagration. William's concern and calculations were proved to be correct. If James had hung onto his throne and if he had decided to throw in his lot with Louis XIV, then England's contribution might well have tipped the scales against the future Grand Alliance during the Nine Years' War. There were harbingers to enhance William's fears. The Anglo-French Naval Agreement of April 1688, whereby Louis undertook to pay part of the cost of the maintenance of an English squadron in the Downs, looked suspiciously like the opening round in a formal alliance between England and France. William took no chances, and used this event as an excuse to fit out the Dutch fleet. The recall into England of the six British regiments in the Dutch service on 14/24 March 1688 did not appear to be the act of a disinterested neutral. Again, William exploited the occasion and raised more troops for the Dutch army without arousing undue suspicion.

However, the condition of England caused equal unease. Through his crude and clumsy combination of increasing the authority of central, royal government whilst attempting to undermine the Anglican Church and introduce a toleration for catholics and protestant dissenters, James created a domestic situation which William totally misunderstood. Indeed, there were many in England who made it their business to ensure that William did misread the omens and William was very much the happy victim of misinformation and biased intelligence. By the summer of 1688, William was fairly certain that the English were going to rebel against the excesses of King James. From this probable scenario William extrapolated the conclusion that such a rising might well result in a republican political settlement, as had been the case in the aftermath of the English Civil Wars. If there was to be a revolt that might topple James, then William had to place himself at the head of that movement to make sure that it was directed onto the course that he required. As the rumours and reports from England grew in volume during the spring and summer of 1688 and the murmurs of possible war increased from the Rhineland and France, William took the decision to intervene in England with the support of a substantial army. It was an enormous political and military gamble which came within an ace of being sunk beneath the waves of the North Sea. Contrary to all expectations, particularly those of James II and Louis XIV, William's amphibious expedition managed to cross the sea, land in Devon, take complete control of events and force James to retire to France in fear of his life. William of Orange had achieved the military and political coup of the century and placed himself on the thrones of England, Scotland and, after 1691, Ireland as well.[17]

However, the corollary of William's dramatic venture was not an English declaration of war on France. William, whose plan was that England should serve as a magazine to fuel the coming war with France, did not appreciate that his expectations did not match those of the English political nation. William had come to England after receiving an invitation signed by just seven individuals and his expeditionary force had been assisted by a conspiracy in the English army, navy and court which might have numbered two hundred people at the very most. The vast majority of the English political classes had not sought or asked for a Williamite intervention in their affairs, did not want that intervention and saw no necessity for that intervention. Even those few soldiers, sailors and politicians who had taken an active part in assisting William's passage into England had intended that the Prince should act as an arbiter between themselves and their errant king. The chosen medium for this mediation was a Parliament, freely elected. Once that body had been summoned and had deliberated, William, supposedly, would be able to return to the United Provinces to pursue his vendetta against Louis XIV. Few seemingly suspected that William sought the crown of England for himself or that his motive was not only dynastic but also to bring England into the war against France on the Dutch side. If Englishmen had divined such aims they would probably not have invited him in the first place but would have endured the remaining years of James II, or taken action amongst themselves. As the Marquis of Halifax explained in 1689, William 'hath such a mind to France that it would incline one to think he took England only in his way.'[18] The Convention Parliament did not see that the offer of a joint-monarchy to William and Mary carried with it the corollary of a declaration of war against France. Luckily for William, events moved in his favour.

Although Louis knew of William's plans to invade England when he launched the Dauphin towards Philippsburg on 14/24 September 1688, he also based his assumptions on false intelligence. By attacking this vital Rhine fortress, Louis thought that the States-General would not allow William to leave the United Provinces undefended and would veto his expedition. Even if this failed to materialise, the French enjoyed the comforting prospect that William's invasion of England would prob-ably result in a civil war which would tie William down, involve Dutch resources on a considerable scale, emasculate England and leave the League of Augsburg leaderless and disunited. Louis's secondary calcu-lations were more precise than his initial thoughts except that the expected civil war occurred in the backwaters of Ireland and Scotland and not in mainland England. William himself had to endure an anxious winter in London as he waited for the Parliament to conclude their constitutional debates. He knew that the United Provinces were at their most vulnerable in winter when the natural defences of the canals, rivers and waterways frequently froze over. It was far easier to attack the Dutch Republic in winter than in summer. Fortunately, the crisis passed.

With Count von Waldeck and the Dutch army guarding the Lower Rhine and General Hans Adam von Schöning commanding the Brand-enburg corps towards the Middle Rhine, the United Provinces were adequately covered from any attempt by Marshal d'Humières's army against the vulnerable south-eastern frontier which had proved the Achilles' Heel in 1672. Also on 12/22 October 1688, Frederick William of Brandenburg, John George III of Saxony, Ernest Augustus of Han-over and Charles of Hesse-Kassel reached an agreement at Magdeburg which mobilised the forces of northern Germany. After the fall of Belgrade on 27 August/6 September, the Emperor Leopold had released the Swabian, Franconian and Bavarian contingents from the Imperial army and had sent them under the command of the Elector Maximilian of Bavaria to defend Southern Germany. The French themselves were far too preoccupied creating the *cordon sanitaire* in the Palatinate to consider serious intervention in the Spanish Netherlands or to move against the south-eastern Dutch provinces along the line of the Rhine.

Louis, by his decision to besiege Philippsburg, granted William six precious months in which to stage and complete his bloodless conquest of England. If Louis had moved towards the Lower Rhine or the Spanish Netherlands or, even better, taken no military action at all, then the States-General would probably have refused William of Orange permission to mount his expedition.

Yet there still had to be some reason, an English reason, for entering into a war with France. William could advise, cajole and bluster but his position in England in 1689 was weak and Parliament had to be convinced in order to provide sufficient funds to finance the war effort. This was the principal stumbling block. Like most European countries, England's national finances had been shattered by the high cost of continental war during the sixteenth and early seventeenth centuries. Henry VIII had started the rot with his gratuitous wars against France and incurred such hideous expenditure that his successors learned to be wary of all foreign entanglements. The wars of Elizabeth I against Spain and in Ireland established massive debts which bedevilled most aspects of the reign of James I, and the 1620s were also overshadowed by the cost of war as James I and Charles I played around on the fringes of the Thirty Years' War. The naval conflicts with the Dutch between 1652 and 1674 had been costly enough but the collective mind of the House of Commons shuddered at what the upkeep of a major commitment of land forces to the continent would involve in order to deflect Louis XIV from the Spanish Netherlands and the gates of the Dutch Republic. However, there were many instruments upon which the new king could play. The expulsion of the Huguenots had been as ill-received in England as elsewhere in protestant Europe and the feeling that England was a part of the protestant brotherhood of nations was strong, especially after the religious experiences during James II's reign. French influence and French gold had been a corrupting influence in English political life during the restoration monarchy and were deeply resented. Above all, it was the activities of ex-King James which sounded the tocsin that swung Parliament behind William's war policy.

Under the Duke of Tyrconnel, Ireland had been turned into a catholic state between 1685 and 1688. Protestants had been dismissed from the army, the civil administration, the judiciary and local government to be replaced by catholic Irish. On the flight of James II to France, Tyrconnel showed every sign of wishing to negotiate with England, probably with the intention of seeking some manner of semi-independent status for his homeland. Tyrconnel, the lion and champion of the new catholic Ireland free from protestant control, soon sensed that his decision to seek a settlement with William and Mary might forfeit the basis of his support. Consequently, he reneged on the discussions and instead decided to utilise the opportunity to rid Ireland of the last vestiges of protestant military power. James II had sought refuge in France where he had been welcomed with open arms by Louis XIV in a calculated display of public sympathy and friendship. The Sun King appreciated the enormity of the strategic weapon which had arrived on his shores. He insisted that James should make immediate endeavours to regain his thrones. With great reluctance, James agreed to try, leaving St. Germain-en-Laye on 15/25 February to journey to Kinsale. By the end of February, the Irish Rebellion was gaining strength and the protestants had been penned back into Ulster and were only offering consistent resistance at Londonderry and Enniskillen. James rode into Dublin on 24 March/3 April. Supported by French gold, French troops, French generals and the leading French diplomat, the Comte d'Avaux, it was abundantly clear that Louis was intending to play James II against the new regime in England for all he was worth.

The States General of the Dutch Republic declared war on France on 27 February/9 March 1689 and this was followed by an offensive compact between the Dutch and the Holy Roman Emperor, the Grand Alliance, on 2/12 May. This accord set out to restore Europe to the boundaries which had been settled at the Peace of Westphalia in 1648 and by the Peace of Nijmegen in 1678. Spain and the Spanish Nether-lands declared war on France on 23 April/3 May 1689. William, as King of England, and the Duke of Lorraine joined the Grand Alliance on 9/19 December 1689 and the Duke of Savoy and the King of Spain added their signatures in June 1690. In August 1689, Christian V of Denmark agreed to a treaty whereby he provided William III with 7,000 troops in return for a subsidy. The Elector of Brandenburg was already allied to both the States-General and the Emperor. The Elector of Bavaria consented to add his name to the Grand Alliance on 24 April/4 May 1690. On 16/26 April 1689, the House of Lords unanimously resolved that if the King thought fit to enter into a war with France, then it would provide every parliamentary assistance. Three days later, the House of Commons concurred and William III and Mary declared war on France on 7/17 May 1689. The English had decided to fight France in order to preserve Ireland and to protect the new regime against the return of James II backed by Gallic soldiers and money. Whereas France had posed no physical danger to England before 1688, after the Glorious Revolution Louis XIV had every excuse to stage an invasion of England in order to help restore the catholic Stuarts.[19]

English politicians had not sought the Glorious Revolution. Left to themselves, the evidence suggests that they would have waited for James to die and then have accepted Mary through the proper channels. The birth of the Prince of Wales on 10/20 June 1688 rather upset this complacency and resignation but infant mortality rates were extremely high in the seventeenth century. Even if the Prince had lived, Parliament could have confounded James's attempts to repeal the Test Acts and the Penal Laws. An insurrection against the King was the very last resort and spoken of by only a few wild men in 1688. Despite all these reservations, by December 1688 the English found themselves deserted by their legitimate sovereign, occupied by a foreign army and faced with a political *fait accompli*. The Parliament effected a constitutional settlement which made the best of a bizarre and unwanted situation, giving William the crown that he craved hedged in by some constitutional safeguards. England went to war with France in 1689 because Louis XIV threatened to overthrow the Glorious Revolution and its precarious political settlement by supporting the old king against the new. Civil war, a horror which many contemporary gentlemen knew from first-hand experience, was to be avoided at all costs even if the only escape from this evil was entry into the massive financial commitment of a European war.

To begin with there was no clear understanding as to what the English contribution to the war would be. Many favoured a purely naval role; it was supposedly cheaper in terms of cash, and it would protect and enhance English trade whilst interrupting that of the enemy. However, there existed a defensive treaty with the United Provinces which had been signed in 1678, a leftover from the time when Charles II had entered the very last phase of the Franco-Dutch War. After announcing 'a sincere, firm and perpetual peace and good relations' between England and the Dutch Republic on land and sea, the treaty pledged both parties to send help to one another within two months of either side being attacked. The scale of this assistance was laid down in the 'Articles Separés'; ten thousand men and twenty men-of-war, either of which could be augmented by mutual consent. These forces were to come under the operational command of the power which was suffering aggression and were obliged to take part in 'all military duties and services of war'. As this treaty had never been repealed by either side, it was the obvious point of reference in deciding the initial English commitment to the armies of the Grand Alliance in the Low Countries and Germany.[20]

Whether the Glorious Revolution of 1688 was a real revolution in

England's political and social structure remains in debate,[21] but it certainly witnessed a reversal in her foreign policy. Louis's pre-emptive strike against Philippsburg witnessed the beginnings of the waning of French power. She was not ready for a major war of attrition in 1688 but was prepared only for a short terror campaign. The resultant Nine Years' War stretched and broke her resources. The passing of French grandeur was reciprocated by the rise of England, and after 1707, Great Britain. From grovelling as a grateful recipient of French subsidies during the reigns of Charles II and James II, England became the source of subsidies during the 1690s with which she maintained troops from Germany and Scandinavia. William III's seizure of England brought his adopted state into partnership with Austria and the United Provinces. Within the space of twelve months from the declaration of war on France, England had ceased to be a minor power and had grown into an international force of the first rank. Whereas both Charles II and James II had dabbled in pseudo-alliances with Louis XIV, William's arrival in England allowed the underlying and majority 'country' interest to demonstrate the deep francophobic tendencies which had really dominated the political consciousness throughout the century and especially since 1667.

The emergence of England as an important international state owed as much to James II as to William III. By seeking refuge in France and then attempting to regain his throne through the invasion of Ireland, King James provided his successor with the ideal instrument with which to convince the English Parliament that entry into a major European war was essential and unavoidable. Provided that Louis harboured James there was always the danger of a French-supported Jacobite invasion which might wither the fragile bloom of the Glorious Revolution. Enough uncertainty and bad political and religious conscience existed in the British Isles to provide active support for Jacobite schemes and the French-Jacobite invasion attempts of 1692, 1696 and 1697 served to keep the central issue of the war permanently before English eyes. For England, the Nine Years' War was basically the War for the English Succession, a war fought to protect the new political order. As the central theatre of conflict was the Spanish Netherlands, 'Flanders' in common parlance, and the campaigns there rarely achieved decisive results, both the signatories of the Grand Alliance and France sought diversionary operations by which they could draw enemy troops away from the Low Countries and so produce the local superiority required for victory and results. In the initial stages of the war, France achieved this through providing limited assistance to the Jacobite forces in Ireland but this theatre was closed by the Treaty of Limerick in 1691. Nevertheless, the two years of the Jacobite Wars in Ireland had given France the opportunity to defeat the armies of the Grand Alliance in two major battles in Flanders and capture a number of important fortresses. Thereafter, plans to invade England itself with the aim of restoring James II assumed a prominent place in French strategy. England rapidly became the lynch-pin of the Grand Alliance supplying the lion's share of its naval requirements, a substantial number of its troops and a good proportion of its financial needs. A successful intervention in England by France would have disrupted the war effort of the Grand Alliance sufficiently to have obliged its component parts to have sought a compromise peace. The restoration of James II would also have rendered the English throne once more compliant to the wishes and subsidies of Louis XIV.

Although England engaged in the Nine Years' War for self-protection, other interests soon became apparent. The foreign policy of the United Provinces did not revolve around territorial expansion but in the maintenance of the international balance. Although there existed certain territorial anomalies in the distribution of her lands which she wished to resolve, particularly around Maastricht, this involved rationalisations of the status quo rather than substantial alterations to international frontiers. William III and the States-General, in their different ways, strove to protect the United Provinces and provide conditions in which trade and commerce could flourish. The strength of the Dutch Republic lay in its economy, not in its territory. The same criteria applied to England. She was not interested in acquiring lands on continental Europe but she was deeply concerned with limiting the power of France in order to defend against a Jacobite restoration and to ensure an international settlement which allowed her to pursue commercial and naval goals overseas, especially in the Atlantic and the Mediterranean. Neither the Dutch nor the English fought France in order to inflict upon her a crushing military defeat. They did not even consider the annihilation of her armies as an objective. The Grand Alliance wanted to restrict French territorial ambitions and force her to obey the Treaties of Westphalia and Nijmegen. Oddly enough, the Nine Years' War saw all its major participants – England, France and the United Provinces – fighting defensive wars. The English and the Dutch wanted to defend the Peace of 1678 whilst France was trying to protect the gains which she had made between 1678 and 1684. Neither side was trying to defeat the other; they were attempting to persuade each other, by military means, to accept their solution to the question of the definition of international frontiers. Perhaps the only aggressive power involved in the conflict was Austria which continued its war with the Turk, thereby extending Imperial authority over Hungary and into the Balkan peninsula.

Although the English war aims were limited, this could not be reflected in the conduct of hostilities. France was a continental power and could only be defeated or restricted by opposing her armies with land forces of equal or greater strength. This committed the major war effort of the Grand Alliance to opposing France's principal armies in the main theatre, the Spanish Netherlands and the Lower Rhine Valley. All other operations were to be subsidiary. Elizabeth I had been the last English monarch to throw armies into France and the Netherlands, at enormous financial cost and for minimal political reward. In the Spanish and Irish Wars of Elizabeth, the navy had proved itself an invaluable defence for the British Isles but it was of little use as a decisive weapon against Spain whose main endeavours were on land in the Northern and Southern Netherlands. The moral was abundantly clear: to make an impact and to be able to impose her will on a European land power, England had to commit forces to the continent and make alliances with European powers, expensive though this was bound to prove. The navy could protect trade, disrupt French overseas commerce and capture colonial territories in the Americas and the West Indies, but it could not defeat the French armies along the Rhine and in the Spanish Netherlands. 'Blue Water Strategy', the reliance upon English sea power rather than fighting on land in Europe, was never an alternative to the 'continental commitment'. It was an adjunct, useful at times as in the intervention of the fleet into the Mediterranean in 1694 and 1695, but it was always secondary to the land war. Blue Water Strategy helped the English to profit from the Nine Years' War both commercially and in the acquisition of new colonial interests but France could not be defeated by having her trade routes cut or her navy blockaded in Brest and Toulon. To a country which was largely self-sufficient in foodstuffs and raw materials, overseas trade was relatively unimportant. Attempts to combine naval and land forces in raids on the French coast, 'descents' as they were termed, proved unsuccessful either because they were ill-planned and poorly executed, as at Brest in 1694, or because they simply could not affect the outcome of the war. Arguably, 'descents' on France were essentially defensive operations. With little trade to protect, the French navy concentrated upon interrupting and destroying Anglo-Dutch seaborne commerce. Rather than adopting a Blue Water Strategy, the British navy was hard-pressed to protect its own merchant marine from enemy depredations. The bombardments of Calais and Dunkirk in 1695 and 1696 were attempts to wreck French privateering bases.

England fought the Nine Years' War to guard the political settlement of 1688. Automatically, this placed her in a defensive posture; she had everything to lose by defeat but nothing positive to gain through victory. William III, who controlled English foreign policy throughout his reign, brought his own Dutch notion of the balance of power into England to find that it was well suited to English concepts of how the war should be fought. To guarantee the financial capabilities of both England and the United Provinces, the naval war had to be fought vigorously to protect trade routes and cross-Channel communications between England and her allies. However, William knew that France could only be defeated on land and he brought this essential fact home to Englishmen and persuaded them that the continental commitment was as important to the war effort as the Blue Water Strategy.[22] England found herself mounting a 'double forward commitment', fighting a war on land and sea with equal vigour and ferocity and at double the cost.[23]

NOTES

1 For a sixth title, see page 26.
2 J. B. Wolf, *The Emergence of the Great Powers* (New York, 1962), pp. 15–53.
3 In particular see, J. C. Rule, *Louis XIV and the Craft of Kingship* (Columbus, Ohio, 1967); Andrew Lossky, 'The Absolutism of Louis XIV: Reality or Myth?', *Canadian Journal of History*, xix. (1984); Paul Sonnino, *Louis XIV and the Origins of the Dutch War* (Cambridge, 1988).
4 Especially, Sonnino, *Origins of the Dutch War*.
5 Henry Guerlac, 'Vauban: the Impact of Science on War', in, *Makers of Modern Strategy from Machiavelli to the Nuclear Age*, ed. Peter Paret (Oxford, 1986), p. 83–6; F. Bluche, *Louis XIV* (Oxford, 1990), p. 246.
6 C. J. Ekberg, *The Failure of Louis XIV's Dutch War* (Chapel Hill, 1979), pp. 110–27; Sonnino, *Origins of the Dutch War*, pp. 166–75, 180, 186.
7 A. C. Carter, *Neutrality or Commitment: the Evolution of Dutch Foreign Policy, 1667–1795* (London, 1975), pp. 19–20; R. Geikie & I. A. Montgomery, *The Dutch Barrier, 1705–1719* (Cambridge, 1930), pp. 3–89.
8 For aspects of the Peace of Nijmegen see, *The Peace of Nijmegen, 1676–1678/9*, ed. J. A. H. Bots (Amsterdam, 1980).
9 Geoffrey Symcox, *Victor Amadeus II* (London, 1983), pp. 80–1.
10 On the siege of Vienna see, John Stoye, *The Siege of Vienna* (London, 1964); T. M. Barker, *Double Eagle and Crescent* (Albany, New York, 1968); Bluche, *Louis XIV*, p. 236
11 On Huguenot emigration see, W. C. Scoville, *The Persecution of Huguenots and French economic development* (Berkeley & Los Angeles, 1960); R. D. Gwynn, *Huguenot Heritage* (London, 1985).

12 *The Habsburg and Hohenzollern Dynasties in the 17th and 18th Centuries*, ed. C. A. MaCartney (London, 1970), pp. 269–74.

13 This section rests heavily upon, Paul Sonnino, 'The Origins of Louis XIV's Wars', in, *The Origins of War in Early Modern Europe*, ed. Jeremy Black (Edinburgh, 1987), pp. 112–31.

14 J. W. Wright, *The Development of the Bastioned System of Fortifications, 1500–1800* (Washington D. C., 1946), pp. 203–5; CMC 4/38, 'Philipsburg avec les Attaques faites par les François au mois d'Octobre, 1688'.

15 John Childs, *Armies and Warfare in Europe, 1648–1789* (Manchester, 1982), pp. 151–2; J. B. Wolf, *Louis XIV* (London, 1968), pp. 451–5; C. Rousset, *Histoire de Louvois* (Paris, 1891), iv. 155–68, 223; see also, Kurt von Raumer, *Die Zerstörung der Pflaz von 1689* (Munich, 1930).

16 On the Anglo-Dutch Wars see, C. R. Boxer, *The Anglo-Dutch Wars of the 17th Century* (London, 1957).

17 On the politics and foreign affairs of Restoration England see, J. R. Western, *Monarchy and Revolution* (London, 1972); J. R. Jones *The Revolution of 1688 in England* (London, 1972); John Miller, *James II* (Hove, 1977); W. A. Speck, *Reluctant Revolutionaries* (Oxford, 1988); John Childs, '1688', *History*, lxxiii. (1988), pp. 398–424; John Childs, *The Army, James II and the Glorious Revolution* (Manchester, 1980); *History Today*, xxxviii. (July, 1988).

18 *The Life and Letters of Sir George Savile, First Marquis of Halifax*, ed. H. C. Foxcroft (London, 1898), ii. 219.

19 Charles Jenkinson, 1st Earl of Liverpol, *A Collection of all the Treaties of Peace, Alliance and Commerce between Great Britain and other Powers* (London, 1785, repr. New York, 1969), i. 267–92; Anchitel Grey, *Debates of the House of Commons, from the year 1667 to 1694* (London, 1763), ix. 87, 96, 108–9, 124, 158–9, 183–6.

20 DCRO, D 60/X12, 3/13 March 1678.

21 See, J. C. D. Clark, *English Society, 1688–1832* (Cambridge, 1985); Joanna Innes, 'Jonathan Clark, Social History and England's "Ancien Regime" ', *Past and Present*, no. 115 (1987); John Brewer, *The Sinews of Power: War, Money and the English State, 1688–1783* (London, 1989).

22 M. Sheehan, 'The development of British theory and practice of the Balance of Power before 1714', *History*, lxxiii. (1988), pp. 24–37; Daniel A. Baugh, 'Great Britain's "Blue Water" policy, 1689–1815', *International History Review*, x. (1988), pp. 33–58; D. B. Horn, *Great Britain and Europe in the Eighteenth Century* (Oxford, 1967), pp. 1–3; Paul Langford, *The Eighteenth Century, 1688–1815* (London, 1976), pp. 43–55.

23 D. W. Jones, *War and Economy in the Age of William III and Marlborough* (Oxford, 1988), pp. 16, 59–60.

II

THE CONDUCT OF
THE WAR IN FLANDERS

The Spanish Netherlands and the Bishopric of Liège covered most of the territory now belonging to Belgium. From Ostend on the North Sea coast to Bastogne, close to the border with modern Luxembourg, is only 273 kilometres. At their widest point, the Spanish Netherlands were just 160 kilometres from north to south. This small and compact geographical area comprised the vital buffer zone between the United Provinces and France, the crucial belt of land which the Dutch viewed as the main defence of their southern frontier.

Between the River Scheldt and the North Sea coast, including the land along the southern shore of the estuary of the Scheldt, lie the polders of Flanders criss-crossed by canals and dykes. Eastwards from the Scheldt, the land lifts from near sea level into the undulating country-side of Brabant. Although the low, rolling plains of the central Spanish Netherlands rarely rise more than 100 metres above sea level, the contrast with the boggy fields of East and West Flanders afforded some startling panoramas. As William III's army approached the River Scheldt at Gavere in 1692, his soldiers

> had a very fine prospect of the whole province of Flanders, which on the other side of the Scheldt is all a perfect level, not as much as a hill to be seen, so that the hills on the Brabant side give a full view and prospect of it. We had the town of Oudenarde, and the hills and plains of Tournai upon our left; Ghent upon our right, and before us all the Low Flanders which gave us such a prospect that we could see as far as Bruges and Antwerp.[1]

To the east of Brussels, the country begins to rise more appreciably as it approaches the foothills of the Ardennes. The line of the River Sambre, running south-west to north-east from Charleroi to Namur, where the

Sambre joins the Meuse, upto Liège, marks the beginning of the wooded uplands of the Ardennes. This massif stretches south-east into the Duchy of Luxembourg and east into Germany where it becomes known as the Eifel and continues to the banks of the Rhine and the Moselle. Although the Ardennes rarely show over 600 metres above sea level, they posed a considerable obstacle to seventeenth century armies. The ancient, eroded block mountains of the Ardennes Forest form a plateau into which numerous rivers have incised deep, steep-sided valleys. This difficult landscape with its wooded ravines was rarely traversed by armies and during the Nine Years' War it was unusual to campaign far to the east of the line of the Sambre and the Meuse. At Liège, the Ardennes swing due east, running their northern edge towards the Rhine to the south of Bonn. The country to the north of the Ardennes, through Liège, Maastricht and Aachen is flat and open reaching into the United Provinces and the North German Plain.

The campaigning theatre was demarcated by a line which ran from Dunkirk, along the North Sea coast and the estuary of the Scheldt to Antwerp; from Antwerp to Roermond on the Meuse; from Roermond south to Liège; from Liège to Maubeuge on the Sambre; and from Maubeuge through Lille and back to Dunkirk. This quadrilateral formed the 'Cockpit of Europe'. At times, the great fortresses in the Generality in the extreme south of the United Provinces came into play as did the Rhineland from Coblenz to Wesel, but these regions tended to be subsidiary to the main arena in the Spanish Netherlands.

As well as being the buffer state between France and the United Provinces, the Spanish Netherlands possessed two other elements vital to the conduct of seventeenth century warfare. The region was rich in waterways, both natural and artificial, and the Spanish Netherlands were not a kingdom in their own right but a province of the Spanish Empire. Armies relied upon water transport for their provisions, heavy baggage, ammunition and siege artillery. Navigable waterways abounded in the Spanish Netherlands, the majority running across the country from south-west to north-east. Only in Flanders did the canals provide significant east-west communications. Because of their importance, each of these waterways was guarded by a succession of fortresses and campaigns were often directed at the capture of successive 'river lines'. Ghent, Courtrai and Menin were the keys to the River Lys; Tournai, Oudenarde, Ghent, Dendermonde and Antwerp commanded the Scheldt; and Ath, Grammont, Alost and Dendermonde governed the line of the Dender. The River Senne was covered by Halle, Brussels, Vilvoorde and Malines, whilst the Meuse, perhaps the most vital artery of all, was protected by some of the strongest fortresses in the Low Countries: Dinant, Namur, Liège, Maastricht, Roermond and Venlo. Maubeuge and Charleroi covered the Sambre, an important tributary of the Meuse. These rivers created great strategic avenues along which French armies could debouch from their northern frontiers and advance upon Brussels and the southern border of the Dutch Republic. Conversely, opponents could march down these rivers towards France. To prevent this unwelcome development, Sebastien le Prestre de Vauban, Louis XIV's principal engineering officer, had built or improved a string of major fortifications along the frontier between France and the Spanish Netherlands. From Dunkirk in the west, this line ran through Ypres, Lille, Tournai, Le Quesnoy and Maubeuge to Dinant on the Meuse. Further French fortresses – St. Omer, Béthune, Arras, Douai, Cambrai, Rocroi and Charleville – stood behind the main frontier defences. In the east, the mighty Rhine was defended by a host of fortified towns – Mannheim, Coblenz, Bonn, Cologne, Neuss, Kaiserswerth and Wesel. The Rhine entered the United Provinces through the fortified gate at Arnhem and the southern stretches of the provinces of Holland, Zealand, Utrecht and Guelderland, as well as the Generality lands, were filled with fortresses guarding against invasion. From Sluys on the Isle of Cadzand, the belt of Dutch defences went from Axel in the west, to Hulst, Bergen-op-Zoom, Breda, Gertruidenberg, Heusden, 's-Hertogenbosch, Grave, Nijmegen, Schenkenschans at the confluence of the Rhine and the Waal, to Bredevoort on the eastern frontier with the Bishopric of Münster. Amidst this maze of fortified towns, fortresses and castles, and only the major posts have been mentioned, siege warfare was the norm.

The Nine Years' War witnessed the culmination of a surge in the size of national military establishments and field armies. The latter had been relatively static in numbers, between 20,000 and 40,000, since the beginning of the 16th century whereas national military establishments had been inching upwards throughout the period from about 1550 to 1689. National military establishments waxed as the political ambitions and the concomitant strategic commitments of first Spain and then France multiplied. The increase in the scale of the field armies drawn from those establishments increased during the second half of the 17th century partly through the political response to French international pressures. Starting in the Franco-Dutch War, 1672–8, coalitions opposed France, a trend which reached its apogee during the Nine Years' War and the War of the Spanish Succession. Numerous small and large states provided troops for the confederate armies resulting in a sudden and massive augmentation of available numbers. France was forced to reciprocate. However, there were also a number of operational and tactical factors which assisted the expansion of field armies. The concentration of the war in the Low Countries meant that larger armies, especially strong in infantry, were needed to attack and defend complex fortifications. Secondly, the Low Countries was one of the few European theatres able to support mass armies. Thirdly, armies lacked hitting power and neither the French nor the Allies possessed a technological superiority; the key to success in both battle and siege lay in numbers. During the opening years of the war, the Allies and the French fought in the Low Countries with armies numbering around 40,000 men. Between 1692 and 1697, when the Grand Alliance was free to focus its full attention on continental Europe, the field armies rarely amounted to less than 100,000 soldiers. The supply of these gigantic bodies by fairly primitive pre-industrial states caused throbbing headaches, so much so that provisioning became a major concern of warfare and a principal restraint upon the manner of its conduct. After the termination of the Wars of Louis XIV in 1714, the average field army in Europe declined in size until the French Revolutionary and Napoleonic Wars brought the combined weight of an industrial, political and demographic revolution to the production of greater hordes.[2]

The larger armies of the Nine Years' War were attracted by the magnetic field of the Low Countries. Although fertile and populous they did not form part of the homeland of any of the principal combatants. It was possible for the armies of the Nine Years' War to subsist in the territory of the Spanish Netherlands without causing much inconvenience to their own, native populations, apart from high levels of taxation. National treasuries also appreciated this arrangement. Years of subjection to foreign armies and campaigns had produced in the Spanish Netherlands the economic and social infrastructure to deal with, and profit from the occurrence of war. Apart from the specialist victualling contractors, the farmers and merchants of the Spanish Netherlands and Liège took advantage of high demand to sell their produce and services to the Allied troops at a premium.[3]

A veneer of civilised manners and behaviour cloaked the Nine Years' War. French and Spanish delegates had met at the village of Deynze, just to the south of Ghent, between September 1676 and February 1678 to discuss ways of controlling the levying of 'contributions' which conquering armies were in the habit of raising from subjected territories. Neither treaty nor official concord emerged from the Deynze Conference but, early in February 1677, Louis decided to abide by the spirit of the proceedings and the Spaniards concurred in the following year. Total contributions from an affected area were not to exceed the peacetime taxation that had been levied in the base-year of 1669. Occupying armies were enjoined to negotiate contributions over wide geographical regions rather than victimise individual towns and villages. If an area could not pay the required sums, then there was to be no physical damage to property in retaliation but an orderly exchange of hostages until all the money had been handed over. This last clause removed the demon of 'brandschatzen', the burning of towns and villages which were slow in meeting their contributions. Overall, Deynze was a brave attempt at trying to regulate the assessment and collection of contributions. Foreign occupation in time of war would naturally remain more onerous than the exactions of peacetime government but some of the gratuitous violence practised by soldiers on civilians was excised. Although the Deynze agreement had as much to do with the preservation of military discipline as it did with common humanity, this introduction of a few of the elements of international law into the conduct of war had some limited effect. Slowly, military men began to realise that there was more to be gained from the systematic exploitation of an occupied region than from razing every building to the ground and destroying all means of livelihood. Unfortunately for the inhabitants of the Spanish Netherlands, Liège and Luxembourg, the high commands of the armies of the Nine Years' War had not been universally converted to the new code by 1688. Even if the collection of contributions had been theoretically regularised, there was nothing to prevent armies from ravaging tracts of countryside for the purpose of tactical advantage or political terror.

The war opened on a sour note with the systematic destruction of the Palatinate and the Rhineland during the winter of 1688–9. The French Intendants of Lille and Dunkirk sent letters into the Spanish Chatellenie of Courtrai, whose authority stretched as far north as Deynze and Ghent, demanding contributions even though these regions were not occupied by the French at that time. The rates charged were computed from those which had been current during the Franco-Dutch War of 1672–8. Not to be outdone, the Spaniards levied contributions on unoccupied French territory, basing their requests on the prices from the Franco-Spanish War of 1683–4. Although an attempt was made in May 1689 to re-introduce the tenets of the Deynze Conference, the French ignored all restrictions and levied contributions as widely as they could throughout the Spanish Netherlands, Liège and Luxembourg. Passports were cancelled, 'brandschatzen' reappeared, hostages were

seized, supplementary contributions were levied and reprisals were regular. As the French assumed the strategic initiative in the Low Countries
in 1689, 1690, 1691 and 1692 their contribution parties grew more
ferocious and rapacious. It took the Duke of Württemberg's raid
through the Lines of the Lys and the Scheldt in 1693 to demonstrate
to the French that their territory was not inviolate. Together with the
waning of French offensive power in 1694, Württemberg's operation
brought the French to a more reasonable attitude towards contributions
for the remainder of the war. In addition to contributions, both the
French and the Allies requisitioned local labour and services. Pioneers
to build roads and fortifications or to dig siege works, waggons, horses,
carpenters, wood for palisades, beds for officers, kitchen utensils, firewood, candles, forage and livestock were all frequently requisitioned.
Generally, the Allies paid for these utilities whereas the French did not.
By 1695, the accumulated war damage to the Spanish Netherlands
amounted to £14,000,000.[4]

The growth of civilian control over armed forces resulted in some
diminution of the burden of foreign military occupation. When civilian
administrators started to accompany armies into the field, civilians
began to deal with fellow civilians and so tended to receive more realistic
treatment. Situated astride the River Meuse and centred on the city of
Liège, the Prince-Bishopric of Liège was frequently the host to foreign
armies. Some came to occupy sections of the province, others simply
marched through making use of the crossing points of the Meuse at
Visé, Argenteau and Hersal, as well as the bridge in Liège itself. In
1690, Prince-Bishop Jean-Louis d'Elderen appointed Jean de Mont as
Military Commissioner for the Principality. His task was to liaise with
foreign armies. When 'visiting' troops entered the Principality, de Mont
met them and then co-operated with their officers and administrators
to make sure that they were housed and fed with minimum disruption
to the civilian population. So important was de Mont's work that he
reported directly to the privy council of the Prince-Bishop.[5]

A number of more limited agreements also enhanced the progress of
humanity in warfare during the 1690s. Louis XIV, the Kreise of Swabia
and Franconia and the Duchy of Württemberg signed a cartel on 22
April/2 May 1692 which banned the use of poisoned bullets and insisted
that all projectiles thrown from hand guns or muskets had to be moul-
ded from lead. It also laid down that contributions should only be
collected by parties of more than nineteen infantrymen or fifteen cavalrymen with at least one officer in attendance; lesser groups might be
treated as robbers and imprisoned for two months if apprehended. A

sceptic might suggest that this particular clause was inspired more by the need to maintain discipline within the respective armies than with the advancement of international law. Indeed, pillaging civilians and exacting contributions by threatening to burn habitations was exceedingly bad for law and order amongst the soldiery, as the French discovered during the ravaging of the Palatinate. The movement towards humanising the conduct of war owed as much to the needs of the military authorities to control their soldiers as it did to more detached and ultruistic motives.[6]

A small French vessel put into Plymouth from St. Malo on 9/19 August 1690 carrying sixty-three English prisoners of war who had been exchanged for an equivalent number of Frenchmen. One month later, a ship of eighty tons delivered a further forty Englishmen. A similar exchange occurred in February 1691 with 150 Englishmen being bartered for a like weight of French. At this stage of the war, it appears that the French authorities held some one thousand English prisoners whilst fifteen hundred Gauls were incarcerated across the Channel. Captives, whether taken on land or at sea, were a nuisance. Important personages – generals, admirals and politicians – might be ransomed for sizeable sums of money but ordinary soldiers and seamen were a pest, and a very expensive pest. The Commissioners for the Exchange of Prisoners complained to the Lords Justices on 29 May/8 June 1696, that there were over 850 French prisoners in the British Isles, 600 of whom were lodged in Plymouth. There was a grave risk of infectious diseases breaking out amongst them and they were proving very costly to feed and shelter. The Commissioners wanted two hundred of the sick and 'unserviceable' French to be swapped for an equal number of British prisoners in France as soon as possible. In June 1691, the French agreed to exchange some Dutch prisoners who had been captured during the Battle of Fleurus in 1690 for some Catholic Irish who had been taken at the Boyne and during the Siege of Cork. The Irish were duly dispatched to Dunkirk but when they arrived the French refused to exchange the Dutchmen for 'such cowards' and left the Irish to starve in the streets. Major-General Jacob van Opdam, the officer in charge of the exchange, relieved the Irish with some cash and eventually persuaded the French to execute their side of the bargain. With exceedingly bad grace the French complied and then, to show their contempt, sent the Irish to serve on board the galleys of the Mediterranean fleet.[7]

This depressing tale typifies the treatment of prisoners during the war. Whenever possible, the armies did not take prisoners. However, if they had no option, as in the aftermath of a siege, prisoners were either rapidly exchanged or paroled and allowed to rejoin their own sides having sworn not to bear arms against their captors for a stipulated period of time or until a formal exchange had been organised. In an age of honour and mock chivalry, these arrangements generally worked quite well and were the standard form at the termination of sieges.[8] No country possessed either the money or the accommodation to retain large numbers of prisoners-of-war. Under the strain of war, gentlemanly behaviour did not always prevail. The Duke of Luxembourg suffered from an outbreak of extreme pettiness after the Battle of Steenkirk in 1692 and refused to exchange prisoners until some Frenchmen in the Tower of London had been released. William III, showing that he could be equally small-minded, then refused to release any French captives at all. The French were also most particular that only persons of the same, or very similar quality could be swapped. The Duke of Ormonde in return for the Duke of Berwick after the Battle of Landen in 1693 was fine but when the Duke of Württemberg had fallen into French hands in the previous year there was no suitable exchange for him and so they demanded a ransom of 2,500,000 florins and the payment of the arrears due on all contributions.[9] During the spring of 1692, an agreement was reached between the French and the English which was ratified into a cartel concerning the return of all prisoners-of-war captured at sea. Under the supervision of the Commissioners for the Exchange of Prisoners in England, all sailors, soldiers and passengers who were taken at sea were to be returned as soon as a sum of money equal to one month's pay for each man captured had been paid to the privateersman responsible for the apprehension. This cartel was renewed in each remaining year of the war.[10] It was punctured now and again but never irrevocably and both sides took a dim view of any *ad hoc* arrangements which were not covered by the cartel.[11] Generally the cartel functioned smoothly and in 1694 an attempt was made to extend its provisions to land warfare although not with equal success.[12]

The English soldiers captured during the abortive attack on Brest in 1694 were returned to Falmouth four months later, 'naked and almost starving'. Richard Hill, the Paymaster of the British forces in Flanders, wrote to Secretary-at-War William Blathwayt on 10/20 January 1697 from Ghent. 'I cannot forbear to put you in mind of our poor French [i.e. Huguenot] officers who are at Dunkirk. Mons. Ponchartrain demands Welch and young Jennings for 'em. I wish his Majesty would give two rascals for a dozen poor gentlemen who suffer extremely.'[13] In June of the same year, the Commissioners were ordered to send a list to the King of all the British prisoners detained in France so that he could select who he would 'pitch on' to be exchanged for Colonel Roger MacElligott, the Irish Catholic.[14] Even when local authorities proved to be ignorant of the terms of the Treaty of Exchange, as when Brigadier Thomas Erle and some of his regimental officers were taken by a Dunkirk privateer, the ransom of 4,000 crowns that each had been obliged to pay to their discourteous captors was returned by the French Agent for Exchanges, Monsieur Dulivier, and all the hostages and prisoners were set free.[15]

At the end of the War, the Lords Justices instructed the Commissioners for Exchange to collect together all the remaining French captives in England and send them back to France as soon as possible. Naturally, there were some anomalies to the general spirit of the cartel. Throughout the conflict, the French had not swapped captured Huguenots who had been serving in the armies of the Grand Alliance. Indeed, the Governor of Nantes, into whose hands fell some Huguenot officers after the Brest Expedition in 1694, said that he had orders from Louis XIV to hang all protestant traitors. The English were equally reluctant to return Roman Catholic soldiers from the Irish Brigade in the French army. These unfortunates balanced one another and a special clause had to be included in the Treaty of Rijswijk to secure their mutual freedom.[16] Even more unlucky was Captain Roger Elrington who, for some unspecified crime, endured six years, four months and eleven days in the Bastille, an incarceration which 'ruined his affairs'. In compensation, he was granted a bounty of £100 by the Treasury and appointed Lieutenant-Governor of Nevis, a post which he retained until 1702.[17]

If exchanges could not be arranged[18] then there were two other solutions to the problem of unwanted prisoners. The simplest was to persuade prisoners-of-war to desert from their previous allegiance and join the ranks of their captors. Sailors, always a more valuable and scarcer human commodity than soldiers, were sometimes offered money to induce them to change sides. Soldiers could expect hard labour on fortifications or road building accompanied by threats and ill treatment until they decided to take the line of least resistance.[19] From his flagship off the Catalonian coast in 1695, Admiral Edward Russell wrote to Lord Shrewsbury that he considered Catalonia to be secure as there was much desertion from the French army and

> to encourage that, I have sent several hundreds of papers in French, Dutch, and English, promising rewards and liberty to dispose themselves as they please, to all such as shall repair to the consul of Barcelona. I make no question but it will have a good effect. I have already supplied

the regiments with one hundred and thirty [French deserters] and have now at Barcelona more than that number waiting for the fleet. Several of them that are come are men taken at the battles of Fleurus, Steenkirk and Camaret [Brest], though many French, Germans and Swiss come away also.[20]

On 18/28 July 1695, the allied garrison of Dixmuyde surrendered to the French after a somewhat weak defence. Along with the nearby garrison of Deynze, which had also capitulated with indecent haste, the French found themselves responsible for over seven thousand captives. By the terms of the surrender, the garrisons agreed to become prisoners-of-war to be released within fifteen days upon payment of a ransom of over £3,000.[21] The French maintained that this sum was never paid, whilst the English were equally adamant that full reparation had been made. Impasse resulted. When the citadel of Namur surrendered, William III arrested and detained Marshal Boufflers, an act contrary to the articles of the capitulation, in retaliation for the non-delivery of the garrisons of Deynze and Dixmuyde. Another clause in the document of surrender, that which undertook to send the French wounded by boat to Dinant, was also ignored. In the meantime, the French made great efforts to induce the Allied prisoners to join the French army and added deliberate cruelty to their techniques of persuasion. On 26 August/5 September 1695, Brigadier Francis Fergus O'Farrell, the commander of the Deynze garrison, wrote to William Blathwayt from his prison in Douai.

> I cannot sufficiently express the ill usage we receive from the French. On Saturday last, Colonel Scheltinga and myself were carried to the common prison. Some time after, the lieutenant-colonels and majors followed us and next the captains and an engineer. They took away our swords and led us with guards as if we had been criminals.
>
> We are in the place where they put their galley slaves and are infected with the stink already by one night's lodging there, so that if we continue we shall all infallibly fall sick.
>
> The subalterns have the barracks for their prison. In fine, I cannot represent the inhumanity we suffer. All manner of access is denied us and all persons forbid to supply us with money so that they resolve to reduce us to bread and water. And yet this does not trouble me so much as the concern for the poor soldiers whose allowance of bread is ordered to be retrenched, thereby to reduce them to a necessity of taking on.[22]

Finally, on 3/13 September, William agreed to send Boufflers to Dinant and the French let the Allied prisoners go free. The troops rendezvoused at Courtrai and marched back to Ghent; well over half the original seven thousand men had been 'debauched' into the French army.

The Nine Years' War was nasty, brutish and long with the participants fighting to their last gasps. England's monetary system all but collapsed in 1695 and 1696; French finances fell apart after 1693; and both English and Dutch commerce was seriously weakened leading to an interruption in the hitherto steady expansion of overseas trade. The Peace of Rijswijk was a truce between two pugilists who had become temporarily exhausted by the middle rounds of a protracted contest.[23] As if the Deynze Conference had never taken place, the French opened the war by ravaging the Palatinate, the Moselle Valley and the Middle Rhine in the winter of 1688–9. During the latter stages of the conflict the French armies inflicted considerable material damage on the Spanish Netherlands, the Duchy of Luxembourg and the Prince-Bishopric of Liège. At the Siege of Mons in 1691, the French promised to excuse the inhabitants of the country around that city from paying contributions provided that they ploughed up their green corn and pastures to deny forage and supplies to the Allied army which was advancing to relieve the blockade. The Dutch occupation of northern and central Flanders was continuous throughout the war and their contributions developed into a regular, annual tax upon the Flemish people. By the spring of 1694, the peasants who lived in that part of Brabant between Brussels, Louvain and the Meuse had suffered so much during previous campaigns 'in which their country had been foraged by the armies, that this year they had neglected the tilling of the ground, being unwilling to work in vain.' William's army 'could hardly find any corn upon the ground but here and there, it may be, half an acre. The Boers had left the country so bare that they boasted of starving both armies into a peace.'[24] Contrary to popular opinion, the war did not grind to a halt each autumn as the armies departed into winter quarters. Operations, mostly small and medium-sized raids, were kept up by both sides during the cold weather in order to levy contributions and gather supplies. Eight hundred French troops from Dinant ravaged the country around Namur in February 1696, and in the 'extreme cold' of January 1693 the French captured the Flemish towns of Furnes and Dixmuyde.[25] Both in winter and in summer, the war consisted of a host of raids, ambushes, limited actions between foragers or contribution parties and attacks on supply and money convoys, interspersed by the occasional formal siege or set-piece battle. It was not a war designed to achieve massive territorial gains or to destroy the opposing field army. Its purpose was strictly political.

Warfare in the late seventeenth century did not seek the destruction of the enemy's army as its principal aim, not because such a result was undesirable but because it was unattainable by contemporary methods. Exceptions like the Battles of Blenheim in 1704 and Ramillies in 1706 proved the rule. The aim was to capture towns or tracts of land which could be traded or negotiated at a peace conference and used in the meantime to gather forage, supplies and contributions in order to sustain the army on an enemy's soil. Territory could only be gained by the systematic reduction of fortified towns and cities. Every major road and water junction in the Low Countries, and to a lesser extent in the Rhineland, was protected by fixed fortifications. They could not be bypassed because to leave an unsubdued enemy garrison in the rear of an advance was to court disaster by leaving vital provision convoys exposed to attack. Every fort, however large or small, had to be besieged and captured. As this was the tried and accepted method of conducting military operations so it became the currency of diplomacy and foreign policy. The objective of armies and therefore of strategy was the siege and reduction of towns and cities in order to retain them for diplomatic ransom. With such aims, warfare was bound to be slow and limited in both scope and ambition. International politics could only follow where its principal weapon led.

As if this geographical, political and military straight-jacket was insufficient, there existed other strictures upon martial mobility and decisiveness. In the first place, armies had outgrown their administrative and command mechanisms. Armies of one hundred thousand men without regular corps or divisional sub-groupings, composed of a multitude of nationalities and commanded by xenophobic princes of royal blood, were resistant to the introduction of unified systems of control and direction. William III spent as much of his time smoothing relations amongst his prickly allies as he did in fighting the French. In July 1696, some Bavarian soldiers and officers 'insulted' the quarters of the Duke of Holstein-Plön, then commanding the Spanish cavalry. The Spaniards supported Holstein 'very warmly' and rapidly escalated the incident into 'a common and national quarrel'. Very soon, the entire Spanish corps in the Elector of Bavaria's army threatened to quit and join the Prince de Vaudemont's camp in Flanders. Luckily, at this crucial moment, Vaudemont himself rode into the Elector's camp and was able to calm down the affronted Spaniards.[26] Marlborough was to find himself facing similar difficulties during the War of the Spanish Succession. An initiative aimed at solving some of these problems emanated from the Elector of Bavaria in March 1691. He advocated the establishment of a regular and organised system of communications between the Allied armies operating in Flanders, Brabant and the Rhineland. Through a central secretariat or chancellery in The Hague, all corps and armies could be circulated with up-to-date news, intelligence, reports and orders. Such a central staff could also have served the needs of the various ministers from the countries forming the Grand Alliance who met frequently in The Hague. This sensible suggestion would have made a valuable contribution to the Allied war effort but nothing more was heard of the idea. The sole spin-off was a set of standing orders, 'Regélment touchant les cérémonies, gardes et ce qui dépend quand l'armée se trouve en campagne', drawn up by Constantijn Huygens on 3/13 April 1691, but this did no more than outline the duties of general officers thereby instituting some uniformity of practice upon the various nationalities in the army.[27] However, the Grand Alliance was not totally without a central administration. After 1689, William III established a permanent Congress at The Hague consisting of representatives from the governments of the Grand Alliance. The Congress met regularly throughout the war. The ministers, envoys and ambassadors accredited to The Hague met with the Raadpensionaris, Anthonie Heinsius, and the Dutch Committee for Foreign Affairs to discuss matters of common interest. Although this body gave some structure to the Grand Alliance, it was mainly concerned with political rather than military affairs.[28] The Elector of Bavaria probably intended his proposed central military staff to be closely attached to the Congress.

Intimately related to the question of co-ordinated staffwork and command was the problem posed by language. Foreign general officers gave orders to British troops in German, French and Dutch, tongues which were not readily comprehended. Contrary to the commonly-held belief that the English upper classes enjoyed a knowledge of French, the lingua franca of civilisation, when the Earl of Portland drew up a list of those peers and members of the House of Commons who could speak and read French well enough to serve as a plenipotentiaries to the peace conference at Rijswijk, he came up with just thirty-one lords and forty-seven gentlemen from the lower house. George Saunderson, 5th Viscount Castleton, colonel of a battalion of foot, had been present on the field of Steenkirk when, 'orders were sent to me in French a language which, I profess, neither I nor any of my officers understood'.[29] Whereas the forces of the Grand Alliance suffered for their lack of an organisation of common command and a common language, the French enjoyed the advantages of a relatively centralised administration and a linguistic unity.

Huge armies operating in a terrain with few good roads and dependent upon water transport, tied down to interminable sieges, often incapable of unanimous action and equipped solely with the horseman and the runner for communication, were unable to move either rapidly or frequently. Weapon technology was a further deterrent to decisive warfare. The inaccurate, short-range muskets had such slow rates of fire that they were impotent to inflict serious damage on opposing infantry. Unbroken foot could not be charged by cavalry. Both field guns and the heavy siege cannon fired solid shot rather than explosive shells making the breaching of earthwork fortifications a long and laborious business. It also took such a length of time to array an army in its battle formation that it was quite possible for the enemy to decide not to fight and leave the field with scarcely a shot having been fired. Battles usually took place with the consent of both parties. Only William's surprise assault on the French camp at Steenkirk in 1692 falls outside this category.

Armies spent much of their lives in camp. In springtime, the component parts of the Allied army gathered from their winter cantonments at a general rendezvous near Brussels whence they marched to their first operational camp. Thereafter, the armies spent the campaigning season trudging from one camp to another blocking attempts by the enemy to besiege key fortresses. A good part of the skill of a seventeenth century commander lay in being able to identify which towns the enemy was likely to attack and then making sure that they were adequately protected and garrisoned. Conversely, the skilful and well-informed general also knew when he could withdraw troops from garrison to reinforce his field army. Superiority in numbers on the battlefield was usually gained by 'drawing in' troops from fortresses and fortified towns which were not liable to attack and siege. From their well-chosen camps, William, Luxembourg, Villeroi and Boufflers sought to achieve an advantage by consuming forage and supplies, thus denying that area to the enemy, or by obliging their opponent to encamp in a location from which foraging was difficult, so forcing him to move camp to an inferior position. In this way, an enemy could be made to lose his tactical balance thus opening the way for a sudden advance to seize territory or besiege a fortress. Armies tried, literally, 'to steal a march' on their opponents. These camps in Flanders and Brabant seem to have been virtually permanent features in the landscape. Earthwork defences, with which many of the camps were surrounded, endured well the ravages of weather and man unless they were deliberately demolished. In 1690, the entrenchments which the Swedes had built near Bichel on the Rhine fifty-six years before were still in evidence, and the battery which had fired the shot that felled Turenne at Salzbach in 1675 'is still to be traced there'. On 25 June/5 July 1695, Major-General George Ramsey marched fourteen battalions towards Namur camping *en route* 'in the retrenchments we made last year at Tourine Bavechein'. At the Siege of Namur itself in 1695, the Allies simply re-excavated the old lines of circumvallation that the French had dug in 1692 'which we found ready cut out to our hands'.[30] Not every camp occupied by the French or Allied armies in the Low Countries was honoured with an enceinte of field fortifications, some were simply overnight stops, but if opposing forces were in the vicinity then most commanders ordered their camps to be entrenched and palisaded. At Anderlecht, Halle, Lembeek, Marie-kerke near Ghent, Harelbeke, Enghien, Parck Abbey, Diegem, Braine-le-Comte, Mont St. André, Bois St. Isaac, Leuse and numerous other sites, the camps were semi-permanent, ready to be occupied by which-ever side required them. They formed the standard, set positions, com-plete with rudimentary fortifications. On the Upper Rhine, where the French and Imperial armies campaigned in Alsace and the Black Forest, the hilly terrain restricted the number of suitable campsites to such an extent that the armies found themselves in the same camping grounds year after year. Warfare came to resemble a board game, possibly chess; there were only a limited number of squares or camp sites within a given theatre with a finite and predictable quantity of moves between them.[31]

Old and established camp sites were preferred. New camps had to be 'prepared' in advance and if the roads traversed woods or marshes then they had to be widened or strengthened before the passage of the main army, clearly revealing the next movement to a vigilant enemy. With well-established camp sites none of these preparations were neces-sary as both the roads and the camping grounds had long been converted to military usage.[32] Flanders to the east of the Lys and the whole of Brabant were heavily forested and dissected by innumerable water-ways.[33] The improvement of roads and the construction of bridges involved the armies in considerable labour and expense. One device designed to disguise the intended direction of a march was the 'marking out' of a number of dummy camps simultaneously to keep the enemy guessing as to the ultimate destination of the army. Villeroi and Bouf-flers employed this trick extensively in the opening stages of the cam-paign of 1696. As the camps could often be eight or ten kilometres in length and encompass three or four villages, confusion sometimes arose over the precise name given to a particular campsite. Usually, the village closest to the centre of the position or the village in which the commanding general pitched his headquarters gave its name to the entire camp.[34]

Few camps were more than sixteen kilometres apart, the most that an army could comfortably travel in daylight. March routes were worked out in precise detail with the roads, the starting times and the river crossings all exactly organised. Armies marched in two divisions – the left wing and the right wing – and each was sub-divided into six or seven columns to make use of all the available roads and tracks. The intention was for one wing to arrive before the other, usually around midday, giving ample time for stragglers to come in and for the fortifications to be dug before nightfall. The artillery and the pontoon bridging train normally led the march. Attacks whilst on the road were not anticipated. By the very nature of 'camp warfare' marches were made away from an enemy or parallel to him so that sudden attacks would fall upon the infantry and cavalry in the rear of a column and not on the 'tin boats' and the cannon in the van. This was the sequence of events at Leuse in 1691, when Luxembourg surprised Waldeck's rearguard during a river crossing.[35] On the rare occasions when an army had to march towards the enemy, then the artillery took station towards the rear of the columns. However, roads and bridges still had to be 'prepared' even when marching towards the enemy; the direction of the march was then camouflaged by 'preparing' a number of roads and bridges to confuse opposing reconnaissance patrols.

All of these limitations on speed and movement which allowed French officers in camp to rise at noon and Field-Marshal the Prince of Nassau-Saarbourg to travel to Spa to take the waters in the middle of the campaign of 1696 pale into insignificance beside the restrictions imposed by supply. Supply – the provision of food for the men, fodder for the horses and ammunition for the guns – dwarfed all other factors in making seventeenth century warfare lethargic in movement and unimaginative in strategy. Put quite simply, a moving army could be provisioned with relative ease but a static army became the commissary's nightmare. Either in camp or besieging a fortress, the armies of the Nine Years' War were frequently motionless for considerable periods of time.[36]

Before the commencement of each campaign in the Spanish Netherlands, the Allies, or Confederates, stocked supply magazines in the principal fortress towns in the southern part of the Dutch Republic, in the towns along the Meuse Valley and in those parts of Flanders and

Brabant which were secure from depredations by the enemy. The French were in a more favourable geographical position and were able to station their magazines firmly within their own national territories. Their main magazines were stationed along the most important acquatic avenues. Cambrai, Valenciennes and Condé moved their stores north-wards along the Scheldt, Maubeuge stood on the Sambre, and Charle-ville, Dinant and Givet operated along the southern Meuse. Brussels was the main Allied base containing 1,260,000 bread rations and 2,700,000 rations of hay in March 1690. Away from Brussels, subsidiary maga-zines were developed at Maastricht, Namur and Liège on the Meuse; Louvain, Ath and Charleroi in Brabant; and Ghent, Bruges, Antwerp and Ostend in Flanders.[37] These vast store cupboards varied in capacity depending upon the probable direction of the coming campaign and whether or not there was a risk that a certain town might be subjected to a siege. Ath, a prime target for French attack in 1696, although it was not in fact assaulted until the following year, was filled with sufficient meal and green fodder in February 1696 to feed 40,000 men for three weeks.

The magazines only provided the basic commodities: ammunition; grain in the form of flour, bread or biscuit; and dry fodder for the horses. In the Low Countries, the commissariat of the British army provided bread for its soldiers but nothing else. Meat, cheese, beer, vegetables, fruit and other foodstuffs had to be purchased by the soldiers from their regimental sutlers or from the local merchants and retailers. In this way, the presence of large armies could create very favourable economic conditions, provided that the soldiers were regularly paid and that they did not overstay their welcome. The Deputy Paymasters of the British army in the Low Countries – Roger Sizer from 1689 to 1692 and Richard Hill for the remainder of the war – deducted 'bread money' from the daily subsistence pay of the men and employed these sums to meet the bills of the provision contractors. From 1694, the bread money was extracted for every day of the year regardless of whether the troops were in the field or in winter quarters as the bread contractors were only prepared to undertake the commitment if they were guaranteed business for a full twelve months. This proved to be unsatisfactory and unnecessarily expensive as the men could provide themselves with cheaper and better bread during the winter months when they were in permanent quarters by buying in the local markets but the system of annual contracts made it impossible for the soldiers to avail themselves of this opportunity.[38]

William's armies in the Low Countries, usually totalling around

100,000 men, needed 150,000 lb. of bread, or its equivalent, per day, 300,000 pints of beer, and 120,000 lb. of other consumables such as wood for fuel, wine, meat and cheese. The horses devoured 1,600,000 lb. of green fodder during the summer months on campaign but had to be supplied with over 624,000 lb, of straw, hay and oats for each of the hundred days that they spent in winter quarters. To provide flour for this amount of daily bread, 270 windmills were required to grind grain for 120 field ovens which were fired by 2,800 waggon-loads of wood and served by 480 bakers.[39] To maintain William's armies in the Low Countries for each year of the Nine Years' War, 400,000 tons of provisions had to be purchased, stored and distributed.[40] By the standards of early modern Europe, this represented a massive national effort which stretched the machinery of state and society to its very limits and, sometimes, beyond those limits. War was the greatest industrial enterprise of the age.[41] Only certain states could afford such a massive expenditure of cash and resources. More fundamental, only a few parts of the continent possessed a sufficient density of urban and rural population to furnish the labour, the services and the financial capital to accommodate war on this enormous scale. The Spanish Netherlands, northern Italy and the Lower Rhineland were the principal regions where warfare between mass armies could be conducted.[42]

England could not afford to provide for her armed forces in Europe through 'direct supply' – the export of home-produced foodstuffs and provisions. Wherever possible, she purchased local supplies and paid local merchants and financiers to undertake the task of supply on her behalf. As far as England was concerned, direct supply was out of the question as it would have tied up over 600,000 tons of shipping a year, leaving the merchant marine almost bereft of tonnage for normal commerce.[43] The most obvious method of providing for an army abroad was to permit the troops to seize supplies from the lands through which they passed but this uncivilised behaviour was unsuitable for war in the Low Countries in the 1690s. The French still collected contributions and lived off the fat of the southern provinces of the Spanish Netherlands and Luxembourg but the armies of William III largely avoided such depredations as they were operating not in a hostile country which they had invaded but in the territories of their ally, Spain. For the British and Dutch soldiers, the Spanish Netherlands represented a friendly state and had to be treated with respect and care. Above all, the Spanish Netherlands was the scene of repeated, annual campaigns; if agriculture and the local economy were severely damaged then the armies would not be able to fight over those territories in future years. The Spanish

Netherlands needed to be cultivated and nurtured by the British and the Dutch, not destroyed. Fortunately, the Spanish Netherlands had been the seat of international war for centuries and she had developed the necessary services, expertise and attitudes to provide for foreign armies at some advantage to herself. This balance of interests only broke down substantially over the provision of green fodder for the horses.

When marching, an army could draw its supplies from local markets and forage for its horse feed but the moment that it came to a halt it devoured the immediately available provisions very quickly indeed. In the Spanish Netherlands, marches were short and infrequent. The armies spent the majority of their campaigning seasons in static camps drawing basic supplies from magazines. Armies did not stray far from their bases — some theorists recommended four day's march as the maximum safe distance — but this was not a serious restriction in the Spanish Netherlands, a small and compact theatre in which both the French and the Allied armies were always within easy reach of their magazines. The lines of communication to and from those magazines had always to be kept clear and secure. The French employed magazines extensively but because the Spanish Netherlands, the Duchy of Luxembourg and the Prince-Bishopric of Liège constituted hostile territory, they did enjoy the additional flexibility of being able to live off the land in an emergency although this was not an option to which frequent resort could be made as it destroyed vital crops and supplies which might be required for future campaigns. For both sides, green fodder for the horses was the main item which had to be garnered from the countryside on a daily basis; no contemporary army possessed the resources or the organisation to lay on green fodder for its field armies during a campaign. Army provision contractors could only supply hay and corn feed during the winter when the horses were in permanent stables. Each of the 80,000 horses which accompanied William III's armies into the Spanish Netherlands munched between forty and sixty pounds of green fodder a day and about half that weight in corn during the winter. In the field, the army had to find its own fodder either by foraging or by allowing the beasts to graze standing crops. The latter course was devastating to the local economy and avoided whenever possible on the obvious grounds that if the regional resources were ruined then that area would be incapable of supporting an army in the immediate future. Foraging, the gathering of hay for the horses, took place once every three or four days when an army was in camp or otherwise immobile. On the march, horses were permitted to graze *en route*. Armies foraged to the flanks and to the front of their camps; the rear areas were left intact to sustain the passage of a retreat. As enemy armies often camped in close proximity, foraging grounds were frequently in dispute and foraging parties had to be escorted and covered by large formations of cavalry and dragoons to hold off opposing patrols. A 'grand forage' could involve virtually an entire army and it was upon such an expedition that the Allied army was supposed to have been engaged when it advanced to take Luxembourg by surprise at Steenkirk in 1692. It was this insatiable demand for fodder which restricted campaigning to the agricultural growing season. Men could fight and march during the cold months but the horses could not be fed for long when away from their stables. This put an end to large-scale operations and limited the winter war to raiding and patrolling.[44]

In good English military tradition, the horses were better cared for than the men. The nutritional value of the soldier's ration was low. Seventeenth century infantrymen fought and marched on 1,700 calories and forty grammes of protein per day. In the 1930s, a soldier on garrison duty was reckoned to consume between 3,200 and 3,500 calories per diem, rising to 3,800 calories and 160 grammes of protein when in action. Our poor soldier was living on the equivalent of a modern slimmer's diet and it was small wonder that he could not march more than ten or twelve miles in twenty-four hours and had to rest every fourth day. Not only was the fare low in calorific value but its nutritional content was ill-balanced. Rye bread was the basic constituent supplemented by hard cheese, beer, some meat and peas. Edward D'Auvergne noted how the quality of the rations improved when the Duke of Württemberg's corps penetrated the Lines of the Lys and the Scheldt and entered France in July 1693. Each battalion was given two cows a week, paid for out of the contributions levied on the local population, with two sheep for the officers and 'corn brandy' in plenty. This was in stark contrast to the monotonous and costive 'ammunition bread' endured in camp. As an infantryman in William III's British forces only received a daily sum of 4*d* in subsistence pay, and this was further reduced by the deduction of the bread money, there was little left for drink, entertainment or the purchase of exotic foods from the sutler's waggon.[45] Some officers recognised both the inadequacy of their soldier's diet and the evils of the pernicious system whereby soldiers in the employ of the state were forced to buy their own food when on active service. Colonel Sir Robert Peyton wrote to George Clarke from Westmeath on 10/20 June 1691 seeking 'an order on the Commissary of Provisions for cheese, it being very hard for poor men that have no pay nor means of their own to live upon bread alone and do duty.'[46]

The commissariat of the British army in the Low Countries scarcely existed. After the supposed peculation and incompetence of Commissary-General John Shales during the first year of the war in Ireland and the débâcle of the Dundalk Camp, even though there is more than a hint that Shales was made the scapegoat for the fiasco when the blame more properly belonged to Schomberg, William put no more faith or trust in the ability of the British army to run its own supply system.[47] A Commissary-General of the Provisions, one Israel Fielding, did function for the army in the Low Countries but he was solely responsible for provisioning the requisitioned transport vessels which ferried troops back and forth across the North Sea and the Irish Sea. Fielding was paid £1 10s a day, and his deputy, John Murray, received £1, high rates of pay for minor functionaries. Such generosity might have been offered in an effort to restrain corruption in officials who wielded considerable power and handled large sums of public money. Fielding's department employed thirty-one storekeepers, bakers, clerks, bricklayers and carpenters. Fielding and Murray worked closely with the Commissioners for Transportation, the department which supervised the requisitioning, hire and deployment of merchant ships for the use of the army and the Ordnance Office.[48] Instead, William turned to a well-established method of indirect supply for an army serving overseas – civilian contractors. Whilst in England and Scotland, or Ireland after 1691, British soldiers paid for and provided their own food and lodging from their subsistence money but once they set foot in Flanders their basic daily bread became the responsibility of the civilian contractors who supplied the entire Allied army.

Resort to civilian merchant syndicates to feed and transport the armies of England, the United Provinces, the Spanish Netherlands, Brandenburg, Bavaria, Hanover, Lüneberg, Celle and Denmark was the ultimate admission that the early modern European state was only a half-modern institution. It was insufficiently developed both in administrative technique and capacity to undertake the maintenance of the armies which it raised to fulfill its diplomatic ambitions. It did not rent the functions of state to private entrepreneurs from ideological commitment but because it was too primitive to administer its own creations. Just as the armies themselves were recruited by the state but administered by the officers whose interests were personal as much as national, so their supply fell into that penumbra where the state was obliged to hire out its basic tasks thereby sacrificing some elements of control. The business of army provisioning had developed out of the Amsterdam grain trade of the sixteenth and seventeenth centuries as well as from the omnipresence of war in the Spanish Netherlands and in the Dutch Republic. By the 1650s, this trade had become the monopoly of the Sephardic Jews, particularly those of Portuguese origin. Jews enjoyed the advantage of being treated as neutrals by both the French and the Allies, enabling them to travel freely all over the Low Countries in search of sources of supply.[49] In addition, Antwerp and Amsterdam were the central entrepôts for the Baltic grain trade and there were always substantial stocks of wheat, barley and rye from the Baltic littoral available for purchase.[50] In a field of human endeavour as hazardous as war, the employment of Jewish victuallers provided military commanders with perfect scapegoats should misfortune attend their operations. Successful campaigns were impossible without prompt supply.

The doyen of all the army contractors of the seventeenth century was Samuel Oppenheimer of Heidelberg (1630–1703). He began his career as the financial agent and contractor to the garrisons of the Elector Karl Ludwig of the Palatinate. In 1673, Oppenheimer formed a consortium which undertook to provision the Austrian Army of the Rhine for the Emperor Leopold I. After 1683, Oppenheimer provisioned the entire Austrian war effort in Hungary whilst his son, Emmanuel, supplied the Imperial garrisons in western Germany during the Nine Years' War.[51] Second only in scale to Oppenheimer's undertakings was the Dutch Sephardic partnership of Antonio Alvarez Machado and Jacob Pereira. From their office in the Lange Voorhout in The Hague, Machado and Pereira supplied bread to the Spanish and Dutch armies throughout the Franco-Dutch War from 1672 to 1678, as well as all the waggons, horses, river barges, warehouses and labour force necessary for its distribution and transport. In 1678, they also provided the British corps in Flanders with its basic provisions and transport.[52] Antonio Alvarez, better known as Moses, Machado was a personal friend of William III frequently accompanying him on campaign and this probably accounts for the fact that Machado and Pereira's first contract with the Dutch army coincided with William's rise to power in 1672.[53] Following the Treaty of Nijmegen in 1678, Machado and Pereira continued to supply the Dutch army during peacetime and they also tendered for, and received, the contract to victual William's expedition to England in 1688.[54] By this time, the firm enjoyed the title of Providiteurs-General to the Dutch army and their retention of the supply contract in 1689 was a formality.[55] As the Dutch army spread its operations into the

Rhineland in 1689, Machado and Pereira came into close contact with the factors of the Oppenheimers who were busy supplying the Imperial garrisons. Jacob Pereira's younger son, Isaac, accepted the contract to supply bread to the Williamite forces in Ireland between 1690 and 1692, a task which even his experience and expertise could not fulfill satisfactorily in such a remote and difficult country. When the initial English contingent of ten thousand men joined the Confederate army in the Low Countries in 1689, naturally it was Machado and Pereira who were entrusted with their supply and they continued to provide for the English army in the Netherlands for the remainder of the war. Isaac Pereira took the contract in Ireland at the rate of 1¼d per man per day, a sum which the paymaster deducted from each man's subsistence pay as the 'bread money'. In return, each soldier received a loaf of one pound in weight or one pound of hard biscuit if no bread was available.[56] In the Netherlands, Machado and Pereira began their contract in 1689 at the rate of 5 sols per man per day rising to 5.125 sols in the following year, a charge which then remained constant until 1697.[57]

A complete service was provided.

> Pereira . . . had already his provision of corn, of ovens and of bakers at Gand [Ghent] as providor to the Danes whom he has fed these two years and Ffonseca [Don Manuel de Fonseca[58]] has the same at Brussels, Louvain, as providor to all the Spanish troops. Ffonseca has the use of 100 waggons as providor and a great many boats to transport his provision. They have commissaries and servants in every town already as they furnish the troops everywhere with bread and for the same reason have credit everywhere. They have provision of corn excise free in all towns, they have waggons to bring 'em in straw and wood as forage. . . . Ffonseca has his own grounds and farms near Brussels where he designed to keep a stock of cattle and bring his provision as he had occasion. He had his own magazines and granaries at Brussels and every town to lay up his provisions.[59]

Magazines were stocked with fodder and biscuit during the winter and, in the campaigning season, waggons complete with drivers and horses were laid-on to take the bread from town bakeries and warehouses to the army in the field. Machado and Pereira supplied the British, the Dutch, the Brandenburgers and the Hanoverians, as well as the contingents from Celle, Hesse-Cassel, Münster, Holstein and Liège.[60] Municipal magistrates from the towns which had been selected as sites for

magazines were ordered by the States-General to liaise closely with
Machado and Pereira to arrange for the hire of warehouses and granaries. Cologne, which forbade Jews to live, stay or trade within its walls
but forced them across the Rhine to reside in the suburb of Deutz, was
obliged by the Dutch government to revoke these restrictions in favour
of the factors of the Dutch contractors.

A good deal of the business was sub-contracted with the two partners
acting as brokers but they did not search further afield for associates
than the Sephardic Jewish mercantile community and its New Christian
adherents. Jacob Pereira's sons, Abraham and David, with Pedro de
Palma, Manuel Pimentel and Jacob Bravusa masterminded the operations from Cologne which served as the central storehouse and distribution depot for the Rhineland theatre. We have seen how Isaac Pereira,
another son of Jacob, conducted the Irish contract. Young Isaac was a
friend of the Duke of Schomberg and he was assisted in Dublin by
David Machado de Sequiera, a relative of Moses Machado.[61] David
Losada Coopman looked after the supply of grain and horses in Brabant
and Maastricht, while Francisco de Cordova and Solomon de Medina
supervised Machado and Pereira's affairs in England.[62] It was a competitive and lucrative business and the partners did not enjoy a monopoly.
Don Manuel de Fonseca was responsible for provisioning the Spanish
forces in the Netherlands. John Heycoop specialised in providing forage
for winter quarters and Pierre Fariseau was another major provider of
fodder. F. V. Mourik was granted the contract for feeding the artillery
and transport horses in December 1690, using Malines as a base, and
in August 1691, F. Castaigne won the right to provide winter rations
for one thousand horses at Namur. G. van den Biesheuvel contracted
to supply hay and oats to the garrisons of Dendermonde and Ghent in
March 1692, but these were all tiny undertakings when set against the
four million rations of winter horse feed stocked in Brussels by Machado
and Pereira in September 1691.[63] Between 1672 and 1697, army victualling in the Low Countries was synonymous with the firm of Machado
and Pereira. Although they continued in business into the War of the
Spanish Succession, the greater geographical and international diversity
of that conflict weakened their monopoly until the firm ceased trading
with the death of Moses Machado in 1707.[64]

These great Jewish merchants were the industrialists of the seventeenth century, the managing directors of that century's equivalent of
the multi-national company. When only three towns in England had
populations in excess of twenty thousand souls – London, Norwich
and Bristol – the army victuallers fed one hundred thousand men and

their horses under the most adverse of circumstances. However, the Low Countries were heavily urbanised compared with England containing more and larger towns, a factor which must have assisted the contractors in acquiring an accumulation of expertise and provided a good deal of the necessary infrastructure for their organisations. The complexity and extent of the contractors' concerns can only be appreciated through a detailed examination of the engagements into which they entered with the English and Dutch governments. William III and Moses Machado signed a contract in 1694 by which Machado and Pereira undertook to provide with bread all the British troops in the Netherlands, together with the train of artillery, the contingent from Hanover and all the German and Scandinavian soldiers who were paid from the English Treasury. The bread was to be baked from 'good Prussia rye' and delivery to the troops in the field was to commence from 31 April/10 May 1694. Each loaf was to be three Brabant pounds in weight baked from the rye which was to be stocked in five or six designated magazines. In those magazines, the grain was to be turned frequently to ensure that the resultant bread was 'good and wholesome'. Naturally, the contractors had to be ready at all times to deliver the bread at the location and time demanded by the army. The bread was to be delivered at the head of each brigade, which usually consisted of three infantry battalions, and 'at the head of the train of artillery', to an appointed quartermaster. Machado and Pereira had to employ a clerk with each brigade and the artillery train to record all the deliveries of bread and to make up fortnightly accounts with the officers concerned. On the basis of these accounts, the Deputy Paymaster reimbursed Machado and Pereira from the bread money; if there were any defaults, then the Paymaster of the Army was empowered to pay Machado and Pereira directly from that unit's subsistence money. The contractors were to be indemnified for any losses to bread, stock or equipment caused by enemy action. In return, Machado and Pereira received 3 stijvers for each three pound loaf, regardless of the actual cost of rye. In 1694 the price was reduced to 2 stijvers and 6 doights but, in compensation, the soldiers had to buy the contractors' bread for the full twelve months of the year and not just during the campaigning season. To provide liquidity, the contractors were granted two advances: 100,000 guilders in the December of the previous year and 100,000 guilders in February. After this, the contractors were paid directly from the bread money deducted from the army's subsistence pay by the Deputy Paymaster. Similar contracts were arranged between Machado and Pereira and the Dutch government to provide bread for

the army of the States-General and for all the Germanic troops paid by
the Dutch Republic. The only real difference from the English contract
was that Machado and Pereira were paid 50 guilders by each company
for its bread rather than being remunerated for each individual loaf.
The whole process had become so standardised by 1692 that Machado
and Pereira issued draft printed contracts.[65]

With their monopoly of bread contracts for the British and Dutch
forces, Machado and Pereira seemed content to allow rival contractors
into the winter forage business. The British forces normally contracted
for two million rations of hay, straw and oats to be stocked in Ghent
and Bruges. Pierre Fariseau and John Heycoop were the main contractors although Machado and Pereira also demonstrated a keen interest.
As soon as the cavalry and dragoon regiments reached winter quarters,
the forage contractors sent the rations by boat or by road directly to
each regiment whose quartermaster received the forage and gave a
certificate to the contractor. These certificates were later presented to
the Paymaster for the Army who settled the bills from the money which
he deducted from the pay of the horsed regiments. Winter feed was to
be provided for two hundred days and each ration of fifteen Brabant
pounds of oats and three 'picotins' of hay was charged at nine stijvers.
The contractors were remunerated with an advance of 300,000 guilders
on signature of contract and then 100,000 guilders at the beginning of
each month of the contract. The forage merchants enjoyed considerable
commercial benefits. They were granted freedom to navigate on all
rivers and canals without having to pay tolls and they were exempted
from the customs and the excise in the Spanish Netherlands, Liège and
the United Provinces.[66]

Payment of the contractors was a regular, usually monthly concern,
and it was recognised as the first priority which had to be met even if
other accounts were left uncleared as a consequence. The cost to the
British army of buying bread, forage and transport services was well
over £200,000 per annum. However, in the disastrous year of 1696,
even this sacred account fell into arrear. In March 1697, Machado and
Pereira were owed £9,544 for the 1696 contract and had yet to be paid
the agreed advance of £17,600 for the 1697 agreement. Heycoop was
owed £40,000 for forage contracts and the English government had
still to meet van der Kaa's bill of £30,000 for the provision of bread
and forage to the auxiliary troops on the Meuse. General Overkirk was
obliged to pledge his personal estates as security in order for the soldiers
to be fed.[67] Fortunately, the shoulders of Machado and Pereira were
broad enough and they weathered the storm without undue hardship.

In the bread contracts with Machado and Pereira for 1695, 1696 and 1697, the contractors were enjoined to export from England an amount of 'rye, oats or other grain . . . as shall amount to the value of the rye and oats to be furnished by him for the service of his Majesty's forces in Flanders or the Low Countries.'[68] This did not mean that English cereals were then ground into the flour which entered the stomachs of the English soldiery for the contracts stipulated that Prussian rye was quite good enough for the diet of the common soldiers. Prussian rye was also the cheapest grain that Machado and Pereira could purchase through the Amsterdam market. As a result of this clause, English grain exports to the Low Countries rose from a negligible £1,600 in 1686 to £57,800 in 1693 and £173,500 in 1695.[69] In return for assisting English exports, Machado and Pereira insisted that all troops and companies which did not wish to buy their bread during the two hundred days of winter quarters had to pay a weekly compensation of fifty guilders. Like all good businessmen, Machado and Pereira bought the cheapest raw materials that they could find. Their contractual purchases of grain were made in England and Scotland up to 1692 but, in the following year, they discovered better bargains in Ireland where wheat cost a mere two shillings a bushel. Irish beef, butter and corn were still flowing into Machado and Pereira's warehouses via Ostend in 1695.[70]

The conveyance of provisions and men from England, Scotland and Ireland to the Netherlands was the task of the Commissioners for Transportation. Surprisingly, Machado and Pereira did not run their own shipping line. The Commissioners requisitioned merchantmen, made sure that they were at the right port at the correct time, and paid for their hire. The Commissioners were jointly funded by contributions from the army and the navy budgets, and they liaised closely with Israel Fielding whose office supplied the provisions for the ships' crews and for any soldiers who were in transit.[71] The Commissioners chartered merchant shipping at the rate of 14s a ton with demurrage of 4d a ton. This was not an unattractive deal and the colliers which plied between Dublin and Whitehaven regarded their redeployment as troop and provision transports for the forces in Ireland as a lucrative arrangement.[72] In face of the dangers from the Dunkirk privateers, all shipping to and from the Netherlands was convoyed.[73] After leaving the Downs or the Thames Estuary, the British ships anchored off the Dutch or Flanders coasts and then lightered their men and stores ashore in specially provided flat-bottomed boats. The sea communications between England and Flanders, although a distance of no more than 150 kilometres, traversed a stretch of water whose weather and moods were extreme.

William III was a very bad sailor and prone to seasickness. He was unable to remain long below decks on his passages across the North Sea and had to sit in a chair, which was tied to a mast, on the open deck. Shivering with wet and cold, his unfortunate courtiers were obliged to remain on deck with their sovereign.[74]

Sea communications were often slow and frequently highly dangerous and tenuous. A brigade of infantry and cavalry sailed from Gravesend on Saturday 19/29 March 1692 and came down to anchor at the Nore where they were to rendezvous with their naval escorts. The latter were not ready: the *Montague* had no pilot and the *Mary* galley wanted provisions. The transports waited patiently at the Nore until their own provisions began to run low at which point they put back to Gravesend to take on more hay for the horses. The wind then changed to the south-east preventing the transports from sailing back to the Nore.[75] Such a combination of bad luck, contrary weather and inefficiency was far from uncommon. Natural disasters were even more frequent. In the year 1692 alone, fifty-five Danish soldiers and forty-five of their women and children were drowned in March; a convoy struck the Goodwin Sands in August; three companies of Lord Cutts's regiment were lost at sea during October; and in June, Robert Wolseley, envoy extraordinaire to the Court at Brussels, nearly failed to take up his new appointment.

> I was in the great storm with the yachts and convoys that sailed out of the river on Sunday senight, and the ship where I was getting into the Goree was drove from her anchors the next morning about nine o'clock and forced ashore. For four hours together 'twas uncertain whether we should save our lives or no. At last, with the ebb of the tide, we waded to land. I was forced to stay a week at Helvoetsluys to get my goods ashore, many of which are spoiled by the breaking of the ship. I write this only to satisfy your Lordship that I got hither as soon as I could.[76]

Even if some human life could be saved from a shipwreck, horses stood no chance of survival. When a horse transport ran aground near the Goree in a storm in May 1697, only seven men lost their lives but all sixty horses were drowned.[77]

Equally as dangerous as the weather were the Dunkirk privateers or 'capers'. William Blathwayt lost his 'family, horses, plate and equipage' to the value of £2,000 to Dunkirk raiders in 1692. His monarch compensated him from the English Treasury and, presumably, the French returned his family upon whom no price could be set. The packet-boat running between Harwich and The Brill was captured twice during July 1695 and ten companies of infantry were taken at sea in March 1696.[78] Perhaps the saddest accident was that which befell the *Spanish Princess*, the packet-boat of twenty guns which plied between Harwich and Ostend. Mistaking an Ostend privateer for a hostile Dunkirk caper, she cleared for action and blew herself out of the water in the process. Sixty died and forty were rescued.[79] The letter post was as important as the convoys of men, horses and stores. A chain of post-horses was permanently stationed along the roads from the Allied camps in Flanders to Ostend, where a packet-boat was always on stand-by to ferry vital news and correspondence to England. Even though William issued instructions that a cruiser should patrol continually between Harwich and The Brill and Harwich and Ostend in order to protect this crucial service, most correspondents still took the sensible precaution of sending duplicates of their letters and papers via an alternative route.[80]

Theoretically, an army of 100,000 men needed 4,000 carts to carry its bread supply for one month. The total provisions for this hypothetical army – bread, forage, sutlers' supplies, beer, biscuit, ammunition and ambulance services – would have required 15,000 carts each month pulled by a total of 100,000 draught animals. This would have created a column 280 kilometres in length. For obvious reasons, no army operated on a monthly scale for its logistics but adopted a basis of between four and seven days.[81] As was the case with the bread and the forage, armies were not equipped with their own transport but rented a complete service from civilian contractors. Again, Machado and Pereira seized the lion's share of the business. At a unit cost of 9 livres per day, Machado and Pereira provided all the draught horses and waggons to convey the food, ammunition, forage and casualties of the British army throughout the war. The waggons were 'such as are usually made in Brabant . . . of sufficient strength and well provided with wheels, axle trees, shaft and shod with iron such as shall carry . . . at least between fourteen and fifteen hundred weight'. Every waggon had to come complete with a waggoneer 'and four good horses, well kept, and each horse to be four years old at the least.' Waggons had to be equipped with 'good harnesses', chairs, ropes, a drag hook to stop the wheels, a hammer, spade, grease pot, a store of iron nails and pins and cords. One spare wheel had to be provided for every ten waggons and each group of fifty waggons had to possess an 'instrument for raising up a waggon'. Machado and Pereira were also instructed to employ two lieutenants, three blacksmiths, two harness-makers and two wheelwrights and they had to have at least six spare waggons and plenty of horses in reserve. By switching its horses and carts from one service to another, the British army in the Low Countries managed with 310 waggons. Two hundred additional carts were contracted by the Ordnance Office to tow the train of artillery. All of the conveyances, horses and equipment were thoroughly inspected by a general officer before they were accepted as fit for service.[82]

The Dutch army was more generous in its provision of waggons. In 1690, the States-General contracted for 224 carts to carry the pontoons and the bridging train; 250 waggons for transporting ammunition; 250 waggons for bread and 12 to serve as field ambulances. These numbers stayed fairly constant throughout the war except that the number of ammunition waggons had increased to 340 by 1696.[83] The Dutch were more lavish in their employment of waggons as their armies were stretched from the North Sea coast to the Rhine whereas the British army in the Low Countries was usually concentrated in Flanders and never served farther afield than Brabant. Machado and Pereira did not own all of the waggons and horses but sub-contracted with merchants like Harman Hardenberg, Jan Boon, Anthony de Ridder, John Heycoop and Cornelius van Menrick.[84] There was a Waggon-Master-General with the British forces in Flanders but he was only responsible for discipline within the waggon train and for supervising the distribution of bread and forage from the civilian carts to the regimental and brigade quartermasters. Robert Barker held this commission for most of the war. There was a separate Baggage-Master, a post assumed by one Bill Pickett, who commanded the baggage train which contained the personal effects of the officers.[85]

The provision of army hospitals in Flanders was another vital service which the English government rented to civilian contractors. The medical arrangements in the Dutch army were far superior to those of the British corps. Dutch sick and wounded were taken straight from the army to one of the two field hospitals which accompanied the troops on campaign. From here, they were transferred to the 'Grootlegerhospitael' in Brussels. This served as a clearing station which nursed the less severely injured back to health but dispatched the more serious cases to the permanent military hospitals in Maastricht, 's-Hertogenbosch, which was the largest, Namur, Breda, Delft, Gouda, Rotterdam, Dordrecht, Gorinchem and Bergen-op-Zoom. The Dutch even provided a special waggon to convey the equipment of each regimental surgeon. One of the reasons for the relative excellence of the Dutch medical organisation was that they had learned during the Franco-Dutch War that the Catholic nuns of Flanders only cared for their co-religionists and refused to look after nasty protestants from Germany, Holland and England.[86] Although the English had participated in the latter stages of that campaign, no-one had remembered this simple lesson.

Sickness was endemic in seventeenth century armies – dysentery, typhus, typhoid, smallpox, venereal disease and food poisoning – and in July 1689, Waldeck reported to William that two hundred of the British corps were sick. However, it was in the aftermath of major battles that the true inadequacy of the pathetic medical service of the British army was revealed. After the disastrous campaign of 1689 in Ireland when raw British recruits died in their hundreds at Dundalk, the Williamite army had established a base hospital in Dublin in 1690 as well as a 'marching hospital' to travel with the troops. Additional surgeons' mates were also appointed to many of the battalions serving in Ireland.[87] The quality of regimental surgeons came in for some serious criticism in Ireland resulting in the institution of a examination before the Surgeon-General for all candidates for medical appointments after 1691.[88] The British corps in the Low Countries failed to take full advantage of these developments. There was an abundance of towns in which to lodge the sick and the wounded obviating the need to pay for an organised network of field and base hospitals. After the Battle of Steenkirk in 1692, British wounded 'were lying with their wounds up and down the streets' of Brussels as the Grootlegerhospitael was filled with Dutch casualties. Luckily there was a Florence Nightingale on hand in the form of the Princess de Vaudemont, the wife of the general of the Spanish forces in Flanders, who went in her coach with the assistance of link-boys and had the wounded moved into the great hall of her palace before calling in her own, personal surgeons and physicians. The Princess and her ladies acted as nurses. It was just as well that this angel of mercy was on hand as Blathwayt described the British hospitals at Malines, Ghent and Bruges as 'miserable', under-funded and badly in debt. French surgeons and apothecaries who were practicing in Brussels had to be drafted to look after British casualties and, needless to say, they were ever properly remunerated. When Blathwayt referred to 'hospitals', he did not imply the Dutch understanding of that word. Instead he meant a few reserved beds in private houses under the vague supervision of a military or a local civilian surgeon. From Brussels, most of the British wounded from Steenkirk were shipped by canal to Bruges and Nieuport before being sent across the North Sea to the Tower of London which served as a giant repository for injured soldiers. It also acted as a prison to prevent convalescent troopers from deserting. Even this progress in repatriating the wounded could be painfully slow and British casualties from Steenkirk were still housed in billets in Flanders as late as April 1693. The situation was no better following the Battle of Landen. Indeed, this action proved injurious to the health of civilians. The huge number of dead bodies left unburied or only partially interred in the wake of this engagement poisoned the waters of the River Hesbaye. Half the population of the village of Montenaken died and serious effects were felt as far away as Liège.[89]

In 1692, a plan was approved for tendering the entire care of the sick and the wounded to a private contractor. Only the regimental surgeons and surgeons' mates were to be retained on the military establishment. Although some progress was made in this direction in 1693 it was not until the succeeding year when the contract was taken by Patrick Lambe that improvements in medical care became noticeable. Lambe provided a total service – premises, equipment, nursing staff, doctors and medicines. By September 1694, Lambe had created hospitals in Ghent, Malines and Brussels and a new station was established at Dixmuyde after its capture late in the campaign. Unfortunately, the surrender of Dixmuyde to the French in July 1695 cost Lambe nearly £500 in lost equipment. Lambe was also responsible for setting up a British hospital at Liège in the summer of 1695 to which the British wounded from the Siege of Namur were shipped by boat down the Meuse.[90] The care of the sick and the wounded certainly improved under Lambe's supervision and the number of soldiers admitted to British hospitals in the Low Countries who ultimately succumbed showed a marked decline after the summer of 1694.[91] However, the subscription to private medical insurance for the common soldier was high. Patrick Lambe charged each patient 4½d a day, a sum which was deducted from the man's wages by the Deputy Paymaster and then forwarded to the contractor. This amounted to slightly more than the daily subsistence pay of the private soldier.[92]

Strategy depended upon supply, supply relied upon contractors, the contractors were paid by deductions from the soldiers' pay and the soldiers' pay rested upon the ability of the Treasury in Whitehall to remit specie across the North Sea. The payment of the troops in the Low Countries was a complex operation. First and foremost it was reliant upon good communications between England and the Netherlands. On one occasion, when five weeks of persistent easterly winds prevented the delivery of letters of credit, Richard Hill had to place the army on half-pay for a fortnight. Roger Sizer acted as the deputy in Flanders of the Paymaster-General in England, the Earl of Ranelagh, until he was dismissed for peculation in April 1692. He was replaced by Richard Hill who held the appointment until the end of the war. Hill enjoyed a daily wage of one pound sterling, which was increased by one hundred per cent in 1694. The Deputy Paymaster's office was in Antwerp where Hill conducted affairs with the assistance of two clerks and a cashier, Theodore Janssen. All payments to the troops were in cash, a process which involved regimental paymasters in ferrying tons of coin to their units from Antwerp. Hill employed the firm of Leman and Paul to provide the waggons although he also used water transport whenever possible. Naturally, these convoys were often troubled by French ambuscades. Security was also a problem for Hill's Antwerp office; carpenters were frequently in attendance to make structural alterations and the paymaster spent considerable sums on the regular acquisition of both new and additional locks.[93] As the men were paid in the local currency, the fulcrum of Hill's operations was to ensure a constant and favourable rate of exchange between the pound sterling, the Dutch guilder and the Flemish pound.[94] Between 1689 and 1691, funds were remitted to the Netherlands through William Schulenberg, Paymaster of the Dutch army, who drew bills on the Earl of Ranelagh in London. With the substantial growth in the size of the British commitment to the Low Countries in 1692 and 1693, there was the need to organise an independent system. From 1692 to 1694, Sir Joseph Herne, a London banker, headed a syndicate which assumed responsibility for the remittance of money to Flanders on a series of six monthly contracts. As government credit began to weaken in 1693 and 1694, the exchange rates started to slip and the business became suddenly less attractive to Herne and his partners. Lord Godolphin opened negotiations with the Bank of England. The result was the establishment of a branch of the Bank of England in Antwerp which undertook the payment of the British army at a fixed and agreed series of rates of exchange. Unfortunately, the exchange rates fell by nearly 20 per cent in mid–1695 and the Bank of England was unable to honour its bills to repay the £200,000 which it had borrowed to pay the troops and contractors during 1696. This ruined national and international confidence in the Bank, at least temporarily, and its Antwerp branch ceased trading having incurred a loss of £130,000 in a little over one year. For the remainder of the war, the army in Flanders was paid by a mixture of loans from financiers in the City of London and substantial short-term borrowings from the States-General of the United Provinces.[95] This fiscal crisis was sufficient to render the British corps in the Low Countries incapable of undertaking any effective action during the campaign

of 1696 and seriously encumbered William's entire strategy for that
particular year.

NOTES

1 D'Auvergne, *1692*, p. 55; CMC 4/39, 44, 46.
2 This is, perhaps, the starting point for a fresh examination of the nature of the
  'Military Revolution' in western Europe during the sixteenth and seventeenth
  centuries, originally promulgated by Michael Roberts, *The Military Revolution,
  1560–1660* (Belfast, 1956). For some additional thoughts see, Simon Adams,
  'Tactics or Politics? "The Military Revolution" and the Hapsburg Hegemony,
  1525–1648', in, *Tools of War: Instruments, Ideas and Institutions of Warfare,
  1445–1871*, ed. John A. Lynn (Urbana, Illinois, 1990), pp. 28–52.
3 See, *Amiable Renegade: The Memoirs of Captain Peter Drake, 1671–1753*,
  eds. P. Jordan-Smith & S. A. Burrell (Stanford, 1960), pp. 48–313.
4 Hubert van Houtte, 'Les Conférences Franco-Espagnoles de Deynze,
  1676–1678', *Revue d'Histoire Moderne*, ii. (1927), pp. 191–215; Fritz Redlich,
  De Praeda Militari: Looting and Booty, 1500–1815 (Wiesbaden, 1956), pp.
  44–8; Hubert van Houtte, *Les Occupations Étrangères en Belgiques sous l'Ancien Régime* (Ghent & Paris, 1930), i. 229–53; ii. 30–4, 52–5, 70–1, 153–4,
  157–202, 217–21.
5 M. P. Gutmann, *War and Rural Life in the Early Modern Low Countries*
  (Princeton, 1980), pp. 22, 64.
6 G. N. Clark, 'The Character of the Nine Years' War, 1688–1697', *Cambridge
  Historical Journal*, xi. (1953), pp. 168–71, 175–6; Richard Kane, *Campaigns
  of King William and the Duke of Marlborough . . . from 1689 to 1712* (London,
  1747), p. 22; HMC, *Finch MSS.*, iv. 73.
7 HMC, *Le Fleming MSS.*, pp. 284–5, 297; Luttrell, *Historical Relation*, ii. 187,
  245–6; *CSPD 1696*, pp. 205–6.
8 Drake, *Memoirs*, pp. 166–87; *Military Memoirs: Robert Parker and Comte de
  Mérode-Westerloo*, ed. David Chandler (London, 1968), p. 109.
9 HMC, *Finch MSS.*, iv. 416; HMC, *Downshire MSS.*, i. 426.
10 HMC, *Finch MSS.*, iv. 73–80.
11 *CSPD 1693*, p. 12.
12 Kane, *Campaigns*, p. 22.
13 BL, Add. MSS. 9,730, f. 23.
14 *CSPD 1697*, p. 260.
15 HMC, *Portland MSS.*, viii. 50; *CSPD 1694–5*, pp. 72–3.
16 HMC, *House of Lords MSS.*, n.s. iv. 232–8; *CSPD 1697*, p. 410; Luttrell,
  Historical Relation, iii. 388; *CSPD 1698*, pp. 17–18; *CSPD 1695*, p. 124.
17 *CSPD 1700–1702*, p. 35; S.S. Webb, *The Governors-General: The English
  Army and the definition of Empire, 1569–1681* (Chapel Hill, 1979), p. 490.
18 The standard rate of prisoner exchange was ten private soldiers in return for
  one lieutenant (Walton, p. 590).
19 HMC, *Finch MSS.*, iv. 323; *CSPD 1695*, p. 277.
20 *Private and Original Correspondence of Charles Talbot, Duke of Shrewsbury*,
  ed. William Coxe (London, 1821), p. 233, 14/24 June 1695.
21 *The Lexington Papers*, ed. H. M. Sutton (London, 1851), pp. 121–3; Luttrell,
  Historical Relation, iii. 506; BCRO, Trumbull Add. MSS. 103, 114.

22 *Memoirs of the Court of France, 1684 to 1720, from the Diary of the Marquis de Dangeau*, ed. John Davenport (London, 1825), p. 287; BCRO, Trumbull Add. MSS. 103.

23 Jones, *War and Economy*, pp. 15–26.

24 D'Auvergne, *1694*, pp. 9–10.

25 LG, no. 3159; *Chronicles of an Old Campaigner, Monsieur de la Colonie, 1692–1717*, ed. W. C. Horsley (London, 1904), p. 26; HMC, *Bath MSS.*, iii. 2–3; HMC, *Denbigh MSS.*, pp. 91–2; *Archives d'Orange-Nassau*, i. 307.

26 HMC, *Buccleuch (Montagu) MSS.*, ii. 373–4.

27 Japikse, iii. 224, 9/19 March 1691; ARA, Heinsius-Archief, 2172.

28 S. B. Baxter, *William III* (London, 1966), p. 288; see pp. 138–9.

29 Japikse (Welbeck), ii. 81–5; *The Parliamentary Diary of Narcissus Luttrell, 1691–1693*, ed. Henry Horwitz (Oxford, 1972), p. 257. On the linguistic abilities of the English gentry and aristocracy see, K. H. D. Haley, *An English Diplomat in the Low Countries: Sir William Temple and John de Witt, 1665–1672* (Oxford, 1986), pp. 11, 23–4.

30 D'Auvergne, *1695*, pp. 46–7; BL, Add. MSS. 61,342, ff. 115–16.

31 Claude Alexander, Comte de Bonneval, *Memoirs of the Bashaw Count Bonneval* (London, 1750), pp. 15–16; BL, Egerton MSS. 3,359, f. 3; BCRO, Trumbull Add. MSS. 103; LG, no. 3188; Luttrell, *Historical Relation*, ii. 536; *Dangeau*, p. 199; D'Auvergne, *1692*, p. 53; CMC 4/59.

32 *Wilhelm III von Oranien und Georg Friedrich von Waldeck*, ed. P. L. Müller (The Hague, 1880), ii. 184.

33 The nature of the countryside in the Low Countries is clearly revealed in, Jean de Beaurain, *Histoire Militaire de Flandre depuis l'année 1690 jusqu'en 1694 inclusivement* (Paris, 1755), i. This first volume consists of campaign maps of the Spanish Netherlands.

34 PRO, SP 77/57, ff. 1–63. Clausewitz says that the camps of the Nine Years' War were regarded as 'off-limits' to attacking armies, refuges where troops could rest safe in the knowledge that they would not be disturbed. As a consequence, he continues, commanders often did not bother to ensure that their camps faced the enemy. This seems a strange conclusion. Although camps stationed several days march from an opponent occupied sites dictated more by the needs of the quartermaster than the tactician, those within reach of the enemy were always positioned in defensible locations with their fronts towards the direction of probable assault. At Leuse in 1691, Steenkirk in 1692 and Landen in 1693, encamped armies were deliberately attacked. Readers will also find many instances where rival generals sought to surprise their encamped adversaries (Karl von Clausewitz, *On War*, eds. Michael Howard and Peter Paret (Princeton, 1976), pp. 297–8).

35 BL, King's MSS. 229; LUL, MS. 12, 'Livre des marches fait par les Armées de sa Majesté de la Grand Bretagne depuis l'an 1689 jusques à la fin de la Campagne 1695'; H. J. van der Heim, *Het Archief van den Raadpensionaris Anthonie Heinsius* (The Hague, 1867–80), ii. pp. xlvix-lii; *Mémoires du Maréchal de Villars*, ed. C. J. Melchior de Mis (Paris, 1884), i. 134–9; *Memoirs of the late Marquis de Feuquières* (Lodon, 1737), ii. 63–6; Bonneval, *Memoirs*, pp. 8–9.

36 G. Perjés, 'Army Provisioning, Logistics and Strategy in the second half of the seventeenth century', *Acta Historica Academiae Scientiarum Hungaricae*, xvi. (1970), p. 36; Martin van Creveld, *Supplying War: Logistics from Wallenstein to Patton* (Cambridge, 1977), p. 25.

37 ARA, Raad van State, 489, ff. 74–8, 168.
38 PRO, WO 24/10, f. 19.
39 Portable iron field ovens were invented by a Dr Keffler around 1666 (Walton, pp. 696–7).
40 This figure is based on Jones, *War and Economy*, p. 31.
41 Geoffrey Parker, *The Military Revolution* (Cambridge, 1988), pp. 45–81; M. S. Anderson, *War and Society in Europe of the Old Regime, 1618–1789* (Leicester, 1988), pp. 135–56.
42 Perjés, 'Army Provisioning', pp. 4–14; Van Creveld, *Supplying War*, p. 24; Walton, p. 697.
43 Jones, *War and Economy*, pp. 28–34.
44 Perjés, 'Army Provisioning', pp. 14–18.
45 D' Auvergne, *1693*, p. 46.
46 Walton, p. 695, n. 2038.
47 Sir John Fortescue, *History of the British Army* (London, 1910–1930), i. 344–8.
48 *CJ*, ix. 451–3; *CJ*, x. 295–6; *HMC, Finch MSS.*, iv. 82; Louis M. Waddell, 'The administration of the English army in Flanders and Brabant from 1689 to 1697' (Doctoral Dissertation, University of North Carolina, 1971), pp. 49–52.
49 Violet Barbour, *Capitalism in Amsterdam in the 17th Century* (Michigan, 1963), pp. 30–1.
50 Jones, *War and Economy*, p. 34.
51 S. Stern, *The Court Jew* (New Brunswick, 1985, 2nd edn), pp. 15–28.
52 PRO, SP 44/52, p. 72.
53 L. A. Vega, *Het Beth Haim van Ouderkerk aan de Amstel* (Assen, 1979), p. 44.
54 Albert M. Hyamson, *The Sephardim of England* (London, 1951), pp. 67–8; GAA, Notarial Protocollen, NP 2259, f. 189.
55 David Franco Mendes, *Memorias Estabelecimento e Progresso des Judeos Portuguezes e Espanhoes nesta famosa citade de Amsterdam*, eds. L. Fuks & R. G. Fuks-Mansfeld (Amsterdam, 1975), pp. 87–8; ARA, Heinsius, 142, 5/15 April 1689, Waldeck to Heinsius.
56 DCRO, Ilchester MSS., D. 124, Establishment, Ireland, 1690; Jonathan I. Israel, *European Jewry in the Age of Mercantilism, 1550–1750* (Oxford, 1985), pp. 124–31.
57 ARA, Heinsius, 142; GAA, Archief der Portugees-Israelietsche gemeente te Amsterdam, PA 334/727, f. 207–21, Machado and Pereira's accounts for supplying the auxiliary troops on the Meuse, June-October 1697. 1 sol = c.¼d.
58 SP 77/56, f. 77.
59 Bod. Lib., MS. Eng. Lib. d. 146(1), f. 7, Richard Hill to William Blathwayt, 12/22 Feb. 1694, quoted in, Jones, *War and Economy*, p. 35.
60 GAA, PA 334/727, f. 204.
61 Israel, *European Jewry*, p. 128; Bernard Shillman, 'The Jewish Cemetery at Ballyborough in Dublin', *Transactions of the Jewish Historical Society of England*, xi. (1924–7), p. 165.
62 GAA, NP 2259, f. 189; GAA, NP 7532, f. 721.
63 ARA, Raad van State, 489, ff. 73–4, 168–72; *The Marlborough-Godolphin Correspondence*, ed. H. L. Snyder (Oxford, 1975), i. 435, 439; *CSPD 1690–1*, p. 7 et passim; BL, Add. MSS. 9,724, f. 45.
64 *NNBW*, vi. 982–3, 1106–7.
65 IESCRO, HD 391/1 (formerly Phillips MSS. 9,999); BL, Add. MSS. 61,333, ff. 1–5, 51–2. For rates of exchange see below, note 94.

66 IESCRO, HD 391/1; BL, Add. MSS. 61,334, ff. 26–7, 29–30, 47.
67 BL, Add. MSS. 9,725, f. 93; BL, Add. MSS. 9,735, f. 61; BL, Add. MSS. 9,730, ff. 81–2; BL, Add. MSS. 61,334, f. 35; *CTP 1697–1702*, pp. 17, 218; Japikse, iii. 427.
68 IESCRO, HD 391/1.
69 Jones, *War and Economy*, pp. 186–8.
70 BL, Add. MSS. 9,735, f. 48; Luttrell, *Historical Relation*, ii. 508, 604–5; BCRO, Trumbull Add. MSS. 103.
71 *CSPD 1693*, p. 278; *HMC, Portland MSS.*, viii. 40; *CSPD 1697*, pp. 398–9; H. C. Tomlinson, *Guns and Government: the Ordnance Office under the later Stuarts* (London, 1979), pp. 150–1.
72 *The Correspondence of Sir John Lowther of Whitehaven, 1693–1698*, ed. D. R. Hainsworth (London, 1983), pp. xxxiv–xxxix, xli–xliii.
73 J. S. Bromley, *Corsairs and Navies, 1660–1760* (London, 1987), pp. 61–73.
74 Luttrell, *Historical Relation*, ii. 386; *The Diary of Abraham de la Pryme*, ed. Charles Jackson (Surtees Society, 1870), pp. 189–90.
75 *HMC, Finch MSS.*, iv. 53, 63.
76 *HMC, Finch MSS.*, iv. 31; Luttrell, *Historical Relation*, ii. 547; *HMC, Rutland MSS.*, ii. 137; SP 77/56, ff. 134–5, 8/18 June 1692, Brussels, Robert Wolseley to Earl of Nottingham.
77 BCRO, Trumbull Add. MSS. 103, 24 May/3 June 1697.
78 BL, Add. MSS. 9,735, f. 50; BL, Add. MSS. 9,723, f. 73; *HMC, Bath MSS.*, iii. 75.
79 *HMC, Finch MSS.*, iv. 404; *The Portledge Papers*, eds. R. J. Kerr & Ida Coffin Duncan (London, 1928), p. 145, 18/28 Aug. 1692.
80 Japikse (Welbeck), ii. 41; *HMC, Finch MSS.*, iv. 90, 186–7.
81 Figures based on Perjés, 'Army Provisioning', pp. 10–11.
82 IESCRO, HD 391/1.
83 ARA, Raad van State, 489, f. 73; ARA, Raad van State, 490, ff. 671–3; BL, Add. MSS. 61,333, ff. 24–38, 76–7.
84 ARA, Raad van State, 1545, ff. 45–9; ARA, Raad van State, 1913/1, f. 280.
85 BL, Add. MSS. 9,724, f. 129; BL, Stowe MSS. 444, ff. 16–22; *HMC, Various Collections*, ii. 176.
86 ARA, Raad van State, 489, ff. 88, 267–71; BL, Add. MSS. 9,723, f. 100; Baxter, *William III*, p. 282.
87 *CSPD 1690–1*, pp. 356–7; Walton, p. 849; WO 24/10, f. 14; Müller, ii. 165; Churchill College, Cambridge, Erle-Drax MSS., 4/18, f. 6; DCRO, Ilchester MSS., D. 124, Establishment 1690. Each British battalion enjoyed the services of one surgeon and one surgeon's mate.
88 Walton, p. 754.
89 D'Auvergne, *1692*, pp. 48–9; BL, Add. MSS. 9,722, f. 30; BL, Add. MSS. 9,724, f. 54; Japikse (Welbeck), ii. 202; BL, Add. MSS. 9,731, f. 7; Luttrell, *Historical Relation*, iii. 189; Gutmann, *War and Rural Life*, p. 165.
90 *HMC, Bath MSS.*, iii. 14; Robert Parker, *Memoirs of the Most Remarkable Military Transactions from the year 1683 to 1718 . . . in Ireland and Flanders during the reigns of King William and Queen Anne* (London, 1747), p. 58; BCRO, Trumbull Add. MSS. 103; BL, Add. MSS. 38,698, f. 173; BL, Add. MSS. 38,699, ff. 23, 88; BL, Add. MSS. 38,700, f. 213.
91 BL, Add. MSS. 9,731, f. 19.
92 Walton, p. 756.

93 L. M. Waddell, 'The Paymaster Accounts of Richard Hill at Attingham Park', *JSAHR*, xlviii. (1970), pp. 50–9.
94 The major currencies in the Low Countries and their rates of exchange against the pound sterling were:
   Dutch: 20 stuijers (stivers, stuivers) = 1 guilder (F1)
   Fl.10 = £1
   Flemish: 39 schellingen (silver shillings) = £1
95 Jones, *War and Economy*, pp. 20–6, 83–4, 161n.36.

III

THE ARMY IN ACTION

William III divided his British army into two distinct sections: the forces in England and the corps in Flanders. After 1692, William assumed personal command over the British troops in the Low Countries and treated them as one of the components of the Confederate army of the Grand Alliance. However, during the campaigns of 1689 and 1690 slightly different arrangements had to be made as the king was occupied in Ireland. During the first year of the war, the command of the British corps in the Netherlands was entrusted to John Churchill, Earl of Marlborough. Although William was present in the Low Countries for much of the campaign of 1691 and assumed overall control of the Allied army, the British corps remained under the direction of Marlborough who was assisted by Lieutenant-General Percy Kirke and four brigadiers – the Duke of Ormonde, James Douglas, George Ramsey and George Churchill. Marlborough fell from grace in 1692 leaving no natural or acceptable successor as commander-in-chief of the British in the Spanish Netherlands. Tired of the xenophobic ambitions of British generals, William left the position vacant for the remainder of the war and simply appointed a lieutenant-general of the British foot and a lieutenant-general of the British horse at the commencement of each campaign. Sir John Lanier was commissioned to command the cavalry in 1692, to be succeeded by the Earl of Portland in 1693 and the Duke of Ormonde in 1695. Thomas Talmash, or Tollemache, was lieutenant-general of the infantry from 1691 to 1693 and he was replaced by Sir Henry Bellasise in 1694. Although these lieutenant-generals, along with their subordinate major-generals, were commissioned specifically to command British troops, in fact they were general officers within the larger context of the Confederate army and as likely to find themselves commanding a mixed detachment of Walloons, Danes and Brandenburgers as a unit of purely native soldiers. The British troops rarely fought together as a separate, national corps. Only at the level of the brigade, which was composed of between three and five infantry battalions or a similar number of cavalry regiments, did British soldiers fight alongside one another. Brigadiers were thus the general officers most likely to command British soldiers in action. The higher general ranks were related to tactical commands within the Allied army as a whole.

The importance of the brigade was mirrored in the administrative organisation of the British forces in the Netherlands. Although each infantry battalion and cavalry regiment was an independent administrative entity, the brigade also possessed administrative functions. Machado and Pereira delivered bread to the brigade and retained a clerk with each brigade who was responsible for supervising the operation. Regiments and battalions were allocated to specific brigades at the beginning of the campaigning season and usually remained with them for its duration. However, if the brigade was the largest building brick in the tactical and organisational structure of the army, as far as the British soldier in Flanders was concerned, his basic loyalty was towards his regiment or battalion. His lieutenant-colonel was king. Each regiment and battalion drew its own pay from Richard Hill in Antwerp and provided its own quarters, clothes, equipment and recruits. On the rare occasions when an overall administrative command for the British corps was required, then William delegated the task to William Blathwayt who travelled to the Netherlands every year in the dual capacity of Secretary-at-War and itinerant Secretary of State. Blathwayt issued orders for the summoning of courts-martial and acted as a clearing house for army correspondence. Blathwayt was simply a secretary who took some limited initiatives but he had no role in military planning or in the conduct of operations after the manner of a modern chief of staff but he did serve as a focus for the resolution of administrative difficulties. Blathwayt was most certainly not an English version of Jules-Louis Chamlay, Marquis de Bolé, whose title of Maréchal Général des Logis aux Campes et Armées du Roi included the responsibilities of chief of the general staff to Louis XIV and Louvois, operational planner and custodian of the Dépôt des Cartes et Plans.

Specific tasks were controlled by commissioned staff officers. Each battalion enjoyed the services of a chaplain, a surgeon, a surgeon's mate, a quartermaster, an adjutant or aide-major and a provost. Cavalry regiments were similarly endowed except that they were allowed a quartermaster for each troop. The principal staff officers of the army in England – the Paymaster-General, Commissary-General of the Musters, the Adjutant-General, the Quartermaster-General and the Judge

Advocate – all appointed deputies to execute their duties with the various overseas operations conducted during the Nine Years' War. The corps sent to Ireland, Flanders and the West Indies all included deputies to the general staff officers in England. The troops in Flanders also benefited from a Chaplain-General as well as a Waggon-Master-General and a Baggage-Master. The same system was applied to the medical staff. A Physician-General, Surgeon-General and Apothecary-General officiated in England but sent deputies to attend the expeditions to Ireland, Scotland, the West Indies and the Low Countries.[1]

Although the battalion, regiment and brigade represented the permanent tactical and administrative sub-divisions of the army, larger tactical groupings were arranged. Before the army took the field, it was divided into a First and Second Line. Each Line was again sectioned into a right wing of horse, a left wing of horse and the infantry. Brigades, both of infantry and cavalry, were given exact positions within one of the Lines which corresponded to their places in the line of battle if the army went into action. As far as possible, the army marched and camped according to the organisation of its Lines. When in camp, the regiments and battalions pitched their tents in two lines, one behind the other, and on the march the brigades trudged along in the formation of the Lines. However, whilst marching, the Lines were referred to as the Right Wing and Left Wing. The Lines, or Wings, were not permanent arrangements. They gave the army some system on marches and in camp as well as quickening its deployment for battle but brigades could be removed from one Line to another or detached from the army altogether to be replaced by new formations. Also, the Line was not an administrative sub-division but possessed only a tactical application.

The question of how many British troops served with the Allied army in the Low Countries during the Nine Years' War has been the subject of some debate.[2] Uncertainties have arisen in three areas. In the first place, how big was a battalion of foot or a squadron of horse? Secondly, the English government's habit of including foreign mercenaries on the English establishment has created difficulties. Thirdly, a clear distinction has to be made between the paper strength of the army as shown in the official establishments and the number of soldiers actually in the field. The Treasury at Whitehall paid the wages of three categories of soldier. The largest portion was of native troops recruited from within the British Isles. This was followed by a substantial corps of foreign mercenaries, mostly composed of Dutchmen and Danes, which was treated as a part of the British army for the duration of the war and whose pay was listed in the official British establishments. The third category consisted of foreign mercenaries who were paid by the English government but who did not appear on the annual establishments. They were not, therefore, regarded as a component of the British army. The annual estimates which the Paymaster-General presented to the House of Commons every autumn indicated the desired strength of the army for the coming year and sought funding to support that number. By using these annual estimates and the resultant official establishments, it is a relatively straightforward exercise to calculate the size of the British army during the war and how much of that army fought in the Low Countries.

James II had raised his army to around 40,000 by early November 1688, although this level slumped dramatically during the latter part of that month and into December. On 1 April 1689, the paper establishment of the British army called for 73,692 men of whom 30,776 were to be British and 42,926 Dutch, German and Danish.[3] When the Earl of Ranelagh read the military estimates for 1690 to the House of Commons on 9/19 October 1689, he asked for 49,238 British subjects to be assisted by 14,788 Dutchmen and 5,610 Danish mercenaries.[4] This figure remained static for 1691[5] but in 1692 the total decreased slightly to 64,924 of which the British share amounted to 48,828.[6] The downward trend continued for 1693. A total of 54,562 troops were supported by the Whitehall government but only 40,863 came from within the British Isles.[7] With pressures growing for a descent on the coast of France and with mounting losses from the unsuccessful campaigns of 1692 and 1693, the British forces were substantially augmented for the season of 1694. The total establishment was increased to 93,635, of whom 68,725 were to be raised in England, Ireland, Scotland and Wales.[8] Out of 83,143 men for 1695, 62,716 were British.[9] This figure was adjusted by only a handful of men in 1696[10] and there was no alteration in the army for the final year of the war in 1697.[11] From 1694 onwards, 4,500 commissioned officers commanded the British forces, an approximate ratio of one officer to every thirteen men. These foreigners within the British army consisted mainly of Dutch and Danish hirelings. 14,778 Dutchmen and 6,530 Danes were entered on the British establishment in 1690, but this had reduced to 7,756 Dutch and 7,540 Danes in 1694. Half of the 8,000 men of the Hanoverian Brigade came onto the British establishment in 1692, having previously been paid by the government of the Spanish Netherlands. Of the 4,000 men raised by the Bishop of Münster, 2,000 were entered onto the British establishment in 1695 and the remainder were paid by the Dutch. Eighteen hundred men from Brunswick-Wolfenbüttel also joined the British army in 1695. Aside from these mercenaries who were counted as parts of the British army, the Treasury also assisted the Dutch in meeting the costs of contract troops from Brandenburg, Hesse-Cassel and Electoral Saxony.[12]

What proportion of these total forces constituted the British contribution to the Allied armies in the Low Countries? 10,972 native horse and foot were sent to join Waldeck's army in 1689.[13] With the war in Ireland entering a critical phase, William was able to spare just 5,360 members of the British army for service in the Low Countries for the campaign of 1690.[14] As the pressures in the Irish theatre eased during the following year, the King enlarged the British corps in Flanders to 11,144 men in 1691.[15] For 1692, 18,466 native privates and non-commissioned officers fought in the Low Countries commanded by 810 officers, in company with 13,926 German and Scandinavian soldiers.[16] This level scarcely altered during 1693 with 19,211 British soldiers and 14,916 foreign mercenaries but there was a sizeable increase in 1694 when 29,100 native troops served alongside 14,916 foreigners, a total corps of 44,016. During 1695, the number of foreign troops in the British corps grew to 15,493 and the abandonment of attempts to land troops in France through amphibious operations released sufficient native troops to boost the total available for the Netherlands to over 40,000. By 1696, the British contingent in the Low Countries had been inflated to 43,156 with an additional 15,493 foreigners, a total corps of 58,649. During the final year of the war, 34,146 British rankers fought with 15,933 mercenaries making a total of 50,349.[17]

All of the figures presented here show the totals stated on the official estimates and establishments. They do not record the actual numbers of troops serving with the army in the field. During the war years, the majority of the infantry battalions on active service in the Low Countries and in Ireland were persistently understrength by a factor of between ten and twenty per cent. This deficiency was caused partly by sickness, desertion, battle casualties and poor recruiting conditions. However, the major reason was the system of mustering the army in the Low Countries. From 1689, all British regiments and battalions in the Netherlands were allowed to 'muster complete'; they were assumed to possess a full complement of officers and men regardless of their true state. This was a useful device in that it gave regiments the chance to build-up a small financial reserve to meet the costs of clothing, damaged equipment and recruitment, but it was also pernicious because it rendered impossible even a half-accurate estimate of how many men were actually serving the King.[18] William Blathwayt calculated that, in the field, a battalion of infantry consisted of an average of 600 men and a squadron of horse or dragoons numbered 130. Although Edward D'Auvergne's figures vary between 650 and 500 men for a battalion in the Netherlands depending upon the state and stage of a particular campaign, the average of his statistics supports the assumption of Blathwayt.[19] In estimating the field strength of the British corps in the Low Countries during the Nine Years' War, and indeed the strength of the Allied army as a whole, Blathwayt's rule of thumb has been adopted. Blathwayt also counted only private soldiers and non-commissioned officers. He justified this on the grounds that although the numbers of men in a battalion or a regiment might vary substantially during a campaign, the complement of commissioned officers remained fairly constant. Again, this practice has been adopted.[20]

The other major component of the military effort of the Grand Alliance in the Low Countries was the army of the Dutch Republic. From a population of only two million people, the Dutch proportionately raised more men than the British Isles even though the latter enjoyed a population that was two and a half times as large. By the end of 1688, the States-General fielded a paper strength of either 64,979[21] or 71,225.[22] No such discrepancy is apparent for 1689 with both major sources agreeing that the army consisted of 64,650,[23] but uncertainty returns in the following year. An English list for 1690 suggests that 75,778 troops were on the Dutch establishment whereas the Dutch Council of State notes only 64,596.[24] The missing 11,000 men are probably accounted for by the fact that the British government paid for a Dutch corps within its own national establishment, a legacy of William's invasion of 1688. The Dutch army was substantially augmented in 1694 to coincide with a similar increase in the British forces. Our two sources mention levels of 97,345[25] and 87,978,[26] with the difference again probably arising from the existence of the Dutch corps in the British army. The Dutch army reached 100,796 in 1695 and 101,880 in 1696 and 1697.[27]

To a greater extent than the English government, the United Provinces employed their commercial wealth to hire considerable numbers of foreign troops. Even in peacetime, the Dutch army was a cosmopolitan organisation containing regiments from Scotland, England, Ireland and Switzerland and this tendency to rely on foreigners to eke out native manpower was exacerbated in time of war. Waldeck's army of 23,620 in the Low Countries in December 1688 contained Dutchmen, Brandenburgers, Swiss, Swedes and Germans.[28] On 5/15 August 1688, the States-General had concluded a contract with the Elector of Brandenburg for the hire of 7,510 troops, a figure which was to be adjusted upwards to 7,884 in 1690. A further treaty, this time with Brunswick-Lüneburg-Celle, was signed on 8/18 August 1688 to provide 2,720 men. A second agreement two years later raised this brigade to 2,868 soldiers. A total of five separate agreements between the States-General and Brunswick-Wolfenbüttel produced 1,300 men in 1688, 1,366 in 1690, 2,587 in 1692, 2,971 in 1693 and 3,457 in 1694. Hesse-Cassel was another participant in the 'soldier trade' renting 2,200 horse and foot in July 1688, 2,442 in 1690 and 4,611 in 1694. The Duchy of Württemberg sold 1,296 men to the Dutch in August 1688 and another 1,386 two years later. Six Swedish infantry battalions entered Dutch service in September 1688, amounting to 6,048 soldiers, and these were joined by further regiments in 1693 to make a total corps of 7,945. Just one cavalry regiment of 468 troopers came from Saxe-Gotha, 456 horsemen rode in from Electoral Saxony, one cavalry regiment containing 456 men was contributed through the combined efforts of Courland and Saxe-Meiningen, a single dragoon regiment of 688 men accompanied the Duke of Holstein-Plön to Holland and two infantry battalions, totalling 1,896 men, were contracted from Slippenbach. In addition, the States-General shared with the English government the costs of the Hanoverian brigade of 8,000 men and bore half the charges of the 4,000 men from Münster.[29] In the aftermath of its expansion in 1694, the Dutch army contained 38,065 hirelings from Sweden and Germany in addition to the Swiss regiments which formed part of the native component. If Britain was beginning to appreciate the benefits of using money to persuade other European states to fight on her behalf, the Dutch were already past masters at the exercise.[30]

The weaponry of the British army in the Nine Years' War was in transition between the pikes and matchlock muskets of the early and mid-seventeenth century and the bayonets and flintlock guns of the eighteenth century. Flintlock muskets had been issued to the whole of the Duke of York's Maritime Regiment of Foot at its foundation in 1664, sea spray not reacting kindly with lighted slow matches. As it was their principal task to guard the train of artillery and ammunition, the Royal Fusiliers, founded in 1685, carried flintlocks for the obvious reason that the hazards of yards of slow match in propinquity to barrels of gunpowder were extreme. The flintlock was shorter in length, lighter to carry, easier to handle and less likely to misfire than the matchlock. Provided that the powder was dry, it could even be used in wet weather. Infantry reinforcements sent to Tangier in 1680 were divided into three equal sections: one was armed with pikes, one with matchlocks and one with flintlocks. In 1683, the First Foot Guards and the Coldstream Guards were rearmed with flintlocks in place of their old matchlocks and all the new regiments raised after 1689 were equipped with the more modern weapon. Although the shortage of muskets in 1689 and 1690 prevented the entire British army from being armed with the more efficient guns, every effort was made to substitute new for old. However, it was a slow and costly process. In May 1693, the train of artillery in the Low Countries carried 3,800 spare flintlock muskets but also 1,700 spare matchlocks.[31] Even in 1702, matchlocks could still be discovered in the British infantry although they were usually confined to garrison companies in the remoter corners of the kingdom.

Pikes, too, persisted into the Nine Years' War. Although Sebastien le Prestre de Vauban had invented the socket bayonet in 1669[32] it was relatively slow in superseding the pike and the earlier plug bayonet. Before 1678, each company of foot, and therefore each battalion, had one third of its men armed with ash pikes, five metres in length, and two-thirds bearing firearms. Gradually, over the next decade, this ratio altered in favour of the musket. A number of the new regiments of 1689 were still armed in the proportion of two muskets to one pike but in 1691 whole companies were equipped with muskets and bayonets. Although it is difficult to generalise in a period when weaponry was changing, supply was frequently difficult and troops were often armed with what was available rather than desirable, the ratio of pikes to muskets fell during the course of the Nine Years' War. Whereas most regiments obeyed the rule of two muskets to each pike in 1689, by the end of the war this had altered to three muskets to every pike. To compensate for the demise of the pike, the new flintlock muskets were fitted with the socket bayonet. The train of artillery in 1693 conveyed 3,960 spare pikes but also 1,500 replacement 'sword bayonets'.[33] This suggests that the socket bayonet was steadily ousting both the pike and the plug bayonet in the middle years of the war. By 1697, virtually all of the British line musketeers were wielding a socket bayonet on the muzzles of their flintlock guns. A similar transformation occurred in the French army. At the opening of the war in 1688, French line infantry battalions were armed in the proportion of one pike to five muskets. The pike was finally abolished in France in 1703. Another important change in the equipment of the foot was the abolition of the dangerous 'collar of bandoliers', the musketeer's shoulder baldric from which had been suspended a number of thin, metal tubes each holding a charge of powder. This was replaced by a leather cartridge box containing a number of measured charges of powder and ball wrapped in a cylinder of thick paper. Each battalion had a company of grenadiers armed with flintlock muskets and small hand grenades, hollow shells of cast iron filled with gunpowder and ignited via a fuse and touch-hole. Grenades were principally used in siege warfare and had no place in open battle.

At the Hounslow Camps in 1686 and 1687, two light, three-pounder brass cannon had been attached to each battalion of foot to serve as 'infantry guns'. This practice seems to have continued during the Nine Years' War. In the field, these infantry cannon were worked by foot soldiers seconded from the battalion rather than by trained gunners supplied by the Ordnance Office. The latter only served the guns situated in the train of artillery. However, the British foot were not always sufficiently fortunate to enjoy the services of infantry guns and much depended upon the supply available from the Tower of London. It appears that when the army was on the march in the Low Countries, all of the heavy cannon and mortars travelled with the train of artillery whilst the light field guns were the responsibility of the infantry battalions and brigades.[34] In selecting its heavy weaponry the army was conservative. Experiments with new-fangled guns were commonplace during this period – multi-barrelled muskets, rifles, rifled pistols, multiple grenade throwers, mortars which threw seven projectiles at once and giant mortars which hurled 500-lb. bombs. Many of these ingenious devices passed their proving trials with flying colours but were then studiously eschewed by the military.[35] The train of artillery for Flanders in 1692 contained eight 12-pounders, ten 6-pounders, twenty 3-pounders and four 8-inch mortars, in addition to ammunition and stores. The train was conveyed by 200 waggons hired in the Low Countries.[36] Two years later, in keeping with the growing British commitment to the Netherlands, the train expanded to twenty 24-pounders, twenty 20-pounders, eighteen 4-pounders, with ten 13-inch mortars and ten 10-inch mortars.[37] In 1695, 1696 and 1697, the train consisted of ten 12-pounders, thirty-six 6-pounders, six howitzers and twenty 3-pounders.[38] The train of artillery also carried all the bridging equipment, 'the tin boats', usually numbering around forty copper pontoons, complete with planking, ropes and tools. In addition to all its own ammunition, stores and gear, the train of artillery conveyed spare arms and equipment for both the infantry and the horse. The train of artillery was effectively the overseas depot of the Ordnance Office. The British train of artillery was very much designed to serve the needs of the British corps in the field and in battle. Although its twenty-four-pounders and mortars were heavy enough to be of use in a siege, the British train did not carry the very heavy and super-heavy breaching cannon that were needed to break down fortifications. During sieges, the British corps had to rely upon the siege trains provided by the Dutch and the Spanish armies.

The weaponry of the mounted troops was not in transition. The heavy cavalry wielded straight sabres in the charge but possessed either a pair of long-barrelled horse pistols or a short-barrelled flintlock carbine for use on picket or reconnaissance duty. Dragoons, befitting their role as mounted infantry, borrowed flintlock muskets and socket bayonets from the foot and horse pistols from the cavalry. The cream of the British heavy cavalry, the Life Guards, sported defensive armour in the form of pot helmets and back and breast plates forged from 'carbine proof' steel. The Royal Horse Guards also wore a cuirass but whether these were reserved for ceremonial occasions or actually worn every day in the field is not clear.

During May 1674, a circular letter was posted to all regimental colonels and garrison governors informing them that a drill manual was about to be issued containing the fruits of the experiences from the Third Anglo-Dutch War. Late in the following year, Thomas Newcomb, the King's printer, published the initial one hundred copies of *The Abridgement of English Military Discipline*. A further 1,500 copies were run off in 1676 and, three years later, the *Abridgement* was adopted for use in the Scottish army. King Charles II was determined to have 'one method established for the exercising of his Forces in all his Dominions . . . He hath already, upon that consideration, appointed an Abridgement of Military Discipline to be made use of by his Forces in his Kingdoms of England and Ireland.'[39] The Abridgement was revised in 1680, a third edition containing the lessons learned during Monmouth's Rebellion followed in 1685 and this was reprinted without alteration in 1686. The section devoted to infantry drill and evolutions was extracted and published separately as *The Exercise of the Foot* in 1690. Three years later, Sir Thomas Livingstone, the commander-in-chief in Scotland, published *The Exercise of the Foot* as the official drill manual for the Scottish army. He added two appendices: an improved and amended 'exercise of the Dragoons' and 'the rules of war for the infantry upon the day of battle', the latter penned by the experienced Lieutenant-General Hugh Mackay.[40] Effectively, the British army fought the Nine Years' War according to the *Abridgement* of 1685 with a few variations. Its spirit was closer to the fashions of France than to the practices of the Dutch.

The *Abridgement* exudes a casual and relaxed tone. There is nothing here of the parade ground of Frederick the Great, no beatings and bawlings from subalterns and sergeants, no attempts to turn human beings into automata who could load and fire their muskets thrice every minute. Instead, words of command had to be given 'leisurely' to avoid confusion and the musketeers and pikemen 'must leisurely and distinctly perform every particular posture'. When moving into battle the troops were enjoined to 'march very leisurely'. As seventeenth century drill was a precise rehearsal of the evolutions which would be required in combat, there is no reason to suppose that this casualness was specially reserved for training. The drill was in keeping with armies which marched but ten miles a day and lay down to rest as often as they could.

Just as the weaponry of the British army was in a state of flux between the old and new, so this was mirrored in the infantry tactics. The battlefield drills and formations were little different from those employed by Gustavus Adolphus at Breitenfeld in 1631. The old Swedish regiment was gradually thinning into a more linear shape but it was a slow process. Charles's soldiers stood with their ranks six paces apart to enable them 'to have liberty to use their arms' and three paces separated each file. This generous allowance of space was dictated by the matchlock musketeers who needed plenty of room to wield their lighted matches without running the risk of igniting their neighbour's cartridge box. As the flintlock replaced the matchlock, the gap between the files was substantially reduced until it was established at just one pace in 1686. The files were now virtually shoulder-to-shoulder. It must be assumed that only those battalions armed with the new gun adopted the closer formation; units which retained the matchlock must have remained in the pre-1686 spacings. Clearly, a battalion could not combine flintlocks and matchlocks. For reviews and inspections, the ranks were drawn up twelve paces apart, sufficient for the reviewing party to ride between them, but the gap was diminished to six paces in battle to present a smaller target to enemy artillery. Even then, the infantry battalion of the Nine Years' War occupied nearly two hundred metres from flank to flank. Whilst waiting in their ranks and files, the soldiers were instructed to 'look lively' and always to keep their eyes on the commanding officer who stood to the front. This latter order was only inserted in the *Exercise* of 1690 in response to the experiences gained from the 1689 campaign in Ireland. 'It must be taken for a General Rule, That nothing be done, nor any motion made, until the last word of every command be fully delivered, then all is to be performed with a graceful readiness and exactness.' The *Exercise* also called for that vital commodity, Silence![41] The matchlock musketeer had to be given thirty-eight separate orders in the task of preparing, firing and loading his gun. However, in action, both the matchlock and the flintlock musketeer were trained to compress all the parade-ground movements within three words of command – Make Ready – Present – Fire.[42] The pikeman had thirty-two set motions which enabled him to 'charge', or point his weapon towards the enemy, at all four points of the compass. In addition to learning how to employ his weapon in action, each soldier was instructed in ceremonial drill, marching, camping and the 'evolutions' by which a battalion manoeuvred on the field of battle. Oddly enough, although the model for all seventeenth century drill manuals, Jacob de Gheyn's *Wapenhandlingen van roers, musquetten und spieesen* (Amsterdam, 1607) conveyed its information almost entirely through illustration, the various editions of the pocket-sized *Abridgement* relied wholly upon the written word.

In handling both the pike and the musket, the soldier had to stand in an 'easy' position with his feet a 'moderate distance' apart for 'if they are too wide asunder, it weakens'. Battalions usually possessed ten, twelve or sixteen companies, each of fifty, sixty, eighty or one hundred men. Guards and the older regiments tended to have the larger establishments whilst the line battalions raised especially for the war enjoyed the smaller. Each company was divided into three wings, two of musketeers, or 'shot', and one of pikemen. At the beginning of the war there were two musketeers to every pikeman but this ratio had lengthened to three to one by 1697. On the parade ground, the musketeers drew up in two wings with the pikes sandwiched between them, the musketeers in six ranks and the pikemen in five. The idea was for the pikes to protect the 'shot' from attack by enemy cavalry whilst the main action was decided by a fire-fight between the rival musketeers. Pikemen also provided a cutting edge to an infantry charge although in such actions the unwieldy pike was discarded in favour of the short infantry sword, or hanger.

The battalion was trained to fire in seven tactical situations: to hold or 'keep' ground; to 'gain' ground; to 'lose' ground or retreat; to fire to the rear should the battalion be taken in reverse; to fire to the flanks whilst on the march; to fire 'in the street way' in a defile; and to fire in all-round defence from a hollow square. To 'keep' ground, the pikemen 'charged' their weapons towards the enemy and all the musketeers knelt down. The sixth rank stood, fired over the heads of the five ranks in front, knelt once more and began to reload. The fifth rank then stood and so the sequence progressed to the first or front rank, by which time the sixth rank would have been loaded ready to resume. There were variations enabling two or three ranks to fire simultaneously, the ranks kneeling, stooping and standing. In 'gaining' ground or advancing, all the six ranks stood. The first or front rank fired and then peeled off to the rear to reform behind the sixth rank and commence reloading. The second rank then marched forward and fired before breaking away to the rear around the right and left flank of the 'wing of shot'. In this way, the battalion inched forward whilst continuing to fire. The same sequence was followed in retreating, except that the ranks did not advance to fire but stood still so that the peeling away of the ranks to right and left allowed the battalion slowly to move backwards. In both advancing and retreating, the pikemen had to keep their ranks level with those of the musketeers on either side. Should the battalion be attacked in the rear, the six ranks of musketeers and the five ranks of pikemen faced about and commenced firing according to the same drill as for 'keeping' ground. Firing to the flank whilst on the march was a very difficult manoeuvre and was reserved for the parade ground rather than the battlefield. The musketeers along the threatened wing turned half left or right and then fired by ranks. 'Firing in the street way' was employed when the battalion was called upon to defend a road, a defile, a hedgerow or operate in a built-up area but it was only safe if there was no danger of a flank attack. The pikemen and musketeers doubled their ranks from five to ten and from six to twelve, so halving the battalion frontage but doubling its depth. Two files of musketeers, each now of twelve men rather than six, one from the left wing of shot and one from the right, marched forward and formed two ranks directly in front of the pikemen in the centre, sheltering under the very tips of the pikes. The front rank knelt, the second rank stood and they gave fire one rank at a time. Both ranks then retired to reform their files and two more files came forward to replace them. The 'hollow square' was a regular evolution, practised to protect an isolated formation from infantry or cavalry assault from any direction. It could be performed by a single company or by a whole battalion. The musketeers formed three ranks on the outside of the square whilst the pikemen stood in three ranks behind them with the officers in the centre. To fire, the first rank knelt, the second stooped and the third stood. If attacked by horse, the pikemen stretched their points over the heads of the musketeers to create a 'hedgehog'.

Given the severe limitations of the seventeenth century military musket and the inflexibility of firing from a formation six ranks deep, the battalion could only fire when halted. Firing on the march was impossible. This meant that the fire-fight in battle took place between two static lines of infantry at ranges of one hundred metres or less. The pikemen were little more than observers of a musketry duel and

frequently its principal victims. Neither firing by rank nor by file produced a heavy weight of shot as only one-sixth of the battalion's firepower was discharged simultaneously. However, it was a prudent
method as a large proportion of the battalion was always loaded and
ready to fire. In many ways, the firing drills were more suited to the
trenches and fixed defences found at sieges than to battle in the open
field. Similarly, in sieges the bayonet and the hanger were handier
weapons than the pike and the musket.[43]

The only real difference between the infantry drill on the parade
ground and battlefield manoeuvre was in the manner of the separation
of the pikes from the muskets. On parade, each company drew up with
its muskets on the flanks and its pikes in the centre. The colonel's
company took station on the right of the line, the lieutenant-colonel's
on the left, the major's next to that of the colonel, the company of the
senior captain next to that of the lieutenant-colonel and similarly
through the order of regimental seniority. A sixteen company battalion,
complete with a grenadier company, was ordered thus.

2 4 6 8 10 12 14 16 15 13 11 9 7 5 3 1 G

The grenadiers always drew up in three ranks only, being armed solely
with flintlock muskets and bayonets, called 'daggers', and took position
to the right of the colonel's company. In battle, the battalion became
as a single company with all its pikemen gathered into the centre and
the musketeers divided into two wings on either flank. The battalion
marched onto the field of battle in column of companies with the files
closed up shoulder-to-shoulder, usually on a frontage of between six
and ten files according to the width of the road. The *Abridgement*
allowed regimental officers discretion to vary the breadth of their columns of companies to suit local conditions.[44]

Although the soldier always commenced his march with the right
foot, 'which is observed to conduce most to keep the ranks even', no
further attempt was made at the maintenance of a cadenced step. Once
it had reached its designated location on the battlefield, the battalion
had to deploy out of column of companies into line of battle with the
additional complication that all the pikemen had to move to the centre
and the musketeers had to be split into two wings. Muddle and confusion must have been the order of the day. It was not surprising that
an army would begin deploying for battle early in the morning and not
be ready for action until the afternoon. Sieges obviated the need for
these involved manoeuvres. Once arranged, the battalion stood in five

and six ranks with the grenadier company on the right so as 'to augment it without intermixing with it, or troubling the order of it, they being a separate number of men that are to be always ready for whatever shall be commanded them.' In other words, the grenadiers were the battalion's shock troops and fire-brigade. By breaking up the companies and throwing their pikemen and musketeers into the battalion line in two different sections, unit cohesion and morale might have been endangered. This was offset by the fact that the companies themselves operated as two distinct entities – the pikes and the shot – and the officers and non-commissioned officers from the relevant sections of each company stood with their men in battle. Officers placed themselves at the head of their sections in the front rank of the battalion line. All officers were on foot with the exception of the major and the adjutant. Only the colonel and the major were permitted to give orders to the whole battalion when it was arrayed in line of battle. The non-commissioned officers were mingled with the troops and placed to the flanks and the rear to prevent straggling, desertion and 'bugging out'.

A theoretical battalion of twelve companies plus a grenadier company, each of fifty men, comprised 400 musketeers and 200 pikemen in 1689 but 450 musketeers and 150 pikemen in 1697. It stood in a line, 200 metres long and 10 metres deep. It was ready for action but at this point the *Abridgement* became very cautious about setting out rules for the conduct of battle. 'Though there can be no certain rules given for any order of battle, which depend chiefly upon circumstances of place, and other accidents that may happen, yet I shall set down some which may serve for an example to show the nature of the thing.' If the aspiring regimental officer wanted ideas on what to do in battle or on how to conduct himself, then he was best advised to put down the *Abridgement* and seek illumination from Sir James Turner's *Pallas Armata* (London, 1683) or *The Treatise of the Art of War* (London, 1677) by Roger Boyle, Earl of Orrery, both of which produced copious examples of the right and wrong methods of combat. Failing these, Richard Elton's *Complete Body of the Art Military* (London, 1650) had been reprinted in 1668. However, the *Abridgement* did lay down some instructions. When the troops stood ready to go into battle, silence was requested and 'none to speak but the commander-in-chief or the major by his order'. As the battalion line advanced towards the enemy, the captains and subalterns had to march in a line in front of the battalion continually checking that the ranks did not tumble into 'disorder'. During the march in battaglia towards the enemy the ranks of the musketeers were to be maintained at two metre intervals but this was to be reduced to one metre when the battalion halted ready to fire. Musketry was to be opened at thirty metres and, at this point, the officers in front of the battalion were instructed to retire into the first or second ranks through the intervals between the files. The major and the adjutant dismounted and took up pikes. The battalions in the battle line were to be sixty metres apart, allowing sufficient space for retreating troops to retire between battalions without hazarding the cohesion of the line. Generally, officers were advised to form two lines of battle for the infantry, the first three hundred metres in advance of the second. A reserve might be placed behind the second line. It stressed, however, that the formation of an army in battle was to be dictated by the nature of the terrain and hard and fast rules could not be established.[45]

A general of the Nine Years' War needed to offer battle on ground of his own choosing and ensure that his force was superior to that of his opponent. These advantages could only be achieved through the acquisition of reliable and accurate intelligence. Waldeck, William, Vaudemont, the Elector of Bavaria, Villeroi, Boufflers, Luxembourg and the other senior general officers from both sides knew the theatre of the Spanish Netherlands and its surrounds intimately. They had campaigned over the region during the Franco-Dutch War and in the Franco-Spanish War between 1683 and 1684 and many of them had been involved in surveys and in the building of fortifications. The very smallness of the area rendered a close acquaintance easy to acquire. Local knowledge, rather than reliance upon the inaccurate and unhlepful maps of the period, was one of the keys to tactical success and generals needed a cognizance of the chessboard of the Spanish Netherlands and all the possible moves. Intelligence of the strength and movement of enemy forces was readily available. Free movement of civilians was permitted throughout the Spanish Netherlands; merchants, sutlers, clergmen and farmers could migrate between rival armies peddling news and gossip as well as commodities. Assessing much of this casual intelligence was fraught with difficulty. 'Just now some Boors come in, that say the French army, or part of it, is advanced as far as Fleurus; but reports of this kind are not immediately to be believed.'[46] More important, the armies were frequently in close physical contact. Reconnaissance patrols were usually within sight of the enemy army or camp enabling the commanders to base their decisions on up-to-date and first-hand information.

Lax security fostered a constant fear of the spy. The extent to which either the Allied or the French commands relied upon the information from spies is debatable but the flow of human traffic between and around the armies and the absence of effective security systems rendered a belief in spies absolute. Undoubtedly there were agents. The number of attempted ambushes indicate clearly that both sides enjoyed a regular supply of 'inside' information. In Ireland in 1690, all Allied soldiers had to travel with passes; if they had no pass then they were treated as spies. A Dutch cornet was hanged in July 1696 for having conducted a secret correspondence with the French and there was always the risk that deserters were really agents and potential saboteurs. The most famous spy of the war was Jaquet, a secretary of the Elector of Bavaria, who was paid one hundred louis d'ors for each of the twenty-three letters he sent to the Duke of Luxembourg. He was unmasked on the eve of the Battle of Steenkirk in 1692.[47]

Despite the emphasis on sieges and the developing weaponry of the foot, the cavalry still had a vital role to play in battle. In the British, French, Dutch and Spanish armies, roughly one third of the troops were mounted as cuirassiers, dragoons or light cavalry.[48] Away from the battlefield, the main task of the mounted troops was to escort food and ammunition convoys and to form raiding parties to attack the supply lines of the enemy. They were also heavily employed in patrolling and in reconnaissance. British heavy cavalry were trained to fire their pistols and carbines from the saddle but to charge with cold steel. In battle, it is not clear whether the heavy cavalry deployed in three ranks or in two, although the former is more likely. The distance between both the ranks and files was six metres, reducing to a close order of one metre and even to a double-close order when the horsemen came knee-to-knee in their files and the ranks were pressed up head-to-crupper. Although the *Abridgement* is very unclear on these points, it suggests that the cavalry charged in double-close order in one rank after the second rank had come into the first rank to fill up the intervals between the files. The third rank probably acted as a reserve and rallying point. The actual charge seems to have been delivered at the trot with troopers riding knee-to-knee in a manner reminiscent of Cromwell's Ironsides.[49]

The British cavalry tactics were probably a compromise between the Cromwellian charge with cold steel and the practice of the 'caracolle'. The French cavalry, still the outstanding mounted arm amongst contemporary European armies and the cream of the French armed forces, combined the caracolle with the charge. They trotted forward in three ranks, gave a simultaneous discharge of fire from carbines or pistols, and then rode on through the smoke, sword in hand.[50] The British tactics were a variant on current French methods although there is no direct reference to the caracolle in drill manuals from the decade of the

Nine Years' War. Cavalry was still the prime force on the battlefield. The French victories at Fleurus, Leuse and Landen were all the direct results of decisive cavalry action. At Fleurus, it was the failure of the Dutch horse which largely decided the day. With the infantry tied to static formations which could advance and retreat only with extreme difficulty, it was the cavalry who charged and broke opposing infantry which had become disorganised by musketry and cannon fire. At Landen in 1693, the French horse seized enemy earthworks which their own foot had proved unable to penetrate and hold. Away from the battlefield, the cavalry was the major weapon in the war of posts and ambuscades. Only during sieges did the role of the mounted arm decline beneath that of the infantry and the gunners. They could take no part in the actual siege operations and had to confine themselves to maintaining the blockade of the beleaguered fortress, ferrying supplies for the besieging infantry or to service with the covering army.

More adaptable and varied in their employment were the dragoons, or mounted infantrymen. Their training was a mixture of heavy cavalry drill and infantry evolutions. When used as cavalry, the dragoons formed up in three ranks and charged home with the sword.[51] When in the infantry mode, the dragoons left their horses with every tenth man, who was known as the 'linkman,' and then formed up in three ranks to fight as musketeers armed with the bayonet. Their infantry drills and formations were similar to those of the grenadier companies as they had no pikes and adopted the thinner three-rank pattern. Dragoons, however, were hardly ever employed as substitute infantry. Complete with mobility and a heavy armanent of muskets, pistols and swords, they were much more useful as multi-purpose mounted troops. The 'little war' of patrols and ambushes was their forte. There was another problem in deploying dragoons as regular infantry. Seventeenth century riding boots were heavy and cumbersome and rendered walking exceedingly difficult. During the Nine Years' War, the dragoons became increasingly to be regarded as simply another form of cavalry, a process which the hard pressed governments of the Grand Alliance were anxious to encourage. Dragoons rode smaller and less expensive horses than the heavy cavalry, they did not wear defensive armour, unless an iron skull cap was sown into the hat, their pay was lower than that enjoyed by the cuirassiers and the troopers could be recruited from lower social strata. By 1697, the dragoons had become a plebeian cavalry.

The function of the artillery in battle was not clearly defined. The British, Dutch and Austrians deployed portable one-and-a-half pounder and three-pounder cannon as infantry guns. During the Nine Years'

War, the British did not have sufficient small cannon to equip every battalion but an allocation was made to each infantry brigade, probably of two three-pounders. These guns were managed by the grenadier companies and they were light enough to be pulled by one horse or man-handled by half a dozen soldiers. It seems that these infantry guns marched with the relevant brigades, complete with their own stores and ammunition, and did not travel with the artillery train.[52] In battle, these cannon fired canister, or patridge shot, in close support of the battalion line. The heavier guns from the train of artillery were arrayed in batteries, usually situated on dominating ground to give a clear and wide field of fire. Batteries typically consisted of between ten and twenty cannon. There was no concept of employing massed batteries to blast holes in opposing infantry formations. The guns covered weak points in the army's position and were seen as an adjunct to infantry firepower and not as a prime weapon in their own right.

Important though pitched battles were in the Nine Years' War, the siege was the principal military and political operation. By the middle of the sixteenth century, gunpowder had rendered the medieval castle all but untenable. Its stone walls and rounded towers were highly porous to artillery and new methods of defence had to be discovered. During the sixteenth century, Italy was one of the major theatres of international war in western Europe and its countrymen understandably came to the fore as the leading innovative military engineers of the age. The fortifications of the Middle Ages had been designed around the basis of a strong, stone curtain wall, or enceinte, flanked at intervals by towers and overlooked by protruding galleries. Heavy cannon firing solid shot made this single line of defence brittle and vulnerable. To begin with, the old stone wall was reinforced by earthen revetments to its rear but it was when these banks of soil were piled up against the front of the wall as well that the key to the new system of fortification began to turn in the lock. The answers to the problem were to give the fortifications more depth, to reduce their height and to construct them from a material that could absorb some of the impact of artillery fire. Increased depth pushed the attacking artillery farther back from the curtain wall and so reduced the hitting power of the attacking guns. Lowering the height of the enceinte presented a smaller target to the inaccurate cannon. Earthworks were quick to build and repair. Unfortunately, the lower ramparts attenuated the field of vision of the defenders and created a substantial amount of 'dead ground' in front of the curtain into which the defenders could neither see nor shoot.

Most of these partially solved difficulties found their final resolution in the adoption of the angled bastion, a polygonal protrusion from the curtain wall which had an obtuse angle at its apex. Based upon earthworks rather than masonry, this structure became the basis for a system of fortification which was known as the 'trace italienne'.[53] By the time of the Nine Years' War, the art of siege warfare and fortification had come to revolve around the career and achievements of the great French engineer, Vauban. He was shadowed only by his Dutch rival, Baron Menno van Coehoorn.[54] Vauban's designs were based upon simple geometry. The shape, or trace, around a fort or surrounding a city or town was polygonal with a bastion at each salient angle. Some detached forts, like Lillo to the north of Antwerp, a few citadels, such as the one at Lille, or the brand-new fortress town of New Breisach, were built as regular polygons and assumed the classic star-shaped trace. This, however, was extremely rare. Most fortifications had to be thrown around existing towns and cities or adjusted to fit awkward terrain and the irregularity of the resultant polygon had to be covered by swarms of outworks which stretched into the countryside. Each bastion possessed an all-round field of fire: out into the country, along the front of the curtain wall or back onto the ramparts and into the fortress itself. Bastions were constructed within supporting distance of each other and if attackers endeavoured to assault the curtain wall at a point between two bastions then they could be engaged by enfilading fire. This was the essential point of fortress design – to ensure that any attackers would be hit in the flank and enfiladed as they attempted to close with the curtain wall. Not an inch of 'dead ground' was permitted within the effective range of the defenders' guns. Everywhere the attacker could be engaged by cross-fire.

To achieve this ideal, bastions were insufficient in themselves and they needed to be covered by works which were detached from the curtain wall. All possible avenues of approach had to be guarded. By 1700, the fortifications around some of the larger towns – Namur, Lille, Bergen-op-Zoom and Dunkirk – had come to resemble military mazes and the over-complexity of their designs led to a certain inefficiency and required enormous garrisons to man all the vital posts. They were on the verge of offending against one of Frederick the Great's favourite maxims: 'he who defends everything defends nothing'. Around the inside of a typical fortress or fortified town ran a military road which gave access to all sections of the *rampart*. This road was at ground-level and the *rampart* was reached by means of wide, gently-inclined ramps. Along the outer edge of the road ran a bank, the *talus*, at an angle of forty-five degrees to the vertical, which then levelled-off to form the main *rampart*. along the top of the rampart was a wide roadway, the *terre-plein*. It was here that the main guns of the garrison were positioned and the *terre-plein* was sufficiently broad to allow for the recoil of the cannon and to permit the marshalling of considerable bodies of troops. The *terre-plein* was protected by an earthen *parapet* fitted with embrasures through which the cannon fired. On the inside of the parapet was a firing-step, or *banquette*, from which the infantry could engage attackers with musketry. Beneath the *terre-plein* and built into the *rampart* were stone-lined casemates which served as magazines, hospitals and barracks. From the summit of the *parapet*, the defences sloped downwards and outwards, giving a field of fire into all the outworks, the *ditch* and the open country beyond the *glacis*.

Below the parapet was a narrow walkway, the *chemin des rondes*, which circumnavigated the exterior of the *rampart*. From the edge of the *chemin des rondes*, the *rampart* fell precipitately into the *ditch* and this steep, almost vertical slope was known as the *scarp*. This was the remains of the medieval town wall, now reduced to nothing more than the revetment containing the back-filling which formed the rampart. It was one of the few brick or stone built structures in the system. The majority of the fortifications were of earth tightly tamped around a timber frame and bound together with turf. Earthworks deadened cannon shot, eliminated the dreaded splinters, were cheaper to build than stone works and were much quicker and easier to repair. The *ditch* was as deep and as wide as the soil excavated for the *rampart* would allow – normally about thirty metres across and three metres in depth – and it was customary to dig a deeper trench along the very centre of the *ditch*, a *cuvette*, to obstruct attackers and oblige miners to tunnel further undergound. The *counterscarp*, the near-vertical upward incline from the *ditch*, was also faced with brick or stone and had a gallery running all around its base. From this *counterscarp gallery* fire could be poured into the backs of any attackers who might break into the *ditch*. At the top of *counterscarp* was the *chemin couvert*, or *covered way*. This was a broad road running along the summit of the *counter-scarp* and it was 'covered' by fire from the *rampart* and by a tall *parapet* complete with a *banquette*. From the *parapet* of the *covered way*, the *glacis* dropped in a gentle slope into the countryside with, occasionally, a second *ditch* at its foot.

Depending upon the size and importance of the place, the horizontal distance from the *talus* to the base of the *glacis* varied between ninety and three hundred metres. Vauban's masterpiece at New Breisach measured two hundred and sixty metres. Similarly, the circumferences of fortresses differed enormously. It took seventy minutes to walk around the ramparts of Coehoorn's Bergen-op-Zoom, a distance of five kilometres, whilst a tour of Strasbourg's curtain wall took twice as long.[55] The profile of all these fortifications was very low, never approaching the height of medieval town walls, presenting a compact silhouette and a difficult target for attacking artillery operating at long range. Unfortunately, the squat fortifications offered little protection to the town from over-shooting or mortar fire and most towns under attack suffered considerable damage. Sometimes the ditch was filled with water, if there was a river nearby which could be conveniently diverted, but this was not encouraged as the customary delicacy of the age permitted the municipal sewage and detritus to be dumped into the ditch converting it into a stinking cesspit. This might have proved the ultimate form of fortification but it was also a serious hazard to the garrison's health. Another feature of these defences was the return to the concept of the citadel, or a castle within a castle. Inside most of the larger fortified towns – Lille, Namur, Casale, Turin and Strasbourg – a separate fort of considerable strength was erected, repeating within a smaller space the familiar sequence of works. Sieges could thus develop into two-stage affairs. Once the actual town had been captured, the garrison withdrew into the citadel which then had to be reduced by a second siege in form. This occurred at Namur in both 1692 and 1695 and it was an excellent ploy as it doubled the strategic value and the time-delay factor of a single fortress. Given the importance attached to the fortress and the siege, it is a wonder that some martial genius did not invent a Russian Doll Fortress consisting of ever-decreasing concentric rings of defences.

The principal outwork was the *ravelin*, also known as a *demi-lune* or *half-moon*,[56] a small triangular work with two faces which was constructed in the ditch to cover the rampart between two bastions. *Counterguards* in the ditch reinforced the apex of the bastion. *Hornworks* and *crownworks* were long, rectangular edifices which reached out into open country beyond the glacis and provided a greater depth of cross-fire. These were most useful in defending irregularly-shaped sites, as at Landau. Hornworks, crownworks and ravelins could become quite separate from the main enceinte and were often independent fortresses with their own garrisons and supplies. From this it was but a short step to the nineteenth century notion of abandoning the rampart and close defences of a town and adopting a more distant protection in the form of a ring, or rings of detached forts. Naturally, within this general pattern of defences there was a fecundity of invention and variation according to the schemes of individual engineers. Some of the larger fortresses has subterranean passages linking the various outworks with the main rampart; stone-lined counter-mine tunnels were built under the ditch and glacis ready to intercept any mines dug by future attackers; *tenailles* could be built into the ditch to serve as infantry posts; detached forts commanded dominating ground outside the main fortress; and, especially in the Low Countries, fortresses often enjoyed the protection afforded by pre-arranged inundations, the necessary sluices being within the control of the fortress or its detached works. Vauban continually experimented with form until he arrived at his most mature expression in the defences of Landau and New Breisach. Here he whittled down the bastion to a slimmer and flatter shape, reinforced at its apex by a *bastioned tower* or *tour bastionée*, a stone-built artillery casemate. *Caponiers*, vaulted galleries of stone, ran across ditches to provide a protected passage for the garrison and to give flanking fire along the length of the ditch. *Traverses* interrupted the covered way. In this field, the British were in the hands of the French and the Dutch. No British engineer was called upon to construct a fortress in the Low Countries, or in the British Isles.

When all this has been said, it must be admitted that we scarcely ever read of an unsuccessful siege. Eventually all these marvellous and expensive works – New Breisach was to cost Louis XIV over four million livres – fell when subjected to sustained pressure. They were not, however, intended to hold out indefinitely, supplies and the endurance of men being finite. Rather, their purpose was to delay the enemy and to interrupt the progress of his strategy. Employing but a fraction of the forces that were needed to seize them, fortified posts tied down huge opposing armies leaving the main field army of the besieged free to recuperate after a battle, redeploy or pursue an alternative objective. A well designed defensive network, such as the French barrier along the frontier with the Spanish Netherlands, could hold up and obstruct a potential invader at relatively little cost to the defenders. To a beaten army, fortresses provided shelter and time. Fortresses were also charged with protection of the massive supply magazines which fuelled the campaigns of both sides. The new style of fortification regained for the defensive some of the initiative which had been lost through the introduction of gunpowder weaponry but as the defence grew more sophisticated so the offense responded by devising new methods.

A siege was a major undertaking and it could prove dangerous. Whilst tied down to a siege, an army was itself vulnerable to attack. The garrison of a beleaguered town usually represented but a fraction of the troops available to that power in that theatre, whereas the besieger was obliged to deploy the majority of his forces to encirlce and assault the fortress. This left the bulk of the comrades of the besieged free to operate in the field, either carrying out separate manoeuvres of attempting to relieve their distressed companions. In response to the latter threat, and it was in just such a situation that Prince Charles of Lorraine and King John Sobieski of Poland relieved Vienna in 1683, it became standard practice for the besiegers to divide their army into two sections. The first conducted the seige and the other 'covered' the besieging corps from the attentions of the enemy's relieving army. To defend themselves more closely, the besiegers constructed *lines of contravallation* around their camps and siege works to protect themselves from sallies and other aggressive reactions from the encircled garrison. If the enemy field army was in the vicinity or raiding parties were harrying the besiegers, then they might also dig *lines of circumvallation* facing away from the besieged town. Thus it could happen that the fortress of the besieged was surrounded by the army of the attackers which was itself defended by two circular belts of field fortifications, one facing away from the town and the other towards the town, with the camp sandwiched in between. This system by which the attacker's defended themselves had been perfected over a century before by the Dukes of Alva and Parma during the Eighty Years' War. At the Siege of 's-Hertogenbosch in 1629, it took eleven hours to make a complete tour of the Dutch lines of circumvallation and contravallation.

The object of a siege was simple – to capture the town or fortress under attack. To effect this, a breach or gap had to be made in the main rampart wide enough for infantry to pass through. Given the limitations of seventeenth century cannon firing solid shot and not explosive shells against earthworks specially designed with sloping faces to deflect projectiles, such a breach could only be made if the heavy siege cannon were firing from the glacis itself. The besiegers had thus to work their way through the outworks, destroy and dismount the cannon of the garrison and steadily advance their own batteries closer and closer to the ramparts. Like most other aspects of the Nine Years' War, sieges were slow and methodical. Only if the nerve of a commander and his garrison collapsed, as at Dixmuyde and Deynze in 1695, or if there was treachery within, which was possibly the case at Mons in 1691 or Namur in 1692, could the grinding slowness and predictability of a 'siege in form' be avoided.

The opening move in a seige was to send a force of cavalry to swoop down on the intended target fortress and establish a *blockade*, preventing reinforcements and supplies from entering. Once the infantry had marched up, a circular camp was established all around the fortress and the soldiers and civilian pioneers set to work to build the lines of contravallation and circumvallation whilst they awaited the arrival of the heavy artillery and the siege train. Engineers then surveyed the fortifications and selected the likeliest sector for assault. This was not usually the subject of prolonged debate as the strengths and weaknesses of the majority of fortresses in the Low Countries were well enough known to the principal generals and their engineers. Louvois kept a special atlas in his office entitled 'Plans et Places Estrangeres', which contained up-to-date maps, plans and intelligence notes on the fortifications in the Low Countries, parts of Germany and Northern Italy. Marlborough campaigned with a chest containing plans of all the major fortresses he was likely to encounter. If there was any doubt then the probability was that either Vauban or Coehoorn had originally designed or modified the fortifications and a consultation with the horse's mouth rapidly produced a solution.[57]

Attackers had approached beleaguered castles and towns along oblique trenches since medieval times, and probably for long before that. By the 1620s, Maurice of Nassau and Prince Frederick Henry had perfected the art of advancing towards besieged fortresses via zig-zagged trenches and had developed a close co-operation between the infantry and the artillery. Vauban did no more than bring a greater sophistication and efficiency to this system, which had evolved during the Eighty Years' War between the Dutch and the Spaniards. His principal innovation was to link the zig-zagged trenches by three wide trenches dug parallel to the ramparts under attack. The Turks had employed a similar system at the twenty-year Siege of Candia, which had finally ended in 1668, and serving on Vauban's staff was a young man who had fought in that operation.[58] However, this is a tenuous connection and Vauban probably drew on the less methodical work of his European predecessors.

At a distance of six or seven hundred metres from the foot of the glacis, the sappers and civilian labourers '*broke ground*' and drove a series of trenches towards the front of the fortress which had been chosen for assault. Some four hundred metres from the glacis, just within the effective range of heavy cannon, a deep and wide trench was thrown out at right angles connecting up all the advancing trenches. This was the *First Parallel*. It was filled with horse, foot, ammunition and stores to form a *place d'armes* sufficiently strong to repulse any sallies that the garrison of the fortress might undertake. Along the line of the *First Parallel* the batteries of heavy siege cannon were constructed. The initial task of these great guns was to dismount the cannon of the defenders which were situated along the terre plein and in the bastions. Vauban liked to fire his guns from this extreme range as the solid shot began to wander off course towards the end of their flight, finding their way amidst the strictly geometric trace of the fortifications. The high elevation of the cannon allowed the balls to drop onto their targets thus negating the best efforts of the designer of the defences. At the Sieges of Namur in 1692 and Ath in 1697, Vauban perfected this technique by ordering his cannon and howitzers to fire on maximum elevation but with reduced charges. This created *ricochet fire*. The solid cannon balls fell into the fortifications and bounced, or ricocheted, leaving few safe corners for the garrison. *Ricochet fire* usually commenced after the main garrison cannon had been knocked from their carriages and it had the effect of driving the defenders away from the sector under attack as well as sweeping communication passages and wrecking palisades and other hidden obstacles on the glacis and covered way. Vauban always spaced his heavy batteries well apart so that fire converged on its targets from several directions and angles.

Once the *First Parallel* had been equipped with a parapet and some redoubts and the heavy guns had begun blasting away at the defenders' cannon, zig-zagged trenches, or *saps*, were driven forward from the *First Parallel* to within about two hundred metres of the glacis at which point a *Second Parallel* was struck. All the equipment, troops and guns from the *First Parallel* were then moved forward to the new line. By this time, the cannon were employing both ricochet fire and direct fire on the point, or points, in the defences which had been selected for assault. From a range of two hundred metres, the cannon would have been making some impact on the earthworks of the covered way. When all was ready in the *Second Parallel*, the *saps* went forward once more. The *saps* had to change direction as often as possible to prevent the trenches from becoming enfiladed and the zig-zags grew more frequent as the range of the garrison's guns closed. Even so, casualties among the highly paid sappers were extensive despite their efforts to protect themselves with *gabions*, wicker baskets filled with earth or sand, *fascines*, bundles of brushwood, and portable wooden shields. As the *saps* wormed ever closer to the defences, a well commanded garrison would have launched numerous sallies upon the siege works, usually at night, to disrupt the operations, dismount cannon and attempt to create some valuable time. The garrisons in the *places d'armes* had to be constantly vigilant to protect the batteries and the sappers.

Within pistol shot of the foot of the glacis, the *Third Parallel* was thrown out and again the infantry, equipment and the heavy siege artillery were advanced at night to the new position. By this time, all the garrison mortars and cannon would have been dismounted and the defenders would have been reliant upon musketry and grenades. The siege guns of the attackers were now close enough to begin the serious work of blasting a hole or breach in the covered way. The batteries had to be positioned as near to the target as possible; even the twenty-four, forty-eight and sixty-pounders could make little impact upon earthworks at ranges above one hundred metres. If all went well, a breach would be blown in the covered way and the time had arrived for the most dangerous and bloody part of the siege – the infantry assault on the glacis and the covered way. Some generals preferred to march their men up the glacis from the *Third Parallel*, others liked to sap up the glacis and attack over a shorter distance. Whatever approach was adopted, casualties amongst the attackers were often high as they advanced over open ground in the face of musketry and grenades from the covered way, the rampart and flanking ravelins and bastions. Every effort was made to provide some covering fire. *Cavaliers de tranchées* were erected along the *Third Parallel,* high earthwork towers which enabled the attackers to fire on the defenders lining the parapet of the covered way.

If the attack was successful – second and even third attempts were sometimes needed – then a *lodgement* was 'effected' on the covered way. The attackers immediately threw up earthen parapets and defences to face the main rampart. The artillery was brought forward to the top of the glacis and began the work of breaching the rampart whilst engineers dynamited sections of the covered way into the ditch to provide a level passage for the infantry. Once the breach in the rampart had been made and the ditch had been partially filled, the attacking infantry possessed a clear path into the town blocked only by the hastily dug *retrenchments* in the rear of the breach. Should the besieging army attack at this stage and gain a victory then it enjoyed the historic right to plunder and burn the town and put the garrison to the sword. Matters rarely reached such an unseemly conclusion. A fortress governor was expected to fight his stronghold for what it was worth and no more; sieges were part of a semi-ritualistic warfare and there was no room for incongruous heroism. Once a *lodgement* had been effected on the covered way then it was accepted that the game was over and the garrison was allowed to surrender on honourable terms in recognition of the fact that they had not caused the attackers unnecessary bloodshed and expense by resisting the inevitable. Sometimes the attackers might be obliged to breach the main rampart before the garrison called it a day, in which case the terms of capitulation were more severe. If the governor failed to exercise sufficient circumspection and forced the attackers to lose large numbers of men in repeated and costly attacks before eventually breaking in, then the town and its defenders could legitimately be put to the sword. There is no recorded instance of this happening in the Low Countries during the Nine Years' War. The defeated garrisons were not taken prisoner, except on rare and bizarre occasions, but were permitted to march to a designated rendezvous from where they were allowed to rejoin their own army after a stipulated interval. The rules of the business were international and were usually obeyed.[59]

Within these general principles there were numerous variations depending upon the forces involved and the topography. Some commanding officers sapped down into the ditch from the covered way and dug across to the scarp. Sometimes the ditch was full of water, in which case it had to be drained or grenadiers had to float across on rafts or manufacture some form of pontoon bridge. Mining was an important element in siege warfare, although in the Low Countries the high water table in Flanders restricted this procedure to the fortresses of Brabant. From the Third Parallel, the engineers and miners tunnelled under the glacis in order to plant explosives beneath the counterscarp and the covered way, a process which was sometimes a great deal quicker than waiting for the cannon. To combat this, subterranean warfare developed as the defenders established listening posts and dug counter mines either to intercept in-coming mines or to attempt to blow-up the Third Parallel. The bigger fortresses were equipped with masonry-lined and vaulted counter-mines which ended underneath the anticipated location of the Third Parallel.

Just as Vauban and Coehoorn were expert at the design and construction of fortifications, so they were adept at their reduction. The system of Three Parallels was first put into operation by Vauban at the Siege of Maastricht in 1673 and it rapidly came to be imitated by all the armies of western Europe. A 'siege in form' came to be a synonymous with the capture of a fortress according to the system of Vauban. Occasionally, the rules governing siege operations were ignored, either by the defenders or the attackers. The surrender of Dixmuyde and Deynze in 1695 contravened convention whilst Lord John Cutts's lunatic assault on Venlo in 1702 succeeded against all the odds as well as the expectations of his own officers, but it saved weeks of digging and numerous casualties.[60] Because of their duration and the fact that the defending and besieging forces were locked on a stationary stage acting a predictable play, sieges became great ceremonial and theatrical performances. Louis XIV 'commanded' as many sieges as he possibly could, taking with him his court, government and ladies for company. Gentlemen volunteers and travellers attended sieges as part of their education, witnessing grand martial manoeuvres from a safe distance spiced with just a hint of danger. The unfortunate Michael Godfrey, a deputy governor of the Bank of England, came to the Siege of Namur in 1695 to converse with King William about financial matters. He entered the trenches by the side of the King to watch the attack on the counterscarp of the town of Namur on 17/27 July only to be struck down by a cannon ball.[61]

NOTES

1 H. J. Cook, 'The Medical Profession in London', in, *The Age of William III and Mary II*, eds. R. P. Maccubbin & M. Hamilton-Phillipps (Williamsburg, 1989), pp. 160–1. On the army in Britain see, John Childs, *The British Army of William III* (Manchester, 1987).
2 D. G. Chandler, 'Fluctuations in the strength of forces in English pay sent to Flanders during the Nine Years' War, 1688–1697', *War and Society*, i. (1983), pp. 1–19; Jones, *War and Economy*, pp. viii, 8–11; Childs, *British Army of William III*, pp. 253, 268.
3 BL, Add. MSS. 15,897, ff. 88–9.
4 *CJ*, x. 430–2.
5 *Portledge Papers*, p. 87.
6 *CJ*, x. 547, 557; *Parliamentary Diary of Luttrell*, pp. 28–9.
7 *CJ*, x. 712–13; Charles Dalton, *English Army Lists and Commission Registers, 1660–1714* (London, 1892–1904), iii. 289–90; HMC, *Westmoreland and Other MSS.*, p. 355.
8 BL, Harl. MSS. 1,898, ff. 40–1; Leopold von Ranke, *A History of England, particularly in the seventeenth century* (London, 1875), vi. 227; *CJ*, xi. 18–20; *The History and Proceedings of the House of Commons from the Restoration to the Present Time*, ed. Richard Chandler (London, 1741–4), ii. 421, 428–9.
9 *CJ*, xi. 176–7; BL, Add. MSS. 61,317, f. 59.
10 HMC, *House of Lords MSS.*, n.s. ii. 131–5; *CJ*, xi. 345–7; SP 8/16, f. 53; BL, Add. MSS. 61,317, f. 59.
11 *CJ*, xi. 569–71; BL, Add. MSS. 61,317, ff. 59, 61–2.
12 HMC, *Denbigh MSS.*, p. 115; HSL, vii. 337–57; Jones, *War and Economy*, pp. 8–9; S.P. Oakley, *William III and the Northern Crowns during the Nine Years War, 1689–1697* (New York, 1987), pp. 77–84.
13 *CSPD 1689–90*, pp. 48, 83, 187, 265; WO 5/5, ff. 103–4; SP 8/17, f. 8; BL, Add. MSS. 15,897, ff. 88–9; Müller, iii. 227–31.
14 Chandler, 'Fluctuations', pp. 7–8; *CJ*, x. 227–31.
15 Chandler, 'Fluctuations', pp. 9–10.

16 Walton, pp. 499–502; BL, Add. MSS. 9,760, ff. 38–9; *CJ*, x. 547, 557.
17 Childs, *British Army of William III*, p. 268; BL. Add. MSS. 9,760, ff. 62, 67; BL, Stowe MSS. 481, f. 24. These figures are revisions of the balance between native and foreign troops previously presented in Childs, *British Army of William III*, pp. 253, 268.
18 Waddell, 'Administration', pp. 45–9.
19 BL, Add. MSS. 9,724, f. 169; Edward D'Auvergne, *The History of the Campaign in Flanders for the Year 1695* (London, 1696), pp. 14, 23.
20 BL, Add. MSS. 15,897, ff. 88–9.
21 ARA, Raad van State, 1932/2, f. 143.
22 *HSL*, vii. 6.
23 ARA, Raad van State, 1932/2, f. 143.
24 Ibid.; Erle-Drax MSS., 4/18, f. 3.
25 Ibid.
26 ARA, Raad van State, 1932/2, f. 143; ARA, Raad van State, 1277.
27 Ibid.
28 Müller, ii. 226; Oakley, *Northern Crowns*, pp. 31, 38–9, 100–16.
29 ARA, Heinsius, 2170; *HSL*, vii. 337–57.
30 *Shrewsbury Correspondence*, p. 132.
31 G. Le M. Gretton, *The Campaigns and History of the Royal Irish Regiment from 1684 to 1902* (Edinburgh & London, 1911), p. 4; Bod. Lib. Rawlinson MSS. A. 349; John Childs, *The Army of Charles II* (London, 1976), pp. 62–3; Walton, pp. 331–2; H. C. B. Rogers, *Weapons of the British Soldier* (London, 1972), pp. 76–89; Howard L. Blackmore, *British Military Firearms, 1650–1850* (London, 1961), pp. 28–44, 261–2.
32 Guerlac, 'Vauban', p. 78.
33 F. W. Hamilton, *The Origin and History of the First or Grenadier Guards* (London, 1874), i. 349; Rawlinson MSS. A. 349.
34 Walton, pp. 733–9.
35 Luttrell, *Historial Relation*, ii. 372; iii. 93, 310; iv. 59; Blackmore, *Firearms*, p. 35; HMC, *Le Fleming MSS.*, p. 267.
36 HMC, *House of Lords MSS.*, n.s. iv. 195–8.
37 Rawlinson MSS. A. 349.
38 BL, Stowe MSS. 444, f. 16.
39 SP 44/41, f. 41.
40 SP 75/5, p. 330; *An Abridgement of English Military Discipline, printed by Especial Command for the Use of his Majesties Forces* (London, 1685, repr. 1686); *The Exercise of the Foot with the Evolutions, according to the words of command as they are explained, as also the forming of battalions with directions to be observed by all Colonels, Captains and other Officers in their Majesties Armies* (London, 1690); *The Exercise of the Foot with the Evolutions, according to the words of command as they are explained . . . Likewise the Exercise of the Dragoons, both on horseback and foot. With the Rules of War for the Infantry upon the Day of Battel* (John Reid, Edinburgh, 1693).
41 *Exercise of the Foot*, pp. 2–3.
42 *Ibid.*, pp. 7–54.
43 *Abridgement* (1686), pp. 161–72.
44 *Ibid.*, pp. 80, 85. The wide column of march is supported by the evidence of the Marlborough Tapestries at Blenheim Palace, particularly that depicting the Battle of Oudenarde, 1708. See Alan Wace, *The Marlborough Tapestries at Blenheim Palace* (London, 1968), pp. 76–7.

45 *Abridgement* (1686), pp. 234–40; David Chandler, *The Art of Warfare in the Age of Marlborough* (London, 1976), pp. 110–14; J. A. Houlding, *Fit for Service: The Training of the British Army, 1715–1795* (Oxford, 1981), pp. 172–6.
46 *HMC, Buccleuch (Montagu) MSS.*, ii. 77; SP 77/56, f. 137.
47 *A Bibliography of Royal Proclamations of the Tudor and Stuart Sovereigns . . . 1485–1714*, ed. Robert Steele (Oxford, 1910), ii. 144, 7/17 Oct. 1690; BCRO, Trumbull Add. MSS. 103; see below p. 194.
48 Chandler, *Art of Warfare*, p. 30.
49 Wace, *Marlborough Tapestries*, pp. 70–1, 79; C. H. Firth, *Cromwell's Army* (London, 1902, repr. 1962), pp. 128–44.
50 Chandler, *Art of Warfare*, pp. 50–1.
51 *Abridgement* (1686), p. 212.
52 BL, Stowe MSS. 444, f. 13.
53 On the development of artillery fortifications and the 'trace Italienne' see, Simon Pepper & Nicholas Adams, *Firearms and Fortifications: Military Architecture and Siege Warfare in sixteenth century Sienna* (Chicago, 1986); Parker, *Military Revolution*, pp. 7–16; J. R. Hale, 'The Early Development of the Bastion: An Italian Chronology, c.1450-c.1534', in, J. R. Hale, *Renaissance War Studies* (London, 1983), pp. 1–29; Christopher Duffy, *Siege Warfare: The Fortress in the Early Modern World, 1494–1660* (London, 1979); Christopher Duffy, *The Fortress in the Age of Vauban and Frederick the Great, 1660–1789* (London, 1985).
54 On Vauban see, Guerlac, 'Vauban'; P. E. Lazard, *Vauban*, (Paris, 1934); Sir Reginald Blomfield, *Sebastien le Prestre de Vauban, 1633–1707* (London, 1938). On Coehoorn see, *NNBW*, i. 620–1; *Het Leven van Menno van Coehoorn*, ed. J. W. van Sypesteyn (Leuwarden, 1860); J. P. C. M. van Hoof, 'Fortifications in the Netherlands, c.1500–1940', *Revue Internationale d'Histoire Militaire*, lviii. (1984), pp. 104–9; Duffy, *Fortress in the Age of Vauban and Frederick the Great*, pp. 63–97.
55 Blomfield, *Vauban*, p. 142. See also, Albert Croquez, *La Citadelle de Lille, Chef-d'Oeuvre de Vauban, 1668–1670* (Paris, 1913); *A Brief Discourse on Fortification* (London, 1668); Wright, *Fortifications*, pp. 26–8.
56 Duffy, *Fortress in the Age of Vauban and Frederick the Great*, p. 299.
57 BL, Add. MSS. 64,108 & 64,109; BL, Add. MSS. 61,342, ff. 139–40.
58 E. M. Lloyd, *Vauban, Montalembert, Carnot: Engineer Studies* (London, 1887), pp. 77–9.
59 J. W. Wright, 'Sieges and Customs of War at the opening of the 18th Century', *American Historical Review*, xxxix. (1933–4), pp. 629–44.
60 *Marlborough-Godolphin Correspondence*, i. 113; Fortescue, i. 404–5.
61 BL, Add. MSS. 9,722, f. 82; *HMC, Downshire MSS.*, i. 515–16.

IV

1689: WALCOURT

The Anglo-Dutch Mutual Defence Treaty was put into effect two months before the House of Commons permitted William and Mary to declare war on France on 7/17 May 1689. An order from William Blathwayt to John Churchill, Earl of Marlborough and Lieutenant-General commanding the British Corps to be sent to the Netherlands, dated 8/18 March, instructed him to assemble nine battalions ready to cross the North Sea. Marlborough accordingly brought together two battalions from the 1st Foot Guards, two from the Coldstream Guards, one from the Royal Scots, Prince George of Denmark's Foot, Charles Churchill's battalion, the Royal Fusiliers and Robert Hodges's Foot.[1] Before these men had reached their embarkation points at Ipswich, Harwich and Greenwich, major mutinies had broken out amongst the Royal Scots and the Prince of Denmark's Foot as well as some minor disturbances in the four battalions from the Guards.[2] On its arrival in the Low Countries, this leading contingent of the British Corps reflected the state of its parent army in England: it was under-strength, of dubious political and religious loyalty to the new regime and somewhat unprofessional. General Georg Friedrich von Waldeck, the commander-in-chief of the Dutch army in the absence of William of Orange, reported that the British Guards battalions 'pretend, commes gardes, ne faire point de service'.[3] All of the British formations were considerably beneath their paper establishments, some to the extent of nearly fifty per cent.

During April, additional infantry was sent from Britain to the Netherlands and, early in the succeeding month, some cavalry was provided in the form of the Royal Horse Guards and the second Troop of the Life Guards. Marlborough himself disembarked in Rotterdam on 17/27 May and immediately travelled the short distance to The Hague. He made his journey in one of the forty passenger boats which maintained a half-hourly service between Rotterdam and Delft and an hourly schedule between Delft and The Hague.[4] The Declaration of War on France obviated the need to abide by the stipulations of the Treaty of 1678. England was no longer an auxiliary but a participant and she was at liberty to put as many men into the Low Countries as she could afford. By the end of May, the Scots Guards, John Hales's battalion, Sir David Colyear's Foot, Edward Fitzpatrick's infantry regiment and Francis Fergus O'Farrell's battalion had been added to the British Corps. The paper strength should now have equalled 10,972 but the corps was already 775 men short of its establishment despite having received drafts from regiments in England.[5] Marlborough earned the praise and admiration of Waldeck for his heroic efforts to train the British soldiers and raise their morale despite the damage caused by sickness and massive desertion. When Marlborough led his corps into the field in July, it contained just 5,200 effective men commanded by 800 officers, less than half its official establishment.[6] This was the price exacted by the Glorious Revolution.

During the winter of 1688 to 1689, Maastricht and the towns of Dutch Brabant were packed with troops.[7] As the French armies along the Rhine razed German fortifications and burned towns and villages, it had become clear that Louis XIV's conception of a limited war had seriously misfired. The destruction of the Palatinate and the Rhineland aroused the fury of the Germans against the French in a way that nothing else could have achieved. Instead of a short war, France was faced with a major conflict involving all the powers of the League of Augsburg with England in addition. Because the French had employed the winter in wrecking the Rhineland and because they had not anticipated that they would be engaged in a major war, their troops were below the necessary strength at the opening of the campaign of 1689. The forces of the Grand Alliance were numerically superior and were deployed in a ring around the north-eastern and eastern borders of France. The problem for the anti-French coalition was the co-ordination of these armies.

In the Spanish Netherlands, the Marquis de Castañaga and the Prince de Vaudemont stood ready with the Army of Flanders. Waldeck was prepared to act in Brabant with a Dutch army of 35,000 whilst the Germans fielded three armies. Elector Maximillian II Emmanuel of Bavaria commanded a corps at Villingen in Baden; Duke Charles V of Lorraine stood on the Middle Rhine at Frankfurt; and Elector Frederick III of Brandenburg-Prussia was based at Wesel. Waldeck envisaged the junction of Castañaga's Spanish forces with his own Dutch army in

order to stage an invasion of France to the south of Charleroi between
Maubeuge and Philippeville. It was hoped that the Elector of Brandenburg would assist this operation by moving towards the Meuse. Waldeck should have known better. Castañaga did not want to join his
Spanish troops with Waldeck's Dutch. His concern was with the protection of the lands and cities of the Spanish Netherlands and not with
the invasion of France. To this end, he wished to maintain a separate
army based in Flanders rather than Brabant. The Elector of Brandenburg was equally unhelpful. Like Castañaga, his first thoughts were for
the integrity of his dominions, in this case his Rhenish principality of
Cleves. The French garrisons in Cologne, Bonn, Neuss and Kaiserswerth
threatened the Duchy of Cleves and Frederick wished to remove these
potential hazards before attempting any more ambitious schemes.
Besides, the German princes had joined the Grand Alliance not out of
a desire to invade France but from the need to resist French aggression
towards the Holy Roman Empire. Waldeck was furious at the lack of
co-operation from his allies but there was nothing that he could do to
change their attitudes.[8] Only a leader with the prestige of William of
Orange could hope to overcome national prejudices and he was busy
in England and Ireland.

   In the Spanish Netherlands, the opposing armies spent much of the
winter months in raiding one another's territory in order to raise contributions. The Dutch garrison of Maastricht levied contributions from
the County of Chimay, south of Charleroi, reaching to the gates of
Maubeuge, whilst the French tried to squeeze 40,000 crowns from the
inhabitants of Aachen. On 8/18 January 1689, fifty Dutchmen from
Maastricht intercepted a similar number of Frenchmen and put them
to flight. The Dutch garrison at Maastricht received intelligence that
the French stationed at Huy on the Meuse were preparing to send a
convoy to Liège to secure arms and stores. By laying an ambush between
Huy and Liège, the Dutch took seventeen prisoners and captured three
waggonloads of weapons and ammunition.[9] Waldeck reported to William on 2/12 February that large French troop movements were under
way towards the Netherlands and towards Coblenz. Fortunately, at this
point 2,000 Swedes arrived on the River Ijsel and five companies of the
forces from the Count of Lippe marched into Zutphen.[10] As the French
began to withdraw from the lands to the east of the Rhine having
carried out their depredations, they also retreated from the Bishopric
of Liège having signed a treaty with the Prince-Bishop which guaranteed
the neutrality of all his territories. As a leaving present, the French
executed a partial demolition of the citadel of Liège. The Liègeois

fortifications at Huy were completely levelled. The French were beginning to concentrate their forces ready for the campaigning season.
Advance intelligence suggested to the Allies that the French were going
to form two main armies, one to operate on the Sambre and the other
to advance along the Moselle in order to attack Coblenz.

John Thibault van Weibnom, the Dutch Governor of Breda, wrote
to William on 8/18 February to report a conference which he had held
with Castañaga. Both feared that Mons might be the opening target for
the French in 1689 but they were satisfied that the Spanish and Dutch
forces were well enough positioned to deflect any attempt or, if the
worst came to the worst, to relieve Mons should it be invested. They
were likewise worried about Namur, seventy kilometres to the east of
Mons, and thought that its garrison ought to be strengthened. Weibnom
was also able to give the good news that the Emperor Leopold I was
hastening the dispatch of experienced troops from Hungary to the Rhine
front.[11] At this point, the Elector of Brandenburg seized the initiative.
Having been reinforced by some Dutch troops under Major-General
Hans Willem van Aylva, General Hans Adam von Schöning led the
Brandenburg forces south into the Electorate of Cologne and occupied
its capital city. This effectively forestalled the French, especially when
Schöning and Aylva extended their occupation into neighbouring Jülich,
ensuring the safety of Cleves, and it dashed any French hopes of invading the United Provinces along the valley of the Rhine. Schöning
intended to clear the French from the Rhine, open navigation and reduce
the French garrisons in the Electorate of Cologne. His army consisted
of 4,000 Brandenburgers and 5,000 Dutchmen.[12]

On 1/11 March, a force of Dutch and Brandenburg cavalry ambushed
a French supply convoy which was transporting corn from the magazine
at Neuss to Bonn. Having successfully persuaded the escorting horse
and foot to retire to Duisburg, the Allied cavalry set out to carry their
spoils back to Wesel. When the news of this humiliation reached Neuss,
the Marquis de Sourdis and Maréchal de Camp Vertillac drew out what
forces they had to hand, 24 squadrons of horse and 7 battalions of foot
totalling 7,000 men, and set off to retrieve the lost convoy. Fortunately
for the Allies, Aylva and Schöning were marching south with 5,000
soldiers to meet the victorious raiders. At the rendezvous, the Allied
generals received intelligence of the approach of Sourdis's corps, and
so they sent the convoy away for Wesel under an escort of dragoons
and drew up their remaining troops in two lines on a wide plain at
Herderbosch, near Neuss, to block the French passage. Major-General
Barfus commanded the Allied right, Major-General Frederick van Slang-

enburg took charge of the left and Aylva and Schöning looked after the centre. On the appearance of the French, the Allies advanced towards them. The battle began with 'brisk firing' by both sides and was close until the French horse became 'disordered'. After their flight, the French foot was exposed and they suffered 2,500 casualties and 500 prisoners. The Allied corps lost around 400 men.

This victory opened the Electorate of Cologne to the Allies. Neuss fell on 4/14 March with a haul of 250 prisoners; Siburg fell two days later closely followed by Zons and Soest on the Ruhr. Kempen succumbed on 6/16 March leaving the French in the Electorate of Cologne with just Bonn, Rheinberg and Kaiserswerth in addition to some smaller posts. Waldeck was not pleased with the conduct of this campaign. Its very success encouraged the Elector of Brandenburg to increase his army to 30,000, by incorporating the troops of the Bishop of Münster and asking for more soldiers from the States-General. To Waldeck's annoyance, the Dutch deputies agreed to send 22 squadrons of horse and 6 battalions of infantry to assist Brandenburg. Before the campaign in the Low Countries had started, the strategic emphasis had already shifted from Brabant to the Rhine. Neither was Waldeck enchanted with the tactical skill of the Brandenburg forces. As the French fell back along the Rhine under the cover of the garrison and guns of Bonn, he considered that the Allied cavalry could have interfered with the withdrawal. Unfortunately, they seemed half-asleep and missed the opportunity. The Elector ordered his army over to a general offensive with the aim of capturing the French bases in the country around Bonn and Cologne and controlling the bridge over the Rhine at Kaiserswerth. The rapid campaign had been a considerable success for the Allies. Despite Waldeck's pique at watching his limelight shift towards the Elector of Brandenburg, the flank of his own intended operations along the Sambre-Meuse had been cleared and the danger of French incursions into Overijsel and Guelderland had been removed. There could be no repeat of the French invasion of the United Provinces of 1672. In addition, some Dutch and Münster troops were sent forward to Stavelot, south-east of Liège, to block French attempts to move reinforcements from the Moselle to the Meuse.[13]

Intelligence that the French were on the move towards Tournai reached Brussels on 12/22 March. River boats had transported the French siege train from Douai on the Scarpe and Cambrai on the Scheldt to a point between Condé and Valenciennes. Waldeck responded by reinforcing Brussels with two regiments and by putting 1,000 Spanish foot into Bruges but he had already resolved to take the field with his main army and encamp at Hasselt in the Bishopric of Liège. From this point he would be able to cover the southern frontier of the United Provinces from attack, observe the line of the Meuse, be close to the vital base of Maastricht and remain in touch with the Brandenburg army in Cologne. Waldeck regarded the French concentration at Tournai as a subsidiary effort.[14] The danger of an invasion of the United Provinces from Flanders could be ruled out because of the barriers posed by the deltas of the Scheldt and the Rhine. Only through Brabant or from Cleves could the Generality lands of the Dutch Republic be endangered. As Waldeck's purpose was to remain on the defensive and protect the United Provinces until William could turn his full attention and energies to the war in Europe, he had to base his operations in Brabant. This meandering and uncertain warfare continued throughout March. The Allies put sizeable garrisons into Namur and Mons and, in Flanders, Castañaga protected Nieuport by opening the sea sluices and inundating the surrounding countryside. Castañaga's greatest fear was for the safety of Ghent and Bruges which appeared at risk from the French corps at Tournai and its accompanying siege train lying in boats on the Scheldt. Waldeck had insufficient troops to assist Castañaga in Flanders. Count Tirimont asked Dyckveldt to use his influence with William to see whether the expected British corps could land in Dutch Flanders in order to cover Ghent and Bruges. This confusion as to French intentions was exacerbated by enemy raids into the Bishopric of Liège in violation of Liègeois neutrality and marches and counter-marches in the triangle between the Sambre and the Meuse. On 22 March/1 April, William felt compelled to ask Waldeck why had had not yet formulated any clear plans for the 1689 campaign. He ordered his general to confer with his senior officers and with the Elector of Brandenburg in order to discover an operational consensus.[15]

In his reply to William three days later, Waldeck seemed somewhat clearer in his interpretation of French intentions. It looked as though the French were going to advance with three corps to attack Flanders and Brabant and counter-attack along the Rhine. In the face of this triple danger, the Allies were short of men and supplies. Schöning's field army still only amounted to 7,000 men with a further 2,000 in garrison in Cologne, although the Bishop of Münster was due to send 6,000 reinforcements.[16] William in London fretted about Flanders, especially Ghent and Bruges, as the Allies simply did not have enough soldiers to meet all their commitments. The only bright spot was the fact that Schöning's army was preparing to undertake the formal siege of Kaiserswerth. The British corps began to arrive at Helvoetsluys and

Rotterdam on 21/31 March and were marched to 's-Hertogenbosch on the next day.[17] Waldeck left The Hague on 26 March/5 April to travel to Brussels to consult with Castañaga whilst Count Adriaan van Flodroff, a Dutch major-general, placed a loose cordon around the city of Liège which had violated its neutrality by 'admitting' a French convoy. In reality, Prince-Bishop Jean-Louis d'Elderen had no choice but to admit the French who were attempting to compromise him into accepting a French alliance. The Holy Roman Emperor promptly wrote to the Prince-Bishop telling him in no uncertain terms that he must decide either for France or the Grand Alliance. He was no longer prepared to recognise his broken neutrality. The Bishop saw both the force of this logic and Flodroff's troopers and declared for the Grand Alliance early in April.[18] He immediately set about raising a Liègeois army of 6,000 men which was commanded by the Walloon mercenary, Albert T'Serclaes, Count of Tilly, the grandson of the Imperial general of the Thirty Years' War.

Upto this point in the campaign, although the French were concentrating their forces both towards the Rhine and towards the Spanish Netherlands and were preparing to enter the field in earnest, Waldeck had yet to make a significant movement. Early in April, he began to form a Dutch army corps of 7,310 men around Hasselt on the River Demer although his own headquarters were at Culembourg on the River Lek in Holland. Schöning in Cologne was reinforced from Brandenburg to bring his army upto nearly 20,000 men. On 4/14 April, Waldeck sent his appreciation of the Allied position to William. Huy on the Meuse, which had passed into Allied possession with the Liègeois declaration of war on France, could not be maintained by less than a full army corps and this was unavailable. Castañaga in Flanders had asked for assistance and Waldeck had responded by sending Count Willem van Hornes with a Dutch corps to co-operate with him and to cover Ghent. A small force of two battalions had been dispatched to reinforce Bruges. Schöning had been strengthened and a Dutch-German army corps was based on the Demer at Hasselt. In the meantime, the arrival of the British troops was anxiously awaited but the only four weak battalions had so far sailed into Helvoetsluys.[19] The Allied position was already showing the weaknesses of coalition warfare and divided command. Waldeck, although William's deputy, was sixty-nine years of age and seemed remarkably dependent upon his master's approval. The resulting lack of confidence and authority exacerbated Waldeck's tendency to react to the initiatives of others rather than forge a strategy of his own. This was in stark contrast to the successful and decisive operations of the Brandenburgers.

The decision of the Prince-Bishop of Liège to join the Allied cause was of the utmost strategic importance. Liège itself was a vital fortress between Maastricht and Namur on the Meuse but almost as significant was the town of Huy, also on the Meuse to the south-east of Liège. If the Allies could hold Huy then it would present them with a bridge across the middle Meuse forming a gateway into the Duchy of Luxembourg and a means of communication with the Rhine and the Moselle. Should Huy fall to the French, then they would be in possession of a bridge and route into Brabant as well as being in a position to threaten Liège and interrupt the navigation of the Meuse making the supply of Namur extremely difficult. Waldeck actually considered abandoning Namur unless the Prince-Bishop could find enough troops to cover the region and garrison Huy. Without the firm retention of Huy, Namur would have become untenable. The French brought together their garrisons from Dinant and Charlemont, to the number of 5,000 men, and tried to surprise Huy on 4/14 April but the Dutch garrison held them off. After the failure of this coup, Marshal d'Humières began to assemble an army corps with the intention of seizing Huy and Liège or, at the very least, destroying the countryside of Liège so that it could not support operations by Allied troops. Waldeck ordered Flodroff and Count Walrad van Nassau-Saarbrück to hold Huy.[20] The Dutch commander-in-chief was assisted in this decision by intelligence that the French were about to abandon Bonn and fall back from the Rhine and the Electorate of Cologne.

Having failed in his attempt to dislodge the Allies from Huy and Liège, d'Humières, who commanded the principal French corps in the Low Countries, fell back to his base and magazine at Philippeville from which he threatened the Allied post at Charleroi. Immediately, Waldeck sent 800 Spanish troops to reinforce the garrison.[21] Castañaga and Waldeck then discussed the command arrangements in the Netherlands. The Spaniard wanted to divide the responsibilities with Waldeck taking charge of the theatres on the Rhine, the Meuse and in Brabant whilst Castañaga assumed command in Flanders. Waldeck did not care for this division and chose to assume overall command in the Low Countries reducing Castañaga to a subordinate role in Flanders. Relations between the two were never quite the same again. However, by 17/27 April Castañaga had grumpily resigned himself to this scheme and the two generals had agreed a rough plan by which to conduct their forthcoming operations. Waldeck was to concentrate his army of

35,000 men at Hasselt leaving Castañaga with a field corps of 6,000 in Flanders and a further 4,000 troops in garrison in Charleroi, Ath, Mons and Oudenarde.[22] Castañaga also had operational control over Count Hornes with his Dutch corps of 12,000 men. Hornes and Castañaga decided to split their forces; Hornes stayed at Brussels with his 12,000 and Castañaga adopted a mobile role with his 6,000 horse to cover the frontier towns of Flanders. Even these dispositions soon proved inadequate to prevent the French from raiding into Flanders as far north as Bruges. With Flanders somewhat tenuously protected, the main army of the Dutch Republic slowly assembled in the triangle formed by Hasselt, Tongres and St. Truiden.

4,000 Frenchmen again raided Huy on 25 April/5 May and although they set fire to the town in four places, they did not press the assault but withdrew to Dinant. On the following day, with the British arriving in strength at Rotterdam, d'Humières sent out a detachment to seize the Castle of Samson, on the Meuse between Namur and Huy. Two days later, on 28 April/8 May, French reconnaissance patrols came into contact with Waldeck's cantonments around Tirlemont.[23] D'Humières's long-range cavalry parties were a nuisance to Waldeck's main army as he was weak in horse and unable to drive the French away. Some Spanish mounted troops had to be diverted from Flanders to his assistance. Despite the presence of enemy horse, the main army of d'Humières was still concentrating between the Sambre and the Meuse and Waldeck was sufficiently confident to write to William expressing a desire to leave a covering force to watch d'Humières whilst he took the main army to the Rhine to assist the Brandenburg forces at the Siege of Kaiserswerth before advancing down the Rhine to destroy the French base at Bonn. After this interlude, he intended to lead his men back to Liège and attack the army of d'Humières. Even Waldeck was now beginning to realise that the path to glory lay along the Rhine. In readiness for the attack on Kaiserswerth, the Allies fortified Neuss and Deutz, the suburb of Cologne on the east bank of the Rhine, and raised a thirty-gun battery on the banks of the river to prevent water-borne interference from the direction of Bonn. As a further preliminary, Rheinberg was captured without a fight. Waldeck ordered troops from the garrison of Maastricht, amounting to 6 battalions and 22 squadrons, to march eastward to reinforce Schöning. A large garrison was no longer required in Maastricht now that the Meuse was guarded by Liège and Huy.

Louis XIV had nearly 250,000 men, both regulars and militia, available for the war in 1689. Louis and Louvois surmised that the major threat in 1689 was likely to emanate from German and Imperial forces along the Rhine rather than from Waldeck and Castañaga in the Low Countries. William of Orange was not present with the Allied army in 1689 and Waldeck was known as a cautious and pedantic general who was not imbued with flair or imagination. He could be relied upon not to take risks. Moreover, the devastation of the Palatinate and the Rhineland, which was to continue into the autumn of 1689, was a recognition that the main danger to France would come from the east of the Rhine. Accordingly, the principal French army assembled around Mainz under the Marshal de Duras, with detached corps positioned on the Moselle, the Saar and in Alsace. D'Humières's army gathered between the Sambre and the Meuse with smaller corps stationed at Courtrai and Condé. Opposing these French armies stood the forces of the Elector of Bavaria in Baden, Prince Charles of Lorraine at Frankfurt-am-Main and the Elector of Brandenburg in Jülich and Cleves.[24] The operations of Castañaga and Waldeck appeared distinctly secondary.

The Brandenburg and Münster forces began to bombard Kaiser-swerth on 13/23 May. In Brabant, d'Humières brought his army of 14,000 foot and 5,000 horse north of the Sambre to Trazegnies, north-west of Charleroi. Waldeck responded by pulling his cantoned forces into a safe camp at Waremme, north of Huy and west of Liège. He was not in an enviable position. The British troops were not yet ready to come into the field, only one of the Swedish regiments was fit for service, the Spaniards deserted in droves through lack of pay and the Province of Zealand refused to raise its quota of fourteen troops of cavalry. It is doubtful if Waldeck had more than 12,000 men at Waremme although his army was supposed to total 35,000. From Trazegnies, d'Humières's army threatened Huy and Liège as well as Ghent and Bruges and he was also in a position to cover any detachments that he might send to reinforce the French position on the Rhine around Kaiserswerth and Bonn. He soon demonstrated the tactical potential of his stance by dispatching Lieutenant-General Calvo with a force of cavalry to Pont d'Espierres on the Scheldt above Tournai. From Ath, the Prince de Vaudemont was sent to cover Calvo with a body of cavalry.[25]

The Siege of Kaiserswerth was well under way by 25 May/4 June; on the day before the Duke of Lorraine had marched his Imperial army before Mainz. Waldeck drew the remains of the Maastricht garrison into his army and reinforced himself as quickly as he possible could, but he still commanded only 16,490 men although the Dutch train of artillery had arrived giving him some sixty cannon. Whilst d'Humières adjusted his camp onto the banks of the little River Piéton, still just to the northwest of Charleroi, Waldeck remained at Waremme, close to Brussels, the Meuse and the Rhine.

D'Humières now stood only 55 kilometres to the south of Brussels and had succeeded in pinning Waldeck. Now he dared not fulfill his original intention of moving to the Rhine to assist Schöning at Kaiserswerth until he knew d'Humières's intentions. Because of Waldeck's shortage of cavalry, he probably did not have a clear image of d'Humières's army and possibly over-estimated his strength.[26] At the most the Frenchman possessed 22,000, much of which was cavalry, and he had no firm intentions except to prevent Waldeck from intervening on the Rhine. To keep Waldeck entertained, the French sent some raiders to burn villages around Tirlemont and, to balance the equation, directed another party towards Ath. On 29 May/8 June, d'Humières broke camp and marched towards Brugelette, south-east of Ath on the Plains of Cambron, as if he intended to link-up with Calvo's corps which was entrenched at Courtrai having lost the race with Vaudemont for Pont d'Espierres. To mask the right flank and direction of his march, d'Humières sent 1,000 cavalry towards Gaasbeek to the south-west of Brussels who burned a few houses before being driven off.[27]

On 1/11 June, Castañaga disobeyed Waldeck's orders by throwing Vaudemont's Spanish corps into Mons. Waldeck did not think that d'Humières was aiming at Mons and Castañaga's insubordination merely tied down valuable men to a useless task at a time when he was short of infantry, cavalry and money. Castañaga's indiscretion and d'Humières's movement towards Flanders ruled out all possibility of Waldeck transferring his weight to the Rhine.[28] However, given the overall strategic situation, Waldeck was decently balanced.

From Waremme he covered Liège, Huy, the line of the Meuse and Brabant, as well as being able to intercept any northward move by the French towards Brussels. The strength of Waldeck's station was reflected in the fact that d'Humières could do no more than launch raids towards Nivelles and Brussels.[29] Waldeck was under considerable pressure from Castañaga to come to his assistance and prevent d'Humières from wasting the countryside to the south of Brussels but Waldeck saw his first duty as protecting the southern frontiers of the United Provinces and that could only be achieved by guarding Brabant and the Meuse.[30] Waldeck pulled his army out of the camp at Waremme on 5/15 June having exhausted the forage, and marched through Landen to Heylissem on the Little Geete.[31] At this point, Waldeck wrote to William outlining his plans. He wanted the Elector of Brandenburg to leave a garrison in Cologne and blockade Bonn after Kaiserswerth had fallen, but to march the bulk of his army to the Meuse to operate in conjunction with Waldeck. It might then be possible to attack Maubeuge or Philippeville. Pique as much as strategic sense lay behind this restatement of Waldeck's earlier views. Waldeck felt that the Elector's successful campaign on the Rhine was giving him a greater independence than Waldeck felt was desirable and was threatening his own position as Allied commander-in-chief. He wanted to see the Elector and Schöning back under his personal eye and command.[32]

The formal siege of Kaiserswerth opened on 11/21 June and, within six days, the French had surrendered. The Allied position on the Rhine was now most advantageous. All of Cologne, with the exception of blockaded Bonn, was now in their hands, the Duke of Lorraine had crossed the Rhine with 20,000 men and was camped before Coblenz, the Elector of Bavaria was within one hour's march of Philippsburg and the Elector of Saxony was in the process of throwing a bridge across the Rhine between Mainz and Oppenheim. In response, the Duke de Duras was forming a considerable French camp between Landau and Philippsburg whilst the Dukes of Choiseul and de Montclair commanded a small corps towards the Black Forest. This was the moment for the Elector of Brandenburg to exert pressure on Waldeck. At a conference near Kaiserswerth, the German generals argued that the time had come for Waldeck to attack d'Humières rather than expect the victorious Brandenburg troops to abandon their campaign on the Rhine and participate in an invasion of France through Philippeville and Maubeuge. Waldeck and his generals strongly disagreed. D'Humières had been reinforced to some 32,000 men and was far superior to the Dutch and Spanish armies in cavalry. Besides, they argued, the troops under Waldeck's command were so unseasoned that to attack the French was to court a disaster from which the cause of William of Orange and the Grand Alliance might never recover. Unable to persuade Waldeck by words, the Elector of Brandenburg turned to deeds. By opening the Siege of Mayence, the Brandenburg generals forced Waldeck to keep d'Humières occupied in order to prevent him from sending reinforcements to the Rhine. It was scarcely an example of Allied co-operation and self-sacrifice. Although his position at Heylissem was perfectly balanced and apposite to the strategic situation, Waldeck had been thoroughly out-manoeuvred by his confederates in the conference room. Waldeck returned to his army in the knowledge that the Brandenburg army would not come towards the Meuse and that he would be unable to march towards the Rhine. For the remainder of the campaign he would have to deal with d'Humières in Brabant and Flanders. Even Castañaga was to be drawn into the web of the Brandenburgers.[33]

It was at this point in the campaign that the British corps came marching into Waldeck's camp. They made quite an impact. From Rotterdam, the British marched in two columns, one commanded by Marlborough and the other by the Duke of Ormonde. The columns trudged through Breda and Loenhout to Lier, south-east of Antwerp, and then to Louvain. As they entered Brabant, the realities of local civil-military relations reared their ugly heads.

> The country began to be dangerous, the Bores, or peasants, being so bloody, rude and surly that, as they find an opportunity, they knock what soldiers they can on the head and butcher them, though they gain nothing thereby but their clothes, as they did two of the Lord of Oxford's Regiment, which lurked behind us and were never heard of after. For which reasons we encamped in a meadow that night and foraged our horses but could get no meat but what we brought from Louvain.

The disappearance of the two troopers from the Royal Horse Guards is probably explained by desertion rather than some grisly fate at the hands of the peasants but Catholic Brabant certainly provided the British officers and soldiers with a sharp blow to their religious and cultural sensibilities. 'We are now come into the Land of Idolatry . . . the Canaanites could never arrive to a greater pitch of idolatry, so that this land can be so fitly likened to nothing as to a Paradise inhabited by Devils.[34] Over the eight years of the British involvement in the war, increased familiarity was to breed a greater tolerance.

If the Allied position on the Rhine was promising, the situation in Flanders was causing concern. Castañaga pressed Waldeck to manoeuvre his army in order to block d'Humières's punishing raids towards Brussels and into Spanish Flanders but the Dutch general was in no mood to comply. Initially, he told the energetic Spaniard that he was short of supplies and would have to forage towards Jodoigne on the Great Geete where the villages were still in a good and supportive condition. However, in a letter to William written on 25 June/5 July, the truth came flooding out. There was trouble in the camp. In William's absence, Waldeck felt that he was the whipping-boy of the factions amongst the Dutch general officers and his camp was riddled with discord which mirrored the political dispute in the United Provinces between the Republican interests and the Orangists. In the midst of all this back-biting, Waldeck confessed that he was tempted to resign his command and go home to the Ederland.[35] Instead, Waldeck did the next best thing. Nothing. Fortunately, his opponent, d'Humières, was not one of the most outstanding of the French field commanders and richly deserved his nick-name of the 'Maréchal sans lumière'. They were well matched.

Waldeck added to his problems by persistently over-estimating the power of the French in the Low Countries. The major French commitment for 1689 was on the Rhine and d'Humières had been entrusted with a holding operation in Flanders and Brabant. Waldeck had been reinforced by 1,200 Spanish infantry and the first four British battalions on 26 June/6 July and by the remaining six British battalions on 29 June/9 July. With these additional troops, his army numbered in the region of 34,000. D'Humières commanded about 32,000 yet Waldeck continued to believe that his opponent was considerably stronger. The Allied army marched forward from Heylissem on 19/29 June in three columns to Perwez, 25 kilometres south of Tirlemont, and it is possible that Waldeck intended to try to attack d'Humières in his camp at Brugelette. The Frenchman's reply was to march back to his central position north of the Sambre between Mons and Charleroi, taking his camp at Trazegnies, three kilometres east of Binche, behind the line of the River Piéton. With d'Humières having been pulled away from Flanders by Waldeck's southward march to Perwez, the way was clear for Castañaga to undertake some offensive action which might oblige d'Humières to weaken his main army by sending detachments to reinforce Calvo at Courtrai or even unbalance his own position. The Brandenburgers were very keen to encourage Castañaga as operations in Flanders would have the effect of further diverting d'Humières's attention from the Rhine.

Simultaneously with Waldeck's move to Perwez, Vaudemont crossed the River Lys at Deynze and was joined on the other side by Count Hornes with 5,000 Dutch foot. The combined detachment then advanced southwards to Harelbeke with the intention of attacking Calvo's corps which was camped near Courtrai. On the approach of the Dutch and Spaniards, Calvo fell back in some haste to a position behind the line of field fortifications which the French had built between Menin on the Lys and Pont d'Espierres on the Scheldt. D'Humières immediately sent some limited reinforcements to Calvo but Castañaga in Brussels also reinforced Vaudemont and Hornes and encouraged them to press Calvo and put the French territory around Lille, Courtrai and Ypres under contributions.[36] This joint offensive by Waldeck's army and the Spanish and Dutch corps in Flanders had been co-ordinated at a conference between Waldeck and Castañaga in Brussels on 22 June/2 July. Despite heavy rains, Waldeck's pioneers cleared the roads to enable his army to march in two columns to Sombreffe, a distance of 21 kilometres.[37] Waldeck's series of southerly advances now came to a halt as he was obliged to send 3,000 cavalry to assist the Brandenburg forces in their blockade and bombardment of Bonn and the bad weather made further large-scale movements difficult. Vaudemont and Hornes, though, remained in offensive mood. They forced the French lines between the Lys and the Scheldt early in July and Calvo again had to withdraw, this time exposing Courtrai to attack.

Taking advantage of the operations in Brabant and Flanders, the Elector of Brandenburg stepped up the tempo of his campaign in Cologne. Flodroff and Schöning captured a fort near Bonn on 1/11 July before moving closer to Bonn itself as if preparing to convert the existing blockade into a siege in form. The Brandenburg army arrived before Bonn on 12/22 July and its batteries opened fire on the city and its fortifications at dawn on the following day. The Duke of Lorraine remained in the vicinity of Mainz.

The British troops with Waldeck's army were already in a sorry state. The field-marshal reported that the British foot numbered only 6,000 effective men whilst the cavalry could muster just four squadrons, the whole corps standing at no more than sixty per cent of its official establishment. He seriously considered sending the British soldiers out of the camp into garrisons and billets to enable them to regain their health, strength and numbers.[38] Shortage of troops prevented Waldeck from ordering this drastic remedy and all he could do was to instruct Marlborough to use his contingency moneys to gather recruits and employ whatever methods he could to check the high rates of desertion.[39] Plots were discovered for British soldiers to desert at Louvain and for Irish soldiers in the Spanish army to run from their colours. Some troopers from the Royal Horse Guards mutinied because they had not been paid, a revolt which was quickly quelled by Major Henry Boad shooting one of the ringleaders through the head. Several Irishmen in the infantry were discovered trying to desert to the French and were executed.[40] Having received some small reinforcements of Spanish and Brandenburg troops, Waldeck commanded 40,000 men with an artillery train of 41 cannon, 4 mortars and 30 pontoons. He was roughly equal in numbers to d'Humières.[41]

Waldeck's army struck camp and marched westwards on 13/23 July in two columns, with the artillery taking a separate route, before encamping in two long lines. Viesville marked the right flank, Mellet the left, and Thiméon was in the centre.⁴² Still on the defensive, d'Humières countered by shifting south-west to Givry, placing outposts at Estinnes and Bray. By this move, the French covered the key magazine of Maubeuge and kept open communications with Calvo's corps to the south of Courtrai. During these marches, there was a skirmish between sixty French horse and double that number of Dutch cavalry whilst a party from the Allied garrison of Charleroi shadowed d'Humières's rearguard during his retirement to Givry. These seemed to be standard tactics. On the eve of a major tactical move and during the actual march itself, numerous cavalry raids and patrols were effected away from the proposed direction of movement in order to confuse enemy reconnaissance troops. Suffering from insufficient weight to defeat Calvo and invade French territory, Vaudemont and Hornes were obliged to withdraw from before Courtrai and establish themselves at Deynze to the south of Ghent on the Scheldt. This freed Calvo to reinforce d'Humières, if his services were required.⁴³ As these adjustments were being made to the positions in Flanders and Brabant, the guns of the Elector of Brandenburg were reducing Bonn to ashes with fires blazing in all quarters and the fortifications along the Rhine were a mass of rubble. The garrison and unfortunate civilian population were living in cellars, caves and in the vaulted casemates beneath the fortifications.⁴⁴ The tactics of terror were not the sole preserve of the French.

Waldeck's position at Thiméon and d'Humières's camp at Givry were separated by a distance of 30 kilometres. Waldeck's camp was in two lines, corresponding to the First and Second Lines of Battle, with a third line containing the artillery and the baggage. Patrols were sent out every night although there was little contact with the French and no reported action. A Dutch patrol under a lieutenant ran away from a French party, for which crime the officer was shot and one in every ten of his men hanged. The local population had adjusted quickly to the presence of foreign armies and were able to protect themselves and their property and take a commercial advantage from the opportunities offered by hungry and thirsty soldiers. 'Here the inhabitants of the country removed what they had into their churches, or rather Temples to their Gods, which alone are free from the plunder of the soldiers having this motto on them, "Altare Privilegiatum". They keep their markets at their churches on the Sabbath, where we might have champagne and Rhenish wine in plenty.' Waldeck's supply position was assisted by the fact that his march from Heylissem to Thiméon had described a quarter of the arc of a circle whose centre was the main Allied base of Brussels. Throughout the march, the Allied army had remained equidistant from its principal magazine. At Thiméon, Brussels was only 32 kilometres away although the road ran through several 'great woods' which 'made our passage dangerous and gave us reason to expect attack from a French party which lay in ambush for us but missed us.'[45]

Although he was conducting his own part of the campaign in a thoroughly competent and professional manner, Waldeck's confidence was at a low ebb. French agents, mostly disguised as clerics, were busy disseminating seditious propaganda amongst his British and German soldiers to try to persuade them to desert, he was short of field artillery and was without any medical services. To make matters worse, he felt that his own authority was not fully respected by his subordinates. He wondered aloud in a letter to William whether the King could stage a 'descent' somewhere on the French coast to drain a few French soldiers away from the Low Countries in order to ease the situation. Tired and unhappy though he was, the old field-marshal was still determined to march closer to d'Humières but he was not prepared to make any movement until reinforcements had reached him from Brussels. His plan was to wait for the Brandenburg army to complete the reduction of Bonn after which some of the German troops might join Waldeck's army in Brabant. The combined force would then cross the Sambre and raid into France. Under the cover of these raids, Waldeck hoped to besiege either Maubeuge or Philippeville in order to provide 'gates', or bases, from which he would be able to launch a full-scale invasion of France in 1690. If this ambitious scheme had been achieved, and with some determination it was not beyond the bounds of possibility, then 1689 would have turned into a decisive campaign and one that would have placed the Allies in a highly advantageous position. However, it could only be executed if Waldeck had a numerical superiority over d'Humières sufficient to conduct a major siege and provide a covering army. For that, Waldeck needed the lion's share of the Brandenburg army on the Rhine but the Elector had other ideas.[46]

From his camp at Thiméon, a good position guarded by a wood and a morass, Waldeck sent his engineers to build a bridge across the Sambre. Some of his senior generals, including Marlborough, were sent on Monday 19/29 July to confer with Vaudemont and Hornes at Deynze in order to co-ordinate the next series of moves. The French received intelligence of this journey and placed four squadrons of horse amongst 'the standing corn' near the road between Brussels and Dendermonde ready to intercept the illustrious party on its return from Deynze. Unfortunately for the French, a relay of fifteen Confederate horse under a lieutenant chose exactly the same spot at which to wait their turn to escort the generals' coaches into Brussels. Quickly realising the danger, the lieutenant charged the French cavalry. He lost eleven men in the process, but one trooper escaped and raced down the road to warn the oncoming generals of the danger ahead. They accordingly returned to Dendermonde for the night.[47]

Strong though the Thiméon camp was in a military sense, in terms of supply it was less than adequate. D'Humières had consumed much of the forage in the region to the north and north-west of Charleroi during his earlier stay at Trazegnies. Waldeck shifted camp to the north on 30 July/9 August marching a distance of twenty-seven kilometres in two columns to encamp around Nivelles, due south of Brussels. Despite his ambitious schemes, d'Humières's earlier consumption of the forage around Charleroi had forced Waldeck away from the Sambre.[48] From Nivelles, Waldeck wrote to William about his plans to cross the Sambre and proceed to a siege of Maubeuge, Dinant or Philippeville and for the Elector of Brandenburg to sweep along the Rhine; he also moaned about the Catholic Irish agents and Capuchins who hovered around his camp working insidiously upon the suspect loyalty of the British troops. The bright spot was the news that Castañaga had signed a contract with the Elector of Hanover for the hire of 5,000 foot and 3,000 horse to serve for the remainder of the campaign.[49] Poor Waldeck was beset by contradictory advice. Castañaga urged him to move closer to Flanders and away from the Rhine, whilst one of the Elector of Brandenburg's colonels, Krusemarch, suggested the opposite course. All this achieved, wailed Waldeck, was to waste precious time in fruitless argument.[50] One of the motives for the march to Nivelles, apart from sitting equally between Castañaga in Flanders and the Germans on the Rhine without obviously favouring either, was to call in his detachments and garrisons in order to build his field army to maximum strength ready for the march south and over the Sambre. With Vaudemont at Deynze with 7,000 men, Hornes at Ghent with 3,000 and Castañaga at Brussels with 12,000, Waldeck felt that Flanders was well enough provided for especially as the only French corps which could mount an offensive was Calvo's dispirited force around Courtrai. Waldeck ignored both the Elector and Castañaga and set off on his own strategy to cross the Sambre and invade France.

One thing was clear; the campsite at Nivelles was positively dangerous. The countryside was heavily wooded and the French cavalry patrolled all around the army to such an extent that the Allies had to camp in 'the round' with the artillery and baggage in the centre instead of adopting the usual formation of two lines.[51] After a major forage on

21/31 July, during which some fourteen cavalrymen had been killed in skirmishes with the French, Waldeck struck camp on 1/11 August and marched in four columns to the Plain of Marche-les-Ecaussines, north of La Louvière. Cavalry clashes occurred throughout the day as French reconnaissance patrols sought to establish the direction and extent of the march. On the following day, 2/12 August, Waldeck moved forward again to d'Humières's old camp at Trazegnies, and he continued towards the Sambre on 3/13 August taking camp in four lines at Fontaine l'Évêque – 'ruined, wasted and decayed' – due west of Charleroi, where he was joined by 3,000 Brandenburg cavalry.[52]

Thus far, Waldeck had not stolen a march on d'Humières whose numerous cavalry had kept him well informed of his opponent's marches. From Givry and Estinnes, d'Humières was retiring south-eastwards towards the banks of the Sambre with the intention of camping at La Buissière and bridging the river. D'Humières was well positioned to block Waldeck's advance south of the Sambre.[53] At this critical juncture, just as Waldeck was steeling himself to back his own judgement and attack across the Sambre knowing that its corollary was going to be either a battle or a siege, came a letter from William III at Hampton Court. Whilst he was sorry to hear of the lack of progress in the Low Countries and sensed that the campaign of 1689 was slipping away without much having been achieved, he did not wish Waldeck to risk a battle with the French. Defeat, given the uncertain state of the British Isles and the shortage of troops available in the Spanish Netherlands, could be disastrous. There was too much at stake for unnecessary risks.[54]

Clearly disturbed by this example of armchair generalship, Waldeck decided to confer with Castañaga before taking any further action. What would d'Humières do now that Waldeck had made his sudden excursion south from Nivelles? He could either move southwards from Givry to cover Waldeck's operations towards the Sambre, or he could take advantage of Waldeck's new commitment to march to Courtrai, link-up with Calvo and wreak havoc in Flanders. The latter alternative would effectively stop Waldeck's plans south of the Sambre and compel him to support the Spaniards in Flanders.[55] Only one fact was certain. If Waldeck wanted to pin d'Humières in the Maubeuge-Philippeville region and prevent him from exploiting opportunities in Flanders, then he had to act fast, cross the Sambre and threaten d'Humières's magazines. To cover himself against all eventualities, Waldeck concentrated his troops in Flanders by ordering the 12,000 Spanish troops in and around Brussels to combine with Vaudemont's 7,000 at Deynze.

As Waldeck balanced his options in the Low Countries, the smooth progress of the Elector of Brandenburg's campaign on the Rhine had come to a juddering halt before Bonn. Without sufficient infantry, he was unable to besiege Bonn in form and had to content himself with the spectacular but ultimately pointless bombardment. He was even considering leaving between 8,000 and 10,000 men to continue the blockade of Bonn whilst the rest of his forces marched to help Waldeck in the Sambre-Meuse. Alternatively, his forces might be better employed moving south to assist the Duke of Lorraine before Mainz. As news came in that Marshal Boufflers was working his way up the Moselle Valley in the direction of Coblenz and had already captured Bernkastel, the latter course of action became more probable.

Waldeck's quartermasters, engineers and senior generals reconnoitred in force over the Sambre and found a suitable camp-site at Ham-sur-Heure, even though the approach to this place ran through a great wood. 'Through lack of time', Waldeck decided to accept this advice despite the hazards. Four pontoon bridges were laid over the Sambre on 6/16 August and, on the following day, Waldeck's army marched south from Fontaine l'Évêque, across the river at Marchienne and camped at Montignies-le-Tilleul, two kilometres beyond. Early on the morning of the 8/18 August, 800 pioneers from the infantry and 100 'volunteer' peasants set out to widen the track through the forest from Montignies-le-Tilleul to Ham-sur-Heure. D'Humières had crossed the Sambre at La Buissière and was marching on a course convergent with Waldeck's line of advance. As the Allied army set out later on the morning of 8/18 August, there was a grave danger that they would be attacked on the march from their right flank by the French, and, accordingly, the army marched in line of battle. Luckily, a fog descended and although the French were very close, the Allied army reached its camp at Ham-sur-Heure without interruption. As Waldeck's men erected their tents, d'Humières's soldiers tramped into Boussu-les-Walcourts, twelve kilometres to the south.[56] Waldeck's army spent the next day, 9/19 August, entrenching the left-hand approaches to the camp and in digging a line of circumvallation. Likewise, the French fortified their position at Boussu-les-Walcourt and cavalry from the rival armies were constantly in contact.

Waldeck now had 35 battalions and 60 squadrons, a total of 28,800 men, whilst d'Humières commanded 28 battalions, 80 squadrons and 7 regiments of dragoons, making an army of 30,700. Waldeck had intended to march forward to Thy-le-Château but the French had already foraged around that area and rendered the site untenable.

Instead, Waldeck organised a major forage towards Thuillies, south-west of Ham-sur-Heure, in which 1,200 foot mowed the hay under the watchful eye of 5,000 covering troops. For a short while it looked as though this forage might precipitate a general action. The French sent forward 25 squadrons and 300 foot and took possession of the Castle of Donstiennes, south-west of Thuillies. However, there was a strong wooded defile between the foragers and the French around Donstiennes and Lieutenant-General Johan Weibnom, Lieutenant-General d'Huby from the Brandenburg army and Major-General Slangenburg posted themselves strongly around Thuillies and the French did not care to press too closely. Only a little desultory firing occurred creating four or five casualties.

After this scare, the 11/21 August was declared a day of rest. On 12/22, Waldeck marched south to Berzée on the River Heure, a manoeuvre effected in battle formation within full view of the enemy. Waldeck had now decided that his target was Philippeville, twenty kilometres to the south-east. From Berzée, Waldeck threw four bridges across the little River Heure at Pry on 13/23 August and marched his army in four columns, the artillery and baggage forming the left wing and thus farthest removed from the enemy, and went into a camp between Thy-le-Château and Laneffe.[57] Waldeck had stolen a march on d'Humières and the two armies were now separated by the River Heure with the Allies on the Philippeville side. The situation was not yet decisive as both armies were equidistant from Philippeville and Waldeck had still to cross the obstacle of the River Yves, a tributary of the Heure, but the advantage lay marginally with the Allied army.

Castañaga led the Spanish reinforcements into Vaudemont's camp at Deynze on 13/23 August, giving the Spanish general a corps of 14,000 foot and 5,000 horse with which to operate defensively or to take advantage of d'Humières's absence in the Sambre-Meuse to attack Calvo in the Lines between the Lys and the Scheldt. Meanwhile, from his headquarters at Thy-le-Château in the forested foothills of the Ardennes, Waldeck exchanged gloomy letters with William in London. The Elector of Brandenburg was the target for their griping. William doubted if he would succeed in taking either Bonn or Mayence in the southern Eifel and his 'irresolution' had condemned Waldeck to a campaign where he could do nothing but prevent d'Humières from crossing the Ardennes. Waldeck replied that valuable time was fast disappearing but he could attempt little against d'Humières as the Frenchman was very strongly posted and Waldeck was short of cavalry.[58] Two days later, on 15/25 August, Waldeck's troops were in action.

The Battle of Walcourt was no more than a large skirmish and only a minority of each army was engaged. However, it was the major action in the Low Countries in 1689 and it marked the British corps's introduction to combat. The camp at Thy-le-Château was protected by a steep ascent to either flank, a river in the rear and a number of settlements to the front, one of which was the walled village of Walcourt. Over five thousand local peasants had flocked into Walcourt to escape from the depredations of the contesting armies. D'Humières had forbidden the peasants to sell any provisions to Waldeck's army in the knowledge that his enemy was at the end of a long and vulnerable line of communication back to Charleroi. The French general also foraged as widely as he could to make virtually impossible any future enemy advance on Philippeville. Feeling the pinch, Waldeck sent two battalions of Brandenburg infantry to Walcourt to explain to the peasants that if they refused to sell their produce to the Allies then their walls and houses would be battered down around their ears. This gentle incentive produced the desired effect and not only did Waldeck gain provisions but a Dutch and a German battalion remained to garrison Walcourt.

Waldeck decided to forage towards Philippeville on 15/25 August and gave the command of the operation to Weibnom, Huby and Slangenburg. Unsure of whether the advance of the Allies to their front heralded simply a forage or an approach march preliminary to an attack on his camp, d'Humières marched his army forwards to meet the enemy. A recent reinforcement of 6,000 men encouraged d'Humières in his boldness. Colonel Robert Hodges and his infantry battalion were stationed amidst the heights of Sleury, some 238 metres above sea level, to the south of Walcourt with 300 Dutch horse under Lieutenant-Colonel Otto Goes riding as outposts before their position. At nine o'clock in the morning, the Dutch cavalry spotted the vanguard of the French army marching towards Walcourt. Two cannon were fired as a signal to the foragers to withdraw and to alert the main army at Thy-le-Château that the enemy was in sight. Although the foragers started to hurry in, the strong wind made the cannon-fire inaudible at the camp. D'Humières's motives are unclear. By foraging widely from his strong camp at Boussu, he had already rendered difficult a further advance by Waldeck towards Philippeville. If he had continued with these tactics, Waldeck's withdrawal to the Sambre was just a matter of time. He may have intended only to interrupt Waldeck's forage in order to increase his problems with supply; he may have been fired by the fact that 15/25 August was St. Louis's Day; he may simply have misjudged the occasion and allowed a limited operation to tumble over into a major action.

There was also the matter of prestige. Waldeck was very close to French territory and neither d'Humières nor his royal master wanted to run the risk of the Allied army raiding into France.

That d'Humières failed in his purpose was largely due to Colonel Hodges and his battalion of 600 men. They were posted at the bottom of a hill and found themselves between the foragers and the advancing French. The supporting Dutch horse were rapidly driven off by the weight of the French cavalry but the English infantry 'lined the hedges' and kept firing from cover for an hour between ten and eleven o'clock. No doubt, they 'fired to keep ground' as laid down in the *Abridgement*. At the end of sixty minutes, Hodges saw that his position had become 'open' to both flanks and so he retired to a windmill atop a nearby hill and again held up the French progress towards Walcourt. Finally, at noon, Hodges withdrew to the main line of battle which Waldeck had been able to form during the time gained by the English foot. Although it was considered a noted feat of arms, Hodges's holding action cost his battalion only one officer killed, one wounded and thirty other ranks killed in two hours of fighting. These figures do not give the impression that the French pressed particularly hard.

Behind Hodges's line of red coats, Waldeck reinforced the two battalions in Walcourt itself and then built his line of battle to the east of the village employing Walcourt as the anchor for his right flank. It was now up to d'Humières to accept a general engagement or to retire having failed in his purpose of surprising Waldeck's army. The marshal made the wrong decision. Waldeck's line of battle was well chosen and difficult for the French to assault. Instead of trying to fight the main Allied line of battle, d'Humières engaged the Allied left and centre with an artillery bombardment whilst he attempted to seize the village of Walcourt by infantry attack. No doubt, he argued that if Walcourt fell then the whole Allied line could be rolled up from the right flank. Nine French battalions made the initial assault at three separate places against the Dutch battalion of Colonel Holle and a Lüneburg regiment. Although Walcourt was ringed by a single stone wall without any modern fortifications, it proved sufficient to defend against infantry who attacked without support or preparation from heavy artillery. At around two o'clock in the afternoon, Brigadier Thomas Talmash led a battalion of the Coldstream Guards and a German regiment into Walcourt to reinforce the garrison. This proved decisive. Although the French continued to batter at the walls, even bringing up a Guards battalion to try to burn down the gate, Walcourt was now safe and Waldeck had a breathing space during which he could ready his forces for a counter-attack. Lieutenant-General Aylva, now returned from the Rhine, took three Dutch regiments, the English Life Guards, two English battalions and Major-General Slangenburg's Dutch battalions around the rear of Walcourt and formed a new line of battle extending to the west of the village. The French battalions involved in the frontal assault on Walcourt were now enfiladed by cannon fire from right and left; in desperation, d'Humières threw some of his infantry into an unprepared and unsupported attack on this new Allied line. This offensive foundered rapidly and the way was open for Waldeck to launch his counter-stroke. At around half past six in the evening, Slangenburg attacked from the west of Walcourt and Marlborough drove in from the east. In the face of this concentric attack which threatened to encircle the infantry assaulting Walcourt, the French began to withdraw. When opposed by a stern rearguard commanded by a Colonel Hector Villars, the Allied army did not press its pursuit and the Frenchmen were left to retire to their camp at Boussu.[59]

Feuquières cited Walcourt as an example to be avoided and it was this crass action that earned d'Humières his nickname.[60] The French lost about 600 men killed and 1,400 in wounded and prisoners whilst the Allies suffered total casualties of between six and seven hundred. The majority of the wounded came from amongst the under-strength British regiments and these unfortunates were bumped northwards in bread waggons to a convent in the village of Les Haies, south of Charleroi. Sadly for the injured men, the nuns had been driven away and so there was no-one to nurse them. Four hundred and thirty wounded soldiers were herded into the convent but the stench soon grew so powerful that no volunteers could be found to care for the patients. Waldeck discovered that the local peasants, or boers, had assisted the French in burying their dead. In retaliation, he allowed his men a temporary license to burn their villages and plunder their churches.

D'Humières appeared anxious to gain a decision over Waldeck to redeem his failure at Walcourt. On 17/27 August, he made preparations for a renewed assault on Walcourt and Waldeck's camp at Thy-le-Château but the German was ready and had posted a strong advance guard before Walcourt. No attack developed but d'Humières did not need to push Waldeck into retirement. Forage and supplies were short and it was clear that the Allies had to retreat from their advanced position. A conference between Waldeck and his generals on 18/28 August confirmed this decision. The Allied high command was extremely concerned to keep its resolutions secret; to throw French spies off the scent, several bridges were built across the Heure at a number of different places. Waldeck's initial task was to draw in his advanced detachments from Walcourt and the surrounding villages and then channel his whole army away from Thy-le-Château through Laneffe towards Gerpinnes. Hopefully, the dummy bridges across the Heure would lull the French into thinking that Waldeck intended to recross that river and withdraw to the Sambre along the route by which he had advanced.

During the very small hours of 19/29 August, Waldeck began his march by the left flank. The garrisons from the small villages and Slangenburg's two battalions from Walcourt were shepherded back to Laneffe by a rearguard commanded by Weibnom. Waldeck had intended to encamp at Laneffe but the French appeared to be too close and so the army marched throughout the 19/29 August until it came to Gerpinnes. The ruse of the false bridges over the Heure had not deceived d'Humières for long and he shadowed Waldeck closely throughout the 19/29 August. The French did not take the same route as the Allies because the forage had been consumed. Instead, they described a wider circuit through Florennes with the intention of intercepting Waldeck when he came to the obstacle of the Sambre. The camp site at Gerpinnes made a long stay out of the question. It was very 'tight' and full of baggage and d'Humières sent out waves of cavalry from Florennes to scour Waldeck's potential foraging area between Gerpinnes and Florennes. Waldeck endured the 20/30 August at Gerpinnes, 'avec bien de l'hazard', in order to give his army a rest and he was saved from French intervention by a fog and heavy rain. Whilst at Gerpinnes, Waldeck received intelligence that d'Humières intended to camp on the Sambre at the identical point to that which he had already selected. This was serious. Flodroff had departed for the Moselle with 3,000 cavalry and Waldeck was drawing flour from the magazines at Namur and Charleroi. If d'Humières reached into the eastern flank of Waldeck's march, then these supplies would have been cut off.

A conference of the senior officers decided to alter the route of withdrawal more to the north-east and attempt both a camp and crossing of the Sambre at Châtelet, south-east of Charleroi. This new axis of retreat was more northerly than had been intended but it made sure that d'Humières could not interrupt the line of communication back to Charleroi. Slangenburg and Quartermaster-General Dopff went ahead to reconnoitre the roads and a possible camp site and the chosen route was then prepared by the pioneers. On 22 August/1 September,

Waldeck's men fell back from Gerpinnes in two columns, preceded by the artillery and the baggage. D'Humières pursued as closely as he dared, but the rearguard, which consisted of one Dutch battalion, the battalions of Robert Hodges and David Colyear, and some cavalry under Aylva, kept the French at bay with musket fire. At one point, Aylva formed his small force into line of battle across a clearing in the midst of a thick wood and drove back the French advance guards with musketry and cannon fire. On arrival at Châtelet, Waldeck decided not to waste time encamping but to stage an immediate passage of the Sambre. Aylva deployed his rearguard in two parties on either side of the main road but d'Humières did not try to interfere with the river crossing although Colonel Villars strongly urged him to take advantage of the situation. Waldeck's weary troops tramped across four pontoon bridges which the engineers had laid over the Sambre and straggled into the haven of a camp at Montignies-sur-Sambre, safely on the north bank.

D'Humières occupied Waldeck's intended camping ground at Châtelet. During the night of 26 August/5 September, d'Humières constructed two batteries, one of ten twenty-four-pounders and one of eight eighteen-pounders. At daybreak on 27 August/6 September, these cannon opened fire on Waldeck's camp. The Allies mounted sixteen guns to return the fire and the cannonade lasted from four o'clock in the morning until an hour before midday. Over two hundred shot and bombs fell into the Allied camp but only two men and one woman were killed.[61] Having beaten off the half-hearted attentions of d'Humières, Waldeck was free to give his attention to the conduct of the remainder of the campaign. His incursion into France had failed but he still had the options of supporting Castañaga in Flanders or moving towards the Rhine where the Brandenburg and Imperial forces had combined to besiege Mayence. An Imperial envoy, the Comte de Borcka, arrived in Waldeck's camp on 28 August/7 September to ask for a diversion which would stem the tide of French reinforcements being sent towards the Moselle. Although the Brandenburg and Imperial troops were investing and attacking Mayence, Boufflers was still steadily advancing along the Moselle Valley and had taken Cochem, no more than twenty kilometres south of Mayence. Relief seemed to be at hand for the beleaguered garrison. To William, far away in Hampton Court, none of this mattered very much as he was already of the opinion that Waldeck could do nothing more in 1689 and should concentrate on making appropriate preparations to ensure that he entered the field before the French in 1690.[62]

Secretly, Waldeck probably wanted to shake off d'Humières and then recross the Sambre with the intention of making a second attempt at a siege of Philippeville but this was just a pipe-dream as the situation on the Moselle, the position in Flanders and the movements of d'Humières gave him no opportunity to forge his own strategy. In Flanders, the Allied cause gave encouragement. On 21/31 August, Castañaga had joined Vaudemont at Harelbeke on the River Lys and the combined corps had set off south along the line of that river to try to drive Calvo out of his defensive lines between the Lys and the Scheldt. Calvo was posted towards the western end of his line near Menin but on receiving news of the advancing Spaniards, he decamped on 26 August/5 September and retired in some haste towards Tournai. This manoeuvre kept open his communications with d'Humières at Châtelet and took him closer to support and succour but it presented the Lines to Vaudemont and Castañaga without a fight. Seizing their opportunity, the Spaniards placed the French countryside towards Lille under contribution and organised the local peasants to level the French Lines. It was in response to the news of this humiliation and the accompanying fall of Courtrai, that d'Humières bombarded Waldeck's camp on 27 August/6 September.

On 1/11 September, d'Humières crossed to the north bank of the Sambre at La Buissière, mid-way between Mons and Charleroi, a movement which took him westwards towards the distressed Calvo and prevented Waldeck from interfering with the communications between the two French corps. Between 28 August/7 September and 5/15 September, Waldeck moved steadily northwards from the Sambre to Genappe, beset by a lack of forage, a weakening army and bad weather. Sickness was rife amongst Waldeck's troops, from eating too much fruit according to one source, and four British battalions and two Dutch regiments were so understrength that they had to be sent from the field army into garrison. On 3/13 September, William wrote to Waldeck telling him not to be ultra-cautious but to take a few risks and try to achieve something from the campaign. This change of tune was caused by knowledge that d'Humières was having to send a regular flow of troops to support the defence of Mayence and Bouffler's drive along the Moselle.[63] The King also penned a note to Marlborough in which he regretted the generally poor showing of the Dutch troops at Walcourt but praised the conduct of the British.[64] Both William and Waldeck still blamed the Elector of Brandenburg for all their ills. First the siege of Bonn and now the siege of Mayence limited Waldeck's options and kept the Brandenburg army away from the Meuse and Brabant. It was all a question of priorities within coalition warfare. Waldeck was entrusted with the defence of the United Provinces and the restriction of French gains in the Spanish Netherlands, whilst the Elector was concerned for the safety of his Rhenish provinces. At least the Elector was positive whereas Waldeck was guilty of dithering and missing his chances. He failed to develop or exploit the success which Castañaga and Vaudemont had achieved at Courtrai and the Lines. He could have manoeuvred to prevent d'Humières from moving to Calvo's aid or even sent substantial reinforcements to the Spanish army. Instead, he wandered northwards from the Sambre allowing d'Humières to march away towards Flanders. William was perturbed by his general's lack of initiative. He felt that the bombardment of Waldeck's camp had been a deep and avoidable humiliation to the Allied cause. D'Humières had hardly revealed the epitome of generalship during 1689 and yet Waldeck was allowing him to dictate the campaign despite his defeat at Walcourt.[65]

Meanwhile, the inexperienced British regiments, riddled by sickness and desertion, were proving more of a handicap than a help to Waldeck. Their lack of field craft, poor medical facilities and inadequate commissariat were as much explained by the fact that the British army had not fought a major European campaign since 1657 and 1658 as by wilful neglect. On 7/17 September, a further four British battalions were pulled out of the army and sent into garrison at Bergen-op-Zoom and Breda in the hope that a spell in early winter quarters would restore them to health and effectiveness.[66] On 4/14 September, Waldeck withdrew north of Charleroi to Mellet and further north to Genappe on 5/15 September. The following day saw a short move of ten kilometres to the west-north-west to the Plains of Bois St. Isaac.[67] During Waldeck's retirement to Bois St. Isaac, d'Humières had marched via Leuse-en-Hainaut northwards to Lessines. This placed him between Waldeck to the south of Brussels and Vaudemont near Tournai. Waldeck had virtually given up the 1689 campaign and was looking forward to 1690. Provided that the Allies achieved an early start to the campaign and that all available troops were concentrated in their starting points on the Meuse, the Demer and at Liège in good time, then all should be well. Success for 1690 also depended on the Elector of Brandenburg co-operating with Waldeck and not conducting his own, separate campaign on the Rhine, and on Castañaga being able to raise a sufficient army to guard Waldeck's flank in Flanders.[68]

Both sides were preparing to put their armies into winter quarters in the most advantageous manner possible. French troops were busy burning and destroying towns, castles and supplies in the Duchy of Luxembourg to deny the area as a wintering ground for Allied forces. William wrote to Marlborough ordering him to place the British infantry into winter quarters in Malines, Bruges and Ghent with the cavalry travelling to Breda.[69] However, Waldeck tried one last throw. On 10/20 September, Waldeck's senior officers reconnoitred the 'grand defile' at Braine-le-Château and then sent 600 pioneers to prepare the road through that danger-spot. Four days later, on 14/24 September, Waldeck took his army along the road to Halle, ten kilometres to the north-west, and then on through Lembeek to Tubise on the next day. Here Waldeck camped, with his right towards Lembeek and his left at Tubise. In the meantime, Castañaga reinforced his garrisons in Flanders and then brought eight battalions of foot and thirty-one squadrons of horse to the north of d'Humières's camp at Lessines, and then around Brussels, through Diegem to enter Waldeck's camp on 15/25 September taking station on the right towards Lembeek. Vaudemont, in command of 3,000 horse, accompanied Castañaga. Flodroff arrived from the Brandenburg army with a further 3,000 cavalry on 19/29 September, bringing Waldeck's total reinforcements to 15,000 men. He was now ready to advance towards d'Humières and attempt to seek a decision by battle. As well as trying to rescue the campaign from oblivion, Waldeck was also induced to march towards d'Humières by Flodroff and Vaudemont who were concerned to stop the heavy French cavalry raids which d'Humières was launching towards Brussels through the country to the north-west of Lembeek.[70]

On 19/29 September, the combined army lumbered forward to Enghien, within fifteen kilometres of d'Humières at Lessines. The Allies attempted to move forward their artillery to cannonade d'Humières in his camp but the heavens opened and in the ensuing downpour the attempt was finally abandoned after the French and Allied outposts had skirmished. On the night of 21 September/1 October, d'Humières pulled back to Leuse on the River Dender. He was now close to Calvo's corps. Waldeck and Castañaga moved up to Silly on 23 September/3 October and then further south-west to Cambron on 26 September/6 October. This placed the Allies within reach of their magazine at Mons whilst their stance at Cambron protected Brussels from cavalry raids.

Waldeck was inclined to attack d'Humières at Leuse but his camp was strongly entrenched and Calvo, now at Roubaix, was busy preparing the roads and the bridges so that d'Humières could fall back to join him in an emergency. Waldeck discussed plans for an attack with his generals but the Spaniards were unenthusiastic thinking it too late in the season to contemplate major engagements. D'Humières's camping ground did not fill the Allies with optimism. It fitted snugly into the angle between the Dender and its confluence with a small tributary and he had fortified the open front with trenches and redoubts. In his rear he had built a number of bridges over the Dender to secure his retreat. However, the Allies reconnoitred the defiles between the two armies and Vaudemont prepared to take 8,000 men forward to engage the French outposts and, hopefully, draw d'Humières from his camp into open battle. Just as Vaudemont was about to set off came intelligence that d'Humiéres was withdrawing from Leuse to take up a new position covering the French frontier at Tournai. The expedition was immediately abandoned. The campaign raised one final flicker when news arrived that Bonn had finally fallen to the Brandenburg army. Perhaps there was still time for Waldeck and the Brandenburgers to advance and take winter quarters in France? This hope was dashed by d'Humières's withdrawal to Tournai and the Elector's announcement that he intended to winter his army on the Rhine around Bonn.[71]

The campaign had ground to a halt. The British corps was to winter in Flanders, the Dutch and Spanish cavalry were to billet in the valley of the River Mehaigne, Charleroi and Namur were to be heavily garrisoned and most of the Dutch infantry was to quarter in the territories of Liège and in Maastricht. All of the British foot was packed into Ghent and Bruges and the cavalry wintered in Breda. The whole design of the disposition of the winter quarters was to enable the Allied commanders to concentrate a considerable force in Flanders, on the Meuse or in Liège within two days should any emergency arise during the winter months.[72] As the troops settled down for a winter of rest and training, the Spanish government in Brussels issued a proclamation forbidding the import or consumption of any French goods or produce. Nothing was to be sold to the French on pain of death.[73]

It had not been a decisive campaign but it had been important. The capture of Bonn by the Imperial and Brandenburg forces on 2/12 October had cleared the French from the Electorate of Cologne and had established an Allied dominance of the Lower Rhine above Coblenz. For the 1690 campaign, the Allies would not have to fear an attack into the United Provinces along the Rhine and they could operate in Brabant without the danger of French interference from the eastern flank. During 1690, the Allies in the Spanish Netherlands would be able to give their full attentions to the French forces to their front.[74] The English regime had also been secured. Waldeck, Castañaga and the Elector of Brandenburg had kept the French fully occupied and had not given Louis XIV the chance to send substantial forces to succour the Jacobites in Ireland and Scotland. From the English point of view, that was the major achievement of the campaign and the object of the war.

NOTES

1 WO 5/5, ff. 103–4; *CSPD 1689–90*, p. 17.
2 Childs, *British Army of William III*, pp. 20–3; Luttrell, *Historical Relation*, i. 507–8.
3 H. R. Knight, *Historical Records of the Buffs, East Kent Regiment, 3rd Foot* (London, 1905), i. 285–6, 14/24 Apr. 1689, Breda.
4 HMC, *Le Fleming MSS.*, pp. 238–9; *LG*, no. 2456; *A Journal of the Late Motions and Actions of the Confederate Forces against the French in the United Provinces and the Spanish Netherlands. . . . Together with an Exact List of the Army, Written by an English Officer who was there during the last Campaign* (London, 1690), p. 2.
5 *CSPD 1689–90*, p. 83; Japikse (Welbeck), i. 62–3.
6 *CSPD 1689–90*, p. 187.
7 ARA, Raad van State, 489, p. 284.
8 *HSL*, vii. 17–20; Waddell, 'Administration', pp. 68–70.
9 *LG*, nos. 2419, 2423, 2424.
10 Müller, ii. 134.
11 Japikse, iii. 98–9.
12 Müller, ii. 142, 24 Feb./5 Mar. 1689; BL, Add. MSS. 61,337, 'Mémoire', ff. 1–2.
13 Müller, ii. 144–5; HMC, *Denbigh MSS.*, pp. 101–2; BL, Add. MSS. 61,337, f. 2; Rousset, *Louvois*, iv. 169–70; CMC 4/40.
14 HMC, *Denbigh MSS.*, p. 103, 15/25 Mar. 1689, Brussels, Count Tirimont to Dyckveldt.
15 *Ibid.*, pp. 104–5; Müller, ii. 148.
16 Müller, ii. 149.
17 Müller, ii. 151; *LG*, no. 2441.
18 Gutmann, *War and Rural Life*, p. 20.
19 *CSPD 1689–90*, pp. 62–3; HMC, *Denbigh MSS.*, pp. 105–6; *Papers illustrating the History of the Scots Brigade in the service of the United Netherlands, 1572–1782*, ed. James Ferguson (Scottish History Society, Edinburgh, 1899), i. 568; BL, Add. MSS. 61,337, f. 2.
20 HMC, *Denbigh MSS.*, p. 106; Müller, ii. 153; CMC 4/39.
21 HMC, *Denbigh MSS.*, p. 107, 12/22 Apr. 1689, Brussels.
22 Müller, ii. 154–5; HMC, *Denbigh MSS.*, p. 108.
23 Müller, ii. 157; *CSPD 1689–90*, pp. 80–1.
24 *Archives d'Orange-Nassau*, i. 16–17, 3/13 May 1689, Heinsius to William; *HSL*, vii. 17–20; André Corvisier, *Louvois* (Paris, 1983), pp. 514–15.
25 *CPSD 1689–90*, p. 109; BL, Add. MSS. 61,377, f. 3; HMC, *Denbigh MSS.*, pp. 110–11, 21/31 May 1689.
26 *CSPD 1689–90*, pp. 119–20; BL, Add. MSS. 61,377, f. 3.
27 HMC, *Denbigh MSS.*, p. 111.
28 *CSPD 1689–90*, pp. 130–1.

29 *HMC, Denbigh MSS.*, pp. 111–12.
30 *CSPD 1689–90*, pp. 142–3.
31 LUL, MS. 12, 'Livres des Marches fait par les Armées de sa Majesté de la Grand Bretagne depuis l'an 1689 jusques à la fin de la Campagne, 1695', ff. 1–3.
32 Müller, ii. 161, 14/24 June 1689, Waldeck to William.
33 BL, Add. MSS. 61,377, ff. 4–5.
34 *Journal of the Late Motions*, pp. 5–8.
35 Baxter, *William III*, pp. 259–62; Japikse, iii. 118–24.
36 BL, Add. MSS. 29,878, 'The Diary of Ensign William Crammond, 1688–90', unfoliated; *HSL*, vii. 9–10; LUL, MS. 12, ff. 4–5.
37 LUL, MS. 12, ff. 5–6; BL, Add. MSS. 29,878; *Journal of the Late Motions*, p. 8.
38 ARA, Heinsius, 142, Waldeck to William.
39 BL, Add. MSS. 34,518, f. 46.
40 *Journal of the Late Motions*, pp. 8–9; BL, Add. MSS. 61,337, f. 3.
41 *HMC, Denbigh MSS.*, p. 114.
42 LUL, MS. 12, ff. 6–8; BL, Add. MSS. 29,878.
43 BL, Add. MSS. 29,878.
44 *HMC, Denbigh, MSS.*, pp. 114–15.
45 *Journal of the Late Motions*, pp. 9–10.
46 Müller, ii. 163–5.
47 BL, Add. MSS. 29,878; *LG*, no. 2475; *HMC, Finch MSS.*, ii. 231–2.
48 *Journal of the Late Motions*, pp. 10–11.
49 Müller, ii. 166–7; *HMC, Denbigh MSS.*, p. 115.
50 Müller, ii. 169.
51 *Journal of the Late Motions*, p. 11.
52 LUL, MS. 12, ff. 10–14; BL, Add. MSS. 29,878; *HSL*, vii. 9–21; *Journal of the Late Motions*, p. 12.
53 BL, Add. MSS. 61,337, f. 5.
54 Müller, ii. 168.
55 *HMC, Denbigh MSS.*, pp. 115–16.
56 LUL, MS. 12, ff. 14–15; BL, Add. MSS. 29,878; BL, Add. MSS. 61,337, f. 6; *Journal of the Late Motions*, pp. 12–13.
57 BL, Add. MSS. 29,878; *HSL*, vii. 9–21; *Journal of the Late Motions*, pp. 13–14; BL, Add. MSS. 61,337, ff. 7–8.
58 Müller, ii. 170–1.
59 BL, Add. MSS. 29,878; *HSL*, vii. 9–21; *LG*, no. 2482; *Journal of the Late Motions*, pp. 14–15; BL, Add. MSS. 61,337, f. 8; William Coxe, *Memoirs of John, Duke of Marlborough* (London, 1820), i. 47ff.; W. S. Churchill, *Marlborough: His Life and Times* (London, 1933–8), i. 314–22; F. B. Maurice, *The History of the Scots Guards* (London, 1934), i. 55; Villars, i. 443–5; Rousset, *Louvois*, iv. 217–20.
60 Antoine de Feuquières, *Mémoires de M. le Marquis de Feuquières, lieutenant général des armées du roi, contenans ses maximes sur la guerre* (Paris, 1737), iii. 176.
61 Müller, ii. 171–2; BL, Add. MSS. 29,878; Villars, i. 445–6; *Journal of the Late Motions*, pp. 15–17; BL, Add. MSS. 61,337, ff. 9–12.
62 Müller, ii. 173–4; BL, Add. MSS. 61,337, f. 12.
63 Müller, ii. 176; *Journal of the Late Motions*, p. 18.
64 BL, Add. MSS. 34,518, f. 46.

65 Müller, ii. 176–8.
66 BL, Add. MSS. 34,518, f. 46; ARA, Heinsius, 142.
67 LUL, MS. 12, ff. 18–22; BL, Add. MSS. 29,878; BL, Add. MSS. 61,337, f. 13.
68 Müller, ii. 179, 11/21 Sept. 1689, Waldeck to William.
69 BL, Add. MSS. 34,518, f. 47; Müller, ii. 180.
70 Müller, ii. 183; *Journal of the Late Motions*, p. 18; BL, Add. MSS. 61,337, ff. 13–14.
71 Müller, ii. 189–93; BL, Add. MSS. 61,337, ff. 15–16.
72 ARA, Heinsius, 142; Müller, ii. 227–31.
73 SP 77/56, ff. 4–5.
74 Japikse, iii. 130, 8/18 Nov. 1689, Whitehall, William III to Elector of Brandenburg.

V

1690: FLEURUS

The armies and navies of the later seventeenth century were relatively blunt weapons. At sea, the limitations of ship-building, gunnery, tactics and the short campaigning season all conspired to render naval warfare indecisive. During the Nine Years' War there were scarcely any battles at sea and, with the exception of the action off Cape La Hogue in 1692, none brought significant results. Partly, this was due to the difficulty of exploiting tactical success. The French victory off Beachy Head led only to the burning of the village of Teignmouth whilst Russell's triumph at La Hogue did not result in the expected major descent on the French coast. However, although navies were not capable of producing dramatic results through battle, they were vital in terms of strategy. The intervention of the British and Dutch navies in the western Mediterranean in 1694 and 1695, although no battles were fought, slowed the French invasion of Catalonia to a halt, retained the wavering Duke of Savoy in the Grand Alliance and emasculated the French navy by blockading its Mediterrnanean squadron in Toulon. The money, mystique and faith which the British placed in their navy was also justified by its role as the protector of overseas trade and as a lifeline to the colonies in America and the West Indies.[1] Land armies similarly were capable of stretegic successes despite lacking the tactical and grand tactical sharpness required to achieve decisive results at an operational level. Crippled by their problems of supply and hampered by weapons which were unable to produce the killing power required to annihilate opponents, armies flattered to deceive. However, in terms of strategy, armies could and did make substantial contributions through siege warfare and the conquest of towns, fortresses and territory. What was that strategy at which these suprisingly ineffective armies and navies were aimed? The answer was attrition. Financial and economic endurance won and lost wars.

To be successful, a strategy of attrition had to be cumulative in its effect and this could only be achieved over a considerable period of time. Unlike Louis XIV, William III did not suffer from the delusion that he was entering upon a short war. Solely through the siege and the acquisition of towns and fortresses could armies realise a consistent and cumulative strategy, whilst navies concentrated upon the protection of their own overseas trade and the strangulation of that of their enemies. William fully appreciated all these factors. His strategy was to draw in French manpower and resources until she was no longer capable of a sustained military effort and would be obliged to sue for peace. In fiscal and economic terms, armed with the productive and growing economies of the United Provinces and England, William held the whip-hand and provided that he did not commit any hideous strategic errors then it was probable that France would eventually succumb. However, it was no certainty. France was a large and prosperous country which did not much rely upon maritime trade for its economic health, whereas English and Dutch seaborne trade was seriously affected by the raiding and privateering of the French navy. In addition, although the English economy was full of potential, the country needed the fiscal machinery and methods to release its power for war. There was also the question of the political will within the British Isles. The ruling classes of England had no experience of major foreign wars and the rapid success of William of Orange's invasion in 1688 may have left them with the erroneous impression that modern armies and navies were capable of achieving rapid political results. They were hastily disillusioned. Parliament had to agree to massive rises in indirect taxation, the Land Tax made its appearance in 1693, and all manner of new-fangled financial devices threatened the economic stability of landed society. In 1696, England witnessed the worst economic crisis since 1672 as the debased and clipped coinage was recalled leaving the country desperately short of specie. No spectacular victories occurred to compensate for these sacrifices. Nothing seemed to happen in Flanders apart from camps and marches; money was seemingly raised and spent for no apparent purpose. Yet Parliament was not in a position to intervene. Foreign policy, the conduct of diplomacy, matters of war and peace and strategy remained within the royal prerogative and were not the business of the Lords and Commons. They might be called upon to vote the necessary funds but policy and its execution were the responsibility of the King. For the English Parliament and for its ruling élite, the Nine Years' War was a time of education in the workings and financing of international war and politics. English attitudes had to mature from those relating to a protected insularity to those of a major participant in Europe. Fortunately for William III, the presence of James II in France reminded his English politicians of the absolute necessity for the war.

Based on attrition, William's strategy was negative rather than positive. He wanted to ensure that the Grand Alliance did not break up under the pressure of war and the insidiousness of French diplomacy but, apart from that, he aimed simply at the physical preservation of the United Provinces, the recognition of his new regime in England and the restatement of European frontiers agreed at Nijmegen in 1678. France too was negative in her strategy. Drawn into a long war which they had neither wanted nor expected, Louis XIV and Louvois lacked strategic goals apart from the preservation of the state of Europe which had been current when the Truce of Regensburg had been signed in 1684. France might have given every appearance of wishing to extend further her frontiers, particularly in the devastation of the Palatinate in the winter of 1688–9 and throughout 1689, but her savagery and aggression were only aimed at acquiring a military dominance from which she could negotiate her own security based upon the 1684 settlement. Both major combatants were fighting to preserve the status quo ante bellum; it was merely a question of which 'bellum' was 'ante' – the Franco-Dutch War of 1672–8 or the Franco-Spanish War of 1683–4. Neither side needed to take risks and had no obvious reason to pursue an aggressive strategy but they could not afford to make major mistakes. Equally important, although contradictory, both sides had to capture towns and cities and tracts of land in order to acquire bargaining counters for future peace negotiations and to commit their opponents into undertaking the extensive and costly operations of war which were essential if the strategy of attrition was to bite.

The Allied campaign of 1690 commenced on an encouraging note with the entry of Savoy into the Grand Alliance on 25 May/4 June. Duke Victor Amadeus II joined the coalition in order to free his principality from French occupation and interference.[2] Three strategic avenues were now available for the invasion of France: from the Spanish Netherlands, through Alsace and via northern Italy. The adherence of Savoy to the Grand Alliance was timely as the British contribution to Waldeck's army in the Low Countries dwindled during 1690. All of the cavalry and five battalions were withdrawn from Flanders in the spring of 1690 and sent to Ireland where William was to command in person in an effort to break the back of Jacobite resistance in one swift campaign. Only six British battalions remained in Flanders – two from the

1st Foot Guards, James Douglas's, the Scots Guards, Robert Hodges's and Francis Fergus O'Farrell's. This small corps had a paper strength of 5,360 men but its effective numbers were nearer to 3,600. Thomas Talmash was in overall command.[3]

During the winter, the 'small war' of attacks on convoys and raids to levy contributions kept both the French and the Allies active and alert. In the week before Christmas 1689, a party of Dutch and Spanish from the garrison of Oudenarde tangled with a patrol of 150 Frenchmen whom they managed to defeat. At the same time, a body of cavalry and infantry from the Allied garrison of Charleroi intercepted some enemy raiders and drove them back behind their own frontier. Seven days later, more French parties were reported, this time burning villages in the vicinity of Ath and Jemappes. The French also looked to the state of their own defences, especially the 'Lines' between the River Lys and the River Scheldt. These Lines, which reached for twenty kilometres from a point just north of Menin on the Lys to Pont d'Espierres on the Scheldt, had been partially destroyed by Vaudemont and Hornes in the previous year. After reconstruction, the fortifications comprised a single rampart and ditch, zig-zagged to create a series of salients and re-entrants. Thirty-four detached redoubts supported the basic fortifications. In themselves, the Lines were not particularly strong but they formed a sufficient obstacle to an attacking army provided that they were adequately garrisoned. The Lines were further covered to their front by a tributary of the Lys, the Heeq Beek, and the Esperiette River which ran into the Scheldt at Pont d'Espierres. These small rivers effectively provided the Lines with a second ditch. On the western side, the guns of the fortress of Menin with its crownwork stretching across onto the eastern bank of the River Lys gave an especial strength to the western end of the Lines. These well-sited defences provided a fixed position from which the French could threaten the heart of Spanish Flanders. With an army inside the Lines, Ghent, Bruges, Ostend and Nieuport were all within striking distance whilst the Lines themselves were closely supported by the magazines at Courtrai and Lille.[4] Working from the foundation of the Lines of the Lys and the Scheldt, the French were greatly to expand their field fortifications in Flanders between 1691 and 1695.

William was pessimistic about the prospects for the 1690 campaign. He himself had decided to assume the conduct of operations in Ireland where Schomberg's pusillanimous performance during the winter of 1689 had convinced William that some royal drive and ginger were required. A rapid resolution of the Irish sideshow would enable William to deploy his British, Danish and German forces in the Low Countries. With his master separated from the Spanish Netherlands by the distance of two seas, Waldeck once more took command of the Dutch-Spanish troops in the Low Countries as well as serving as the liaison with the Brandenburgers on the Lower Rhine. Although Waldeck was still fit and lean, never went to bed before midnight and was always up and dressed by five o'clock in the morning ready to receive reports, he was nearly seventy years of age and had already proved unable to exert his will on the operations of 1689.

> To take a post or select a camp, to subsist an army, to preserve order and discipline, to execute a march or a forage, no-one could approach the Prince de Waldeck. However, the glory of qualifying as a master of war did not rest in just these talents but also in trying to seek advantage through battle. In this he was often rash in his preparations and in his dispositions.[5]

William soon detected that the Allied military preparations in both the Spanish Netherlands and in the United Provinces were progressing very slowly. Everywhere he looked, all he could see was sluggishness and negligence leading to the conclusion that the French were bound to beat the Confederates into the field. Waldeck was a trifle more sanguine. He thought that the Netherlands could be successfully defended provided that Mons and Charleroi were reinforced and substantial magazines of bread and forage were established at Namur and Brussels. The Earl of Portland was endeavouring to hire more troops to augment Waldeck's army. A cavalry regiment and two thousand infantry were secured from Brunswick-Wolfenbüttel and the Elector of Brandenburg agreed to continue his army of 18,000 men on the Lower Rhine. A further 6,000 became available as the army of Liège completed its organisation and recruitment. Despite all this, William remained pessimistic and thought that Waldeck's only chance lay in entering the field before the French and then seeking an early decision by battle. With luck, he hoped that the Elector of Bavaria might be able to draw some French troops to the Upper Rhine whilst the entry of Savoy into the Grand Alliance might also provide some alleviation.[6] To make matters worse, the Allies in the Low Countries looked to be short of manpower. On the Meuse, Waldeck's army would consist of the majority of the Dutch horse and foot, 6,000 Brandenburgers, the detachments from Celle and Liège and some Spanish dragoons and cavalry. In Flanders, Castañaga would command 5,000 Spanish horse,

4,000 Dutch infantry, the small British corps and the Hanoverian Brigade of 8,000 men. The Brandenburg army on the Lower Rhine was to be composed of 18,000 soldiers drawn from Brandenburg, Sweden, Swabia, Franconia, Württemberg, Münster, Paderborn, Cologne, Neuburg, Hesse and Brunswick-Lüneburg.[7]

During late February and early March, the French and the Allies began to stir from their winter quarters. The French established considerable magazines at Dinant and Philippeville which made Waldeck inclined to expect an advance up the Meuse towards Huy and Liège. In response, the Allied frontier garrisons in Mons, Charleroi and Namur were reinforced and active patrolling was encouraged. For this year, the command of the principal French army in the Netherlands was entrusted to the Duke of Luxembourg, the foremost general officer in Louis XIV's service, and he undertook to cover the movements of Waldeck's main army. A secondary body under Boufflers was to form a 'flying camp' on the Meuse and support Luxembourg as well as guarding his eastern flank from interventions by the Brandenburg forces between the Rhine and the Moselle. After his poor showing in the previous campaign, d'Humières was relegated to commanding the corps stationed in the Lines of the Lys and the Scheldt. 'Flying camps' were designed 'for sudden onsets, or for seizing of passes or towns, or else for joining the main army on all occasions. They consist generally of good horse and dragoons and are seldom encamped above ten or twelve hours march from the main body'. Luxembourg concentrated his main army around Valenciennes. It consisted of 37 battalions and 91 squadrons, about 25,000 men.[8]

Following the disruption of the campaign of 1689 which had been caused partially by the inability of Castañaga, Waldeck and the Elector of Brandenburg to work together, William resurrected the idea of establishing a planning congress, or standing conference, at The Hague. William had experimented with such a scheme in 1683 and 1684 and he suggested its readoption on 20/30 August 1689. He proposed to Heinsius that the four main partners in the Grand Alliance – England, Spain, the United Provinces and the Empire – should appoint permanent representatives to the congress assisted by ministers from the smaller partners. Probably, William wanted the congress to function as a superior planning authority which could lay down agreed schemes of operations for each year, allocate troops to the various armies and theatres and liaise between rival commanders and national interests. No standing orders were ever formulated to define the work of the congress. It was to prove useful in such tasks as allotting winter quarters but its proposed planning function was undermined by the lack of military expertise amongst its members and the fact that the Imperial envoy, Count Berka, lacked the confidence of his political masters and had to refer all matters back to Vienna for final decision. The Hague Congress came to be further weakened by the development of a rival institution in Vienna in which members of the Emperor's Council began to sit with Allied diplomats and consider both operations and peace negotiations. Because of its more flexible structure, the Vienna Congress enjoyed greater effectiveness and, as the war progressed, it became more important than its rival in the west. In fact, the Hague Congress only really came to life in the spring when William III attended in person and summoned his senior generals and fellow-rulers of the Grand Alliance to come to The Hague and work out the details and objectives of the coming campaign. Once this short session was over, the Hague Congress lapsed into suspended animation for another twelve months. It suffered still further from the habit of Waldeck, Castañaga, William, the Elector of Bavaria, Vaudemont and the Elector of Brandenburg in seeking *ad hoc* conferences in the field during the actual campaigning season. If the Hague Congress could have been translated into a central, general staff responsible for planning, co-ordination and liaison then it would have performed a valuable role within the coalition but this would have involved seconding senior military officers to serve at its board. This was never attempted and the Congress remained basically a diplomatic organism.[9]

Castañaga assembled his Spanish, Dutch and Walloon forces at Ghent with the intention of marching against the French Lines of the Lys and the Scheldt, a repeat of his strategy in 1689. He then intended to penetrate the French frontier with the support of the British and Hanoverian forces which had wintered in Malines and Bruges. Waldeck concentrated his army on the Demer and around Maastricht, with the aim of marching south to cross the Sambre and invade France. Again, this was largely a repetition of the previous year's schemes. The Elector of Brandenburg, whose troops had wintered in Jülich, Cologne and Cleves, was expected to make a diversion between the Meuse and Moselle, possibly towards Mont Royal, and then operate in support of Waldeck's manoeuvres on the Sambre. This plan was agreed during a conference at The Hague which concluded its deliberations in mid-March. The opening move was to be the siege of Dinant by Waldeck's army. Within ten days of these resolutions, the Brandenburgers were having second thoughts. Dankelmann, the Brandenburg envoy at the Hague Congress, wrote to Waldeck on 25 March/ 4 April hinting that Waldeck ought to think in terms of operating in three corps during 1690, two on the Rhine and only one on the Meuse. As in 1689, it looked as though the Elector of Brandenburg was going to exert every possible pressure to be allowed to conduct his own independent war on the Lower Rhine with scant concern for the needs of Waldeck and Castañaga.[10]

Whilst the Allies were conferring, dining and dancing in The Hague, the French gave a strong clue as to their strategic intentions which was not sufficiently noticed. A powerful French corps showed an unhealthy interest in the Castle of Boussu but the Governor of Mons, situated some ten kilometres to the west, gained intelligence of the enemy movement just in time and hurried a reinforcement into the castle. Thwarted in this attempt, Boufflers's corps then launched a major raid by 2,500 horse and 1,500 foot across the Sambre at Floreffe, nine kilometres west-south-west of Namur, with the intention of raising contributions in Brabant. Each trooper carried enough oats to feed his mount for three days. Again, Waldeck's earlier precaution of strengthening his major frontier garrisons paid off and the Governor of Namur was able to oppose the French passage of the Sambre and then force Boufflers to retire.

Despite this manifest evidence of increasing French acitivity and pre-paredness, the Allies lagged well behind. John Andrew Eckhart, the English Resident in Brussels, wrote to the Earl of Shrewsbury that Castañaga lacked intelligence of French movements although he was certain that they would make a big effort in Flanders now that William was tied down in Ireland.[11] On 20/30 April, the French once more sent a sizeable detachment towards the Sambre but the Governor of Namur's antennae again received news of their march in good time and was able to dispatch a body of horse to observe them. The French retired as soon as they realised they had lost the element of surprise. Further indications of the French intentions to operate on the Sambre and the Meuse were gathered when news was received in Brussels of a large provision convoy which had recently arrived at the magazine of Dinant on the Meuse, twenty-two kilometres south of Namur. The information that the town was well stocked was a grave blow to Waldeck's scheme to besiege Dinant. By 27 April/6 May, Luxembourg had moved his headquarters to Condé on the Scheldt whilst his army concentrated at St. Amand on the Scarpe, a few kilometres to the west.[12] At the same time, the Dutch infantry, which had wintered in its home territories and had then con-centrated around Bergen-op-Zoom, marched to its assembly areas between Liège and Maastricht. Luxembourg moved his camp a little northward to Mortagne-du-Nord on 7/17 May whilst he and his staff rode to Leuse where he ordered a camp to be marked out and a bridge laid over the Scheldt. Now that the enemy commander had seemingly revealed his intentions, Vaudemont, the Marquis de Bedmar and Count Tirimont travelled to St. Truiden to confer with Waldeck about the appropriate Allied response.

Luxembourg's elaborate preparations for an advance to Leuse were only a feint and after his soldiers had destroyed the forage in the lands around Ath and Leuse, he decamped, recrossed the Scheldt and marched to Harelbeke on the Lys, just to the north of the Lines. From this central position he sent out detachments to Deynze on the Lys and towards the Bruges-Ghent Canal where 'they destroy all the corn and country'. Castañaga replied as rapidly as he could by marshalling his forces at Dendermonde and then advancing to Ghent to observe the corps of 20,000 Frenchmen at Deynze. This threat was sufficient to oblige Luxembourg to order his two detachments to retire to the principal camp at Harelbeke, where he was close to the support of d'Humières's corps within the Lines of the Lys and the Scheldt.[13] It later transpired that Luxembourg's sudden advance into the Spanish Netherlands had been occasioned by strong suggestions that the civic authorities in Bruges, Ostend and Nieuport were considering surrendering their towns to the French. Whatever the reason for Luxembourg's foray into Flanders, it pulled the focus of the campaign away from the Sambre-Meuse. Waldeck sent his vanguard as far as Wavre, to the south-east of Brussels, in order to be ready to support Castãnaga at Ghent but his main army continued to assemble to the west of Maastricht. At this point, the Allies were cheered by news of a great fire in Philippeville, one of the principal magazines of the French. By 25 May/4 June, Waldeck had brought his whole army of 40,000 forward to Wavre. In Flanders, Luxembourg continued in camp at Harelbeke whilst Castañaga remained at Ghent with 20,000 men. In the last week of May, he sent a raiding party of 2,000 infantry and 600 horse under Don Francisco de Castillo which succeeded in penetrating the French defences between Ypres and Dunkirk.[14] This demonstration revealed the vulnerability of Luxembourg's western flank at Harelbeke and he withdrew under the guns of Courtrai and linked-up with d'Humières's men within the Lines. Boufflers, whose corps of 7,000 had been stationed in a camp on the Moselle to cover any movements by Imperial or Brandenburg forces towards Mont Royal and Trier, now reappeared in the Netherlands and camped between Dinant and St. Vith at Marche-en-Famenne.

With Luxembourg under some pressure from Castañaga and Boufflers commanding only a weak corps of observation, there was a chance for

Waldeck to slip over the Sambre and execute the siege of Dinant. He and Castañaga met in Brussels for a conference on 26 May/5 June. Although we have no record of their deliberations, the two generals probably wanted to launch Waldeck's army over the Sambre whilst Castañaga guarded Flanders. Unfortunately, such a strategy was hamstrung by two vital considerations. In the first place, if Castañaga was to occupy Luxembourg's attention in Flanders and allow Waldeck the time to besiege Dinant, then he had to act offensively but to effect this he needed substantial reinforcements. Secondly, the Lines of the Lys and the Scheldt, provided they were properly garrisoned, effectively guarded the French frontier and threatened Spanish Flanders enabling Luxembourg to turn away from Flanders and pursue Waldeck. Faced with these dilemmas, Castañaga and Waldeck agreed to a compromise manoeuvre: Castañaga was to defend Flanders passively and at least prevent d'Humières from being able to abandon the Lines and reinforce Luxembourg, whilst Waldeck threatened to advance south over the Sambre. In accordance with these decisions reached at Brussels, Castañaga shifted his camp eastwards to Wieze, between Dendermonde and Alost behind the line of the River Dender, and on 2/12 June Waldeck marched south from Wavre to Genappe, a distance of fifteen kilometres.[15] Castañaga's retirement and Waldeck's advance automatically shifted the emphasis of the Allied campaign from Flanders to Brabant, a development which was marked by a considerable weakening of Castañaga's army to reinforce that of Waldeck.

On 12/22 June, Waldeck decamped from Genappe and ventured south to Pont-à-Celles on the Piéton River to the north of Charleroi. Sensing the danger to Philippeville and Dinant, Boufflers marched his corps to within twelve kilometres, one march, of the latter fortress. Luxembourg was equally quick to appreciate the threat from Waldeck's manoeuvres and he hurried his army from Courtrai through Leuse, Perulwelz and Quiévrain and then over the Sambre to encamp close to the fortress and magazine of Maubeuge on 13/23 June. After feeding troops to Waldeck, Castañaga's army at Wieze numbered between 13,000 and 14,000 men, roughly equal to the strength of d'Humières's corps within the Lines. The Spanish general would have relished the prospect of raiding towards Dunkirk and Ypres in order to raise contributions but he was prevented from taking aggressive action by the fact that the entirety of the small British Corps lay within his command. The British Corps had no money, could not pay its debts and was unable to march. With nearly one-third of his troops ineffective, Castañaga had to lay aside his offensive ambitions. All remained quiet on the Rhine.

The German contingents assembled in the Eifel near Cologne where they waited for the Brandenburg troops to take the field from their winter quarters.[16]

Waldeck waited in his camp at Pont-à-Celles for four days, taking delivery of an artillery train of 120 cannon which had been dispatched down the Meuse from Namur. On 19/29 June, the Governor of Namur received intelligence that Luxembourg had marched north from Maubeuge and was about to cross the Sambre. Quickly appreciating the proximity of the two main armies and the fact that Waldeck might be taken by surprise, he drew out three battalions of foot and two squadrons of horse from his garrison and sent them to observe the French and report their movements. These 2,000 men found the French in the act of crossing the Sambre on seven bridges at the Castle of Fromont, to the east of Charleroi, and stayed long enough to watch them go into camp at Velaine, just to the north of the river, with their front to the north-west. Luxembourg's camp was nine kilometres in length with its left resting on the village of Lambusart and its right on the stream of the Orme Bach. Once this was reported to Waldeck, he rapidly realised that Luxembourg had succeeded in marching around his left flank and had now camped towards his rear. To make matters worse, the French had placed themselves across Waldeck's communications with Namur, a vital magazine and fortress, and they had severed the line of the Sambre-Meuse. Waldeck was now isolated from his own major garrisons on the Meuse and from contact with the Brandenburg and Imperial troops on the Rhine and the Moselle. If Waldeck retired northwards to cover Brussels he would automatically expose Charleroi, Namur, Huy and Liège to the possibility of siege and attack. He had little option but to force Luxembourg to withdraw.

The French marshal was also under some pressure to seek a decision through battle. Information had reached him that the Brandenburgers were advancing towards Mont Royal with the intention of undertaking a siege and he suspected that Waldeck was entrusted with the task of preventing him from marching away from Brabant to bring relief. Should Mont Royal have fallen, then the valley of the Moselle would have become yet another avenue along which France could have been invaded. In a successful attempt to provide himself with a numerical superiority for the expected battle, Luxembourg ordered d'Humières to leave just 3,000 men to guard the Lines of the Lys and the Scheldt and march his remaining 10,000 to join the main army. D'Humières's camp, complete with tents and camp fires, was left in situ and Castañaga's scouts and patrols assumed that all of d'Humières's troops were still in residence. This carelessness in reconnaissance made certain that Luxembourg was substantially reinforced whereas Waldeck had to fight with Castañaga's corps of 14,000 men standing uselessly between the Lys and the Scheldt. D'Humières joined Luxembourg as he was crossing the Sambre.[17] Waldeck decamped from amidst the grain fields around Pont-à-Celles and Herlaimont, sending his cavalry ahead to secure the crossings of the River Piéton. The infantry marched as rapidly as they could and the whole army went into camp in two lines facing to the south-east with the right resting on the Piéton and the left on a small stream. The village of Mellet lay to the left front. The two armies were now less than ten kilometres apart and both were intent on battle. Waldeck believed his army to be equal in numbers to that of Luxembourg, remaining in ignorance of the arrival of d'Humières's corps.

Early on the following morning, 20/30 June, Waldeck sent Brigadier Count Albert van Berlo on a reconnaissance towards Mazy, just to the north of Luxembourg's extreme right wing on the Orme Bach. Not surprisingly, Berlo ran into considerable French forces around the village of Fleurus. He immediately reported his encounter with the enemy to Waldeck who sent Count Flodroff to support Berlo with a body of cavalry. Luxembourg, thinking that Berlo's reconnaissance in force was in fact the vanguard of the whole Allied army on the march towards him, put his army of forty-one battalions, eighty squadrons and several regiments of dragoons into line of battle. Once this had been accomplished, the French cavalry on the left charged into Berlo's troopers, killing the Brigadier and obliging them to retire in some considerable disorder. Waldeck then delayed making his next operational decision, a delay that was to prove disastrous. His camp at Mellet was not particularly strong and, given the proximity of Luxembourg's army, he should have moved immediately to a more advantageous position. Instead, he waited for the remainder of 20/30 June before giving orders to advance to a new camp site between Trois Bareilles and Ligny on the morning of 21 June/1 July. Again, having failed to observe Luxembourg's movements in a systematic manner, Waldeck was unaware that during the night of 20/30 June to 21 June/1 July Luxembourg had marched forward and encamped on the very ground that Waldeck had selected. Whether Waldeck now stayed in his camp at Mellet or advanced, Luxembourg was well situated to attack his exposed left flank. As Waldeck pushed forward from the Mellet camp on the morning of 21 June/1 July, he found Luxembourg's army in line of battle stretching across and beyond his left wing. In a great hurry, Waldeck put his army into line of battle with his left flank anchored on the village of Wagnèlée and his right on Wagnée. His final formation described a convex curve with the wings slightly retired and the centre bowed outwards pointing at the village of St. Amand. Despite the long and curved Allied line of battle, Luxembourg's army stood concentrated against Waldeck's left wing and left centre. Frederick the Great would have admired the 'oblique order'.

On this highly unpromising ground, Waldeck had to give battle. At the most, his army numbered 30,000 men whilst Luxembourg commanded 40,000, the difference being the sum of d'Humières's corps. Waldeck's cavalry had been seriously weakened during Berlo's reconnaissance on the previous day, presenting Luxembourg with another major advantage. The Allied position occupied a low ridge which rose a little to the right, sloped quite sharply to the rear and fell gradually to the front. At ten o'clock in the morning, the French cavalry of the right wing opened the action by charging the Dutch horse on the Allied left. There was virtually no resistance and the Dutch horsemen fled from the field exposing the left flank of the Dutch infantry in the centre of Waldeck's line of battle. Having disposed of the whole of the Allied right wing, Luxembourg switched some squadrons from his right flank to his left to reinforce Monsieur de Gournay who commanded the French cavalry on the left wing. As soon as this manoeuvre had been completed, Luxembourg launched his infantry against the left flank and front of the Dutch infantry in the Allied centre and ordered Gournay to attack the Spanish horse on the Allied right. Gournay found the Spaniards to be a very different proposition to the Dutch. Lieutenant-General d'Huby had no more than two thousand cavalry under his command but he succeeded in repulsing two lines of the French horse and captured ten light cannon. Although the resistance of the Spanish horse covered the right of the Dutch infantry, their left, front and rear were all open to French attack. For over six hours, the Dutch foot soldiers fought three ranks deep, firing to three sides simultaneously. Late in the afternoon, having absorbed a series of French assaults, both the Dutch infantry and the Spanish cavalry managed to disengage and retire north-westwards towards Nivelles in a giant hollow square. As Waldeck commenced this manoeuvre, he received a timely reinforcement of nine battalions under Major-General van Aylva, who had advanced from Nivelles, and three thousand fresh Spanish horsemen directed by Lieutenant-General van Weibnom and Vaudemont. Although these troopers arrived too late to affect the outcome of the battle, they were able to cover the withdrawal of Waldeck's beaten forces and discourage the French from pressing their pursuit. Waldeck brought fifteen battalions back to Nivelles and he was gratified to learn that most of the disgraced Dutch cavalry had found its way to the safety of Charleroi.

Waldeck's retreat had caused him to leave behind most of his cannon, his heavy baggage and his bridging train, complete with its expensive copper pontoons. During the night, after Luxembourg had withdrawn his own soldiers from the battlefield, detachments from the garrison of Charleroi rescued some of the forfeited equipment. Waldeck's performance had not been distinguished. The dashing Hector Villars thought that Waldeck's conduct of the battle had demonstrated his 'inbécillité ordinaire' and he castigated the Allied generals as 'old fools', most of whom were over eighty years of age. Despite the pardonable hyperbole, there was much truth in these remarks. In the first place, Waldeck had failed to maximise his field strength and concentrate all his available weight at the decisive point of battle. When he knew that a general action was imminent, he should have drawn in all his out-lying and detached forces, particularly the garrisons of Charleroi and Namur, and added them to his main army. Castañaga also deserved a sharp reprimand for allowing d'Humières's corps to leave the Lines unobserved, a failure which added 10,000 men to Luxembourg's army but deprived Waldeck of 14,000. The Earl of Portland was of the opinion that if another 2,000 horses had been present at Fleurus then the result of the engagement might have been different. In complete contrast, Luxembourg's pre-battle manoeuvres had been masterly. He had drawn in d'Humières from Courtrai, Gournay with 6,000 cavalry from Condé, Tilliardet with a small corps from Maubeuge and Boufflers's troops from near Dinant to bring his maximum weight against Waldeck. Secondly, through inadequate reconnaissance and carelessness, in the two days before the battle Waldeck had allowed himself to be thoroughly out-manoeuvred by Luxembourg until he was finally trapped and outflanked on a disadvantageous battlefield. For a man of Waldeck's experience and supposed prudence, it was not an outstanding demonstration of the art of war. As with so many battles, the victors lost almost as many men as the vanquished, perhaps 7,000 killed, wounded and prisoners on each side.[18]

Waldeck's first task was to reform his army. As far as was possible, he sent the shattered regiments back to the United Provinces to recruit and recuperate and drew new formations from the home garrisons. The new army concentrated around Diegem, on the north-eastern edge of Brussels, whilst Vaudemont stood at Halle to the south of Brussels with 3,000 cavalry to observe the movements of Luxembourg at Velaine.

Castañaga rapidly rallied to the emergency. The five British battalions were shipped on bilanders at Ghent, sailed up the Scheldt and then down the Canal of Brussels to Vilvorde, a voyage which lasted four days. The British then camped at Perk, close to Diegem, a ruined castle which had once been used as a prison for the nobility and people of quality. The Prince of Hanover was dispatched to Tirlemont to cover Waldeck's eastern flank and Castañaga reinforced the garrisons of Bruges, Ghent and Mons.[19] Luxembourg, who had also suffered a casualty rate of nearly twenty per cent, needed time to regroup and gather reinforcements. He adjusted his camp to lie along the Sambre between Charleroi and Farciennes and sent d'Humières back to the Lines of the Lys and the Scheldt. On arrival, d'Humières took advantage of the departure of the Hanoverian and British battalions to advance outside the Lines to Avelgem having drawn in the Courtrai garrison. As the two armies licked their wounds it was time to consider the strategic balance after the Battle of Fleurus. The Allies had suffered a considerable reverse. Waldeck had been forced to abandon any thoughts of invading France and besieging Dinant or Philippeville and he had left exposed the major fortresses of Charleroi, Namur, Huy and Liège. He had also been obliged to vacate Brabant making it impossible for him to support any move by the Brandenburgers towards the Moselle. For Luxembourg, his victory at Fleurus had reduced the likelihood of a Brandenburg attack on Mont Royal and the Moselle Valley and had opened up a series of tempting and important targets along the Sambre-Meuse.

Belatedly, the Brandenburg forces marched into the campaign. Under the personal command of the Elector, 23,000 troops arrived at Visé on the Meuse on 7/17 July. This corps, or small army, had been late entering the field and had attempted nothing of consequence on the Rhine. Had the Elector made an earlier decision to march to the Meuse and co-operate with Waldeck, then the Battle of Fleurus need never have taken place and Luxembourg would have been forced onto the defensive by a numerically superior opponent. Although their tardy arrival could not compensate for the lose of a battle, their presence put new heart into Waldeck. His own Dutch, Spanish, Hanoverian and British army around Diegem and Vilvorde now numbered thirty battalions and forty squadrons, a total of around 25,000 men, and he, could now count on 23,000 Brandenburgers and a Liègeois corps of 8,000. After a conference with the Elector and Castañaga at Liège, Waldeck resolved to march against the enemy whilst Castañaga undertook to advance from Dendermonde towards the French frontier. The

Brandenburgers crossed the Meuse on 12/22 July with the intention of meeting the Dutch army as it marched eastwards towards the Hanoverian corps at Tirlemont. In response, Luxembourg shifted a little to the westward and took up a camp of observation at Quiévrain, between Mons and Valenciennes. Boufflers was given command of a detached corps to observe the march of the Brandenburg army.[20] The Brandenburg troops reached Tongres on 12/22 July, the same day that Count Tilly led the 8,000 Liègeois into Waldeck's camp at Diegem. True to his word, Castañaga moved south-west to Gavere on the Scheldt with 18,000 men to observe d'Humières in his advanced position at Avelgem. In readiness for the combined assault on the French frontier, the Allies laid in stocks of corn at the magazines of Mons, Oudenarde and Ath.

Waldeck's army marched from Diegem southwards to Overijse on 18/28 July. On the following day, Castañaga brought 16,000 men from his corps at Gavere to co-operate with Waldeck, leaving just 2,000 to watch over Flanders. This change in plan had been made possible by Luxembourg's decision to order the corps of d'Humières to retire within the Lines of the Lys and the Scheldt and then to disperse. A sufficient garrison was left to man the Lines whilst the majority of the corps marched to join Luxembourg at Quiévrain and d'Humières left the field to take up his government of Lille. The French marshal thought that the Allies would be unable to undertake any substantial movements in either Brabant or Flanders after their defeat at Fleurus and he was under considerable pressure to send reinforcements from his army to Germany. He was content to spend the remainder of the campaign on the defensive. Waldeck rode to Aachen to confer with the Elector of Brandenburg on 21/31 July.[21] As this conference was taking place, Waldeck's army marched from Overijse to Wavre where the Brandenburgers joined on 23 July/2 August. Castañaga brought his corps to Halle, south of Brussels; he was to command independently but had agreed to work closely with both Waldeck and the Elector. To make certain of his own position, Luxembourg ordered Boufflers, who had returned to Dinant after the Battle of Fleurus, to cross the Meuse on 17/27 July to cover Maubeuge and Philippeville but to be ready to march to Luxembourg's support. The main French army adjusted its position to Bavay, between Maubeuge and Valenciennes, and Luxembourg drew in sufficient garrison troops to bring his numbers closer to those of the combined army of Waldeck and the Elector. On 24 July/3 August, Waldeck's army moved to Genappe. To this camp came the cheerful news of William's victory at the Boyne Water. All the cannon and muskets in the army fired a salute and Mr. James Johnston, the

English envoy extraordinaire to the court of the Elector of Brandenburg, gave a banquet and alcoholic celebration at his quarters in the castle of Bousval.[22]

During the army's soujourn at Wavre, a series of meetings were held between Waldeck, Castañaga and the Elector of Brandenburg in an attempt to hammer out a common course of action. Relations between the Spanish and Dutch on the one side and the Elector on the other were somewhat strained, not just over questions of strategy but also about the payment of £10,000 a month which the Elector thought he was being denied.[23] On 29 July/8 August, Waldeck shifted his camp to Bois St. Isaac, within two hours' march of Castañaga at Halle, and another grand council of war was held on the following day. A resolution was taken to march towards the French frontier near Mons. Luxembourg was still busy calling in his detachments and garrisons but, even when Boufflers arrived from Dinant, he would only possess around 40,000 with which to face Waldeck and the Elector's 45,000 in addition to the 16,000 of Castañaga. The whole Allied army merged on 2/12 August, forming a camp over eight kilometres in length stretching from Halle to Lembeek and containing 61,000 men. Immediately, the senior commanders conferred.[24] They decided to make two marches towards Luxembourg and then encamp about Soignies and Roulx, to the north and east of Mons. The Allies did not intend to fight but they wanted to show aggression in order to keep their opponent on the defensive. Having borne the brunt of the fighting and the casualties during the summer, the Dutch Field Deputies refused to consider another major action. It was also the opinion of the conference that Luxembourg would not fight again that year unless he could secure a heavy superiority in numbers. The only hope of loosening the corset which bound operations in the Low Countries was if the corps composed of troops from Jülich and Münster, which was supposed to operate on the Moselle, opened its projected campaign. To face that eventuality, Luxembourg would have to release Boufflers to deal with the threat and something might then be attempted against Luxembourg's inferior army. However, there were few signs that this German operation would develop. Another problem was the Elector of Brandenburg. He said that he was keen to fight and felt 'that his honour is engaged' yet he was acutely conscious that his army had been raised and trained by his father and if he destroyed it in the Netherlands then he would have to surrender his Rhenish provinces and be insulted by his numerous enemies in Germany. Waldeck himself was more disingenuous than he appeared. He regarded both the Elector and Castañaga as rivals and badly wanted to reserve for himself the chief command in the Netherlands. Although he moaned to William about the lack of co-operation demonstrated by the Elector, Waldeck secretly encouraged him to look to the Rhine rather than the Meuse. Amidst all these cross-currents, the previous resolve to advance to the Sambre and seek battle with Luxembourg weakened. To make the Elector feel even more uncomfortable, reports came in that the French were raising contri-butions from the city of Aachen and were burning villages in Jülich.[25]

The weather then came to everyone's rescue. For six-days thunder and lightening split the air and the rain poured down 'so that we could hardly stir all that while out of our tents unless booted'. Major troop movements were out of the question. Fortune played a second card to the pusillanimous Allies when Luxembourg sent a detachment of 2,000 horse to establish a post at Soignies, the next intended camp site of Waldeck's army, from which they could observe and reconniotre the Allied positions at Halle and Lembeek. The French diversions in Jülich and around Aachen also had their effect; the Liègeois corps left Wal-deck's army and recrossed the Meuse on 8/18 August in order to cover the Prince-Bishopric against French incursions from the east. Tilly's troops intended to join with the forces of the Duke of Neuburg and the Bishop of Münster and the Elector of Brandenburg promised to send some regiments to assist. However, Luxembourg was also beset by contrary considerations. The Court at Vienna wanted to stage a late season effort along the Moselle from Coblenz aiming at Mont Royal and Trier under the command of the Elector of Bavaria, whilst the Duke of Saxony stood on the defensive along the Middle Rhine and Louis of Baden occupied the Lines of Stollhofen on the Upper Rhine.[26] On receipt of this intelligence from Paris, Luxembourg shifted his camp to Blaton, between Leuse and Condé, and dispatched Boufflers to the Moselle with 10,000 men on 15/25 August to forestall any Imperial intentions. At Halle, these rapid changes in the strategic situation reduced the once-resolute generals to indecision: Castañaga still advo-cated pressing on towards the French frontier, Waldeck now urged caution and the Elector of Brandenburg looked over his shoulder towards the Rhineland.[27] From the information that was reaching Wal-deck at Halle, it looked as though a major French offensive was under way. Opposite Philippsburg, the Dauphin had crossed the Rhine and was seeking battle with the Imperial and Saxon troops under the Duke of Saxony. Luxembourg marched north to Ligne, between Ath and Tournai, and then continued to move north-eastwards to Lessines on the Dender, a balanced stance from which he could attack into Flanders in the direction of Ghent and Bruges or menace the Allied position at Halle. Suspicions of Luxembourg's aggressive intentions were heightened by reports that he was stockpiling bombs and carcasses as if he intended a siege or a bombardment.[28] Then the rains intervened once again. Waldeck moved his headquarters from Halle to Lembeek on 22 August/1 September but the bad weather had brought the campaign to a standstill. Five thousand Brandenburg troops under General Spaen were detached from Waldeck's army on 12/22 September to link-up with Tilly's Liègeois corps to protect both the Prince-Bishopric and Cleves and Jülich from enemy incursions.

Luxembourg withdrew from Lessines on 30 September/10 October to Renaix, between Tournai and Oudenarde. From here he tried to tempt Waldeck out of the Halle-Lembeek position by launching raids into Spanish Flanders. He detached 8,000 men under Montbrun to cross the canal which ran from Bruges to Ostend and ravage the 'Pays du Nord'. As Montbrun approached the canal on 1/11 October, he was intercepted by two small, Dutch 'frigates' and some Dutch and Spanish soldiers. The fire from the cannon of the frigates was sufficiently heavy to persuade the French to abandon the scheme.[29] This was the final throw of the campaign and both sides began to think of winter quarters. Waldeck left Lembeek on 10/20 October to find more forage as the country around Halle had come to resemble 'a desert'. He marched a few kilometres south to Tubise 'which we found almost like a Garden' but the continuance of the vile weather caused Waldeck to order the break-up of the army shortly afterwards and the soldiers dispersed into their winter quarters.[30] The Brandenburgers left ten battalions to winter in and around Brussels whilst the remainder of the corps marched back to the Rhineland. The five British battalions were sent to lodge in Bruges under the command of Thomas Talmash, close to their communications with England. The French distributed their men amongst their frontier garrisons but a large corps was put into billets between Luxembourg City and the Moselle to cover any Imperial winter campaign from Coblenz towards Mont Royal.

James Johnston thought that the Allies had endured a grisly campaign and had ended the season in a grim condition. They had lost a major battle; the Hanoverian troops were marching back into Germany having failed to agree terms with Castañaga for their retention into 1691; there were fewer English and Dutch troops than in 1689; and the Spanish cavalry were turning to robbery for lack of pay.[31] To add to the litany of woes, the British and Dutch fleet had been beaten by Tourville off Beachy Head, Teignmouth had been burned and the new ally, Savoy,

had been defeated by Catinat at Staffarda. The sole promising augury
had been William's triumph at the Boyne leading to the reasonable
expectation that the Irish War would be concluded during 1691. Progress in Ireland also meant that William himself would be free to
command in the Netherlands in the next campaign and more British
troops would become available as the commitment to Ireland was
reduced. William's presence in the Low Countries was badly needed;
he was the recognised leader of the Alliance and the only person who
could bring some unity of purpose to the factions within the coalition.

No sooner had the armies settled into their winter quarters than
the 'little war' commenced. Twelve hundred French horse marched to
Enghien in the last week of November whilst another large patrol
travelled to Grammont, to the south-west of Brussels, with the intention
of burning villages but the Allied command in Brussels quickly concentrated sufficient troops from the winter cantonments to force the French
back over the frontier. These winter raids, usually executed by cavalry,
could not be sustained into major operations as it was almost impossible
to discover horse feed in the countryside. The raiding parties had to
carry oats and forage with them, a factor which seriously curtailed their
range and endurance; a mere show of force by the defenders was
normally enough to persuade the marauders to return to their bases.
Destruction of supplies and forage was the principal objective with the
raising of contributions as a secondary motive. In one way or another,
most of the winter raids sought to gain a strategic or a tactical advantage
before the onset of the next campaigning season. If the agricultural and
human resources were stripped from great swathes of land, then the
enemy would find it difficult to operate in those regions during the
coming campaign. As a bonus, the booty and the cash raised through
forced contributions gave a welcome boost to the French intendants
and paymasters. The French 'forages' during the winters of 1690 and
1691 were extremely severe and virtually depopulated the countryside
around Louvain and the along the valley of the River Dender. The only
crumb of comfort for the Dutch and Spanish defenders was that a
careful analysis of the areas depredated could give a clue about the
probable direction of enemy advance during the following spring and
summer. Boufflers's occupation and fortification of the small town of
Thuin on the Sambre, twelve kilometres south-west of Charleroi, and
a series of raids around Mons during the winter of 1690–1, ought to
have given the Allies a clear indication that the French intended an
offensive against either Mons or Charleroi early in the season of 1691.[32]

From England, William responded to the French activity by preparing to send twelve British battalions across the North Sea. Castañaga reinforced his frontier garrisons and set about building additional fortifications.³³ Although concern was expressed that the enemy would venture over the Ghent-Bruges Canal and put East Flanders under contribution, most of the intelligence pointed to extensive French preparations on the Sambre and the Meuse, an early indication that a substantial effort was planned for that region in the summer of 1691. The storm burst on 3/13 December. Taking advantage of the bitterly cold weather which had turned the rivers and canals into solid ice and translated the roads from thigh-deep mud into passable highways, the Comte de Bouteville, Luxembourg's son, drew 8,000 men from the frontier garrisons and marched to Grammont where he left 2,000 infantry. With the remaining 6,000, most of whom were mounted, he raided Alost before venturing into Brabant where he burned seventeen villages, regardless of whether or not they had paid their contributions. This marauding continued for two days, the party withdrawing to Tournai on 6/16 December. The Spanish were surprised by Bouteville's descent. They scratched together a force of cavalry at Ninove, to the south of Alost, and this may have been influential in curtailing Bouteville's activities. Further French troops gathered on the frontier from Valenciennes to Dinant. Boufflers took the main corps of 10,000 men and six cannon across the Sambre at Auvelais, to the east of Charleroi, on 5/15 December. He left Ximenes at Auvelais with 5,000 foot and 500 horse to guard the crossing and pressed on into Brabant with 4,500 cavalry and the artillery. He scourged through Walloon Brabant, burning villages and even threatening the town and abbey of Louvain. Lieutenant-General d'Huby drew together 15,000 Spanish and Dutch horse at Nivelles, to the south of Brussels, but was unable to intervene effectively. Simultaneously, Villars assembled 8,000 men at Tournai and raided around Grammont, Halle and the region to the south of Brussels. Villars and Boufflers were supposed to unite south of Brussels but the Comte de Valsassine, who commanded Boufflers's advance guard, bungled a simple river crossing in the face of light opposition placing Villars's corps in some temporary jeopardy. After this débâcle, Boufflers and Villars returned to French territory, the former in something of a hurry as a sudden thaw threatened to render the Sambre impassable.³⁴

At this stage, the Allied generals might have asked themselves why the enemy had carried out two major depredations across the Sambre to the east and west of Brussels. The local inhabitants took the hint and abandoned many of their smouldering villages and farms to shelter in the larger towns, preferably those with fortifications and garrisons, fearful that the French raids were preparatory to major offensives. In distant Kensington Palace, William failed to analyse the French movements. When Waldeck sent him a paper which listed Castañaga's proposed troop dispositions for the remainder of the winter, William was horrified when he saw that the Spaniard intended to cover the whole frontier from the banks of the Sambre to the North Sea. The King thought it 'ridiculous' to try to defend such a large area with so few troops. Instead, William advised Waldeck, Castañaga should be conserving and resting his men ready for the next campaign and concentrating his winter defence only on his most important fortresses. As Frederick the Great might have said, 'he who defends everything defends nothing'. Perhaps, instead of criticising Castañaga's understandable wish to protect his own government, William should have pondered more deeply about the nature and directions of the enemy raids.[35]

NOTES

1 Geoffrey Symcox, *The Crisis of French Sea Power, 1688–1697* (The Hague, 1974), pp. 67–8.
2 Geoffrey Symcox, *Victor Amadeus II: Absolutism in the Savoyard State, 1675–1730* (London, 1983), pp. 100–6.
3 BL, Add. MSS. 29,878; Chandler, 'Fluctuations', pp. 7–10.
4 See the map of the Lines by Nicolas Visscher, *Afbeelding van de Linien of Retrenchemenien door den Koning van Vranckryk Louis de XIV in de Jaren 1692 en 1693 maken* (Amsterdam, no date).
5 *Mémoires du Feld-Maréchal Comte de Mérode-Westerloo* (Brussels, 1840), i. 67; William Sawle, *An Impartial Relation of all the Transactions between the Army of the Confederates and that of the French King in their last summers Campaign in Flanders with a more particular respect of the Battle of Fleury* (London, 1691), p. 3. Sawle was the chaplain of Robert Hodges's Foot.
6 Japikse (Welbeck), i. 105–7; Müller, ii. 215.
7 Ibid., ii. 218–19, Feb. 1690, Waldeck to William; SP 84/221, f. 100.
8 Beaurain, ii. 7–10; Sawle, *Impartial Relation*, p. 4.
9 NCMH, vi. 171–2, 237–8; Baxter, *William III*, p. 288.
10 Beaurain, ii. 5–6; SP 77/56, ff. 31–2; SP 84/221, f. 100.
11 SP 77/56, ff. 40, 45.
12 Ibid., ff. 48, 51; Beaurain, ii. 10.
13 SP 77/56, ff. 57–8.
14 Ibid., f. 60; SP 84/221, f. 141.
15 SP 77/56, f. 63; LUL, MS. 12, f. 44.
16 SP 77/56, f. 64; Sawle, *Impartial Relation*, pp. 4–5; Beaurain, ii. 20–3; BL, Add. MSS. 9,723, f. 5.
17 Sawle, *Impartial Relation*, pp. 5–6.
18 Japikse (Welbeck), ii. 199–200; Feuquières, ii. 55–9; Villars, i. 447; *LG*, no. 2570; Müller, ii. 81, 232–4; LUL, MS. 12, ff. 49–50; Eduard van Biema, 'Eenige bizonderheden over den slag bij Fleurus van 30 Juni en 1 Juli 1690',

Oud-Holland (1914), pp. 55–71; HSL, vii. 27–8; Sawle, *Impartial Relation*, pp. 7–9; SP 84/222, ff. 122–3; BL, Add. MSS. 61,306, ff. 1–2; Beaurain, ii. 29–38; Rousset, *Louvois*, iv. 402–15; *Mérode-Westerloo*, i. 66–8; PRO, MPH 16/Part 1.

19 BL, Add. MSS. 9,723, f. 71; LUL. MS. 12, f. 50; Japikse, iii. 176; Sawle, *Impartial Relation*, pp. 10–11; SP 84/222, ff. 122–3.

20 SP 77/56, f. 67; *Archives d'Orange-Nassau*, i. 75–6; BL, Add. MSS. 9,723, ff. 9–10.

21 SP 77/56, ff. 66, 70; HMC, *Finch MSS.*, ii. 380–1.

22 SP 77/56, f. 71.

23 HMC, *Hastings MSS.*, ii. 215–16.

24 LUL, MS. 12, ff. 60–2.

25 BL, Add. MSS. 9,723, ff. 11–13; HMC, *Hastings MSS.*, ii. 219:

26 Sawle, *Impartial Relation*, p. 16; BL, Add. MSS. 9,723, ff. 16–17.

27 SP 77/56, f. 74; BL, Add. MSS. 9,723, f. 18.

28 HMC, *Finch MSS.*, ii. 432; BL, Add. MSS. 9,723, f. 14; SP 77/56, ff. 77–8; Beaurain, ii. 51.

29 SP 77/56, ff. 83, 85.

30 Sawle, *Impartial Relation*, p. 17.

31 HMC, *Finch MSS.*, ii. 468, 12/22 Oct. 1690.

32 Van Houtte, *Les Occupations Étrangères*, i. 229–53.

33 HMC, *Downshire MSS.*, i. 366, 5/15 Dec. 1690.

34 Beaurain, ii. 59–60; Villars, i. 124–6.

35 Japikse, iii. 192–3, 28 Nov./8 Dec. 1690, William to Waldeck; HSL, vii. 21–38.

VI

1691: MONS
AND LEUSE

William crossed the North Sea to the United Provinces, a dangerous journey amid fog and ice floes, to arrive in The Hague on 21/31 January 1691. Riding beneath triumphal arches flung over streets lined with cheering crowds, William returned to his homeland for the first time since his conquest of England in 1688.[1] He came to reassert his authority within the Netherlands and as commander-in-chief of the Grand Alliance, whose military efforts it was his initial task to co-ordinate. The Congress at The Hague had been in semi-permanent session since April 1690 and had already completed some of the necessary preparatory staff-work when a galaxy of international politicians and rulers descended on the Dutch capital for a grand planning conference. The Electors of Brandenburg and Bavaria were the most senior and below them appeared the Landgraves of Hesse-Darmstadt and Homberg, the Princes of Lüneburg, Württemberg and Ansbach, the Dukes of Holstein, Courland and Saxe-Eisenach, the Marquis of Castañaga and all the resident ministers and envoys of the member-states of the Grand Alliance. The usual difficulty with gatherings of this nature concerned matters of precedence and dignity but William succeeded in persuading all the participants to waive ceremony and talk to one another as equals. In retrospect, this may well have been William's greatest achievement in the whole of the 1691 campaign. Now that the war in Ireland was effectively over, although Limerick was not to fall to Ginkel until September, William could turn his full attention to the Netherlands and Germany. He opened the conference with an aggressive speech.

> The states of Europe had too long indulged themselves in a spirit of division, or of delay, and of attention to particular interests. But, while the dangers which threatened them from France reminded them of past errors, they pointed out also the necessity of amending them for the

future. It was not now a time to deliberate but to act. Already the French King had made himself master of the chief fortresses around his kingdom, which were the only barriers to his ambition; and, if not instantly opposed, he would seize the rest. All ought, therefore, to be convinced that the particular interest of each was comprised in the general interest of the whole. The enemy's forces were strong and they would carry things like a torrent before them. It was in vain to oppose complaints and unprofitable protestations against injustice. It was not the resolutions of diets, nor hopes founded on treaties, but strong armies and firm union among the allies which alone could stop the enemy in his course. With these they must now snatch the liberties of Europe out of his hands or submit for ever to his yoke. As to himself, he would not spare his credit, his forces, or his person, and would come in the spring at the head of his troops to conquer or perish with his allies.

With these bellicose words ringing in their ears, the delegates agreed to bring 220,000 men into the field in 1691. The Emperor, Spain, Brandenburg and England would contribute 20,000 apiece; the Dutch Republic's share would be 35,000; Savoy and Bavaria could manage 18,000 each; the Elector of Saxony bid 12,000; the Palatinate raised 4,000; Hesse-Cassel recruited 8,000; the Circles of Swabia and Franconia put 10,000 men into the field; Liège and Württemberg both agreed to 6,000; the Bishop of Münster sent 7,000; and the Hanoverians stretched their combined resources to provide 16,000. Although these commitments represented pious hopes which frequently failed to materialise into actual soldiers in the field, William had at least succeeded in goading his allies into making a substantial public declaration of intent. Not satisfied with this, the delegates then resolved not to lay down their arms until France had restored everything that she had taken from neighbouring nations since the Treaty of Münster in 1648. The existence of the Treaty of Nijmegen of 1678 was seemingly overlooked by the conference in its fervour for the common cause. In addition, the Allies stated that they wished to see the parlements, clergy, nobility, towns and people of France restored to their ancient privileges and Louis XIV was recommended to make reparations to the Pope for the injuries he had received at French hands. On this ringing note, but with scant regard as to how the military operations in the Low Countries, Germany, Italy and Catalonia were to be conducted, William retired to his palace at Het Loo, just to the north of Apeldoorn, to hunt and rest.[2]

On 9/19 January 1691, Boufflers and Villars mounted another grand raid deep into the heart of the Spanish Netherlands. Villars assembled

the garrisons of Tournai, Valenciennes, Douai and Lille before marching
up the right bank of the Lys, crossing to the left at Deynze. Boufflers
drew out the garrisons of Ypres and Dunkirk and headed for Bruges;
the combined French corps numbered 13,000 infantry, 6,000 cavalry
and sixteen cannon. The ice on the Ghent-Bruges Canal was sufficiently
thick to withstand the passage of 19,000 men enabling Villars and
Boufflers to invade East Flanders and the Pays de Waas, levying contributions. Only a sudden thaw caused Boufflers to withdraw his contribution parties, who had ranged from the North Sea to the estuary of
the Scheldt and burned a suburb of Ghent. Reputedly without the
loss of a single soldier, Boufflers's raid had netted 1,800,000 livres in
contributions. Two weeks later, the Allied governor of Ath partially
returned the compliment by bridging the Scheldt in order to burn and
plunder between Antoing and Mortagne-du-Nord.[3]

As William was whipping his fellow rulers into a frenzy of positive
thinking at The Hague, Louvois was holding his own planning conference at Versailles on 16/26 February. This gathering ended not in empty
rhetoric but in the decision to surprise and attack Mons. It also decided
to commit 70 battalions and 204 squadrons to the Netherlands, a total
of around 66,000 men. Mons had been selected as it was a major Allied
frontier garrison and its capture would point an arrow directly at
Brussels, the main Allied base. It was also a tempting target because it
was relatively isolated; the supporting garrison of Ath was twenty-two
kilometres distant and the important post of Charleroi was thirty-six
kilometres to the east. Mons also lay close to France so there would be
no Allied forces between the attackers and their magazines; the French
lines of communication would be entirely secure during the seige. Above
all, Mons was a comparatively soft option as it fortifications were rather
out-of-date. Something very rare was achieved by the French at Mons
– complete secrecy and total surprise. From the planning conference,
Boufflers was sent a long list of orders. The Intendants of Flanders and
Hainaut were to supervise transport and the officials in Lille, Dunkirk,
Maubeuge and Amiens were instructed to provide a corps of 21,500
civilian pioneers to labour on the siege works. A magazine sufficient to
feed fifty-three squadrons for three weeks was laid in at Maubeuge and
a total of 1,150,000 hay rations was accumulated in garrisons between
the River Scarpe and the Scheldt. Megrigny, the Governor of Tournai,
was let into the secret and entrusted with organising sufficient boats
and bridges to ship the supplies along the Scarpe, the Haine and the
Scheldt towards Mons. Louvois did not forget to allocate two battalions
to guard the locks on the River Haine. Tournai became the forward

magazine for the besieging army, stocking huge quantities of bread and other foodstuffs, including 220,000 round Dutch cheeses. A train of 130 cannon and forty-five mortars was assembled at Douai, Tournai, Valenciennes and Condé. Boufflers himself was made responsible for the concentration of the troops and was also entrusted with the tracing of the lines of contravallation and circumvallation around Mons in conjunction with Vauban and Chamlay.[4] Had he known anything about them, William would have envied the efficiency with which these vast preparations were executed – the fruits of an absolute government. Remarkably, everything was completed on time and without the Allies gaining any definite intelligence. So profound was their ignorance that they did not even reinforce the threatened fortress; Mons was to be defended by the 5,000 troops who had lodged there for their winter quarters.

Boufflers brought 40,000 men before Mons whilst d'Humières stood in the Lines of the Lys and the Scheldt with 16,000 to prevent the Allied garrisons in Flanders from sending troops to the relief of the besieged town. A further French detachment of 7,000 was positioned in the Sambre-Meuse to observe any Allied movements from Namur, Huy, Liège and Maastricht, and d'Harcourt concentrated 3,000 cavalry at Trier which had the effect of detaining the Brandenburgers in their winter quarters in Jülich and Cleves. The first intimation of the threat to Mons was not received by the Allies until Castañaga penned a hurried letter to Portland on 5/15 March from Brussels containing the news, received directly from the Prince de Berghes, the Governor of Mons, that Boufflers had invested the town on that very same morning. At day-break, wrote Castañaga, French cavalry had completed a blockade of Mons. Castañaga stressed the importance of Mons as a link-town between the Allied frontier along the Scheldt and the Allied fortresses on the line of the Sambre-Meuse. He felt sure that William would march to its relief for the second time in eleven years.[5] The King was more doubtful and did not reflect Castañaga's optimism about an early relief. He knew that there would be 'extraordinary difficulties' in operating to save Mons and his pessimism was increased when he learned that Louis XIV was travelling to attend the siege in person. The Sun King never 'commanded' a siege that was likely to fail.[6]

The Marquis de Bedmar hurried to Brussels on 6/16 March to receive William's orders concerning the organisation of a possible relief expedition.[7] French cavalry had already closed all the roads into and out of Mons and on 8/18 March the corps of conscripted labourers arrived to begin work on the lines of contravallation. Vauban supervised

the formal opening of the trenches on 14/24 March. Despite the close
attentions of the French, the blockade was not watertight and the Prince
de Berghes managed to send word to Brussels that the garrison and the
townspeople were in good heart and should be able to hold out for
long enough to allow William to assemble an army and march to the
rescue.[8] Reflecting these buoyant spirits, Berghe's Spanish soldiers sallied out to disrupt the progress of the trenches on a number of occasions
during the early stages of the siege.[9] William strained every nerve to
concentrate a relief army. The Elector of Brandenberg informed him on
9/19 March that he was prepared to co-operate fully and he had ordered
his 6,000 men in Maastricht and 4,000 troops from his garrisons on
the Meuse to join-up with William. Castañaga breathed more easily
when he found out that William had resolved to go to the rescue of
Mons but he could not resist pointing out that the operation was fraught
with problems, although the French were not guaranteed success.[10]

Mons was built on a low hill, surrounded by marshy ground. It still
retained its old medieval wall, complete with turrets, but its new artillery
fortifications were irregular in trace and had not been well conceived.
There were too many fronts and there were a number of areas of dead-
ground which were not covered by cross-fires. In addition to these
difficulties, the outworks were only 'sodworks' lacking masonry revetments. Mons relied heavily on enveloping itself within a corset of
inundations. The weakest sector lay to the east where a spur of higher
land, Hiom Hill, approached close to the Bertemont Gate, a factor
which Louvois and his planners had realised as far back as 1683.[11]
Accordingly, Vauban launched his main attack towards the Bertemont
Front. The 20,000 labourers were set to dig 'drains' to direct the flood
waters into two new 'canals' which in turn led into the River Trouille.
Once this engineering feat had been accomplished, Vauban mounted
his siege batteries on wooden rafts to prevent them sinking into the
saturated ground. The guns first opened fire on 17/27 March and started
a number of fires in the town. No sooner had the batteries commenced
their work than the garrison re-opened the sluices and inundated the
eastern sector once more, causing one whole thirty-gun battery to dis-
appear into the mud. Vauban had the sense not to repeat the exercise
but instead changed the direction of his attack a little to the north
where the two hornworks before the Bertemont Gate could be assaulted
from the spur of higher land.

Mons had a population of around 5,000 souls, roughly equal to the
size of its military garrison, and it began the siege well-stocked with
food and ammunition. However, the earlier high morale began to waver

as French mortar fire reduced much of the town to ashes and the garrison cannon were disabled by the attacking barrage. Whilst the batteries blazed away at the town and the ramparts of the hornwork, a windmill on Hiom Hill, five hundred metres beyond the glacis, became the scene of some bitter fighting. The French made seven attempts to dislodge the small Spanish garrison of this outpost and finally succeeded at the cost of 2,000 casualties.[12] As Vauban's trenches worked closer to the hornwork, William rode south from The Hague to Vilvorde and then to Halle where he had ordered the army to assemble. It was still much too early in the year for an army to be able to forage in the field and so William was entirely dependent on the transport of winter horse-feed which Castañaga had undertaken to arrange. The Spaniard failed utterly to realise his promises. Without fodder, William's 50,000 men were unable to advance from Halle. Even if Castañaga had delivered the necessary supplies, Luxembourg stood covering the siege with 50,000 soldiers. The odds were stacked heavily against both William and Mons.[13]

To begin with, the siege progressed extremely slowly. This was caused partly by the re-flooding of the marshes but also by the fact that the French had not quite finished their preparations when Boufflers had moved forward to complete the investment. Apparently, Louvois had advanced the date of the Mons operation by two weeks on receipt of intelligence that two Spanish battalions were *en route* to reinforce the garrison.[14] However, these early setbacks were soon overcome and once the power of the French artillery had established itself and was battering the hornwork and the ravelin before the Bertemont Gate, the towns-people began to grow uneasy. Already, the military authorities had discovered one plot to blow-up the powder magazine but thereafter civilian pressure on the garrison increased. Only the English sources mention these developments. At some time during the first week of April, a large crowd of townspeople, led by two priests, remonstrated with the Prince de Berghes and demanded that he surrender to save their town from further damage. He showed them a letter from the Prince of Orange which stated that within three or four days his army of 50,000 would be ready to march to challenge the French before Mons with hopes of lifting the siege. As the Governor tried to prevaricate, the crowd said that they would rather surrender to the French King than be rescued by a heretic prince. It is only fair to point out that Mons lay within the French-speaking provinces of the Spanish Netherlands and both religiously and linguistically its people had far more in common with the French than with the Flemings and Dutch to the north. No doubt Louvois's public announcement that Mons would be fined 100,000 écus for each day of the siege also had its influence. With his garrison reduced by casualties and now heavily outnumbered by the burghers, the Prince de Berghes had no option but to bow to pressure and seek terms with the French.[15]

The French version of the capture of Mons is more heroic. According to Villars, by this time a maréchal de camp, the defence of Mons had been feeble from the outset. After three weeks, much of which had been spent in draining the marshes, the French cannon made a partial breach in the hornwork by the Bertemont Gate and duly launched an infantry assault which gained a lodgement. Because of the negligence of a guards regiment, a sally by the garrison retook the hornwork and ejected the French; the French cannon had to resume firing for a further forty-eight hours until a proper breach had been effected. A second infantry attack gained a secure lodgement on the hornwork and the Prince de Berghes sued for terms on 29 March/8 April. An honourable surrender was quickly arranged enabling Louis XIV to return to Versailles in triumph having defeated his arch-enemy, William III, in the field.[16] The whole episode had been deeply humiliating to William. After all the grand rhetoric at The Hague in January, the Grand Alliance had proved dilatory in rallying to the relief of Mons and he himself, and all his senior generals, had been totally out-witted by the French strategy. Castañaga had also failed when faced with a crisis. Even worse, the French were now the rulers of Mons, a lever between the Allied lines along the Scheldt and the Sambre-Meuse.

It was still very early in the campaigning season. A garrison of 10,000 foot and 2,000 horse was put into Mons and pioneers and the civilian labour corps busied themselves in repairing the fortifications and demolishing the siege lines but the remainder of the French army retired into winter quarters. The Allies followed suit and the campaign lapsed into inactivity. During the course of the siege of Mons, the British corps had begun to assemble in the Netherlands. Although the war in Ireland was not concluded, William still felt able to double the size of the British contingent in the Low Countries to 11,144, twenty per cent of the Allied total of 56,270 available in that theatre.[17] Three regiments of foot and a battalion of replacements sailed from Leith to Ostend, the Duke of Leinster's horse embarked at Gravesend and the Earl of Bath's foot was transferred from the Channel Islands to Flanders. Contingency plans for moving the bulk of the forces in Ireland to the Netherlands were drawn up in February and throughout the year a steady trickle of troops was translated from the one theatre to the other.[18] By the end of April, the British corps in the Low Countries amounted to fifteen battalions and two regiments of cavalry.[19] Many of these infantry formations were in a sorry state. The Cameronians, commanded by the Earl of Angus, landed at Veere on Walcheren in mid-March 1691 only to be attacked immediately by the 'Walcheren sickness' – malaria. The battalion became so under-strength that the soldiers feared that it would be disbanded and used to fill other units. They possessed neither arms nor equipment until Major Daniel Kerr was dispatched into Holland to purchase these items with the colonel's own money. When they finally marched to join the army at Halle they mustered only 400 men, two-thirds of their paper establishment.[20]

William retained an army corps to the south of Brussels but moved back from Halle to Anderlecht on the south-western fringe of the city. With Mons in French possession, William's strategic options were severely restricted. D'Humières's corps in the Lines of the Lys and the Scheldt obliged the Allies to retain a considerable body of troops in Flanders to garrison the principal fortresses, especially Ghent and Bruges, whilst the Mons garrison and Luxembourg's field army meant that Brussels was always in danger of insult from the south. From Mons, the French were already summoning contributions from Soignies, Halle and Enghien and the whole of Hainaut was passing under enemy domination. So worried had the Allies become, that Castañaga was prepared to move the seat of his government from Brussels to Antwerp. The French seemed to have every advantage and could dictate the course of the campaign. On 5/15 May, the Allies detected French preparations being made between Dinant and Mézières suggesting that they intended to operate along the Meuse, possibly aiming at Namur. Five days later, 6,000 French cavalry crossed the Sambre and began gathering contributions from Brabant. Information was also received that Luxembourg had shifted westwards and was concentrating his field army around Harelbeke, to the north-east of Courtrai. This was a very flexible position as it threatened Spanish Flanders and Brussels and was closely supported by d'Humières's corps in the Lines of the Lys and the Scheldt.[21]

If Luxembourg, d'Humières and Vertillac in Mons could pin William and Castañaga to the defence of Flanders and Brussels, then the way would be left clear for Boufflers to operate against the Allied garrisons on the Meuse and the Sambre – Charleroi, Namur, Huy and Liège. To achieve freedom of action for Boufflers, Luxembourg had to ensure that William was tied to the defence of Brussels and thus unable to reinforce his posts along the Sambre-Meuse. Should Luxembourg fail to persuade

William that Brussels and Flanders were in danger, then the Dutchman would have been at liberty to draw in the garrisons of Ghent and Bruges and march to support his fortresses on the Meuse. There was even the prospect that William might attempt the recapture of Mons. On 9/19 May, Luxembourg decamped from Harelbeke, gathered his artillery from Douai and proceeded to bridge the Scheldt on 15/25 May and encamp at Renaix. He quickly pressed on to Lessines, to Enghien on 18/28 May and finally to Halle on the following day. Waldeck, in command of the main army during William's absence, thought that Luxembourg, d'Humières and Boufflers had all joined forces and failed to realise that Boufflers was still based at Dinant with 20,000 horse and foot, thirty-four cannon and twelve mortars waiting for Luxembourg to create the strategic opportunity for him to begin his campaign along the Meuse. For the second time that year, William hurried from the pleasures of Het Loo to take control of a rapidly deteriorating situation. Again, the Allied weakness in cavalry and reconnaissance had been the cause of this perilous development. Luxembourg's march from the Lys had not been particularly rapid and yet Waldeck found himself with only 18,000 men concentrated at Anderlecht and the garrison of Halle cut-off by Luxembourg's arrival. On the night of 20/30 May, the five battalions marooned in Halle managed to creep away under cover of darkness and rejoin Waldeck's lines. Luxembourg intended to attack Waldeck's weak army at Anderlecht but the front of the Allied camp was covered by a marsh and the headwaters of the River Senne. With Waldeck posted in line of battle on high ground, Luxembourg would have been obliged to attack a defile in the face of the enemy. Never a man to take unnecessary risks, even though he outnumbered Waldeck by more than two to one, he returned to Halle and contented himself with demolishing its weak defences and burning most of the town.[22]

Departing from Het Loo at two o'clock on the afternoon of 21/31 May, William journeyed all night to reach Breda by noon on the following day. Not sparing himself, he again rode through the hours of darkness to arrive in Anderlecht at 8.00 a.m. on Saturday 23 May/2 June. Immediately, he went to visit Waldeck who was ill in bed having spent the two previous days in the saddle awaiting an attack from Luxembourg. The old soldier had made his dispositions so skilfully that he had been able to thwart Luxembourg's intention of assaulting the city of Brussels itself. By the time of William's arrival, the Allied army at Anderlecht had increased to 50 battalions of foot and 100 squadrons of horse, a total of around 42,000. Luxembourg's strength was similar.[23] As William and Luxembourg faced each other from Anderlecht and

Halle with their armies actually in sight, Boufflers moved down the Meuse to bombard Liège. Louis XIV had selected Liège as a target partly because it was an important Allied magazine but also because the Prince-Bishop had departed from his promised neutrality and joined the Grand Alliance. Boufflers's mission was one of terror: to bombard the city and do as much damage as possible both as vengeance upon the Liègeois and to reduce the Allied magazines to ashes. Strategically, Boufflers would have been better employed in capturing Huy or Charleroi. With 20,000 men, Boufflers took possession of Fort Chartreuse on the right bank of the Meuse and promptly demanded a contribution of 2,600,000 livres from the city. Not surprisingly, this outrageous demand was refused and so Boufflers constructed batteries at Fort Chartreuse and opened fire on 25 May/4 June. Red hot shot and mortar bombs rained down on Liège and one whole street was consumed by flames. However, the Prince-Bishop was determined to make a fight for his capital city and resolved not to wilt before French blackmail. All citizens whose loyalty was suspect were rounded-up and the Prince-Bishop himself commanded his garrison of 8 battalions and 3,000 horse in making preparations to endure a full siege. Fortunately, help was already on the way. The Count of Lippe was advancing towards Liège with 7,000 soldiers from the Brandenburg and Imperial army on the Rhine and William dispatched 2,500 cavalry from the main army at Anderlecht. When these detachments marched into Liège, Boufflers found himself opposed by equal numbers and he deemed it prudent to retire. He burned the suburbs as a parting gift and Villars captured the garrison of 500 men from the Fort de Chenée, but Liège had been saved from destruction and capture, the magazines were intact and the line of the Meuse remained in Allied control. The Prince-Bishop had won a considerable victory. With Allied cavalry pressing lightly on the rear of his columns, Boufflers withdrew to his base at Dinant. He was to spend the remainder of the campaign observing the movements of the German troops on the Rhine and the Moselle in order to cover Luxembourg's eastern flank.[24] After the depression and humiliation of the French capture of Mons, Prince-Bishop Jean-Louis d'Elderen's rebuff to Boufflers at Liège and Waldeck and William's check to Luxembourg before Brussels had at least restored some stability to the campaign.

Luxembourg accepted the inevitable on 26 May/5 June and marched southwards to Braine-le-Comte, a distance of eighteen kilometres. As he was retreating in the face of an enemy who possessed a strength equivalent to his own, the marshal took considerable precautions to secure his passage. During the night, patrols of cavalry were sent forward to St. Pieters Leeuw to reconnoitre William's camp at Anderlecht and report any movements. A battalion was also advanced into the woods which separated the rival armies. So concerned was Luxembourg that William would gain intelligence of his intended march and try to attack, that he sent infantry and cavalry to occupy the line of the River Senne in his rear which was to form the left flank barrier of his march south. In addition, after the army had crossed the Senne, one of his columns would have to pass through the Forest of Houssières to the north of Braine-le-Comte. This was occupied by infantry before the march began. With his vulnerable left flank thus made safe, the marshal marched early in the morning, his troops divided into nine columns which soon merged into six. The Senne was crossed at Tubise on six pontoon bridges and the army then formed three columns for the remainder of its journey. To cover his withdrawal, the marshal posted a strong rearguard of cavalry supported by twenty cannon. Undoubtedly, William would have intervened to attack or disrupt his opponent's retirement if it had been possible. However, the information which reached William suggested that the French were merely sending a strong detachment to Enghien and it was therefore suspected that the retreat was really a feint to draw the Allies away from their strong position at Anderlecht. In fact, William's scouts had encountered Luxembourg's extreme right hand column which did indeed make a considerable detour towards Enghien in order to make use of the available roads. William and Waldeck sat tight. His march safely accomplished, Luxembourg went into a strong camp between Steenkirk and the Forest of Houssières which covered his front as well as his right flank.[25]

Between them, the combined efforts of the French and the Allies had exhausted the forage to the south of Brussels. Now that Luxembourg had shifted well to the south of Brussels and Boufflers was occupied watching the Brandenburgers, William thought it safe to leave the security of Anderlecht. He moved round and through Brussels on 7/17 June to take up a camp on the north edge of the city between Diegem, Vilvorde and Perk. He extended parts of his left wing to Bethlehem Abbey, to the south-west of Louvain, on the following day.[26] Both armies were devouring the resources of Brabant, the heartland of William's supplies, at an alarming rate and it had become imperative for William to shift the campaign towards the frontiers of France and oblige Luxembourg to draw from his own magazines. William was mentally prepared to achieve this objective either through manoeuvre or by battle. On 8/18 June, the whole army edged eastward to Bethlehem

Abbey, a march which was completed by three o'clock in the afternoon, and then rested for twenty-four hours.[27] A short hike of nine kilometres brought the army to Beauvechain on 11/21 June. Luxembourg made no move from Braine-le-Comte being well balanced to intercept William should he try to go south towards the Sambre, attempt to force an engagement, or consider a siege of Mons.[28] The Allies marched further south to Malèves on 13/23 June and onto Gembloux on 16/26 June. At Gembloux, the troops of the Landgrave of Hesse-Cassel joined William's army. Luxembourg still remained at Braine-le-Comte even though William was now forty kilometres, two or even three marches, to the east. However, William and Waldeck received some vague intelligence that Luxembourg had sent his quartermasters to mark out a camp on the Plains of Cambron to the west of Braine-le-Comte.[29]

This turned out to be false information. Luxembourg correctly devised that William intended to bring the campaign to the borders of France. In order to achieve this, Luxembourg thought that his opponent would attack across the Sambre towards Dinant and Philippeville. As a counter, he ordered Boufflers to bridge the Meuse at Givet and come towards Beaumont, south-east of Mons. The main French army fell back in step with William, moving over the Sambre to Haine-St. Pierre, just to the north of Binche between Mons and Charleroi. Luxembourg and Boufflers were now in close mutual support and within easy reach of the fortresses and magazines at Mons, Dinant and Philippeville. At this point, Luxembourg's carefully balanced stance was upset by political interference. Anxious for some public and dramatic act, Louis XIV pressed Luxembourg to advance northwards and bombard Brussels, a move which would have achieved nothing in terms of the campaign and might well have led to the French losing Dinant or Philippeville to an Allied siege. Against his better judgement, Luxembourg marched over the Sambre to Soignies but he reinforced his position by ordering Villars, who commanded the Lines of the Lys and the Scheldt with fifteen battalions and thirty squadrons, to march to Baudour to the west of Mons.[30] Through no efforts of their own, the Allies suddenly found themselves in an advantageous position. In the wake of his junction with the forces of Hesse-Cassel and Liège, William had 90,000 men whilst Castañaga guarded Flanders from near Brussels with a sizeable corps. The French were unbalanced. Boufflers and Villars had been drawn too close to Luxembourg's main army in order to provide additional strength in the face of William's 90,000 men. Even worse, Luxembourg was in an unsound position being too far to the north and at least one march behind William should the latter decide to cross the

Sambre and lay siege to Dinant or Philippeville. At length, the French court relented and Luxembourg hastened to regain his tactical balance marching south to reach Estinnes, west of Binche, and then onto Merbes-le-Château on 26 June/6 July. From the camp at Merbes, Luxembourg built three bridges across the Sambre to his front to be ready to march towards Dinant and Philippeville. William responded by ordering Castañaga to advance west from Brussels to Gavere on the Scheldt; this obliged Luxembourg to send Villars back to the Lines to cover the French frontier in Flanders. William had succeeded in forcing Luxembourg to split his forces once more.

During Luxembourg's reluctant movement north to Soignies, William had summoned his siege train from Namur and intended to exploit his unexpected advantage by attempting the siege of either Dinant or Philippeville.[31] The rapid reversal of French plans and Luxembourg's return to the banks of the Sambre put an end to these dreams. On 10/20 July, William advanced from Gembloux towards the Sambre, camping close to the previous year's battlefield at Fleurus. The army departed from Fleurus at 1.00 a.m. on 11/21 July and marched into Montignies-sur-Sambre six hours later. The engineers threw two bridges across the Sambre and the troops crossed immediately and encamped on the Plains of Gerpinnes. Luxembourg did not learn of William's night march until 10.00 a.m. on 11/21 July and he immediately decamped and crossed the Sambre on the pre-laid bridges and marched to a camp between Florennes and Philippeville, around Heptinne and St. Aubin, nine kilometres south of the Allied position. Here he prepared his army for battle, sending the heavy baggage south to Mariembourg.[32] When the Allied reconnaissance patrols investigated the French position on 16/26 July, they found its front covered by a thick wood and deep ravines and the left wing so placed that it would be able to wheel back on Philippeville should it be forced to retire. The position looked far too strong to be attacked and this interpretation was confirmed when Boufflers's corps of 8,000 marched into camp on Luxembourg's right.[33] Stalemate ensued with neither side able to attack the other and the issue could only be resolved by the question of food and forage. Provisions for the soldiers were readily available as the Allies were close to their magazines at Charleroi and Namur and the French stood at the gates of Philippeville, but forage for the horses was more difficult. Boufflers, commanding a detachment of 4,000 cavalry, destroyed the forage in the country between Gerpinnes and Dinant whilst Vertillac, the Governor of Mons, devoured the forage from Gerpinnes to the Sambre. Although deserters reported that the French army was also short of forage, the

Allies felt the greater need and were compelled to be the first to move camp.[34]

On 28 July/7 August, William marched south-west to Cour-sur-Heure to stand between Luxembourg and Mons, threatening both the French frontier and a siege of the latter town.[35] William was within a short march of the small fortified town of Beaumont on the River Heure which dominated the river crossing of the main road from Mons to Philippeville, the route that Luxembourg would be bound to take if he was to interpose his army between William's troops and the French frontier. Beaumont lay just in French territory – William was close to invading France and enjoying the luxury of living from his enemy's resources. A grand strategic opportunity had opened before William to be instantly squandered through carelessness and dithering. Instead of pressing on to Beaumont with his whole army, William lingered at Cour-sur-Heure and only sent the Saxon General Heinrich Fleming with 2,000 men to occupy Beaumont and watch the crossings of the Sambre at Thuin and La Buissière. Whilst William took his time, Luxembourg executed a forced flank march through the foothills and forests of the Ardennes to Beaumont where he crossed the River Heure and camped on the left bank of the river along a ridge within two kilometres of the town. At a leisurely pace, the Allied army advanced through the forests on 31 July/10 August on tracks cut by the pioneers and pressed civilian labourers. As the troops emerged from the trees into the valley of the Hantes at 4.00 p.m. they found, not sleepy Beaumont resting on its hill-top, but Luxembourg's entire army laid out in battle array. William had brought his troops under walls of Beaumont by 7.00 p.m. and built bridges across the river during the night. He was determined to attack in the morning.[36] At sunrise on 1/11 August, the Allied generals under-took a reconnaissance of the ground and the French positions and rapidly came to the conclusion that the attack was impossible without great hazard to the army. In frustration, the Allied cannon fired a few desultory shots at the French camp and the compliment was returned. William had a narrow escape; a cannon ball landed on the very spot where he had been sitting but two minutes previously.[37] William's army returned to Cour-sur-Heure during the 1/11 August only to meet with further problems that night. A Frenchman concealed himself amongst the artillery waggons and, at 10.00 p.m. when the camp was quiet, he lit a brace of bombs and tossed them into two waggons, each of which was loaded with thirty grenades and two barrels of powder. Alongside were six more carts similarly burdened, and next to them stood the ammunition store for the whole army. Some artillery officers reacted with great presence of mind by pulling the burning waggons out of the column and overturning them before they exploded. This quick work prevented the fire spreading to the rest of the ammunition train. According to one report, Luxembourg's army stood to arms all night waiting to hear the massive explosion which was their cue to advance. The French incendiary, who had been paid 100,000 livres by Luxembourg, was apprehended and burned alive.[38]

Following Luxembourg's victory at Mons and then William's failure to invade France, the campaign entered its third phase. William's main army stood at Cour-sur-Heure, with General Fleming at Marchienne, north of the Sambre on the outskirts of Charleroi, and Castañaga was at Gavere on the Scheldt. Luxembourg's army was encamped at Leugnies, two kilometres to the south-west of Beaumont, supported by Boufflers at Rance, a small village fifteen kilometres further south. General Ximenes commanded a corps at Maubeuge on the Sambre to the west of Beaumont and Villars occupied the Lines of the Lys and the Scheldt. William effected a slight forward movement on 13/23 August, which Luxembourg did not oppose, in order to bring off the garrison of Beaumont and demolish the fortifications before the whole army marched back to Gerpinnes.[39] Consistently aggressive, William marched due east to St. Gérard on the following day as it to threaten Dinant but a small corps was left behind at Ham-sur-Heure to secure the passage over that river should the main army be forced to retreat. Luxembourg's intelligence service was in its customary sparkling form and he received notice of William's advance to St. Gérard before it had actually occurred. Accordingly, he moved his principal force to Strees, close to Gerpinnes, and dispatched Boufflers to Dinant.[40] Although Lord Sydney could report to the Earl of Nottingham that 'we are here in the enemy's country, eating their forage', this was the limit of William's achievement. His stance was threatened by Boufflers from the south, Luxembourg to the west and his intended retreat through Ham-sur-Heure was intercepted. Despite Sydney's optimism, there was little forage in the region for either the French or the Allies. The campaign had now moved into the forested foothills of the Ardennes, far removed from the fertile plains of Hainaut and Brabant. The relatively scarce provisions of forage that had existed in the frontier regions had long since been gathered into French magazines. This had the double effect of giving the French armies some limited supplies of forage from their own bases whilst creating an operational desert for enemy forces. It took but a short time for William's horses to devour the existing green fodder and the King had no option but to retreat into his own foraging areas in Brabant.[41]

The heavy baggage and the artillery departed from St. Gérard on the afternoon of 24 August/3 September, with the main army following on the next day. The first camp was at Velaine, north of the Sambre to the east of Charleroi, and the second was at Mellet, to the north of Charleroi, on 26 August/5 September. After a day's rest, the army withdrew northwards to Bois St. Isaac on 28 August/7 September. William reached his objective, Lembeek south of Halle, on 29 August/8 September. He was now in rich foraging country, close to his main base of Brussels, and within supporting distance of Castañaga at Gavere but he had forfeited the campaign. In response, Luxembourg made a long march of fifty kilometres, crossing the Sambre, and coming to camp at Feluy, eighteen kilometres south of the Allies' stance at Lembeek. With their frontier now secure, the only slight concern for the French was that William might try to combine with Castañaga and make a joint effort towards the Lines of the Lys and the Scheldt. To reduce the danger of this occurrence, Luxembourg adjusted his camp to Ninove, directly between William at Lembeek and Castañaga at Gavere. This adjustment also brought the Frenchman into richer foraging country; even at Feluy he had felt the savage influence of the scorched earth policy which his countrymen had executed around their frontiers.[42]

Sensing that the season was drawing to a close, both sides began to consider their dispositions for winter quarters. At Lembeek, William released the Brandenberg regiments and the Hessians to commence their march towards cantonments along the Rhine. The Allies advanced to Enghien on 31 August/10 September and further forward to Ghislenghien two days later, taking the opportunity to throw some reinforcements and supplies into Ath. From a respectful distance, Luxembourg covered William's tentative movements, coming back from Ninove to Grammont before marching to Pont d'Espierres to gain contact with Villars's corps which was holding the Lines of the Lys and the Scheldt. William pushed forward to Leuse on 3/13 September.[43] Even at this late stage, William was attempting to salvage something positive from a disappointing campaign. His wanderings from Brabant into Hainaut and then into Flanders were designed to bring Luxembourg to a general action – the desire to decide an issue by combat was William's standard response when he had been thwarted by manoeuvre. However, Luxembourg had gained enough from the campaign and was too cautious to rise to his opponent's bait. He had captured Mons and protected France from invasion, at the same time further increasing the security of the French frontier by devouring the forage from the Lys to the Meuse. In keeping with the basically defensive intentions of his royal master,

Luxembourg's achievement was all that could have been asked. William was also hamstrung by the nature of the Flanders countryside which made it easy for a reluctant army to avoid battle. "tis such a country that if both parties have a mnid to it, 'tis impossible they should ever meet. . . . Our army is in a very good condition and their's, they say, is in a very bad one, which will make us try all the ways we can to get to them.'[44] On 9/19 September, with Luxembourg still encamped between Pont d'Espierres and Tournai and his own army at Leuse, William effectively abandoned the campaign. Leaving the army in Waldeck's charge, he rode for Breda and Het Loo to prepare himself to return to England in time for the opening of Parliament in October.[45]

The two armies were divided by twenty-five kilometres of flat but wooded country. Luxembourg personally reconnoitred Waldeck's position on 8/18 September and came to the conclusion that he was about to decamp and withdraw, probably towards his base at Brussels as a prelude to dispersing his army into winter quarters. The French marshal also detected that Waldeck seemed to be taking no precautions to cover his flanks and rear in readiness for the march as he clearly thought that the distance between the armies was too great for the French to be able to interfere. Luxembourg decided otherwise. The knowledge that Waldeck had replaced William as commander-in-chief must also have encouraged Luxembourg. The King had put up a reasonable show during 1691 and had even, temporarily, out-manoeuvred Luxembourg around Beaumont but Waldeck's performance at Fleurus in 1690 marked him out as a slow and often careless general. He would not be looking for the unexpected. On 9/19 September, still under discreet observation by enemy cavalry, Waldeck prepared to retreat eastwards to Cambron.[46] On the previous evening, Luxembourg had ordered 400 horse under Lieutenant-Colonel Marcilly of the Gardes du Corps to ride to Waldeck's camp, reconnoitre and send back reports. Marcilly took station on the Leuse road. Luxembourg also instructed Villars to take four battalions of foot and two regiments of dragoons to support Marcilly. When these forces were under way, Luxembourg drew sixty squadrons from his field army and readied himself to march rapidly to support Marcilly and Villars.

Early on the morning of 9/19 September, Luxembourg set out from near Tournai with 7,000 cavalry, including the Maison du Roi and the Gendarmes, taking the Leuse road leaving Antoing on his right. On the march, Luxembourg received news from both Marcilly and the 'country people' that Waldeck had broken camp two hours before dawn and was heading for Cambron. Luxembourg quickened his pace. Behind

him, the main body of the French field army with all its infantry and
artillery was also on the road; the aim was to pin the Allied rearguard
with a cavalry action, oblige Waldeck to abandon his march and draw
him into a general engagement. Villars joined Marcilly at 8.00 a.m.
with his six squadrons of dragoons, having left his four battalions of
foot to make as good a speed as they could manage. His first task was
to tell a somewhat surprised Marcilly of Luxembourg's plan. By this
time, the Allied artillery and infantry were crossing the Catoire Brook
at the rear, or eastern extremity of their camp. Waldeck had placed
fifteen squadrons of horse to the west of the brook to serve as a
rearguard. The entire Allied dispositions exuded an air of slackness.
The rearguard was very weak, only eighteen hundred men, without any
artillery or infantry support, and the rearguard commander had sent
no patrols west of the Leuse River towards Luxembourg's position
around Tournai. The approach of Marcilly, Villars and Luxembourg
was undetected and unexpected. To make matters worse, Waldeck had
positioned no infantry at the bridges across the Catoire Brook in case
the cavalry rearguard had to fall back and traverse the brook under
pressure. From Marcilly's detailed intelligence, Luxembourg seems to
have been aware of all these weaknesses and clearly thought that it
would be possible to beat the Allied rearguard before Waldeck could
bring up support from the main army which had crossed the Catoire
and was marching off towards Cambron. Villars, very much the man
of action, ordered Marcilly to advance his 400 horsemen to within 500
metres of the Allied rearguard and form a line of battle whilst Villars
brought his 700 cavalry into a second line, some 1,000 metres to the
rear. The rearguard must have presented a sorely tempting target to the
aggressive Villars as it was not formed into a line of battle but was
shuffling about in a vague column stretching back to the banks of the
Catoire. On the sudden appearance of the French, the rearguard began
to muster into something resembling a line of battle and seemed to be
under the illusion that they were facing the 2,000 cavalry from the
garrison of St. Ghislain under the command of Brigadier, the Marquis
de Bezons.

However, the Allies were probably saved by a sudden bout of nerves
from Villars. He thought that the combined force of himself and Marcilly was insufficient to attack the rearguard and he waited for Luxembourg's cavalry vanguard to arrive. Very soon, the Duke of Berwick
galloped up with the Maison du Roi and the Regiment de Tessé and
Villars sought his advice. Berwick recommended the dragoons on the
right and the cavalry on the left but, more importantly, he brought

orders from Luxembourg that Villars was to wait until he had enough men and a favourable terrain. Luxembourg then marched onto the scene with the main body of the horse and deployed to the south of Waldeck's army directly threatening the southern flank of its intended line of march. The remainder of the French army was hurrying down the Leuse road under the command of Lieutenant-General Conrad von Rosen. The Marshal could hardly believe his luck that he had achieved total surprise and had succeeded in isolating the Allied rearguard from the main force. He knew that he could not afford to wait as Waldeck was already showing signs of pulling in his left wing and reinforcing his rearguard. He sent some more troops to Villars and ordered him to attack. With the Duke de Choiseul commanding his right and Lieutenant-General Guy d'Auger responsible for the left, Villar's first line crossed a small depression to their front and then charged towards the Allied rearguard which was still not fully deployed to receive them. The French broke through and pressed the Allied horsemen back towards the bridges over the Catoire. Unfortunately for Luxembourg and Villars, they had delayed for just too long and Waldeck had managed to bring considerable bodies of infantry back towards the Catoire to support the cavalry of the rearguard and enable them to cross the bridges to the safety of the east bank. As Villars's first line began to withdraw between the intervals in the second line, the second line prepared to charge but already the odds were excessive and Luxembourg called off the action. Although the engagement had lasted for no more than forty-five minutes, the French suffered four hundred casualties out of the 700 cavalry involved, with the loss of officers being particularly high. General d'Auger was killed. Villars himself, or so he boasts in his memoirs, suffered seventeen sword cuts. Having narrowly missed his immediate purpose, Luxembourg withdrew and reached his camp at Tournai at 6.00 p.m. Waldeck continued on his march to the Plains of Cambron.[47]

The Battle of Leuse was a serious affair. Armies camped at action stations so that, in an emergency the troops could run out of their tents and form into the two main lines of battle at a moment's notice. This was to be part of Luxembourg's salvation at Steenkirk in the following year. When leaving a camp, armies suffered a period of extreme vulnerability as they deployed into marching columns from their lines of battle. If two opposing armies were in sight of one another or otherwise in propinquity, commanders took exceptional precautions to secure their decampment through the employment of deception and the advance positioning of rearguards and bodies of troops at key points and features. Above all, armies needed to maintain extensive reconnais-

sance patrols. Waldeck seemingly ignored most of these standard proce-
dures and his soldiers had only just escaped from Luxembourg's trap
at the cost of 500 casualties. According to Allied accounts, the early
morning of 9/19 September was foggy and this was one of the reasons
why Villars and Luxembourg were able to approach the rear of Leuse
village and deploy without being spotted by the rearguard. Waldeck's
letter to William of 10/20 September was pathetic. He explained that
he renounced all responsibility for the battle as he was not personally
at the scene of the action and did not direct the course of events. If
William wanted a more detail description of Leuse and what had gone
wrong, he continued, then he must write separately to the lieutenant-
generals involved. This was an appalling admission from a supposed
commander-in-chief. Any combat involving his own army was his
responsibility and the matter of arranging for the safety of a march was
a primary duty of the senior officer. Waldeck was utterly negligent in
this, one of the most important functions of a commander-in-chief.
Because Luxembourg was distant by one long march and the campaign
appeared to be petering out, Waldeck assumed that he could leave a
camp, cross a river in its rear and march off without taking any particular precautions. Even the basic provision of cavalry patrols towards the
enemy was ignored. Leuse must have done much to convince William
that Waldeck was too old and incompetent. In future years he would
have to command the army himself throughout a campaign and discover
some more reliable and able subordinates. Whilst William was no military genius, he was in a different class to Waldeck.[48]

Leuse brought the campaign to an effective conclusion. From his
camp between Brugelette and Cambron, Waldeck moved to Ghislenghien and Silly on 13/23 September and then back to Pollare and Zandber-
gen on the Dender, just to the west of Ninove, on 18/28 September and
19/29 September. In the meantime, Luxembourg advanced to Renaix
on the Scheldt.[49] The armies lingered in these stations for a further
month before drifting into their winter quarters. The forces of Lippe
and Liège joined with the Brandenberg regiments under General Fleming
and marched to take up their billets in the Duchy of Luxembourg
and in Jülich and Cleves. Waldeck put 15,000 in Brussels and further
protected his main base by quartering 5,000 men in Louvain, 2,000 in
Vilvorde, 4,000 in Malines and 3,000 in Dendermonde. Flanders was
guarded by 10,000 in Ghent and 5,000 in Oudenarde and the frontier
with France received substantial garrisons in Namur, Charleroi and
Ath. Just as the campaign in Flanders was ending, the British and Allied
troops released from Ireland began to arrive in the Low Countries in

significant numbers. Four British regiments were housed in Bergen-op-Zoom and Breda, Danish battalions lodged in Nieuport and Danish cavalry was sent to Malines.[50] Hard on the heels of the departing soldiery came intelligence that Vauban had been spotted in Dinant supervising the storage of bombs, carcasses and other siege materials, indicating that the French would probably operate on the Sambre-Meuse in 1692. Charleroi and Namur were the obvious targets.

NOTES

1 'A Description of the most glorious and most magnificent Arches erected at The Hague for the reception of William the Third, King of Great Britain', *Harleian Miscellany* (London, 1810), v. 387–93; Govert Bidloo, *Komste van Zyne Majesteit Willem III . . . in 's-Gravenhage* (The Hague, 1691) contains a number of Romeyn de Hooghe's coloured engravings of William's ceremonial entry into The Hague.
2 Luttrell, *Historical Relation*, ii. 136–9; *The Life and Diary of Lieut. Col. J. Blackader*, ed. Andrew Crichton (Edinburgh, 1824), p. 115; Sir John Dalrymple, *Memoirs of Great Britain and Ireland* (London, 1790, repr. 1970), iii. 137–40; *HSL* vii. 38–53.
3 *HMC, Rutland MSS.*, ii. 132–3; *HSL*, vii. 42; Villars, i. 124–6; Beaurain, ii, 60; Van Houtte, *Les Occupations Étrangères*, i. 242.
4 Beaurain, ii. 61–3; Duffy, *Fortress in the Age of Vauban and Frederick the Great*, p.29.
5 Japikse, iii. 213; Baxter, *William III*, p. 293. The first Williamite relief of Mons had occurred in 1678.
6 Gilbert Burnet, *History of His Own Time* (Oxford, 1833), iv. 132.
7 Japikse, iii. 214.
8 Ibid., iii. 218–19.
9 *HMC, Downshire MSS.*, i. 369.
10 Japikse, iii. 217–18; *HMC, Denbigh MSS.*, p. 85, 12/22 Mar. 1691, Castañaga to William III.
11 *Journal of the Late Motions*, p. 22; Wright, *Fortifications*, pp. 171–4; Beaurain, i. section 1, pl. 1 & 2; BL, Add. MSS. 64,108, ff. 70–4.
12 *The Correspondence of John Locke*, ed. E. S. de Beer (Oxford, 1976ff.), iv. 246; Beaurain, ii. 69–70.
13 Burnet, *History*, iv. 132; Rousset, *Louvois*, iv. 459–67.
14 *HMC, Finch MSS.*, iii. 32–3.
15 *HMC, Downshire MSS.*, i. 369–70, 9/19 Apr. 1691, The Hague, Nottingham to Trumbull; Burnet, *History*, iv. 132; Baxter, *William III*, p. 294; BL, Add. MSS. 61,341, ff. 2–9.
16 *Mémoires du Maréchal de Berwick, écrits par lui-même* (Switzerland, 1778), i. 60–1; Villars, i. 126–8; Beaurain, ii. 69–73.
17 Chandler, 'Fluctuations', pp. 9–10.
18 *CSPD 1690–1*, pp. 266–7; *HMC, Le Fleming, MSS.*, p. 319; *HMC, Hastings MSS.*, ii. 333.
19 Walton, p. 184.

20 S. H. F. Johnston, 'A Scots Chaplain in Flanders, 1691–1697', *JSAHR*, xxvii. (1949), pp. 3–5.
21 SP 77/56, ff. 104, 106.
22 *HMC, Finch MSS.*, iii. 70, 11/21 May 1691, Het Loo, Sydney to Nottingham; Beaurain, ii. 75–84; PRO, MPH 17/Part 2, f. 11.
23 *HMC, Finch MSS.*, iii. 73, 76.
24 Japikse, iii. 240; *HMC, Finch MSS.*, iii. 82–3; Villars, i. 129–30; *HMC, Marchmont MSS.*, p. 122; *Archives d'Orange-Nassau*, i. 180–1.
25 Walton, p. 189; Beaurain, ii. 84–9.
26 LUL, MS. 12, ff. 82–5.
27 Japikse, iii. 240–1; *HMC, Finch MSS.*, iii. 104–5.
28 *HMC, Finch MSS.*, iii. 108.
29 LUL, MS. 12, ff. 85–93; *HMC, Finch MSS.*, iii. 113.
30 Walton, p. 191; *HMC, Finch MSS.*, iii. 119; Beaurain, ii. 96–102.
31 *HMC, Finch MSS.*, iii. 132.
32 LUL, MS. 12, ff. 93–6; SP 77/56, f. 112; *HMC, Finch MSS.*, iii. 149, 154; Beaurain, ii. 103–11.
33 SP 77/56, f. 116; *HMC, Finch MSS.*, iii. 158.
34 *HMC, Finch MSS.*, iii. 165.
35 LUL, MS. 12, ff. 96–8; *HMC, Finch MSS.*, iii. 179, 187.
36 Walton, pp. 196–8; SP 77/56, f. 117; Beaurain, ii. 114–17.
37 *HMC, Hope-Johnstone MSS.*, p. 58.
38 *HMC, Finch MSS.*, iii. 191, 202, 225–6; *HMC, Marchmont MSS.*, pp. 122–3.
39 LUL, MS. 12, ff. 102–5; *HMC, Finch MSS.*, iii. 199.
40 LUL, MS. 12, ff. 105–6; *HMC, Finch MSS.*, iii, 204; Beaurain, ii. 122.
41 *HMC, Finch MSS.*, iii. 212–13; SP 77/56, f. 118.
42 LUL, MS. 12, ff. 106–12; *HMC, Finch MSS.*, iii. 225–6, 243; Beaurain, ii. 123–6.
43 LUL, MS. 12, ff. 113–17.
44 *HMC, Finch MSS.*, iii. 249; Japikse, iii. 252–3.
45 SP 77/56, f. 120; *HMC, Finch MSS.*, iii. 256.
46 LUL, MS. 12, ff. 118–20.
47 Feuquières, ii. 63–6; Heim, ii. pp. xlvix-li; Villars, i. 134–9, 449–50; Bonneval, *Memoirs*, pp. 8–9; Berwick, i. 60–9; Beaurain, ii. 136–8; PRO, MPH 17/Part 1.
48 Japikse, iii. 255–6; *HMC, Finch MSS.*, iii. 266; *HMC, Marchmont MSS.*, p. 123.
49 SP 77/56, f. 121; LUL, MS. 12, ff. 120–5.
50 Japikse, iii. 266.

VII

1692: NAMUR
AND STEENKIRK

When the Treaty of Limerick brought the war in Ireland to a close on 3/13 October 1691, the British army became available almost exclusively for service in the Low Countries. Expecting to be faced with numerically superior French forces, William sought a means to negate this advantage and employ the superior mobility provided by the Anglo-Dutch fleets. His eyes lighted on Dunkirk. The privateers from this heavily fortified port were already a nuisance to Allied shipping in the English Channel and the North Sea and its defences were unfinished. In terms of the war in the Low Countries, the capture of Dunkirk would have turned the seaward flank of the French frontier with the Spanish Netherlands giving the Allies a huge victory. William first toyed with the notion of attacking Dunkirk in 1691. He planned to use the troops released from Ireland and make his move early in 1692, before the French had come into the field. An elaborate and detailed plan was drafted in January 1692 but the scheme was suddenly dropped. Either the Earl of Marlborough, or some other Jacobite sympathiser or agent, betrayed the plan to Versailles or the complex assault on this massively fortified target was considered beyond the Allies' capabilities so early in the campaign. However, the profit to be gained by a successful attack on Dunkirk did not go away but stayed prominently in William's mind for the remainder of the war.[1] The abandonment of the Dunkirk enterprise decided William to commit the surplus forces from Ireland directly into the Low Countries.

Louis XIV had other ideas. He had not entertained James II at great expense merely out of a sense of sympathy and ultruism – James had to earn his keep. Once the considerable diversion of the Irish Wars had ended, Louis decided to employ the Irish Brigade of 12,000, which had been released to France by the Treaty of Limerick, supported by a similar number of French troops, as the spearhead of an attempted invasion of England. A reluctant and uncertain James II was politely requested to accompany the expedition. Although Louis began to organise this operation in February 1692, not until 19/29 April were the ministers in London convinced that the enemy concentration in the Cotentin Peninsula was aimed at an invasion of England rather than the occupation of the Channel Islands. The ensuing 'invasion scare' seriously interfered with the transfer of troops from Ireland to the Low Countries and a number of regiments which had already made the journey had to sail back to England to reinforce the home army. Two cavalry regiments were recalled from transports in the Thames and three battalions were diverted from Leith to the Isle of Wight. Three more battalions – William Selwyn's, William Beveridge's and Edward Lloyd's – were returned from Flanders and William placed a further six British battalions on stand-by to embark at Willemstadt. In the event, these six battalions were not required as over 10,000 soldiers were already packed into the countryside around Portsmouth and the Isle of Wight, sufficient to deter the invader. The French scheme collapsed when Admiral Edward Russell's victory over Tourville's fleet off Cape La Hogue on 19/29 May and 20/30 May denied the French the essential prerequisite of command of the English Channel. Although the twenty-three additional battalions in England were then theoretically free to sail to the Low Countries, they were retained in order to mount a counter-operation against the French coast at St. Malo in an effort to divert enemy troops from Flanders. The affairs on either side of the Channel had been closely connected to events in the Netherlands. The French invasion attempt had been launched to draw Allied troops away from Brabant so that the siege of Namur could occur, whilst the Allied counter-thrust had been brought about by William's need to weaken the French armies so that he could try to relieve that same, beleaguered city.[2]

French strategy continued to be basically defensive although opportunist with both Louis and Luxembourg prepared to employ the tactical and grand tactical offensive to achieve that objective. The campaign of 1691, and indeed that of 1690, had revealed a major weakness in the French frontier defences. From the North Sea to Mons, the French frontier was guarded by a string of fortresses sheltering behind convenient rivers and waterways. Between the Lys and the Scheldt this system broke down but here the French had built a line of field fortifications to block this 'gate' into France. From Mons to the east, the frontier was less imposing, running through Maubeuge, Philippeville, Dinant and Charleville, all situated well to the south of the main river

barrier along the Sambre and the Meuse. With the principal fortress of
the Sambre, Charleroi, in Allied hands along with the main Meuse
fortresses – Namur, Liège and Maastricht – the French found it difficult
to dominate the awkward country between their frontier and the Sambre-Meuse, the districts known as the Marlagne and the Condroz. This
simple fact of geography had enabled Waldeck and William to operate
south of the Sambre in the first three years of the war to the considerable
disadvantage of their opponents. Although the seizure of Mons had
dislocated the Allied frontier defence in the south of the Spanish Netherlands, it had not presented control of the lower Sambre to France. This
could only be achieved by the ultimate acquisition of Charleroi, a strong
and heavily garrisoned post. Initially, it made more sense to tackle
Namur, positioned at the confluence of the Sambre and the Meuse to
the east of Charleroi. Once Namur was in French hands, Charleroi
could be squeezed between that city and Mons until it became untenable. Allied armies would experience great difficulty in operating in
support of Charleroi and a successful French siege would be relatively
easy to accomplish. Also, the French occupation of Namur would give
them another foothold on the Meuse above their own fort at Dinant
and deny most of the Sambre and the middle Meuse to Allied navigation. Perhaps even more important, the possession of Namur and
then Charleroi would advance the French frontier to the Sambre-Meuse
and bring all of the Marlagne and the Condroz under their control.
The Allies would still hold the line of the Meuse above Huy but if they
wished to invade France then they would have to attack out of Flanders
and tackle the fortress barrier or advance from east of the Meuse
through the Ardennes. Louis had an even deeper and more defensive
purpose. He thought that the combination of the capture of Namur
and the threat to invade England would force the Maritime Powers,
England and the United Provinces, to sue for peace.[3] To achieve a
sufficient numerical superiority in the Low Countries, Louis drew heavily from his armies in Savoy and Germany, relying upon the fact that
the German forces were usually very slow to come into the field, and
hoped that James II would produce results in England.

The intense cold of January brought forth the customary series of
French raids to disrupt the winter quarters of the Allies. Already, the
early signs indicated that the French would open the campaign with a
siege on the Sambre-Meuse. A party of French smashed the sluice of
Grignon, on the Sambre between Namur and Charleroi, and advanced
towards the latter fortress until a thaw forced them to retire. Rumours
were rife in The Hague that Louis XIV was expected to be at Mons by

the end of February – the presence of the Sun King could only foretell the imminence of a major siege. In Spanish Flanders important changes had taken place. The Spaniards were no longer able to pay for the troops from Brandenburg and Hesse and this burden was assumed by England and the Dutch Republic. More significantly, Castañaga was replaced as Governor of the Spanish Netherlands by Max Emmanuel, the Elector of Bavaria. Castañaga's patriotism had not been in question but he was inefficient and his failure to support fully William's attempt to save Mons in the spring of 1691 was a major factor in his dismissal. Bavaria's appointment dated from December 1691.[4] Not only did the new governor demonstrate more energy almost immediately, establishing a 'fire brigade' of 6,000 men in Flanders ready to march to repel French winter raids, but he had a less independent mind than his predecessor giving William a greater control over the whole theatre of war. The departure of Castañaga elevated the influence and prestige of the Prince de Vaudemont, William's ally and favourite amongst the ranks of the Spanish army in the Netherlands. Vaudemont and Bavaria were to cause the Spanish army to function in William's interest and Vaudemont became one of the King's most trusted and able subordinate commanders.

Intelligence reached The Hague and Brussels that the French were filling considerable magazines with hay and oats at Dinant and Charlemont and were assembling a train of artillery at Philippeville. Even more worrying, Louis ordered twenty battalions of foot, four regiments of horse and two of dragoons to be recalled from Catinat's army in Savoy to reinforce his troops in the Low Countries. This prompted William to contact his envoy in Vienna, Lord Paget, to ask him to press 'very earnestly' the Imperial government to appoint Prince Eugene of Savoy to command the Allied forces in Italy and oblige them to act offensively in 1692. Otherwise, the French would continue to reinforce their armies in the Netherlands from this reservoir. It was estimated that Louis XIV would field 60,000 under Luxembourg in the Netherlands supported by Boufflers with 15,000 on the frontiers of Liège. A corps of 8,000 men would guard the Lines of the Lys and the Scheldt and a further 7,000 troops would be stationed on the Moselle. Rather optimistically, the Allies hoped to have 180,000 men available for Germany and the Low Countries, with perhaps as many as 100,000 of these forming William's command in Flanders and Brabant. The Duke of Saxony was to control the Allied corps on the Rhine, consisting largely of Saxon and Brandenburg soldiers. So considerable and aggressive did the French preparations appear, that even James II was shaken from his guilt-ridden lethargy. 'There is like to be great armies in Flanders', he wrote to the Electress Sophia of Hanover on 3/13 February, 'and consequently something very considerable will happen there which may be very decisive to my concerns, and to those of all Europe.'[5]

February was dominated by a spell of exceptionally cold weather. Most of the rivers in England and the Low Countries froze, including the Thames. 'Several persons went over in different places; great snows also fell during that time which made the roads impassable. The northern post came not in a post or two, and the western mail, beyond Exeter, came not in above a week together, the snows were so deep.'[6] Although the North Sea became a solid mass of ice for some distance off the Dutch coast making it almost impossible to berth a ship, the intrepid soldiers were not distracted from their winter marauding. A party from the Allied garrison of Charleroi rode fifty kilometres to the south and burned 1500 cartloads of hay in the French magazine at Chimay.

On 26 February/8 March, King William held a conference at White-hall for all the officers of the artillery who were to go to Flanders to command the English train which, for the first time, was to be deployed in Flanders. During the last two weeks in February and the first seven days of March, the battalions and cavalry regiments of the British army which had been earmarked for service in Flanders were assembled and shipped across the North Sea as soon as the ice broke. 'Many officers and others fill the court daily to receive orders and dispatches for Flanders', reported Luttrell.[7] Sixteen regiments embarked in the Thames between Wednesday 24 February/5 March and 1/11 March, to be shipped to Ostend. Regiments from Scotland landed at Willemstadt. The train of artillery was put on board ship at Tower Wharf and disembarked in Helvoetsluys, where the guns and equipment were transferred into bilanders to sail via river and canal to the army and the siege park. One of the transports conveying 200 Danish soldiers to Ostend ran aground with the loss of fifty-five soldiers and as many women and children. On Friday 4/14 March, William III travelled by coach to Harwich where he embarked on the *Mary* yacht. He sailed in convoy on the following morning and landed at the Oranje Polder on Sunday 6/16 March after a crossing of twenty-five hours. William reached The Hague that evening, ready for a series of planning conferences.[8] All of the British infantry destined for Flanders had been shipped by 21/31 March and three troops of the Life Guard were also embarked to be in position to protect the person of the monarch throughout the coming campaign. The remainder of the cavalry was retained in England until the grass was growing strongly in the Low Countries, thereby reducing the burden on the provision contractors.

In spite of their fears of an Allied descent on the Channel coast and the 24,000 troops reserved for the invasion of England to restore James II, the French could still spare 83,960 men for their armies in the Spanish Netherlands: 31,260 cavalry, 8,400 dragoons and 44,300 infantry. A further 30,000 were to operate on the Rhine, 45,000 in Piedmont and 13,000 in Catalonia. Brabant and Flanders were becoming 'extremely thronged' with soldiers as William and Bavaria concentrated their forces ready for the opening of the campaign. Indeed, finding quarters and cantonments for the troops within convenient reach of the magazines and the provision contractors' waggon trains was not a simple matter. When Sir Charles O'Hara of the 1st Foot Guards stepped ashore at Willemstadt on 13/23 March, he could find neither money nor orders nor billets. His officers had no spare cash and he doubted whether discipline could be maintained if the men were not supported.[9] Colonel Thomas Erle's battalion received a very rude reception. Under the command of Lieutenant-Colonel Robert Freke, the battalion landed at Ostend and set out for Bruges but the French learned of their arrival and intended march and laid an ambush on the road. In turn, the battalion discovered the enemy plan and set a counter-ambuscade with such success that the battalion of 650 men drove off some 4,000 French horsemen after a sharp engagement, taking fifty prisoners and a number of horses. The animals were promptly sold and the proceeds distributed amongst the men, making a handsome addition to the bounty of twenty shillings which each man had already received for agreeing to serve in Flanders.[10] Abraham Kick from the Office of Tents and Toils, reported to Blathwayt on 30 March/9 April that the tents for the British Corps were ready and in good order.[11] As the Allies shuffled their forces into some sort of shape and tried to accommodate the growing number of troops from England and Ireland, the French remained quietly in their frontier garrisons and did not overtly reveal their intentions.[12] On 16/26 March, the Elector of Bavaria entered Brussels and William departed from The Hague three days later in order to travel to a conference with the new governor.[13]

Louis XIV left Paris on 30 April/10 May for Luxembourg's camp at Givry, having sent the ladies of his entourage to the safety of Mons, nine kilometres to the north. Louis then brought his entire court to review the combined armies of Luxembourg and Boufflers, a total of 115,000 men arrayed in two lines nearly fifteen kilometres in length. After this spectacular advertisement of French power, the armies separated and the ladies retired to the protection of Dinant.[14] Boufflers departed for Rochefort, on the River Lomme twenty-five kilometres south-east of Dinant, with 10,000 foot and 8,000 horse. From this post in the wooded Ardennes he was ideally placed to move north to the Meuse to protect the flank of any siege operations around Namur from intervention emanating from Liège, Maastricht or Cologne. Boufflers's post also provided a communication with the Marquis de Joyeuse who was to stand on the Moselle and observe the Hessian and Brandenburg forces under the Duke of Saxony. A thin guard was to be left in the Lines of the Lys and the Scheldt and the French garrisons in Dixmuyde, Furnes and Courtrai were under orders to evacuate those places if they came under attack in order not to stretch resources too far. The French siege train consisted of 196 cannon and 67 mortars.[15] Luxembourg's main army was to divide into two corps: the Marshal's own force of 66 battalions and 209 squadrons was to cover the siege and the King's Army of 40 battalions and 70 squadrons, actually commanded by Vauban, was to undertake the capture of the town.[16]

'The motions of the French' caused William and his generals to hurry into Brussels on 9/19 May and they left for the army on the next morning. William's British, Dutch and German army was concentrating around Anderlecht whilst the Elector of Bavaria's Spanish army was gathering between Ghent and Dendermonde. The royal army at Anderlecht numbered no more than thirty-two squadrons and forty battalions, less than 30,000 men. To make matters worse, the threat of an invasion of England by the 24,000 French and Irish soldiers in the Cotentin peninsula was now so alarming that William had to dispatch Lieutenant-General Thomas Talmash from Flanders to take command of the home army and three British battalions were ordered to Willemstadt to sail for England. A further six British battalions were held around Willemstadt as a reserve should the situation in England deteriorate. Already, Louis XIV's diversionary tactics were working smoothly.[17] William established his headquarters at Koekelberg, between Anderlecht and Brussels, on 12/22 May. Bavaria's army, under the temporary command of Major-General Willem van Zuylestein, consisted of just 23 battalions stationed between Dendermonde and Baasrode to guard Spanish Flanders. The only cheering news was the arrival of 2,000 Brandenburg cavalry at Malines, to the north of Brussels.[18]

With his preparations well behind those of his opponent, William could only watch in frustration and anger as Luxembourg began to manoeuvre towards the Sambre-Meuse. Intelligence reached William on 13/23 May that Luxembourg had marched that morning and gone into camp near Piéton. He was clearly aiming at either Charleroi or Namur. If it was to be the latter then William vowed that he would try to relieve it 'at all costs', but if it was to be Charleroi he would only be able 'to see what he can do'.[19] The English train of artillery arrived in Koekelberg on 13/23 May and awaited orders for deployment.[20] By 16/26 May, the situation had clarified slightly and Blathwayt wrote to the Earl of Nottingham that Charleroi could no longer be the target as Luxembourg's army had moved from Trazegnies to Gembloux. Namur or Liège were threatened. In either event, the required direction of William's relief march was now obvious and he was determined to attack.[21] Accordingly, on 17/27 May, the main Allied army marched through the streets of Brussels, over the Antwerp-Brussels Canal to Diegem where the 2,000 Brandenburg cavalry from Malines joined-up.[22] The following day saw the royal standard move to Bethlehem Abbey to the south-west of Louvain. Satisfied that both Luxembourg and Boufflers were operating on the Meuse and that only a token force had been left in the Lines of the Lys and the Scheldt, the Elector of Bavaria decided to come to William's assistance. From Dendermonde, he marched his army to the Brussels-Louvain road and camped within three kilometres of the royal army on 22 May/1 June. Five days earlier, Bavaria had sent General Hugh Mackay to William's camp with 16,000 Dutch and British troops. That same day, the Duke of Württemberg led eight Danish battalions into the Bethlehem camp. William advanced to Parck Abbey, to the south of Louvain, on 24 May/3 June and sent the heavy baggage to Arschot preparatory to marching towards Namur.[23] By this time, the French had invested Namur, opening the trenches on 19/29 May. Louis XIV's army, commanded by Vauban, blockaded the north side of the town; Ximenes, who had escorted the artillery train, occupied the region between the Sambre and the Meuse; and Boufflers moved north from Rochefort to stand along the eastern flank. Bridges were laid across the Sambre and the Meuse to link the three corps. Luxembourg covered the siege operations from a position to the north-west of Namur with his front facing directly towards Brussels. A small cavalry corps at Châtelet, south of the Sambre to the immediate south-east of Charleroi, kept an eye on that troublesome garrison.[24]

Namur lay at the confluence of the Sambre and the Meuse. The town rested on the north bank of the river junction whilst the citadel was sited on a steep, rocky outcrop in the angle formed by the meeting of the two waterways. The east side of the town was defended by the wide River Meuse with the Sambre and the citadel covering its southern edge but, to the north and west, it was overlooked by a ring of higher ground, the Heights of Bouge. To push potential attackers away from the main fortifications and to negate the disadvantage of the proximity of this feature, a line of lunettes had been constructed along the Heights of Bouge, cleverly situated on the reverse slope facilitating command of the higher ground without being silhouetted on the crest. The citadel and the main works around the town had been built under the direction of Menno van Coehoorn in 1679. A deep, wet ditch surrounded the north and west of the town linking the Sambre with the Meuse to form a complete corset of water around Namur. On the northern and western sides the Verderin Brook ran across the front of the glacis providing further aquatic protection. Opposite the system of lunettes along the Heights of Bouge, the main fortifications of the town were not elaborate, consisting of four bastions, three ravelins, the ditch and an extra ravelin guarding the strip of lowland along the shore of the Meuse. To the west, where the higher ground was more distant from the town but lacked the protection from detached works, the enceinte boasted three bastions and ravelins. The citadel was an exceptionally strong position. On its eastern and northern sides, the rocky hill on which it stood dropped precipitously into the Sambre and the Meuse. However, towards its western and southern fronts, the hill slipped more gradually towards the marshy bottom of the valley of the Sambre. The principal fort was called the Terra Nova which boasted a triple line of bastions and ravelins. Before this stood the Coehoorn Fort, attached to the Terra Nova by a series of trenches and palisades. Namur was a formidable obstacle.[25]

The garrison of Namur numbered 9,000 men, a mixture of five weak Spanish battalions and ten rather better Brandenburg and Dutch regiments. The place was commanded by Octavius de Ligne, the Prince de Barbançon. It was an unenviable assignment, the garrison being too small to man the lunettes and trenches on the Heights of Bouge, the defences of the town and the citadel. As the Allies had not expected Namur to be attacked, but had thought in terms of Liège or Charleroi, the garrison had not been adequately reinforced. However, Barbançon possessed some advantages. Coehoorn had supervised the strengthening of the citadel during the winter of 1691–92 and the engineer was present in Namur during the coming siege to advise and assist the defence. Vauban wanted to pursue a traditional, two-stage operation – the capture of the town followed by the reduction of the citadel – but the Baron de Bressé thought that the town and the citadel should be attacked simultaneously. Almost certainly, this opinion was based on intelligence about the size and effectiveness of the garrison. There was a suggestion of treachery from within the garrison and Bressé must have appreciated that the small number of defenders could have been stretched to breaking point by co-ordinated attacks on both the town and the citadel.

Whilst the French threw lines of contravallation around Namur, opened their trenches and argued about the order of assault, William remained at Parck Abbey. The arrival of some Bavarian cavalry on 25 May/4 June gave him sufficient strength to begin his forward march to challenge Luxembourg's covering army. On 26 May/5 June, he advanced to Meldert and then trudged further east to camp at Lincent on the next day. William had been unable to march due south towards Namur as Luxembourg had destroyed 'the first forage' around Gembloux and he had to move to the support of the Brandenburg corps under General Fleming and the Liègeois contingent under Count Tilly who were in danger of being cut-off from the main Allied army by Luxembourg's patrols and raiders. The 14,000 Brandenburg and Liègeois reinforcements marched into William's camp at Lincent on 28 May/7 June. From Lincent the Allied generals, who had now been joined by the Elector of Bavaria, could see that Luxembourg's army was on the march towards the River Mehaigne 'by the great dust it raised in the air, it being now dry and hot weather'. Patrols soon confirmed that the Frenchman had brought his covering army to Hemptinne and William gave orders for his quartermasters to ride forward and mark out a new camp. On 29 May/8 June, the Allied army marched towards the French. The two armies came into sight of one another at 2.00 p.m. in the afternoon and William's troops immediately took the initiative. His left wing seized all the posts along the narrow but deep River Mehaigne forcing the French to keep back from the river bank and shelter in two villages surrounded by thick hedges. Onto the quarter-mile of flat land between the French-occupied villages and the river rode some French cavalry but they were driven back by a swift cannonade. William then advanced his guns to command the bank of the river. All was now ready for the Allies to force a river crossing in the face of the enemy and orders were issued that each battalion and regiment was to build its own bridge so that the whole army could traverse the Mehaigne quickly whilst maintaining a semblance of line of battle.[26]

William was in a most promising position. With 78,000 men opposing Luxembourg's 60,000, his camp stretched from Lattine in the east, eight kilometres from Huy on the Meuse, through Soleil in the centre to Thisnes in the west. From his headquarters at Viller-le-Peuplier in the centre-front of his camp, William could see that his right flank over-lapped Luxembourg's left by a considerable margin.²⁷ His good luck was not to last and dispatches brought ill-tidings on 30 May/9 June. Blessed with fine weather and a hot sun, Boufflers and d'Humières, under the direction of Vauban, had operated with such effect against the town of Namur that Barbançon had sued for a capitulation after just eleven days of siege. Accordingly, on 26 May/5 June, the garrison was allowed forty hours within which to retire from the town into the citadel. Louis XIV took advantage of the interval to shift his camp into a pleasant meadow on the east bank of the Sambre within 500 metres of the Abbey of Marlaigne from where he commanded an excellent view up the slope to the Coehoorn Fort and the Terra Nova in the citadel. He would have a grandstand seat from which to witness the glorious capture of Namur. To the French, St. Médard enjoyed the same baleful reputation that the English attached to St. Swithin: if rain fell on St. Médard's Day then it would continue for forty days and forty nights. The saint enjoyed his feast on 29 May/8 June. A few drops fell during the day but, after sunset, the deluge began accompanied by strong winds. It might not have rained for forty days but it certainly lasted for eight; the Mehaigne turned into a raging torrent and the low-lying water-meadows on either bank became bogs eight hundred metres wide. William's regiments had begun to construct their bridges on St. Médard's Day but on 31 May/10 June, all plans to cross the Mehaigne were postponed.²⁸ Luxembourg had been saved by the weather.

The best and most obvious way by which the French could attack the citadel of Namur was from the town itself but the French had signed away this approach in the articles of surrender. Both the defenders and the attackers had agreed not to fire into or out of the town. Denied the chance to take the citadel in the rear whilst their guns and gunners were protected by the town walls, the French had to set up their batteries in the land between the Sambre and the Meuse and to the west of the Sambre. It was only at this point that the sheer physical strength of the citadel imposed itself on the French. To add to their woes, the same rains which washed away William's bridges over the Mehaigne slowed the siege operations to a crawl. Causeways of fascines had to be laid between the tents in the French camp and renewed daily as they sank into the mud. Trenches filled with water and it took three days to move cannon from one battery to another. Water-logged roads became impassable and ammunition for the siege guns and mortars had to be transported by water. The countryside around Namur was reduced to a quagmire and a serious shortage of green fodder developed; even the horses of the King's household had to eat leaves. Namur and its environs were something of a quartermaster's nightmare at the best of times being basically wooded rather than cultivated but the incessant rains made foraging impossible and horses had to be sent away from the camp into more suitable cantonments leaving the army short of transport. Waggon wheels refused to turn; only pack-horses and mules could negotiate the mud. Even worse, the earthwork fortifications more readily absorbed the solid shot from the attacking cannon instead of allowing them to bounce and ricochet. The inadequate supply of ammunition and the ineffectiveness of the fire brought the siege to a virtual halt by the end of June. Vauban approached the King with stark alternatives: either abandon the siege or break the articles of surrender and attack from the town side. Here the citadel's defences were relatively weak and the French batteries could be supplied directly from boats on the rivers guaranteeing a respectable rate of fire. Louis dithered. He did not want to nullify the agreement but he was sorely tempted.

Louis decided upon a judicious compromise. Vauban was ordered to make all the necessary preparations prior to shifting the heavy cannon to the town ramparts whilst the infantry were instructed to launch one final, legitimate assault. The Coehoorn Fort had fallen on 2/12 June after a bombardment of six days and a breach had been effected in the 'Priest's Cap', a small work close to the Terra Nova. In response to the royal call for one last effort, French infantry attacked the covered way of the Priest's Cap and gained a lodgement, the garrison withdrawing into the Terra Nova after a single volley. The foot soldiers spent the night filling the ditch between the Priest's Cap and a partial breach in the hornwork of the Terra Nova. Seemingly on his own initiative, a lone French soldier wandered forward to reconnoitre the small breach in the hornwork and, to his surprise, discovered a single sentry, half asleep. It appeared that the garrison of the hornwork retired every night into an underground passage to shelter from the rain and the cannon and mortar fire. They customarily left just one man to watch over the breach which they thought was insufficiently advanced for the French to risk an attack. The enterprising Frenchman reported his discovery and led back a lieutenant, a sergeant and twenty grenadiers. The dozing sentry was captured and persuaded to lead the Frenchmen to his sleeping comrades in return for his life. These unfortunates were put to the sword. Two mines, which had been intended to render the French assault on the breach most uncomfortable, were defused and the hornwork was then searched but no more defenders were found. Rapidly, the French reinforced the hornwork in expectation of a major counter-attack at dawn. None came. Instead, the Prince de Barbançon panicked and ran up the white flag asking for a parley. It was 21 June/1 July, the twenty-seventh day of the siege. The garrison agreed terms on the same day and marched out of the breach at 10.00 a.m. on 22 June/2 July. Louis breathed a sigh of relief and went off to celebrate with his ladies at Dinant. It had been a close run thing. The French army was exhausted and if the garrison had held on for a further week or ten days then the attackers might well have been obliged to lift the siege as they were very short of forage and their logistics were grinding to a halt in the endless downpours. Luckily for the French, the weather proved to be a more substantial opponent than Barbançon who conducted a pusillanimous defence of one of the strongest citadels in the Netherlands.[29]

Out of sixty French engineering officers who had been employed at Namur, only twenty-two survived the siege. The French army lost 2,500 men killed and 3,000 wounded. Their 151 cannon and mortars fired 50,000 solid shot and 11,000 bombs. Louis appointed the Comte de Guiscard as the first French Governor of Namur and provided him with a garrison of twenty-five battalions. His immediate task was to level the siege works, repair the fortifications and convince the citizens that French rule was just as unpleasant as they had feared. In mid-July, the garrison was labouring 'night and day' on the works and building up considerable magazines of ammunition and provisions. Guiscard sent all the Allied sick and wounded out of the town and a number of the principal citizens left voluntarily. To the Allies, it seemed that the French expected William to launch an immediate counter-attack on Namur.[30]

During the siege, William and Luxembourg had continued to observe one another across the swollen Mehaigne. Numerous French deserters, as many as two hundred per day, came into the Allied camp to tell of the shortages of food and forage being endured by both Luxembourg's army and the siege troops as the French steadily devoured the country between the Meuse and the Mehaigne. Until the fall of the town of Namur Luxembourg was numerically inferior to William but his problems eased with its fall. The siege of the citadel required fewer troops and the surplus were released from the siege lines, along with their supplies, to bolster Luxembourg. Even if the weather made William impotent to interrupt the siege, the garrison of Charleroi did its best to intercept enemy provision convoys. Because of the weather and the lack of forage around Namur, the French had to provision both the covering army and the besieging forces from their magazines at Dinant, Philippeville, Mons and Maubeuge. These convoys, numbering between fifty and two hundred waggons, required heavy escorts in the face of almost daily menace from the energetic soldiers from Charleroi. On 6/16 June, William wrote to Heinsius that he intended to shift his camp to the right on the following day to see whether Luxembourg could be unbalanced and an alternative method of crossing the Mehaigne discovered.[31] This move on 7/17 June brought the centre of the Allied position to Ramillies with the right at Perwez and the left at the ford of Branchon on the Mehaigne. William seemed to be attempting to manoeuvre around Luxembourg's left wing in order to force him into an engagement. The Frenchman responded by coming closer to the Mehaigne at Boneffe on 9/19 June but he placed his new camp behind a wood and some higher ground so that he was out of sight of the Allies. By this stage, Namur had fallen and the garrison was penned into the citadel. This provided Luxembourg with reinforcements from the shortened siege lines but also gave him a freer operational hand. Before Namur citadel, Louis XIV's siege corps was sheltered behind the Sambre – Luxembourg no longer had to worry about the safety of French soldiers to the north and west of the Sambre-Meuse. Whereas Luxembourg's task grew easier, William's became more difficult. To be effective and interrupt the siege, William now had to march around Luxembourg's left flank, cross the Sambre in the face of serious opposition and then attack the royal siege camp. Although this was a near impossibility, William sent Count Tilly across the Meuse at Huy. His 6,000 horse were to ride down the east bank and attack the bridge of boats below Namur. The French soon learned of his presence and Tilly withdrew in the face of mounting opposition.[32]

On 11/12 June, Luxembourg decamped and moved a little closer to Namur, taking a position at Gembloux on the River Onoz, a left bank tributary of the Sambre. The French right was now close to the Allied right. William responded on 12/22 June by marching across Luxembourg's front and half-round his left flank to Sombreffe, but the French marshal pivotted on Gembloux and stretched his front as far south as Mazy. William's new camp reached from Sombreffe, through Ligny to Fleurus, his right slightly over-lapping the French left. To correct this imbalance, Luxembourg ordered Boufflers from Namur to take post at Auvelais on the Sambre and bridges were thrown over that river at Jemeppe and Floreffe to link the two corps. Despite slightly altering his stance westwards to Mellet on 14/24 June, William was thwarted. His sole compensation was the report that a French convoy of 130 waggons loaded with wine, meal and oats *en route* to Namur had fallen into the hands of a raiding party from the garrison of Charleroi.[33] Privately, in two letters written whilst the army was based on Ramillies, Blathwayt admitted the hopelessness of his master's cause.

> The early setting out of the French at land and the strength of their armies have made it impossible for the King to attack them with prudence, and the base of the town of Namur have given the French the advantages. We can hardly overcome so soon. All this is occasioned by the backwardness of the Emperor and the German princes to send their forces to the Rhine whereby some diversion might be made and the French have not the opportunity of drawing all theirs into these parts.

Against 120,000 Frenchmen in the Low Countries, 20,000 of whom were before Namur citadel, William's 80,000 were insufficient. Salvation could come from only two sources. Perhaps the German armies would make a timely demonstration and divert French forces from the Netherlands to the Rhine. Failing that, there remained the possibility that the 23 battalions in England could mount an operation against the French Channel or Atlantic coasts large enough to cause Louis concern about the defence of his homeland. However, considering the mess that was being made of the administration and command of the projected descent, this was a forlorn hope.[34]

During a rearward forage towards Trazegnies on 20/30 June, the sound of firing from the direction of Namur informed the Allies that the citadel was continuing to resist.[35] News of the surrender reached the camp at Mellet on 22 June/2 July.[36] William had been unlucky but also out-generalled. Almost within sight of the besieged city, he had been unable to manoeuvre Luxembourg away from the natural defences of the Mehaigne. Some armchair generals thought that the King could, and ought to have done more to try to relieve Namur.[37] The weather had saved Luxembourg until the fall of the town but, thereafter, his superior numbers and greater skill had given him a full command of the situation. William's only chance had rested in forcing the Frenchman to a battle but he was careful to post his camp in strong positions and William dared not risk attack. The garrison of Namur was allowed to march out with reasonable honours of war and was conducted to Maastricht and Louvain. When he reached the latter town, the Prince de Barbançon was examined about his conduct at Namur and asked to justify his premature surrender of the citadel. He blamed Vaudemont who, said Barbançon, had been negligent in providing sufficient stores and ammunition. This was almost certainly rubbish – William did not believe it – as Namur had fallen not through want of provisions but because the governor had lost his nerve when the hornwork of the Terra Nova was seized by a coup de main. In fact, the careless practices exercised in that hornwork suggest that Barbançon was a lazy and incompetent commander who should not have been entrusted with such a vital appointment. According to Robert Wolseley, the English envoy extraordinaire to the Court of Brussels, William had asked for the replacement of Barbançon before the 1692 campaign had opened 'as he knew he was not fit to be trusted'. Unfortunately, the patronage lay with the Governor of the Spanish Netherlands. Castañaga, who had appointed Barbançon, had been relieved and his successor, the Elector of Bavaria, was too inexperienced to heed William's warning. The blame fell squarely, and unjustifiably, on Vaudemont.

'Handsome, dashing, witty and urbane,' Charles Henri de Lorraine, the Prince de Vaudemont, had been born in 1649, the illegitimate son of Duke Charles IV of Lorraine. He was a brother of Duke Charles V, the Imperial general and saviour of Vienna from the Turks in 1683. He entered the Spanish army and first came to William's attention by his successful command of the rearguard of the Dutch-Spanish army at the Battle of Seneffe in 1674. As he matured, he became one of only five generals whom William was prepared to trust with independent authority – the others were Marlborough, Waldeck, Ginckel and the Duke of Leinster. A personal friend of both William and the Duke of Luxembourg, Vaudemont had been presented with a capacious palace in Brussels by his Dutch patron. Between 1688 and 1697, Vaudemont was the commander-in-chief of the Spanish forces in the Netherlands.[38] Suddenly finding himself the object of the odium of the people of Brussels, who were incensed by the loss of Namur, Vaudemont prudently retired to Aachen to take the waters for the alleviation of his rheumatism. There were rumours that an attempt might have been made on his life had he remained in Brussels.[39]

William was angry and uncertain. Deeply hurt and humiliated by the loss of Namur, he searched for instant revenge. He toyed with the notion of launching an immediate counter-attack on Namur but this was impossible in the face of Luxembourg's dispositions and the fact that there was no forage within an operational radius to the north and west of the confluence of the Sambre-Meuse. He then considered trying to seize Mons by a coup de main. This made more sense. Its fortifications were still relatively weak, indeed there was still an unrepaired breach from the siege of the previous year, it was garrisoned by Swiss mercenaries and the inhabitants were uneasy under French rule wanting a return to Spanish suzerainty. During 22 June/2 July, a strong detachment was made of sixty men and three officers from every battalion in the army, ostensibly to cover a grand forage on the following day. This attempt at spreading disinformation was immediately negated by the construction of numerous scaling ladders. During the night of 23 June/3 July – 24 June/4 July, the force of 12,000 men marched towards Mons and halted at 1.00 a.m., one hour short of its objective. The command of the operation had been given to Ferdinand Wilhelm, the Duke of Württemberg-Neustadt, a lieutenant-general in the Danish Army who directed the Danish contingent within the Allied forces.[40] On resuming his march towards Mons, Württemberg encountered French outposts. The Comte de Vertillac, the Governor of Mons, had received news of Württemberg's expedition and had positioned Lieutenant-General the Marquis de la Valette with 52 squadrons of horse in readiness. Württemberg realised that the game was up and trudged back to Mellet. The operation had been doomed from the outset. One Grandval, or Jaquet, the secretary to the Elector of Bavaria, was a French spy. After the Battle of Steenkirk when he was tortured, he admitted having sent twenty-three letters to the Duke of Luxembourg since the beginning of the 1692 campaign describing the movements, encampments and intentions of the Allied armies. For each epistle he received one hundred louis d'ors, about £80 sterling. He was discovered when he dropped one of his incriminating letters which was picked up by a peasant and found its way to the tent of the Elector of Bavaria. He was 'turned' and employed as a double-agent to the advantage of the Allies on the eve of Steenkirk, but after that action he was court-martialled, convicted and hanged from a tree at the head of the army.[41] It was Grandval who had informed Luxembourg of the attempt on Mons. The French marshal had rapidly reinforced the garrison with cavalry and alerted the governor. When Württemberg arrived all hopes of surprise had vanished and he had no option but to abandon the enterprise. On the return march, two British colonels, Sir Robert Douglas and Francis Fergus O'Farrell, lost their way in the dark and fell in with an enemy cavalry patrol which promptly took them into Mons as prisoners.[42]

William now had no alternative but to attempt to salvage something from the campaign by seeking a general action. Morale was low. French cavalry swarmed around the camp at Mellet, cutting off foragers and messengers, and it was only safe to venture forth in large parties.[43] The initial requirement was to regroup in a safe position from which the army could forage, gather reinforcements and restore its balance before beginning to manoeuvre against Luxembourg. In wet weather the artillery was sent north to Genappe on the Dyle on 25 June/5 July and the remainder of the army followed on the next day. The new camp was guarded by woods to either flank and the Bois de Soignes stood in its rear. The battalion tents were ranged across a cluster of low hills. Although Genappe offered plentiful forage and a shortened supply line to Brussels, William had to weaken his army by dispatching Tilly and Fleming with the Brandenburg and Liègeois corps back to Liège which was now open to attack after the fall of Namur.[44] Luxembourg's army was also in need of rest. The wear and tear of duty in the flooded trenches before Namur had debilitated the men and the shortage of forage had weakened the horses. In addition, the French had to find 25 battalions to garrison Namur and a further 41 battalions were required to reinforce the French armies on the Rhine. Luxembourg dismissed plans for more offensive action and settled down to fight a defensive campaign supported from the resources of Spanish territory. This, he thought, would be best achieved by manoeuvreing closer to the support of the Lines of the Lys and the Scheldt.[45] He also wanted to come north of the Sambre to prevent the Allies from attacking Mons and to consume the forage around that vulnerable city. He crossed the Sambre and marched south of Charleroi to Ham-sur-Heure. From this familiar staging post, the French soldiers re-bridged the Sambre between Thuin and La Buissière and camped at Merbes-St. Marie. On 29 June/9 July, Luxembourg pressed on to Roulx before camping at Soignies on 1/11 July. His lines faced to the north-east, with Naast on his right wing, Chausée-Notre Dame to his left and the small town of Soignies to his front. From this camp, the Comte d'Harcourt was sent with a corps to observe General Fleming, who was positioned on the Meuse near Huy. Boufflers commanded a flying camp between Luxembourg's post and the Sambre to watch the movements of William's main army but also to reinforce Luxembourg should the occasion arise.[46] Luxembourg had moved to Soignies to cover Mons and be close to his major magazines and the Lines of the Lys and the Scheldt but he also intended to threaten Brussels knowing that William dared not march to the Meuse to attempt the recapture of Namur if his opponent could then advance upon Brussels during his absence. Luxembourg had been twisted into this expedient as the countryside of the Condroz and the Marlagne had been so wasted during the operations against Namur that major French troops movements were out of the question. Luxembourg could not have defended Namur. If William had known this, he might well have risked a counter-siege.

However, William responded more conventionally. Expecting the campaign to develop into Flanders, Count Hornes travelled to Ghent with 10 battalions and some cavalry to secure the forage for future Allied use. At Genappe, the weather cleared, 'for these two days fair which is more, I think, than has happened since we are come into the field'. Despite the more cheering metereological outlook, Blathwayt could see 'little prospect of any success. The rest of the allies being so supine as to leave the whole weight upon the King and the States and now begin to make an improvable noise upon the Rhine more for the sake of winter quarters and the formal answering their obligation to the Empire than for any harm they can hope for.'[47] Between 7/17 July and 10/20 July, William reviewed the English and Scottish horse and foot at Genappe. Then the incessant rains started once more. The King travelled to Malines in dreadful weather on 8/18 July to consult with the Elector of Brandenburg, who was lodging at Turnhout. He returned to Genappe in the same, miserable conditions but, at least, the downpour extinguished a fire which had started in a pile of forage close to some ammunition waggons. Between 16/26 July and 19/29 July, no forage orders were issued, a certain sign that a change of camp was imminent. It was not before time, as the Bois de Soignes between Genappe and Brussels was full of French cavalry patrols. The bridging train left the camp on 20/30 July and orders were given for the rest of the army to march at dawn on the following day. Yet again in that awful summer, the rain teemed down as the army wound out of Genappe heading for Halle to the south-west of Brussels. The artillery train, having left camp at 6.00 a.m., bogged down on a steep hill near Ophain and had to stay where it was for the night, the gunners sheltering by the roadside. Sharp orders from one of William's aides-de-camp on the morning of 22 July/1 August to get the guns moving had their effect but the waggons attached to the artillery train were obliged to take a different road, the one which the main army had used on the previous day. It was a sea of knee-deep mud and the progress of the transport was not assisted by some Hanoverian troops who marched across the front of the train imposing further delay.[48] Not until late in the evening did the artillery lumber into the camp at Halle. On the same day, Luxembourg edged north to Enghien.[49]

In the absence on a significant diversion in Germany or Savoy, there was no prospect of William attempting a siege. His sole chance of success lay in forcing Luxembourg to battle. Given the cautious and skilful nature of his opponent, surprise appeared to be William's best option. The coming encounter was not the result of subtle manoeuvre by William but was contrived from opportunism: the march from Genappe to Halle had been undertaken to find new foraging grounds,[50] whilst Luxembourg's move to Enghien could not have been accurately predicted. However, the series of marches brought the armies close together. The Allied camp stood in two lines on the west bank of the River Senne, the left resting on the village of Tubise and the right on the main road from Brussels to Halle. Lembeek, the royal headquarters, lay in the left rear and Halle, the billet of the Elector of Bavaria, was towards the right rear. Fifteen kilometres to the west was Luxembourg. His camp occupied a long and prominent ridge, the watershed of the drainage systems of the Senne and the Dender. The ground between the opposing armies was basically a plateau which had been etched by a series of small streams creating fairly steep-sided valleys, ravines or defiles in contemporary parlance. The resultant landscape was one of the low, rounded hills. The largest ravine belonged to the Senne, running from the right wing of Luxembourg's line of battle to the left flank of William's encampment at Tubise. The valleys ran roughly east to west, their broader reaches towards William's position and the steeper and narrower aspects close to the French camp. Luxembourg's right was advanced to the little village of Steenkirk on the north bank of the Senne. His right flank then stretched in a north-westerly direction to the valley of a small brook. The centre reached from this feature to the village of Marq and the left was anchored on Biévène. The whole position was twelve kilometres long and the centre sheltered behind the unfortified town of Enghien. Much of the plateau was wooded and the extensive Bois de Triou covered the front of Luxembourg's left and centre rendering those sectors virtually invulnerable. More inviting was the French right wing where the woods gave way to a landscape of small fields enclosed within thick hawthorn hedges. Four defiles, containing streams, ran east at right angles from the French right. The slope from the valley of the Senne upto the Plaine St. Martin, on which the extreme French right above Steenkirk was positioned, was relatively steep.

Luxembourg had chosen a strong camp site but it was not a terrain on which he would have chosen to do battle. The major advantage, from William's point of view, was that the country favoured infantry, the strongest feature of his army, rather than cavalry, which was the French strength. With his preponderance of horse, Luxembourg would have preferred a flat and open battlefield. By any stretch of the imagination, the selection of the Enghien position for a attack was a desperate throw. William could only assault the extreme right wing of the French line with the aim of over-lapping it and achieving a local success. To expect more was unrealistic. Even this modest ambition was wrecked by William's carelessness and lack of professionalism. He did not rec-

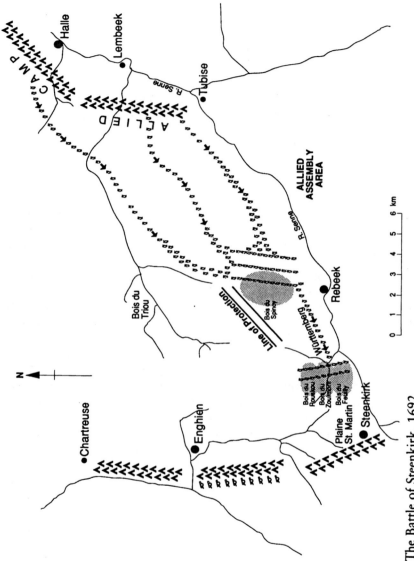

The Battle of Steenkirk, 1692

onnoitre the ground and when his foot marched towards Steenkirk they found the land more broken, more heavily wooded and more enclosed than they had anticipated. As a result only a partial deployment proved to be possible and the eventual attack occurred on a very narrow frontage. It was the measure of William's desperation that he was prepared to act against the advice of the Dutch Field Deputies by risking a general action at such an unpromising place as Steenkirk. Only the Elector of Bavaria supported him, anxious to protect Brussels from attack.[51]

One way to make the odds more even was to employ subterfuge. Jaquet, Bavaria's treacherous secretary, was required to perform a task for the Allies before he met his end. He wrote a letter at William's dictation on 23 July/2 August which informed Luxembourg that on the following day the Allied army would undertake a grand forage towards his lines. The information from the reliable master-spy was swallowed and Luxembourg was very slow to respond when the attack developed towards his right flank.[52] On the evening of 23 July/2 August, William issued orders for the following day. He planned to march his infantry in three columns, from his right, centre and left, some ten kilometres to a point between the Senne and the Bois de Spinoy. Here, the right and centre columns were to form into line of battle facing to the north-west to observe Luxembourg's centre and left and to cover the open northern flank of William's left-hand column which was detailed to undertake the main attack against Luxembourg's right on the Plaine St. Martin. William's own left flank was to rest on the Senne. Although he did not commit his precise objectives to paper, William can only have been aiming at a local, tactical victory sufficient to oblige Luxembourg to withdraw from the Enghien position. Interestingly, William's scheme of attack looked forward to the 'oblique order' of the mid-eighteenth century.

The artillery began the Allied march at 2.00 a.m. but the lack of reconnaissance condemned the guns to a route that was so poor and 'rotten' that they could not deploy in time to take a major part in the ensuing battle. During the night and the previous evening six battalions had laboured to prepare the roads and routes along which the three infantry columns were to march. At 4.00 a.m. on 24 July/3 August, the Duke of Württemberg led the advance guard of six battalions, 4 British and 2 Danish, out of the camp along the most southerly route. His column was preceded by 400 pioneers who did their best to clear a path. The remainder of the infantry marched at day-break. At much the same time as Württemberg left the Halle position, Luxembourg advanced some of his infantry to line the hedges and ditches to his right front and brought forward some cannon. Even if the Allies were only conducting a grand forage, it was still a good idea to disrupt their activities as much as possible. He also sent patrols towards Tubise which reported the movements of William's left-hand column as well as indentifying a fake foraging expedition travelling southwards in the direction of Ronquières. All of this made Luxembourg sufficiently suspicious to ride over to his right wing in the middle of the morning to carry out a personal reconnaissance.

At eleven o'clock, Württemberg's advance guard cleared the cover of the woods and appeared before the French right wing at the Bois de Rouskou. Even at this late stage, such a small force might have been no more than an infantry cover for a forage but Luxembourg thought otherwise. As Württemberg went into line of battle, placing three battalions north of a stream in the Bois de Zoulmont and the other three to the south in the Bois de Feuilly, the French troops poured out of their tents into an impromptu line of battle. Luxembourg sent orders for his left wing to advance clear of the twin rows of tents and form a line of battle facing east with nine battalions thrown obliquely to mask Enghien itself. The French centre and right were pulled down towards the Plaine St. Martin and thrown into *ad hoc* battle formations, eventually to be seven lines deep on the extreme right flank by Steenkirk. Because of their haste, the French line of battle was a piecemeal affair and lacked co-ordination. However, Luxembourg's men had the advantage of high ground and they were protected from a full-blooded assault by the cluster of woods, hedges, ditches and enclosures. Above all, the Allies could only attack frontally. The River Senne prevented the French right from being out-flanked whereas there was always the danger that the unengaged French left could descend and irritate the more open right flank of William's army.

As Württemberg stood awaiting reinforcements, the Allied infantry began to debouch from the woods between the Bois de Spinoy and the Bois de Stoquoy but then a combination of bad planning and poor staff work halted their progress. Lieutenant-General Hendrik, Graaf van Solms-Braunfels, a great-uncle of William III, had been placed in charge of the complicated process whereby the three marching columns deployed into line of battle as they cleared the cover of the woods. It was a difficult assignment but through either incompetence or sheer bad luck he allowed a body of cavalry to move ahead of the infantry in one of the approach defiles despite William's strict instructions that the foot were to be in the van and all the horse in the rear. The narrow road at the point of deployment, where physically the three approach roads became one, was rapidly choked with cavalrymen and the infantry battalions had to break ranks and filter past as best they could. Not only did this misfortune considerably slow the deployment but, even worse, the line of battle was formed too far from the French position. Solms brought his infantry into double line two and a half kilometres from Luxembourg's battalions, when he should have pressed on in column whilst the French were still recovering from the shock of finding themselves under attack. William had not envisaged the horse taking any part in the offensive action; they were only to be brought onto the field to cover a withdrawal. Luxembourg took every advantage of his opponents' embarrassment. The infantry of his right tumbled out of their tents into a double line of battle just in front of their encampment and dismounted dragoons rushed to plug the gap between the banks of the Senne and the slope upto the Plaine St. Martin. Guns were hurried from the artillery park, which was situated in the rear of the middle of the French position, and additional battalions were drawn from the centre and pushed into the line to reinforce the extreme right flank. Self-possessed and confident, Luxembourg instructed his infantry to fell trees and create breastworks to strengthen the natural defences of the hedges and the ditches.

By midday, seven battalions had managed to struggle through the traffic jam to join Württemberg's original vanguard, giving him a total of nearly 8,000 men. He also made use of the unwanted cavalry and formed a brigade from all the British horse then with the Allied field army to cover his rear and right flank. Württemberg began a frontal attack with all his battalions in a single line at 1.00 p.m. His closest supporting infantry was still two kilometres away and arrayed in battalia which meant that when they did advance to his aid they would only be able to march very slowly across the broken and difficult ground. The attack was uphill, through hedges, over ditches and into the teeth of French musketry and cannon fire. Württemberg's battalions rapidly lost their linear formations and the units soon became separated from their neighbours. The Cameronians attacked behind a thin screen of soldiers from the Royal Scots and the English Guards. They advanced through a small wood, probably the Bois de Zoulmont, before they reached a hedge which they were ordered 'to line'. The French came upto the other side of the thicket and the fighting appears to have occurred through and over this hedge, musket barrels virtually muzzle-to-muzzle. We can only assume that the Cameronians fought in the 'street way'. The battalion which was to have supported the flank of the Cameronians retired too early and the French brought up a regiment of dragoons 'without boots or shoes' which the Scotsmen initially mistook for Dutchmen, 'their apparel being the same'. Despite the increasing weight of numbers against them, the Cameronians continued to line the hedge until they were ordered to retire. It was during the withdrawal that the battalion suffered the majority of its casualties as the soldiers struggled through 'thick, thorny hedges' whilst under fire from the French dragoons and artillery. Once the regiment reached the safety of the Bois de Zoulmont, it rallied and reorganised but there was no French pursuit. Out of their 600 men and 40 officers, the Cameronians lost their colonel, the Earl of Angus, Lieutenant-Colonel John Fullerton, Major Daniel Kerr, two captains, two lieutenants, one ensign, two non-commissioned officers and 91 other ranks killed and 109 wounded. One third of the battalion had fallen.[53]

The experience of the Cameronians was repeated along Württemberg's thin line. The tenacity and courage of the British and Danish infantry almost carried them into the French camp and it took the personal exhortation of the Duke of Luxembourg and his senior officers to stiffen the foot and dragoons who were now massed seven lines deep on the Plaine St. Martin. After the repulse of the augmented vanguard, further progress depended upon Württemberg being substantially reinforced, or a fresh attack developing towards Luxembourg's vulnerable centre. Neither option was taken. Twice, Württemberg sent messengers asking Solms for additional battalions but he refused to take action. Quite why he denied Württemberg the much-needed support is not clear. He was 'a proud, haughty man and not at all grateful' to the British and it seems that he disliked Württemberg and coveted the command of the vanguard for himself.[54] Solms certainly had no affection for the British and was perhaps somewhat indifferent to their mounting casualties.[55] Although Solms had his faults and it is possible that he was influenced by pique against the British and Württemberg, there are more convincing explanations for his failure to order forward reinforcements. As we have seen, the main body of the infantry was deploying from column into line of battle about two kilometres behind Württemberg, too distant to offer prompt assistance. Rapid movement in line of battle over the very rough ground was impossible. Having prematurely committed his men to line of battle, Solms's only realistic option would have been to re-deploy the lines into column, advance and then deploy once more into linear formation. This would have consumed hours, not minutes. In contrast, Württemberg had taken his men in column as close as he dared to the French camp before going into line.

Secondly, the planning blunder which had allowed the cavalry to march ahead of some of the infantry meant that the first available troops to reinforce Württemberg happened to be horse rather than foot. Solms did order the horse forward to support the vanguard. The trouble was that cavalry were quite useless on the Plaine St. Martin and could do nothing but form-up and wait in Württemberg's rear. Dismounted dragoons might have been more efficacious but were unavailable. William, as commander-in-chief, was back with the columns before they debouched from the defiles, sufficiently close to see what was going wrong but not near enough to influence events. According to one of his pages, William 'in great passion bit his nails, and with tears in his eyes said, that he could not have his orders obeyed'. However, there is no record of the King riding forward to take personal command. Neither did Solms show any inclination to go upto Württemberg's position to seek clarification or to reconnoitre. Solms can be charged with incompetence, a lack of professionalism and a shortage of imagination and initiative but it is hard to sustain the accusation that he allowed the British to die on the Plaine St. Martin out of hatred and callousness. Much of the dirt subsequently thrown at Solms was *ex post facto* and came about through the campaign of political generals like Marlborough and Talmash to rid the British army of Dutch domination. Lieutenant John Blackader of the Cameronians, who was in the hardest part of the action, merely noted that Solms could not advance his infantry through 'the narrow ways'. British and Danish soldiers died before Steenkirk village because the command arrangements and the staff work of the army were amateur. William and Solms were attempting to fight a battle with their army in a long column of march when by both training and design it was supposed to engage in a long linear formation. It was a battle fought from political desperation and operational frustration ending in a total mess.[56]

The weight of the French army proved too great for Württemberg's thirteen shattered battalions and they began to fall back down the hill towards their starting points in the Bois du Rouskou and the Bois de Zoulmont. Still Solms could not push sizeable bodies of infantry forward and although there was cavalry behind Württemberg's centre they could not charge over the enclosed ground. The 4th Dragoons, Eppinger's Dutch Dragoons and the Horse Grenadier Guards came forward, dismounted and assumed infantry positions to the right of the Bois du Rouskou. This small measure of assistance helped Württem-

berg's right wing to swing backwards whilst a Lüneburg battalion
performed a similar supporting role for the left wing. There was no
attempt to pursue Württemberg's tired battalions from the field. The
French had been taken by surprise and were neither deployed in the
correct formation nor in the right frame of mind to consider pursuit.
The enclosed ground would also have made pursuit impractical and
costly. As Württemberg was conducting the remains of his command
away from Steenkirk, Luxembourg began to move his unengaged left
wing closer to Enghien. For a short time, there appeared the danger
that the Frenchman might try to attack the open right flank of Württemberg's withdrawal. To combat this, the cavalry which had waited help-
lessly in the rear of Württemberg's original attack was shifted half-right
as a flank guard. This was sufficient to stop Luxembourg's half-hearted
scheme.

William now formed 'a line of protection' facing to the north-west,
composed of the infantry battalions that had finally struggled through
the defiles. This line was designed to prevent Luxembourg from interfering with the retirement of the vanguard as it deployed out of line
into column ready for the return journey through the defiles. French
cannon played upon these covering battalions with some effect but the
enemy foot and horse kept their distance. At around 7.00 p.m. the 'line
of protection' began to file off into the 'narrow ways' under the cover of
a rearguard consisting of the grenadier companies from all the engaged
battalions. Occasionally the rearguard faced about to discourage the
French from pressing too closely upon the rear of the retreating columns
but there was no systematic attempt at disruption and the coming of
darkness brought the battle to an end. By 10.00 p.m. the Allied army
was back in its camp.[57] Considering that less than half the infantry in
William's army had been engaged, the casualties were extremely heavy.
Müller suggests that 5,286 officers and men were killed and 2,353 were
wounded, whilst Atkinson has 4,469 officers and men killed and 3,452
wounded.[58] Seventeenth century casualty statistics do not lend themselves to dogmatic interpretation; that both the French and the Allies
each lost around 8,000 men is a sufficient testimony to the ferocity of
the fighting on the Plaine St. Martin.

Once back in his camp, William ordered a two-day forage towards
Haute Croix and then settled down to write to the Earl of Nottingham
instructing him to co-ordinate some sort of operation in the English
Channel against the French coast. Any demonstration, anywhere after
the humiliation of Steenkirk – St. Malo, Dunkirk or Calais – it did not
matter but something had to be rescued from the mire of 1692.[59] In

the interim, the battlefield was cleared up. The eight guns which had been abandoned by the Allies as they withdrew were recovered without opposition and the wounded were piled into waggons and jolted away to Brussels on 26 July/5 August. Luxembourg pulled back to Ghiselenghien on 1/11 August.[60]

The French withdrawal was observed by Allied cavalry patrols which then entered the old camp at Enghien and discovered a number of wounded prisoners who had been abandoned in the town.[61] Another retirement on 2/12 August brought the French army to Lessines where Luxembourg made a detachment of 30,000 charged with watching the coast around Dunkirk and Calais in case the Allies attempted a descent on this region. Despite Luxembourg's retirement towards the Lines of the Lys and the Scheldt and the threat of an amphibious operation against the French rear, William remained extremely nervous and cautious. The twin blows of Namur and Steenkirk had drained his self-confidence. Not until 9/19 August did the Allied army move from Halle towards the north-west taking a camp about St. Kwintens-Lennik and St. Martins-Lennik, some fifteen kilometres west-south-west from Brussels, a site 'remarkable only for the retrenchments which remain there, which Prince Waldeck caused to be made some time before the army's breaking up in 1690'. This movement had been dictated by the requirement for fresh foraging grounds rather than by any aggressive intent. The following day saw the Allied army inch forward to Ninove on the Dender.[62] During this march, the artillery and heavy baggage were routed via St. Pieters-Leeuw whilst the army took the main road through Peppingen and Leerbeek. Although Luxembourg was encamped at Lessines, French cavalry patrols hovered around the Allied army in sufficient strength to attempt a surprise attack on a Saxe-Gotha cavalry regiment which was camped in an isolated position along the west bank of the Senne on the night of 2/12 August.[63]

After a demoralising campaign, the tide turned partially in William's favour during the autumn. The attempt to organise an attack on St. Malo had been called off releasing 12,000 British troops for the Low Countries. Complete with their own train of artillery and bomb vessels, these forces arrived at Ostend and Nieuport between 21/31 August and 22 August/1 September. The Duke of Leinster was in command. William dispatched Thomas Talmash from the main army with 8,000 British soldiers to give his grace a corps of 20,000 men.[64] This improvement in Flanders was reflected on the Meuse. The Brandenburg and Liègeois troops concentrated in the Principality of Liège gathered artillery as if they intended to make an attempt on Namur. Although Fleming and

Tilly were not strong enough to risk such a manoeuvre, their forward
deployment had the affect of pinning the French garrisons along the
Sambre and the Meuse and preventing them from reinforcing Luxembourg's army at Lessines.

On 14/24 August, the heavy baggage was sent to Ghent and the
Allied army marched on the following day. As the Allies left Ninove,
Luxembourg marched from his camp between Grammont and Lessines
and the two armies moved on parallel tracks towards the Scheldt. Again,
William was extremely careless as his left flank was open to serious
attack throughout the day but Luxembourg did not interfere. That
night, William camped at St. Lievens-Houtem, some fifteen kilometres
south-east of Ghent. At 6.30 a.m. on 16/26 August, the Allies crossed
the Scheldt at Gavere and pressed on across the very 'close ground'
between the Scheldt and the Lys, full of trees and defiles, which forced
the soldiers to march slowly. That night's rest was taken at Nazareth,
south of Ghent. Count Hornes joined William from Ghent on 17/27
August and the army marched westwards to cross the Lys at Deynze
and go into camp between that town and Grammene. A short march
on 18/28 August brought the army into its pre-selected position at
Drongen on the western edge of Ghent. Luxembourg had meanwhile
crossed the Scheldt and taken post at Harelbeke, close to the guns of
Courtrai and in supporting distance of the Lines of the Lys and the
Scheldt.[65] From this strong camp by Ghent, William put into action his
plan to make some progress in Flanders, culminating, he hoped, in an
attempt on Dunkirk by Leinster and Talmash's British corps.

Brigadier George Ramsay took six British battalions to Bruges on
21/31 August where he was joined on the following day by Talmash
with five British and five Dutch battalions. This force marched through
Bruges on 24 August/3 September, travelled along the Ostend-Bruges
Canal, turned left onto the Nieuport Canal and camped at Oudenburg.
Leinster had come ashore at Ostend with fifteen battalions on 22
August/1 September and had journeyed to Middelkerke, between
Ostend and Nieuport. Talmash advanced to Newendam, a small Spanish fort outside Nieuport, and sent the Dutch Colonel Jacques Noyelles
to occupy the town of Furnes. On the following day, Talmash moved
to within cannon shot of Furnes and Leinster brought his corps to Oost-
Duinkerke (Ost-Dunkirk), no more than two kilometres from Talmash's
position. Talmash and Leinster were now almost ready to launch an
attack down the coastal plain towards Dunkirk in conjunction with a
bombardment squadron drawn from the British and Dutch navies.
Leinster's task was not enviable. Dunkirk contained a large garrison, a

separate corps was camped outside its gates and Boufflers stood with 30,000 at Bergues, ten kilometres to the south. The Duke had to entrench his camp at Oost-Duinkerke to guard against French patrols moving through the sand dunes between his right flank and the sea whilst more enemy parties harassed the left of Talmash's position around Furnes. The British corps was in an isolated and exposed stance but, just as during the summer of 1692 when he had been in command of the projected descent on the French coast, Leinster was happier in pointing out difficulties than in proposing and executing solutions.[66] Despite Leinster's whining, partially supported by Coehoorn who considered that there was a great deal of preparatory work to be done before an attack on Dunkirk could be launched, William ordered the reluctant duke to march on Dunkirk and attack in conjunction with the naval squadron 'if at all possible'.[67] Lord Galway also began to express doubts. He knew from experience that Allied bombs and cannon fire could do little damage to Dunkirk's harbour or installations and he realised that the naval segment of the plan was wholly dependent upon the chance of wind and weather. Boufflers's corps at Bergues posed a very definite threat to Leinster and Talmash. Indeed, the British corps as in greater danger than the fortress of Dunkirk.[68]

William cared little about operational niceties. He had nothing much to lose and everything to gain from a success in Flanders. If he could just rescue some crumb from the 1692 campaign to wave before Parliament and the Grand Alliance then he would go into winter quarters in an improved political condition. To deflect French attention from Flanders, General Fleming led 15,000 Brandenburg and Liègeois troops on a terror raid through Maubeuge into Picardy, but Luxembourg refused to alter his balance around Dunkirk. William himself now began to have second thoughts and wondered aloud what would be gained from bombarding Dunkirk, bearing in mind the risks involved. A movement of eight French battalions to Ypres helped to make up William's mind but the deciding factor was the measures which the French had taken to render the projected operation untenable. All the grain, cattle and forage in the region between the Allied camp at Oost-Duinkerke and Dunkirk had been seized by the French quartermasters and the whole countryside had been wasted to render Allied movements impossible. Right upto the banks of the Ghent-Bruges Canal, the French soldiers had ruined the agriculture and depopulated the villages. There was little option but to abandon the plan. Satisfied that William could now achieve little or nothing before Dunkirk, Luxembourg removed Boufflers from Bergues and sent him scurrying eastwards to the Meuse to observe General Fleming's raiding corps.[69]

On 4/14 September, William wrote to Portland that the Dunkirk operation was now no longer feasible yet something had to be accomplished to allay criticism from within England that the entire 1692 campaign had been a total waste of time and money. He suggested moving Leinster's corps from Oost-Duinkerke on the coast to a point between Furnes and Dixmuyde from which it could attack and reduce Fort Knokke (Kenoque), drawing its supplies by sea and canal through Nieuport. As a preliminary to this operation, Furnes and Dixmuyde needed to be fortified so that they could be employed as bases for a possible renewed attempt on Dunkirk early in 1693. Speed, however, was essential as the season was fast drawing towards a close.[70] Furnes, a town the size of Ostend, had been seized by Noyelles in the face of minimal opposition. Three thousand 'boor pioneers' had been set to work to dig fortifications. By 7/17 September, the ditch had been cleared and three new ravelins had been constructed. Furnes was then equipped with a garrison of five battalions and some light cannon before the work force was moved onto Dixmuyde. The refortification of this town had now become a matter of some urgency as the French had reinforced the garrison of Fort Knokke to ten battalions and hastily built two new ravelins and erected palisades.

One hundred men from each battalion were detailed as assist the three thousand civilian labourers in repairing the defences of Dixmuyde. The River Ijzer covered the western part of the town and the Nieuport Canal was equipped with sluices to inundate the southerly approaches. Dixmuyde was connected to the bridge over the Ijzer by a causeway. The bridge itself was protected by a bastion, on the western bank, and a square sconce on the town side, both works possessing ditches and palisades. The vulnerable sectors to the north and east were guarded by an enceinte of five bastions, each covered by counter-guards, with ravelins in between. A double-ditch completed the works. By 23 September/3 October, Leinster's work force of 5,000 men had strengthened and raised the delapidated bastions and widened and deepened the ditches. The task was far from easy. Portable mills had to be provided to draw the water from the ditches before they could be dredged and all work was brought to a halt on 8/18 September when an earthquake occurred at 2.00 p.m. At first, it was unclear whether 'the very great shaking of the earth' had been caused by an exploding magazine, a French mine under Dixmuyde, the accidental blowing-up of one of the 'machines' to be employed against Dunkirk or natural tremors. The soldiers suffered severely in the wet weather and the sickness rate increased dramatically as they laboured amidst the malarial polders of Flanders.[71] Once Dixmuyde had been restored to a defensible condition, Leinster inserted a garrison of ten battalions before taking his remaining fifteen battalions into camp closer to Nieuport. To oppose Leinster and Talmash in Furnes, Dixmuyde and Nieuport, the French had stationed ten battalions in Fort Knokke supported by 12,000 men under the Comte de Choiseul at Roesbrugge-an-der-Ijzer. The siege and capture of Fort Knokke was now an impossibility. On hearing this, William began to think in terms of establishing advanced winter quarters in Flanders in order to be in a position to open the 1693 campaign with an attack on Dunkirk. In the meantime, Het Loo and some enjoyable hunting beckoned. The King left the army on 16/26 September, passing command to the Elector of Bavaria. His first set of orders put the main army on the road from Drongen to Gavere on the Scheldt.[72]

The Allies appeared to have abandoned the campaign. Colliers brought five thousand 'cauldrons' of coal from Newcastle to Flanders for the use of the Allied troops in their winter quarters and 'great quantity of deals' were purchased locally to construct huts. However, there remained a nagging fear that the French had not reached the same decision as the Allies and might try some late adventure, possibly against Charleroi. The activities of Boufflers tended to support this suspicion. As Fleming's raiders retired, Boufflers crossed the Meuse and pillaged the southern part of Liège before withdrawing to Dinant. Despite this, all appeared normal in Flanders, especially as the weather had turned very wet and stormy. Leinster sent 14 of his battalions back to England from Ostend and Nieuport and on 29 September/9 October Talmash led more British battalions into their winter quarters at Bruges. Luxembourg's army also seemed to be separating into its winter billets.[73] All was quiet and peaceful until 6/16 October when William received an express that Boufflers was moving against Charleroi, the fortress which had been a thorn in the French flesh throughout the year. Bavaria responded rapidly marching his remaining troops to Brussels whilst William hastened from Het Loo to resume command. In the event, there was nothing much that William could do. Boufflers, who had been reinforced by Montal, did not intend a full siege but bombarded the lower town destroying many of the buildings.[74] Boufflers stayed south of the Sambre and fired on Charleroi from the French side, challenging William to cross the Sambre and hazard a battle at the end of long supply lines and in atrocious weather. Taking a calculated gamble that if the Allies refused to play then the French would soon stop shooting at Charleroi, William left Brussels for The Hague where he found Sir Cloudisley Shovell with the royal yacht ready for the voyage to England. Left in charge once more, the Elector of Bavaria marched his small army south from Brussels to Waterloo and onto Genappe. This was sufficient to persuade Boufflers to pack away his guns and consider winter quarters.[75]

The campaign still refused to die. Boufflers and d'Humières conferred at Lille on 6/16 November and the fruits of their deliberations resulted in orders to raise 10,000 new troops from the 'conquered territories' in the Spanish Netherlands. These soldiers were to be employed in reinforcing Mons, Tournai, Valenciennes and Cambrai. The French also began to concentrate considerable forces on the Rhine leading the Allies to fear for the safety of Cologne, Coblenz and the fortress of Ehrenbreitstein. The Emperor convened a conference of Allied generals at Cologne on 9/19 December to decide how to respond. Solms, Tettau and d'Arco attended and resolved that the best course of action was to try to persuade the Elector of Saxony to commit his troops on the Middle Rhine. The French then developed a double winter attack. Boufflers suddenly invested Huy with 18,000 on 26 December 1693/5 January 1693 but drew off three days later when he learned of the approach of the Elector of Bavaria and Count Tilly with 32,000 men. In Flanders, the Allied garrisons in Furnes and Dixmuyde were heavily attacked in the most sustained and extensive winter campaign of the war.[76]

NOTES

1 BL, Add. MSS. 61,337, ff. 19–31, 'Mémoire touchant le Siege de D:. Fait au mois de Janvier, 1692'. It is interesting that this plan of the attack on Dunkirk is extant in the archive of John Churchill, 1st Duke of Marlborough. See, Churchill, *Marlborough*, i. 391–3; Garnet Wolseley, *The Life of John Churchill, Duke of Marlborough* (London, 1894), ii. 263–6. On Dunkirk see, *Atlas Portatif*, p. 14; PRO, MPHH/27, f. 3, Plan of the town, citadell and port of Dunkirk and Fort Louis, by Pierre F. Carpeau.

2 Childs, *Army of William III*, pp. 175–6, 208–18; J. G. Simms, *Jacobite Ireland, 1685–91* (London, 1969), pp. 258–61; P. Aubrey, *The Defeat of James Stuart's Armada* (Leicester, 1979); *HSL*, vii. 53–64.

3 Beaurain, ii. 149–50; Walton, pp. 203–4; Edward D'Auvergne, *A Relation of the Most Remarkable Transactions in the Last Campaigne of the Confederate Army. . . . in the Spanish Netherlands, 1692* (London, 1693), pp. 2–3.

4 Baxter, *William III*, p. 294.

5 *HMC, Hastings MSS.*, ii. 338–9; *HMC, Finch MSS.*, iv. 11; *Memoirs of Mary, Queen of England, 1689–1693*, ed. R. Doebner (London, 1886), p. 90.

6 Luttrell, *Historical Relation*, ii. 353, 356–8.

7 *Ibid.*, ii. 366–9.
8 *HMC, Finch MSS.*, iv. 22, 27, 29, 31.
9 BL, Add. MSS. 9,723, f. 29.
10 Luttrell, *Historical Relation*, ii. 295–6.
11 BL, Add. MSS. 9,273, f. 51.
12 *HMC, 4th Report, Appendix*, p. 325.
13 BL, Add. MSS. 9,735, f. 48.
14 *Mémoires du Duc de Saint-Simon* (Paris, 1881), i. 5–6.
15 Walton, p. 204; Beaurain, ii. 151–2; PRO, MPH 18/Part 1.
16 Jean Racine (?), *Relation de ce qui s'est passé au Siege de Namur* (Paris, 1692), pp. 10–11.
17 BL, Add. MSS. 9,735, f. 55; *HMC, Finch MSS.*, iv. 135.
18 *Ibid.*, iv. 146.
19 Japikse (Welbeck), i. 170.
20 BL, Add. MSS. 9,723, f. 123.
21 *HMC, Finch MSS.*, iv. 161.
22 LUL, MS. 12, ff. 132–4.
23 D'Auvergne, *1692*, pp. 6–10; Japikse (Welbeck), i. 171; LUL, MS. 12, ff. 134–9.
24 Walton, p. 205; Beaurain, ii. 152–8.
25 Wright, *Fortifications*, pp. 182–4; Walton, pp. 291–2; CMC 4/58; BL, Add. MSS. 64,108, ff. 105–10; Fortescue, i. 377–8; PRO, MPH 18/Part 2, f. 10.
26 LUL, MS. 12, ff. 134–44; BL, Stowe MSS. 481, ff. 3–23, Jacob Richards's Journal of the Marches of the English Artillery in Flanders in 1692; *HMC, Finch MSS.*, iv. 179–80; Duffy, *Fortress in the Age of Vauban and Frederick the Great*, pp. 29, 63; D'Auvergne, *1692*, pp. 11–13; Beaurain, ii. 167–9.
27 *Archives d'Orange-Nassau*, i. 278; *HMC, Finch MSS.*, iv. 186–7; D'Auvergne, *1692*, p. 14.
28 BL, Stowe 481; PRO, MPH 18/Part 2, ff. 10–11.
29 *Colonie*, pp. 14–25; *Saint-Simon*, i. 6–11; *Blackader*, pp. 118–20; *Dangeau*, p. 234; Beaurain, ii. 163–80; Karl von Landmann, *Wilhelm III von England und Max Emanuel von Bayern im Niederländischen Kriege, 1692–97* (Munich, 1901), pp. 10–14; Racine, *Relation*, pp. 35–40.
30 BL, Stowe MSS. 444, Journal of the Campaign of 1692 by Colonel J. Richards; SP 77/56, f. 137; Beaurain, ii. 160–1.
31 D'Auvergne, *1692*, pp. 15–16; *Archives d'Orange-Nassau*, i. 279–81.
32 BL, Stowe 444; SP 77/56, f. 134; Racine, *Relation*, p. 30.
33 LUL, MS. 12, ff. 147–9; *HMC, Finch MSS.*, iv. 228–9; D'Auvergne, *1692*, pp. 18–20; Beaurain, ii. 172–6.
34 BL, Add. MSS. 9,724, f. 24; BL, Add. MSS. 9,722, f. 13.
35 *HMC, Finch MSS.*, iv. 246; *HMC, 4th Report, Appendix*, p. 325; D'Auvergne, *1692*, p. 21.
36 *HMC, Finch MSS.*, iv. 258; SP 77/56, f. 139.
37 Burnet, *History*, iv. 174–7.
38 *Lexington Papers*, p. 52n.; Baxter, *William III*, pp. 115–18, 156; H. & B. van der Zee, *William and Mary* (London, 1973), p. 420; N. A. Robb, *William of Orange* (London, 1966), ii. 11.
39 Japikse (Welbeck), i. 199.
40 K. Danaher & J. G. Simms, *The Danish Force in Ireland, 1690–1691* (Dublin, 1962), pp. 141–2; John Jordan, 'Württemberg at Limerick, 1690', *Studies*, xliii. (1954), pp. 219–25.

41 *HMC, Finch MSS.*, iv. 321; Luttrell, *Historical Relation*, ii. 530, 532; D'Auvergne, *1692*, pp. 29–30. Jaquet enjoyed the doubly apt nickname of the Chevalier de Millevoix because of his great love of music and ability as a singer (D'Auvergne, *1692*, p. 50).
42 BL, Stowe 444; BL, Stowe 481.
43 BL, Stowe, 481.
44 LUL, MS. 12, ff. 152–3; D'Auvergne, *1692*, pp. 31–2.
45 John Mackay, *The Life of Lieut.-General Hugh Mackay, Commander-in-Chief of the Forces in Scotland, 1689 and 1690* (Edinburgh, Bannatyne Club, 1836), pp. 128–9; *HMC, 4th Report, Appendix*, p. 325.
46 Walton, pp. 211–12; D'Auvergne, *1692*, p. 34; Beaurain, ii. 183–9.
47 *HMC, Finch MSS.*, iv. 292–3; BL, Add. MSS. 9,274, f. 31; D'Auvergne, *1692*, p. 33.
48 BL, Stowe 444.
49 *HMC, Finch MSS.*, iv. 301, 306–7; D'Auvergne, *1692*, p. 36; BL, Stowe 444; Beaurain, ii. 193–6.
50 *HMC, 4th Report, Appendix*, p. 325.
51 *Relation du Combat de Stein-Kerke* (Paris, 1692), pp. 35–6.
52 *Blackader*, pp. 120–4; Berwick, i. 74; Beaurain, ii. 196–208.
53 S. H. F. Johnston, 'The Cameronians at Steenkirk, 1692', *Scottish Historical Review*, xxvii. (1948), pp. 70–6; PRO, MPH 18/Part 1.
54 *Parliamentary Diary of Luttrell*, pp. 255–6; Japikse (Welbeck), i. 63.
55 Burnet, *History*, iv. 175–7; Walton, p. 224; Mackay, *Life*, p. 129.
56 Bod. Lib., Ballard, MSS. 39, f. 87.
57 This account of the Battle of Steenkirk is based on: Walton, pp. 219–27; *HMC, Finch MSS.*, iv. 339–40; Feuquières, ii. 66–74; *Correspondence of the Family of Hatton*, ed. E. M. Thompson (London, Camden Society, 1878), ii. 181–2; *HMC, Rutland MSS.*, ii. 135–6; *Blackader*, pp. 120–4; *HMC, Portland MSS.*, iii. 493–4; *Relation du Combat de Stein-Kerke*, pp. 33–120; Müller, ii. 236–7; Paul Rapin de Thoyas, completed by Thomas Lediard, *The History of England* (London, 1732–7), iii. 424; *HMC, Downshire MSS.*, i. 412; BL, Add. MSS. 9,274, ff. 37–9; Berwick, i. 74; BL, Stowe 444; D'Auvergne, *1692*, pp. 38–49.
58 Müller, ii. 238–41; C. T. Atkinson, 'The British losses at Steenkirk, 1692', *JSAHR*, xvii. (1938), pp. 200–4.
59 *HMC, Finch MSS.*, iv. 345–6.
60 BL, Stowe 481; BL, Stowe 444; *HMC, Finch MSS.*, iv. 359.
61 D'Auvergne, *1692*, p. 50.
62 BL, Stowe 444; LUL, MS. 12, ff. 157–9; BL, Stowe 481; D'Auvergne, *1692*, p. 53.
63 *HMC, Finch MSS.*, iv. 383; Beaurain, ii. 210–13.
64 SP 77/56, f. 141; *HMC, Finch MSS.*, iv. 394, 411, 421–2; D'Auvergne, *1692*, p. 57.
65 BL, Stowe 444; LUL, MS. 12, ff. 162–6; D'Auvergne, *1692*, pp. 54–6.
66 Japikse (Welbeck), ii. 201–2; D'Auvergne, *1692*, pp. 56–8.
67 Japikse (Welbeck), ii. 68–9; *HMC, Finch MSS.*, iv. 431, 444, 448.
68 Japikse (Welbeck), ii. 203–4.
69 BL, Stowe 444; Japikse (Welbeck), i. 172–3; ii. 204.
70 *HMC, 4th Report, Appendix*, p. 325; Japikse (Welbeck), i. 173–4.
71 *HMC, Finch MSS.*, iv. 449, 454; SP 77/56, f. 143; BL, Stowe 444; Japikse (Welbeck), ii. 204–6; D'Auvergne, *1692*, pp. 59–64.
72 Müller, ii. 220; SP 77/56, f. 143; Japikse (Welbeck), ii. 207–8.

73 SP 77/56, ff. 145, 147; BL, Add. MSS. 9,273, f. 31; *HMC, Finch MSS.,* iv. 480; D'Auvergne, *1692,* p. 64.
74 *Catalogue of the Collection of Autograph Letters and Historical Documents formed between 1865 and 1882 by Alfred Morrison,* ed. A. W. Thibaudeau (Privately printed, 1883–92), i. 106, 9/19 Oct. 1692, camp before Charleroi, Boufflers to Vertillac; *HMC, Finch MSS.,* iv. 483; BL, Stowe 444.
75 *HMC, 4th Report, Appendix,* p. 325; *HMC, Finch MSS.,* iv. 484.
76 SP 77/56, ff. 148, 156; *HMC, Denbigh MSS.,* pp. 91–2.

VIII

1693: LANDEN
AND CHARLEROI

The French economy was deteriorating under the pressures of war. By 1691, the army of France numbered 273,000 men but it scaled new heights to 395,000 in 1694 and 1695.[1] Taxation had to be extended and increased to meet these military demands at a time when France was short of precious metals to convert into coin. More worrying, the decade of the 1690s witnessed a run of poor harvests, especially in France. Between 1689 and 1691, the harvests in some regions had been distressing failures but in 1692 the whole of the national harvest was indifferent on account of the extremely wet and cold summer. Catastrophe struck in the autumn of 1693 when virtually the entire French grain harvest failed. As agriculture collapsed the crown's revenues declined, both peasants and landlords struggling to meet rising taxation. The growing and parasitic army in Flanders, Germany, Italy and Spain still required its magazines to be filled with grain and flour and the military were granted priority over civilians in the allocation of scarce foodstuffs. From the winter of 1692–3, Louis XIV's thoughts turned increasingly to the acquisition of a quick yet advantageous peace. His country could no longer afford to support an open-ended struggle for dynastic objectives, such as had occurred between 1635 and 1659 in the war against Spain. Yet Louis was true to both himself and his times. He was not the responsible governor of a nation of independent individuals but the head of a dynasty who happened to possess the human and economic resources of one of the largest and richest countries in western Europe. Louis had no intention of throwing in the towel. On the contrary, the writing on the economic wall drove him into exaggerated efforts to bring the Grand Alliance to the negotiating table and accept a conclusion to hostilities on French terms. Increasing economic problems persuaded Louis to make 1693 the year of the offensive.

William's enthusiasm for the war had also diminished by the winter of 1692. Ireland and Scotland had been secured and his hold on the throne of England was now relatively sure. The urgent necessity to beat France in the field in order to hold onto England was largely over by 1693, especially after the French naval defeat at La Hogue and the scattering of Louis's attempt to invade the south of England. James II began to look a hopeless and forlorn figure. As William's political expectations from the war came close to fruition, so the potential damage that France could inflict on England diminished. One of the most obvious consequences of dwindling resources was the abandonment of the French 'double forward commitment', the staging of major military efforts by both land and sea. In order to economise, Louis recognised that France was principally a land power and that peace would only be achieved through land action. Accordingly, he cut the budget of his navy by a swingeing amount thereby obliging his admirals to abandon the fleet, decommission their larger vessels and switch the lighter craft to privateering, 'la guerre de course'. Privateering also implied a high level of private enterprise, undermining the central authority of the French navy. Although the Dunkirk privateers made unhealthy inroads into English and Dutch shipping between 1693 and 1697, in terms of strategy the adoption of the guerre de course was an admission by France that she no longer envisaged winning the war by an invasion of the British Isles. The weapons by which she could seek to command the narrow seas were laid up in Brest and Toulon. Politically, it was a tacit admission that William of Orange was now King of England and there was little that France could do to alter that state of affairs. Despite the facts that William regarded his sovereignty in England as un-negotiable and Louis found it distasteful to recognise William's new title, it was fairly clear from 1693 that some form of words would have to be discovered which could break the deadlock and recognise realities. There were still to be French attempts to invade England but after 1692 they lacked political and military credibility and were only relevant to the state of the war in the Low Countries.

William was suffering from a degree of disillusion. Thus far, the Grand Alliance had been spectacularly unsuccessful even though France was diplomatically isolated, had no allies and was suffering severe economic hardship. Waldeck and William had been defeated at Fleurus and Steenkirk and they had allowed their enemy to break through the fortress barrier of the Spanish Netherlands with the capture of Mons and Namur. Little had been achieved in Germany or along the Rhine apart from the eviction of the French from the Electorate of Cologne.

During 1692, the combined forces of the Empire, Spain and Savoy had managed a very limited invasion of Dauphiné and had even held the fortress of Embrun for a while, but the operation had ended in confusion and total withdrawal from French territory in September. Only at sea, with the victory of La Hogue, was there cause for an Allied cheer. Impressive though it looked on paper, the Grand Alliance did not seem capable of decisive military action. To reduce William's confidence further, some serious cracks appeared in the tissue of the Grand Alliance in 1692. Desperate for troops, the Emperor had secured 6,000 men from the Duke of Hanover only at the price of promising to elevate that ruler to the dignity of the ninth Elector of the Holy Roman Empire. This had disturbed the Elector of Saxony, who, together with the equally jealous rulers of Denmark, Brunswick-Wolfenbüttel, Saxe-Gotha, Hesse-Cassel and Münster, formed the League of Corresponding Princes to resist the innovation. Louis exploited this piece of good fortune by sending the Comte d'Avaux, one of his most accomplished diplomats, to Stockholm. His mission, which was satisfactorily concluded, was to persuade Sweden to mediate in the Nine Years' War by developing this fissure within the Empire. Not only did France now possess Swedish good offices to secure first negotiations and then peace, but she also reaped the benefit of ending Sweden's support for the Grand Alliance. After 1692, William received no more Swedish soldiers. Against this unpromising background, William too began to search for a path out of the war. Realising that the full achievement of the aims of the Grand Alliance was unattainable, he moved towards a via media which looked for a settlement somewhere between the Treaty of the Pyrenees of 1659 and the Peace of Nijmegen of 1678.

Diplomacy along these lines might have brought an earlier end to the war but for three sticking points. William and Louis shared a mutual antipathy which amounted to chronic distrust; Louis refused to recognise William as King of England; and there was no agreement about how many towns and fortresses in the Spanish Netherlands amounted to a 'just equivalent' for the French retention of the Duchy of Luxembourg. In practice, this meant that Louis would not negotiate directly with William or Englishmen – he would only deal with the States-General. In the late summer of 1693, a French merchant named Daguerre opened informal talks with Dijkveldt but Daguerre was soon replaced by the more experienced diplomat, the Abbé Morel. Simultaneously, François de Callières approached François Mollo, a Polish resident in Holland, who revealed the important intelligence that the Amsterdam merchants were tired of war and anxious for peace. These exploratory discussions identified the principal areas of difference. William let it be known that the English succession was not negotiable and the two sides made no progress over the provisions that should be made for James II, his wife and son.[2] However, from the autumn of 1693 regular diplomatic contacts between the French and the Dutch occurred and military operations became more firmly attached to the realities of diplomacy.

Most of the French martial manoeuvres in 1693 were geared to these ends. Louis intended to launch a 'peace offensive' by offering generous terms – including concessions to William III – in the wake of a vigorous military campaign on all fronts. The Comte de Lorge was instructed to capture Heidelberg and then act decisively in Germany, risking battle if necessary. Similar orders were intimated to Luxembourg in the Low Countries including the option to seek a general engagement if he thought that success could thereby be achieved. Louis even took the trouble to travel to the Low Countries in person to give the impression that some spectacular coup was afoot.[3] In the event, nothing came of Louis's plans as Lorge, although he seized Heidelberg and sacked it for the second time in four years, failed to press the Imperial forces to battle and his devastation of the Palatinate retarded rather than advanced the desire for peace in Germany. In Italy, the French offensive fared much better. Prince Eugene designed the capture of the fortress of Pinerolo followed by an invasion of France. Instead, the attempted siege failed and Catinat crushed the Italian and Imperial forces at Marsaglia on 24 September/4 October. This defeat convinced Victor Amadeus II of Savoy that he had backed the wrong horse in joining the Grand Alliance and during the winter of 1693–4 he opened clandestine contacts with the French general, the Comte de Tessé.[4] In the Low Countries, Luxembourg conducted an aggressive if flawed campaign which placed the Allies under continual pressure.

The Allies agreed to commit 40,000 troops to northern Italy and Piedmont, 58,000 to the Rhine and 122,000 to the armies in the Netherlands.[5] During the winter the French had raised twelve new single-battalion regiments of foot from the 'conquered territories' and, in March, Louis XIV created seven new Marshals of France – Choiseul, Villeroi, Joyeuse, Boufflers, Tourville, Noailles and Catinat. The Order of St. Louis was introduced to help improve the morale of the troops and a range of promotions occurred across the officer corps. Everything possible was attempted to improve the fighting spirit of the troops.[6] General Nicholas de la Brousse, Comte de Vertillac, might also have been amongst the new Marshals of France had he not met his death in action whilst escorting a convoy from Mons to Namur.[7]

Reflecting Louis's aggressive intentions, there was no break between the campaigns of 1692 and 1693 in the Netherlands. Luxembourg decided to fight through the winter, attacking both in Flanders and on the Meuse. On 16/26 December 1692, a French corps of 14,000 under the Comte de Guiscard had invested Huy and seized that section of the town which lay on the west bank of the Meuse. The Elector of Bavaria managed to scrape together enough troops from the winter cantonments to advance towards Huy and scare Guiscard into a retirement.[8] This was of scant concern to Luxembourg as the operation against Huy had only been a feint to distract Allied attention from Flanders. Covered by Villars from the Lines of the Lys and the Scheldt, Boufflers swooped on Furnes on 19/29 December 1692 with 37,800 men, investing the town and camping 'in the Downs' between Furnes, Nieuport and the North Sea. Despite the attentions of Leinster and Talmash earlier in the year, Furnes was ill-fortified. It had two small, weak bastions facing towards the sea whose angles were too sharp and flanks were too short. However, it possessed a good wet ditch and a number of well-designed ravelins did something to cover the poorly conceived bastions. The Elector of Bavaria promptly ordered the garrisons of Ghent, Dendermonde and Malines to concentrate and march to the relief of Furnes but they only made very slow progress. The weather was frightful. Rain poured down and the Allied relief corps sunk upto their thighs and waists in the quagmires that passed for roads. Horses could not move and waggon wheels refused to turn. Reinforcements were also summoned from Brussels. Slowly, the columns of cold, mud-stained and saturated soldiers marched into Nieuport which Bavaria had selected as his base from which to attempt the relief of Furnes.[9] So bad were the conditions that the Allied soldiers had only made one day's march in every four.

Furnes was covered on its northern and western sides by inundations which were controlled through sluices operated by the garrison of Nieuport. Contemporary opinion considered that Furnes was only tenable if its northern side was well flooded. Through negligence, the Governor of Nieuport did not let sufficient water through his control gates to make the flooding completely effective. Boufflers opened his trenches on 22 December 1692/1 January 1693 and although his men had to paddle knee-deep in water some of his cannon began to fire on 24 December 1692/3 January 1693. Three days later, most of the French siege batteries were pounding Furnes.[10] From Nieuport, no more than twelve kilometres distant, the Elector of Bavaria ordered the Governor of Furnes, Count Hornes, to surrender with his garrison of five Dutch battalions. Given the weather and the rapid advance of the French siege works, relief was impossible. Hornes marched out on 28 December 1692/7 January 1693 with the dignity of two cannon and joined Bavaria at Nieuport. Dixmuyde was simultaneously evacuated as it had become untenable with the enemy ensconced in both Furnes and Fort Knokke.[11] Bavaria was now seriously concerned that Boufflers would attack Nieuport and indeed he did approach sufficiently close to throw in a few bombs, one of which wounded Lieutenant-Colonel Robert Jackson of the Earl of Argyll's Foot, before retiring. Following the sad year of 1692, this unpromising beginning to the next campaign filled William with despair. He admitted to Heinsius that all he could do was to hope and pray that after the fall of Furnes and Dixmuyde the French did not take advantage of the feeble condition of the Allies in Flanders to attack a major town like Ostend or Bruges. William was lucky. Boufflers submitted a project to Louis XIV for the siege of Nieuport but Louis dithered and said that he preferred a scheme against Ostend. By the time that he had reached a decision, France was busy preparing for the main summer offensives and no men could be spared for subsidiary operations in Flanders.[12]

Obeying the directive from Versailles, Boufflers and Luxembourg continued to keep up the pressure. Robert Wolseley reported to the Earl of Nottingham on 7/17 January 1693 that a French patrol had lately razed some villages close to Louvain whilst another party had suddenly materialised at Zellick, just ten kilometres from the centre of Brussels, 'upon the hearing of which the boat that was going to Antwerp came back and did not set out again until yesterday morning'.[13] By 10/20 January, the weather had turned extremely cold and the Allied garrisons were placed on the alert. The villages on the road between Brussels and Tirlemont were instructed to keep some of their stables and barns empty ready to accommodate any parties of Allied horse that might be sent in pursuit of French marauders. A false report that enemy cavalry were advancing to burn Anderlecht sent the inhabitants scurrying into Brussels for safety. On 14/24 January, a thaw set in and the threat of further raids receded. The French broke up their troop concentrations in Namur, Dinant and Charlemont* dispersing the men into quarters in the villages along the banks of the Meuse and the Sambre in order to control river traffic and force the local people

---

* Fort Charlemont lay on the west bank of the Meuse, opposite Givet.

to pay their contributions.[14] The Allies were consistently at a grave disadvantage during these winter wars of raids and patrols. Their opponents dominated the frontier from Dunkirk, through Courtrai to Mons whilst Namur gave them access to the middle-Meuse. The French could thus raid into Spanish and Liègeois territory at will whilst the Allies were restricted to counter-raiding into France through the gap between Mons and Namur, via Charleroi. Their only other option was to raid into those parts of the Spanish Netherlands, principally in Flanders, which were occupied by the French but this was tantamount to attacking and antagonising a friendly population. Even so, the Allies did little to co-ordinate the defence of their territories during the winter months. They rarely received intelligence of French operations and the fact that they allowed Halle and Louvain, both within easy reach of Brussels, to be attacked smacks of pusillanimity as well as incompetence.[15]

From distant Kensington, William surmised that the French would attempt a major campaign in the Low Countries as soon as the weather improved. It was imperative that the Allied Forces came early into the field and were in position to block the opening French moves.[16] In the Netherlands, the Allied commanders began to take some belated measures to improve their local defences. Major Jacob, 'the famous party man', took a patrol over the Dyle towards Gembloux to hinder the French from seizing corn which rightly belonged to the peasants. Some of the general officers inspected posts around Brussels to ascertain appropriate locations for small parties of soldiers who might be able to discourage the French raiders from venturing too close to the city. So serious had the French winter activities become that there was a real fear that Brussels might be bombarded and a full council of war met at Vaudemont's house, in the presence of the Elector of Bavaria, to discuss possible counter-measures.[17]

French preparations were pointing menacingly towards the Meuse, possibly aiming at Charleroi or Huy. Reports filtered in of the French moving large stores of oats from Lorraine into Charleville and Mézières and then down the Meuse by boat to Givet and Dinant. Great quantities of bombs, carcasses and ammunition were being stored in Namur.[18] Charleroi appeared to be the logical target. Its acquisition would link the French frontier defences between Mons and Namur and plug the gap through which the Allies might be able to mount an invasion of France. It would also remove one of the most active and irritating of the Allied garrisons. Reinforcements were hurried to the threatened fortress. Under General Nicolas van 's-Gravenmoer, 3,000 cavalry and a close escort of three battalions brought a convoy of forty waggons safely into Charleroi on 26 January/5 February.[19] Given the poor state of the fortifications of Nieuport, it was fortunate that all was quiet in Flanders and there were no signs that the French intended another major effort in that region.[20] This was partly due to the weather which continued very wet. On 1/11 March, more evidence arrived in Brussels that the French intended to limit the campaign to the Sambre-Meuse. Having demolished the mill of Grignon on the Sambre in the previous year, the French now appeared to be busy repairing the damage. Clearly, they wished to control the flow of water in order to maintain navigation towards Charleroi. Two hundred men from the Charleroi garrison set out to undo the work but the Comte de Guiscard, the Governor of Namur, received notice of this expedition and sent considerable reinforcements to Grignon which proved sufficient to deter the Allies from launching an attack.[21] It is quite probable that the French did intend to surprise Charleroi before the opening of the main campaigning season after the manner in which they had seized Mons in 1691 but they were prevented by the inclement weather. From the beginning of March, the French garrisons of Mons and Namur were under orders to march for Charleroi at short notice and the siege train was embarked on boats along the banks of the Meuse.[22]

During this period of shadow-boxing occurred one of those incidents that renders the distinction between soldiering and boy-scouting very slight. Seven French infantrymen had surprised and captured eleven Bavarian cuirassiers near Dendermonde, north-west of Brussels, an indication of how far and wide the French raiding parties were permitted to range. Three Spanish dragoons heard of this and placed themselves to the rear of a small eminence past which the Frenchmen had to march with their captives. As they sauntered along, two of the dragoons broke cover and levelled their muskets at the Frenchmen. They shouted fiercely and looked so menacing that they appeared to be but the advance guard of a large patrol. Cleverly, the third Spaniard remained out of sight behind the hill periodically calling out to his comrades to give the impression of greater numbers. The intrepid duo shouted to their companion that there was no need to bring up the remainder of the patrol as the Frenchmen had already surrendered. How the infantrymen must have felt when only three horsemen came forward to take possession of both themselves and their Bavarian captives is not recorded. Not content with this effrontery, the dragoons then claimed the horses of the Bavarians as their legitimate spoils of war. The Elector of Bavaria was so amused by the story that he granted their request.[23]

William left London on 25 March/4 April to travel to The Hague via
Harwich.[24] On his arrival he found a letter from Sir Henry Bellasise,
the Governor of Bruges, announcing that there were few French troops
remaining in Flanders, most of them having marched off in the direction
of Mons. As a leaving present, they had demolished the fortifications
of Dixmuyde. Unknown to either Bellasise or William, Luxembourg
and Boufflers had abandoned their attempt to 'bounce' Charleroi and
the troop concentrations in Mons and Namur had been stood down.
Between them, the two French marshals were to command 133,000
troops in the Netherlands theatre in 1693. Towards the end of April,
Luxembourg's army was moving towards its concentration area around
Givry and Boufflers's men were coming into a camp between Antoing
and Mont Trinité on the outskirts of Tournai.[25] For the first time,
William was not beaten into the field. William issued orders for his
main army to concentrate at Diegem and Vilvorde to the north Brussels
and for the Earl of Athlone to bring a corps of horse into camp between
Tongres and Maastricht. The Duke of Württemberg was given command of the army in Flanders in the absence of Vaudemont who was
ill with the gout and had been given leave by the King of Spain to seek
a water cure in Italy. This army contained most of the British troops,
under the control of Talmash, who had been garrisoned in Ghent,
Bruges and Ostend. By 7/17 May, they had come into 'a good and dry
camp' near Ghent, 'thought not a very regular one and the greatest
want is a hospital'.[26] The British troops from Bruges had joined the
camp on 4/14 May to find the train of artillery and Colonel James
Stanley's battalion from Ostend already in residence. Between 6/16 May
and 7/17 May, two bridges were laid across the Ghent Canal to allow
the British corps of twenty-two battalions to march to Brussels via
Alost, should William require reinforcements, and to permit foragers
to enter the foraging grounds should the stay at Ghent be protracted.
The artillery horses and waggons arrived from the contractors on 9/19
May and, on the next day, four battalions were detailed to march to
the main army at Diegem. Each of these battalions was allowed one
bilander[27] to transport its baggage on the Ghent Canal to Terneuzen,
then along the Scheldt and south down the Antwerp Canal to Diegem.
A further four battalions departed for Diegem on 11/21 May to be
replaced by five regiments of Dutch horse.[28]

Despite William's timely preparations, the French were the first to
move. Boufflers stood at Tournai with 46,000 and Luxembourg was at
Givry, to the south-east of Mons, with 66,000. The Marquis de la
Valette guarded the Lines of the Lys and the Scheldt with 4,500 and a

corps under the Duc d'Harcourt was stationed east of the Meuse to observe Allied movements towards the Rhine and the Moselle. The French plan was to threaten and possibly besiege one of the major Allied fortresses on the Meuse – Huy, Liège or even Maastricht – in order to draw the Allies away from Flanders and the weaker sections of the French frontier. Operations towards the Meuse would also permit the French armies to forage in enemy territory and the Brandenburg and Liègeois forces would be forced to guard their own lands and would not be available to combine with William's main army. Boufflers left Tournai on 20/30 May and marched eastwards through Leuse, Cambron and Obaix towards Gembloux.

Luxembourg set off one day later than Boufflers, marching north to Nivelles and then eastwards to reach Gembloux on 28 May/7 June.[29] As both the French armies had passed close to Charleroi, there was a sigh of relief amongst the Allied generals when the French troops concentrated at Gembloux instead of investing that city. Luxembourg was now just to the north of Namur and at the head of his principal supply line along the River Meuse from Lorraine. William had to react swiftly if Luxembourg was not to seize the initiative and besiege one of the Meuse strongholds. On receipt of intelligence describing the direction of Luxembourg and Boufflers, William instructed his army to march to the Parck Abbey position, six kilometres to the south of Louvain, which covered Brussels, Malines and Louvain. Usually, William allowed his army two days to march from Diegem to Parck, stopping overnight at Bethlehem Abbey. Such was his haste on 26 May/5 June, that the King drove his soldiers the whole distance in a single day; several men died from heat exhaustion. Parck Abbey was a well known and long established position blocking any advance towards northern Brabant. The right of the camp rested on the River Dyle at Havre, a country house belonging to the Duke of Arschot where the Elector of Bavaria took his lodging, and the left was at Bierbeek. Across the front and around the left stretched the Meerdael Wood. Through the centre of the wood ran the main road from Louvain to Namur.[30]

On advance intelligence that Boufflers was preparing to march to the Meuse and was not about to advance into Flanders, the Duke of Württemberg ordered his corps at Ghent to be ready to march at 2.00 a.m. on 19/29 May. A single battalion was left to garrison Ghent and another was dispatched to Bruges. The infantry marched from Ghent in a long column, winding through Dendermonde and Lebbeke. The artillery followed on the same road and in the rear came the bread waggons and the baggage. Lord Leven's battalion acted as rearguard.

The corps continued its journey on 22 May/1 June around the north of Dendermonde but the guns had to find an alternative route as the countryside about Dendermonde was still suffering from the effects of inundations which the governor had made on a false report of a French approach during the winter. After further delays occasioned by difficulties in constructing pontoon bridges and the poor state of the roads, Württemberg led his corps of 15,000 men into the Parck Abbey camp on 27 May/6 June.[31] Even with the addition of Württemberg's men and Athlone's cavalry force, William possessed no more than 50,000 men at Parck although General Fleming was to the east at Tirlemont with 27,000. William's shortage of soldiers was a direct consequence of Luxembourg's aggressive move to the Meuse which had caused William to leave sizeable garrisons in Huy, Liège and Maastricht. Luxembourg and Boufflers enjoyed the support of 110,000 men, having denuded nearly all their major fortresses of troops.

It seemed evident that Luxembourg and Boufflers intended to besiege some major fortress as Louis XIV was personally attending the campaign. Once Luxembourg had reached Gembloux, Robert Wolseley reported that the French stood 'on the great causeway that leads either to Liège or Charleroi'. The former was the more obvious target as Charleroi was too insignificant for the great Louis to capture in person. A siege train of three thousand waggons was reported to be ready outside the Brussels Gate of Namur. Bad weather as much as anything may have interfered with French schemes at this point. Liège was a powerful fortress additionally strengthened by an entrenched camp which was garrisoned by Brandenburg and Liègeois forces. Memories of the Siege of Namur in 1692, when pouring rain had nearly ruined the operation, must have been in the back of Luxembourg's mind. A further problem concerning a possible siege of Liège was that the Allies held both Huy and Maastricht, above and below Liège on the Meuse. Before Liège could be invested, Huy had to be captured but this would be a minor and unglamorous affair, not at all what Louis had travelled to the Meuse to witness. To rationalise the inevitable, Louis held a planning conference at Gembloux. Chamlay, now high in Louis's confidence after the death of Louvois, argued that Germany represented a better road to peace than the Low Countries, especially now that the Comte de Lorge had taken Heidelberg. If the Holy Roman Emperor could be forced to end hostilities, said Chamlay, the rest of the Grand Alliance would have to follow. Strategically, the bold and forceful Chamlay painted a bleak prospect on the Meuse. Although Liège was the next logical target, Huy would have to be besieged first thereby presenting William with sufficient time to reinforce Liège. Louis, whose health was too poor to enable him to remain with his armies, accepted Chamlay's advice. The Dauphin was sent to Germany with 30,000 men from Luxembourg and Boufflers's armies whilst Louis retired to Versailles. Luxembourg was left to continue the campaign as best he could with 96 battalions and 201 squadrons. He was given vague instructions by Louis to hold up the Prince of Orange, possibly along the River Dyle, but he was not told whether to conduct either a defensive or an offensive strategy.[32] The French campaign was suddenly without a rudder or an engine. Probably, Luxembourg should have attempted to come to grips with Charleroi or Huy but he had now lost his numerical superiority over William. Instead, he chose to march closer to Louvain to observe the Allies and restrict their movements. On 5/15 June, he marched north from Gembloux to camp at Bossut behind the River Nethe, no more than ten kilometres south of the Allied position at Parck Abbey. Luxembourg stretched his right towards Tirlemont, placed his left near the Dyle at Bossut and established his headquarters at Meldert. The thick and extensive Bois de Meerdael separated the two armies. William received news of Luxembourg's move to Meldert on 5/15 June and he immediately marched out with some horse to reconnoitre. They bumped into 6,000 French cavalry foraging, a clear indication of the accuracy of the intelligence.[33] Safe in the knowledge that Luxembourg had turned away from the Meuse, William felt able to thin his garrisons in Liège and Maastricht to form a field corps. This he placed east of the Meuse to interrupt the passage of French troops from the Rhine marching back to reinforce Luxembourg in the Netherlands.[34]

In oppressively hot weather, interspersed by violent thunder storms, William and his generals reviewed their camp and dispositions on 10/20 June. Some slight adjustments were made to the location of the left wing which was over-lapped by Luxembourg's right. News of the departure of Boufflers's 30,000 for Germany reached William on 12/22 June but as his source indicated that a large contingent of waggons and pioneers had accompanied Boufflers, he assumed that the corps was going to besiege Maastricht or Liège whilst Luxembourg blocked the path of relief at Meldert. Luxembourg was unable to attack William's left whilst the Allies had built so many bridges over the Dyle that if he did succeed in mounting an attack then they could withdraw towards Brussels sufficiently quickly to avoid being sucked into an action. It was a stalemate. The Allied garrisons on the Meuse were big enough to discourage Luxembourg from attempting a siege and William's army covered Brussels and northern Brabant. In an admission of defeat, the French returned the siege train to Namur. Neither was there much prospect of one commander surprising the other. Deserters slipping through the woods between the camps kept the supply of information constant and up-to-date. Swiss escaped from the French lines to be replaced by Irish catholics from the Allied ranks. Proclamations, rewards and executions failed to stem the flow. As an additional precaution against sudden attack, William had the battalion guns dragged from the artillery park and positioned in the brigade lines, complete with ammunition. A battery of six-pounders was drawn-up in the centre of the camp to fire down the Louvain-Namur road. Luxembourg improved his security by establishing a listening post at the Monastery of Valdue in the middle of the forest.[35]

For once, William seemed to be in a superior position as French supplies began to run short. William was close to his main base and magazine at Brussels and could forage in northern Brabant, a rich and fertile region virtually untouched by war. Luxembourg stood at the tip of a seventy kilometre supply-line which reached back to Namur and Mons and the countryside between his camp and the Sambre had been foraged, raided and devastated over the previous four years. Deserters came into the Allied camp on 7/17 June with information that the French commissariat was in difficulties; if the Allies could interrupt the communications between Meldert and the Sambre-Meuse then Luxembourg would have no option but to fall back.[36] Luxembourg's problems were compounded by the stormy weather which slowed his convoys on the muddy roads. He tried to establish a forward base at Jodoigne, south of Tirlemont, but the provisions still had to trek from Namur. Much of Luxembourg's army was employed in escorting these convoys in the face of vigorous patrolling by the Allied garrisons from Charleroi, Huy and Liège.

However, it was imperative for Luxembourg to retain his position. He intended to consume all the forage between Louvain and the Meuse in order to prevent the Allies from being able to operate in that direction. At a later date, this might present Luxembourg with the option of besieging one of the Allied Meuse fortresses. Secondly, a premature retirement to the Meuse would have allowed William to gather in his Meuse garrisons and shift the focus of the campaign to Flanders where the French frontier defences were most vulnerable. After a month of standing passively before the Bois de Meerdael, Luxembourg resolved to threaten Huy or Liège.[37]

Although the French supply restrictions were more severe, the Allies became less comfortable as their stay at Parck Abbey extended into July. The forage to the west of the Dyle had been consumed by 9/19 June and, three days later, the quality of the forage from other areas had become so poor that William had to order stocks of oats and dry fodder from Holland. The heavy rain irritated both sides. Thunder storms on the night of 14/24 June demolished tents and affected the sutlers very badly as their waggons had been parked in a hollow lane. The rising rivers flooded both the French and the Allied camps during 15/25 June and General Overkirk was nearly washed away whilst out riding. To the delight of the British, the quarters of Count Solms were inundated. Reports from deserters indicated that the French would soon move and at 1.00 a.m. on 28 June/8 July, Luxembourg silently slipped away from his camp and marched eastwards to a new position near Jodoigne and Heylissem in the land between the Great and Little Geete. William drew out some horse but was too late to bother the French rearguard.

> The King rid into the enemy's camp and viewed it. Some of our Refugiés (i.e. Huguenots) officers came near enough to speak with some of their acquaintance in the French army which they found straggling behind. A very deep way remained between them which hindered any other action but compliments on both sides. They consented mutually to a truce to have a little discourse together but a small party of our horse, which knew nothing of the agreement, came up another way, fired amongst them and broke the conference.

Once he had received intelligence of Luxembourg's new position, William summoned all his detachments to Parck Abbey. Major-General Julius von Tettau came with his Liègeois corps of observation from the Meuse, General Fleming marched in with the Brandenburgers who had been observing the Dauphin's army and Count Tilly arrived with 3,000 horse from Tongres. Having concentrated, William needed to draw Luxembourg's attention away from the Meuse before he invested one of the denuded fortresses. The best method was to stage a major diversion in Flanders. This strategy enjoyed the added attraction that contributions might be raised from French Flanders, a necessity at a time when the Treasury in London was dry and confidence in the money markets had been wrecked by the destruction of the Smyrna Convoy. William's soldiers had to raise contributions or go without pay and basic provisions.[38]

The Duke of Württemberg was given command of a corps of 13

battalions and 40 squadrons, 8,000 infantry and 6,000 horse, and ordered to march to Oudenarde. There, he was to gain intelligence of French dispositions in Flanders, taking especial note of enemy strength within the Lines of the Lys and the Scheldt. If he discovered that the Lines were not held in overwhelming force, then he was to approach, force a passage and proceed to levy contributions on the French country-side over as wide an area as he could manage. When all this had been successfully accomplished, Württemberg was to re-concentrate his corps and march to Warneton where he was to bridge the Lys and travel to Roeselare. Should the opportunity present itself, Courtrai was then to be attacked. If, by some miracle, all was still going to plan, a detachment was to be dispatched to Deynze to open communications with Ghent. However, and how Württemberg must have breathed a sigh of relief when he heard this, if the Lines were too strongly garrisoned he was to try to attack Courtrai but at all times he was to avoid an open encounter with a superior force.[39] Württemberg was assisted by three major-generals: Frédéric Henri de Suzannet, Marquis de la Forest, Johan Ellenburg and van Wymberg. Four British regiments found themselves attached to this expedition – Lord Castleton's Foot, the Earl of Argyll's Foot, Lord Bath's Foot and the Duke of Schomberg's Horse. In filthy weather and accompanied by a train of twelve cannon, of which two were twelve-pounders, Württemberg's corps marched from Parck on 1/11 July. Their place in William's army was taken by General Tettau's thirteen battalions which had been stationed in the entrenched camp by Liège. Württemberg's column travelled around the north of Brussels through Vilvorde, Mellem and Alost to bridge the Scheldt at Oudenarde. Twelve battalions from the Allied garrisons at Charleroi, Bruges, Ath and Brussels combined with Württemberg on the banks of the Scheldt.

Since 1690, the French had spent the winter months in extending their system of defensive lines in Flanders. By 1693, conscripted peasants had dug zig-zagged trenches, ramparts and redoubts from the Scheldt to the Lys, then onto Ypres, through Berg St. Winnox to the sea at Dunkirk. Following the capture of Mons in 1691, more lines were constructed, although not so strong as those in Flanders, between Mons and Tournai with an extension reaching to the Sambre at Maubeuge. The sector between the Lys and the Scheldt was the most formidable of all these field fortifications as it protected the rich lands around Lille and Cour-trai against the powerful Allied fortress of Oudenarde. The elderly lieutenant-general, the Marquis de Calvo, commanded the entirety of the lines in Flanders but the Lys-Scheldt section was under the local control of the Marquis de la Valette with a garrison of 10,000 men.

Württemberg crossed the Scheldt with his cavalry on 4/14 July and camped within sight of the Lines opposite the village of Dottignies. Ellenburg led the foot over the Scheldt on 5/15 July and, the same day, Count Hornes arrived from Ghent with a convoy of ammunition, stores and bridging pontoons. Württemberg's horse had encamped to the west of Kooigem, very close to the Lines, but Ellenburg brought the foot into a camp at St. Denijs, four kilometres to the north, with the intention of marching to join up with Württemberg during the hours of darkness. That night, a violent thunder storm flooded the little valley which separated Württemberg from Ellenburg. Count Hornes's battalion waded through the inundation but a number of men were drowned. Temporarily, the Allies were in a predicament. In the face of 10,000 men within the Lines, Württemberg's small cavalry force and Hornes's depleted battalion were cut-off from Ellenburg's infantry corps and were highly vulnerable should the French learn of the situation. Hornes's battalion showed great presence of mind in using their drums to beat the English, Scottish, Danish and Dutch marches to simulate Ellenburg's corps arriving in the advanced camp. They also lit a number of camp fires to increase the deception. The ruse fooled the French and by 3.00 a.m. the floods had sufficiently subsided for Ellenburg to bring his whole corps forward to support Hornes and Württemberg's horse. Before any attack could be contemplated the infantry needed a rest. They had marched continuously for eight days 'in very foul weather' and they were glad to collapse inside their tents on 6/16 July and 7/17 July. 'To cheer up our soldiers', Württemberg, 'who took great compassion', issued six gallons of 'corn brandy' to each company. This must have induced some sleep despite the incessant rain which churned the streets of the camp into knee-deep mud.

Württemberg planned to attack in two columns. The western force under van Wymberg was to assault the redoubts of Beau Verd and Haute Plante, whilst the eastern column under Ellenburg tackled the Kooigem Redoubt. In the centre, the Danish Brigadier, Count d'Alfeldt, commanded a four battalion attack on the redoubt at Pont David. This was the most important point on this sector of the Lines as a road ran through the fortifications and there were permanent bridges over both the wet ditch and the River Espierrette. Between the columns was a small, wooded eminence called the Bois de Bray. Württemberg and his generals set to work to devise a method for crossing the Lines now that all surprise had been lost and de la Valette had concentrated his garrison against the threatened sector. Each of the three columns was headed by an advance guard of grenadiers, commanded by a captain, who were charged with traversing the river and the ditch in order to mask the bridging operation. Behind this thin screen, thirty pikemen from each battalion in the column carried bundles of fascines, large numbers of which had been delivered to the camp by the local peasants on 7/17 July. The pikemen were ordered to tie their pikes into bundles of four, place them over the river and the ditch to form a frame on which they were to lay fascines at right angles to make a bridge. This task was to be performed under cover from the advance guard of grenadiers. The remainder of the grenadiers waited to charge over the bridge of pikes and attack the redoubts. The main body of the infantry battalions were towards the rear, ready to support the grenadiers and exploit any success. The cavalry were at the back of the field, unable to take part in the action until openings had been effected in the Lines. From the Bois de Bray, nine cannon assisted the left attack and three guns supported the western assault.

In improving weather on the morning of 8/18 July, the three Allied columns advanced to the attack. Within musket shot of the Lines, they halted and fired three cannon as a signal that they were ready to proceed. The cannon then fired on the redoubts and on the French cavalry who were deployed to the east of Dottignies behind the Lines. Two houses before the fortifications were set on fire by the French to prevent them being used to shelter Allied soldiers. The Earl of Argyll's grenadiers headed d'Alfeldt's attack on the Redoubt du Pont David, losing a quarter of their number dead as they fought their way over the river, the ditch and up to the ramparts. The Earl of Castleton's grenadiers led the way towards the Beau Verd Redoubt on the right. Count d'Alfeldt committed his four battalions in support of Argyll's grenadiers before Pont David and after half an hour's stiff resistance from a Swiss battalion, de la Valette ordered a withdrawal from the redoubt. As soon as the redoubt was clear, Württemberg ordered his cavalry along the road to form up in the rear of the French Lines. To the right of Pont David, the Earl of Castleton's grenadiers assaulted the Beau Verd Redoubt. The garrison resisted manfully until the retirement from the neighbouring Pont David Redoubt threatened the right flank of the defenders and they too began an orderly retreat. Württemberg had waited to launch Ellenburg's column until both d'Alfeldt and Wymberg's attacks had developed. The Earl of Bath's grenadiers struggled across the swollen Espierrette River and marched up to the palisades of the Haute Plante Redoubt under the covering fire of the supporting battalions on the north bank of the river. At this point, with the Pont David and Haute Plante Redoubts already in Allied hands, de la Valette began to evacuate the Haute Plante and the Earl of Bath's grenadiers broke in as the garrison was retiring. Württemberg held his men in check and reformed his battalions and squadrons before calling in an army of peasant-pioneers to level the Lines between the Haute Plante and Beau Verde Redoubts and build bridges over the river. During this delay, de la Valette led his troops to safety through St. Léger and down the road towards Tournai. Thwarted in their pursuit, the Allied troops turned to plunder. Twelve villages behind the Lines were burned including the churches at St. Léger and Evregnies 'where the Boers had heaped all their moveable goods'. In the evening, the Allied corps camped in two lines at Dottignies whilst de la Valette took a position at Pont a Tressin, on the River Marque, five kilometres to the east of Lille. Württemberg instructed his pioneers to level the whole eighteen kilometres of the Lines of the Lys and the Scheldt 'which they have done though not so thoroughly as it should have been'. The smoke from the burning villages persuaded the inhabitants of the district of Courtrai to volunteer contributions to Württemberg before they too suffered.[40]

Württemberg's depredations into Hainaut were not the only indignities suffered by France during Luxembourg's embarrassment in Brabant. On 23 June/2 July, 900 horse and 500 foot from the garrison of Charleroi passed into France through the Lines between Mons and Maubeuge, putting seven redoubts out of action on the way. They burned several villages before returning unmolested with 1,000 head of cattle, 120 horses and over 100 prisoners. Five days later, Major-General Louis du Puy again led out the cavalry of the Charleroi garrison and intercepted a French convoy carrying money and provisions near Beaumont. To begin with, all went well and the escort was driven off but a French reinforcement of thirteen squadrons suddenly appeared, before which du Puy deemed it prudent to beat a hasty retreat.[41]

Luxembourg adjusted his camp to Waremme (Borgworm), on the River Geer, to be closer to the Meuse. There was nothing that he could do about Württemberg in Flanders or du Puy before Maubeuge, so he continued with his own, local strategy. Whilst at Waremme, Luxembourg learned that Count Tilly had arrived in Tongres with five regiments of Liègeois horse and three of dragoons, marching to join William at Parck. The Marshal drew out 10,000 cavalry and rode to intercept Tilly. Fortunately, the Liègeois corps was on its guard and, discovering Luxembourg's approach, succeeded in slipping away from the trap. Frustrated in his design, Luxembourg sent horsemen in swift pursuit but they only managed to skirmish with Tilly's rearguard. However, Tilly's eight regiments escaped not towards William at Parck but to seek refuge in Maastricht. From Waremme, Luxembourg sent d'Harcourt to invest Huy on 9/19 July.

'A dirty, poor town', Huy stood on both sides of the Meuse. An antique castle was situated in the middle of the old town on the east bank but the whole of Huy was commanded by a ring of adjacent hills. Until the French capture of Namur in 1692, Huy had only its medieval stone walls for defence but the Allies had added several ravelins and retrenchments during the previous twelve months. The Baron de Reneffe commanded a garrison of 2,000 men who were expected to put up resistance for seven or eight days. On d'Harcourt's arrival, Reneffe abandoned the new town on the west bank and retired into the old town, breaking down the bridge across the Meuse. A single day's bombardment was sufficient to persuade Reneffe to surrender the town on 10/20 July and retire into the castle. Although the castle was out-of-date and dominated by low hills, it was very difficult to approach and even if the French artillery did effect a breach, infantry assault would be far from easy. The out-lying Fort Picard capitulated on 13/23 July and d'Harcourt's cannon and mortars hurled shot and bombs into the castle. Grenadiers from the Régiment d'Orléans took a tower within one hundred metres of the castle walls, opposite the point at which the cannon were trying to make a breach. This was sufficient for Reneffe who sought terms on the following morning. Reneffe requested permission to march his garrison to Liège but Luxembourg was in no hurry to allow reinforcements to reach William's depleted army and so he detained the garrison on the feeble pretence that the town owed money to the Cardinal von Fürstenberg, one of the canons of Liège. The Prince-Bishop was less than impressed with Reneffe's performance and ordered the governor and many of his officers to be examined by a council-of-war. Dutifully, the court imprisoned Reneffe for three months and suspended him from employment for one year.

Now that the French had possession of Namur and Huy, William feared that Luxembourg's next target was Liège and, possibly, Maastricht. The Allied army left Parck on 10/20 July, as soon as the news of the investment of Huy was received, and encamped at Tirlemont. The 11/21 July saw the army cross both the Great and the Little Geete to camp at Neerheylissem. William pressed on to Wellem, to the east of St. Truiden, on 13/23 July and it was here that he was informed of the fall of Huy. Luxembourg moved eastwards through Les Waleffes and Vinalmont arriving at Lexhy on 15/25 July. From here he conducted a reconnaissance of the Lines which had been built around Liège as a consequence of Boufflers's raid in 1691. The Allies responded rapidly by dispatching Brigadier von Schwerin to Liège with ten battalions from the main army and a further three battalions were sent from Maastricht. This brought the garrison of Liège up to thirty battalions. Even though the Lines were poorly designed and constructed, Luxembourg found them too strongly held and withdrew to his camp at Lexhy. With a sigh of relief, William returned from Wellem to the more central position at Neerheylissem. This spate of manoeuvres had given Luxembourg a huge advantage. He had both secured Huy and forced William into depleting his army by ordering detachments to Liège and Maastricht, not to mention Württemberg's absence in Flanders. Luxembourg's skill had produced a local superiority of force sufficient to merit the risk of a general action, the necessity for which increased as news came in of the damage and humiliation that Württemberg was inflicting on Hainaut.[42]

Württemberg decamped from Dottignies on 12/22 July, crossed the river at St. Léger on pontoon bridges and advanced to within two kilometres of Tournai. On the following day, Brigadier Johann Huybert was instructed to force a passage of the River Marque at Pont a Tressin with 1,200 horse, 600 foot and three cannon. Tressin was three and a half kilometres from Lille on the road between that city and Tournai. The well paved highway ran along a causeway elevated two metres above the surrounding fields. The French had erected palisade barriers on the bridge and had turned a number of houses into strong-points. Huybert's cannon drove the defenders from both the causeway and the block-houses but they succeeded in taking up positions behind the palisades on the bridge. Two hundred grenadiers, supported by the artillery and musketry from the houses, rushed the bridge and the French took to their heels and dashed for the safety of Lille. Huybert camped at Tressin and began to levy contributions from as far south as Douai and the Sambre. Württemberg brought the main corps to camp alongside Huybert on 17/27 July. He was planning deeper raids into France when news arrived on 20/30 July of the disaster at Landen and he hastened back through Pont d'Espierres, Oudenarde and Alost to rejoin the remnants of the main army.[43]

With William in his camp between Neerwinden and Neerhespen, now known as Neerheylissem, on the Little Geete, Luxembourg decided that the moment to strike had arrived. Liège had gobbled up 17,000 Allied soldiers, Württemberg commanded as many in Hainaut and the garrison of Maastricht amounted to 5,000. William's field army consisted of no more than 50,000 men, or fifty-two battalions and 150 squadrons. He was opposed by 66,000 Frenchmen in eighty-six battalions and 210 squadrons. On the afternoon of 17/27 July, Marshal de Joyeuse took

10,000 men towards Waremme, there to feint in the direction of Liège to induce the notion that Luxembourg was intent on an investment and siege. To keep William guessing still further, Lieutenant-General Montrevel led a detachment into a flying camp slightly to the west of Luxembourg's main position around Latinne, as if he was contemplating a challenge to Württemberg in Hainaut. Luxembourg had intended to march to attack William on 17/27 July, but heavy rain caused a twenty-four hour postponement. In brighter weather, Luxembourg's army marched in seven columns early on the morning of 18/28 July. Two columns of horse guarded the flanks and the infantry and artillery occupied the centre. Joyeuse and Montrevel marched independently towards the battlefield, providing wider flank cover for the main force. The army crossed the River Jeker near Waremme and at 4.00 p.m. the cavalry advance guard came into sight of William's camp from a vantage point near Oberwinden. William was not taken by surprise as his mounted patrols had come into contact with the French march around Waremme. However, William had little time in which to adjust his position and rather than be attacked as he tried to retreat across the Great and Little Geete, he decided to stand and fight before his camp even though he was heavily outnumbered. During the evening, the French army trudged into Landen, Overwinden and St. Gertrude after a march of over thirty kilometres.

Not only had William been caught with his trousers down in not having his available forces concentrated in the face of the enemy, but he had allowed himself to be trapped on a very bad battlefield. Three kilometres to the rear of his position ran the Little Geete, a small river but one with stretches of marshland along its banks. Five kilometres to the west of the Little Geete was its Great neighbour. Fixed and permanent bridges spanned the Little Geete at Overhespen and Eliksem and although the Allies had built a number of pontoon structures there remained insufficient crossing points for the whole army to retreat simultaneously. Should the army be forced back, there were bound to be severe bottlenecks at the bridging points. The battlefield was also too shallow from front to rear not giving William enough space to manoeuvre and switch forces from one flank to the other. There were no positions from which an orderly withdrawal over the few bridges could be covered by a rearguard. The Neerwinden-Landen camp had been chosen by William as it commanded good foraging towards Louvain and Tirlemont and because of its balanced stance between the Meuse and Brussels. As at Steenkirk in 1692, except that the tables had been reversed, one general had been trapped by another on a battlefield

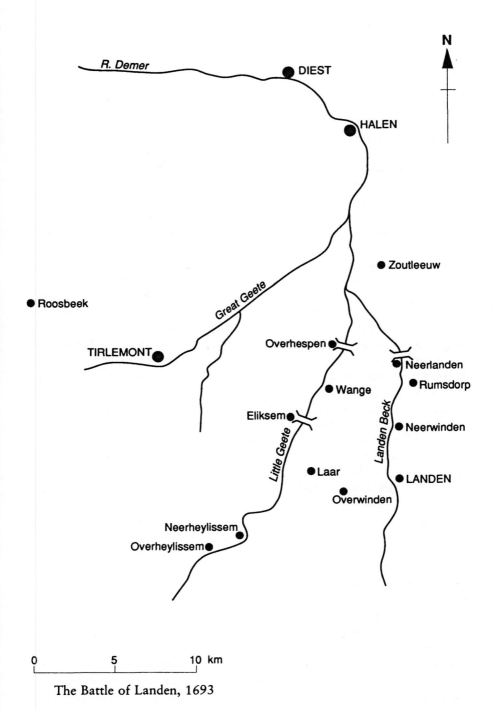

N

R. Demer
● DIEST
● HALEN

● Zoutleeuw

● Roosbeek

Great Geete

TIRLEMONT ●

Overhespen ●
● Neerlanden
● Rumsdorp

● Wange

Eliksem ●

Little Geete

Landen Beck

● Neerwinden

● Laar
● LANDEN

●
Overwinden

Neerheylissem ●
Overheylissem ●

0   5   10 km

The Battle of Landen, 1693

which had been initially selected for its merits as a camp-site. To make up for his lack of soldiers and for the short-comings of the topography, the Allied troops spent the night of 18/28 July in digging trenches, building breastworks and in fortifying the villages.

The land about the battlefield of Landen, or Neerwinden, is flat with areas of slightly higher ground barely perceptible to the naked eye. William's left rested on the hamlet of Neerlanden and the Landen Beck, which drained into the Little Geete at Zoutleeuw (Leau) to the north. The banks of this stream were boggy and the sole bridge was at Neerlanden. The Landen Beck virtually refused the Allied left but William took no chances and placed some cavalry in its rear. The main line ran south from Neerlanden and the left was reinforced by the tiny village of Rumsdorp which lay in advance of the battle positions and was garrisoned by British infantry. William's right was at ninety degrees to his left, the pivot being the larger settlement of Neerwinden; this post was the key to the field. Neerwinden was supported by the village of Laar which stood to the front of the main line and was once more occupied by British foot. Cavalry plugged the gap between Laar and the Little Geete. Two lines of horse drew up behind the centre about Neerwinden but the restricted space and the wet ground within the Allied lines were unsuitable for cavalry manoeuvres. The defence of the Landen position was to depend on infantry. This was probably deliberate as William feared the numerical strength and efficiency of the French horse whilst his own army was short of mounted soldiers. The breastworks and entrenchments with which the Allies sought to improve their defences were feeble affairs. Only 1,500 men were detailed as pioneers and the resultant fortifications were such that 'they could only serve to hinder horse from riding into our camp, but not cover our men either from cannon or small-shot; a man could easily have jumped over them, ditch and all.'[44] Similarly, the so-called 'defences' of Neerlanden, Rumsdorp, Neerwinden and Laar consisted of hedges and the mud walls with which the inhabitants of Brabant habitually separated their plots of land. A few loopholes were knocked through the walls of some houses.

Luxembourg's initial scheme had been to force the Allied centre between Neerwinden and Rumsdorp and exploit the opening with his cavalry. When he reconnoitred the battlefield at dawn on the morning of 19/29 July, he noticed that the hurriedly-dug entrenchments, although pathetic, would disrupt cavalry; they would have to be levelled before horse could advance, a difficult and potentially costly operation in the face of enfilading fire from Rumsdorp and Neerwinden. Luxembourg changed his plans. His infantry would attack Neerwinden and Laar with the intention of destroying the hinge of the whole line as well as the right wing. Once the foot had broken through, the horse could advance across the rear of the Allied position and cut-off any retreat to the bridges over the Little Geete. To stretch the Allies further, he designed to assault Rumsdorp and pass dragoons over the Landen Beck at Neerlanden to search out the possibility of outflanking the left of the Allied centre.

During the night, William concentrated ninety cannon towards the centre of his line about Neerwinden, outnumbering by twenty the French artillery. The Elector of Bavaria strongly advised William to slip out of the trap in the hours of darkness and withdraw over the Geete but the King refused and, indeed, thought he had selected a rather good field on which to emasculate the French cavalry. The action opened at 4.00 a.m. with a cannonade which lasted two hours. Luxembourg organised an initial assault by 18,000 infantry and 8,000 horse against Neerwinden with 15,000 foot and 2,000 dismounted dragoons operating towards Rumsdorp and Neerlanden on the Allied left. Opposite Neerwinden, the French deployed into eight lines, two of infantry and six of cavalry. Because of the smallness of the battlefield and the shortage of space within which to deploy a massed army, Luxembourg not only brought his troops onto the field in column but he also attacked in column rather than in line. Although this enabled him to manoeuvre his men more rapidly and effectively and allowed quick reinforcement of local successes or reverses, it had the disadvantage of only permitting him to bring into action a limited proportion of his forces at any one time. This tended to level the numerical disparity between the armies, a balance which was turned further in the Allies' favour by the occupation of higher ground, sturdily-built villages, hedges, walls and primitive field fortifications. For all his enormous skill and occasional brilliance in marching and manoeuvre, on the field of Landen Luxembourg was reduced to crude, battering tactics.

At 6.00 a.m., Luxembourg ordered the French left to advance. Three columns of infantry marched steadily towards Neerwinden whilst six regiments headed in the direction of Laar. In support of this main attack, the French cavalry stood in the rear of their foot although some squadrons began to pass through the hedges between Laar and the Little Geete in order to engage the Allied cavalry of the right wing to prevent them from succouring the defenders of Laar and Neerwinden. The leading ranks of the infantry columns carried fascines with which to fill the shallow ditches around the villages. As soon as they were

near the earthen walls of Neerwinden, the infantry charged and carried
the initial line of obstacles but there the attack stuck. In close fighting,
reminiscent of Steenkirk, the battle flowed through Neerwinden as
infantry fought amidst the walls, hedges and loop-holed cottages. The
fighting was hand-to-hand and muzzle-to-muzzle. Twenty-six French
battalions faced just nine Allied battalions but the attackers were unable
to deploy their full weight within the cramped streets of Neerwinden
and the Allies were at an advantage as the French formations lost
cohesion and momentum. The First Foot Guards, the Scots Guards, a
battalion of the Dutch Blue Guards, and six Hanovarian battalions
hung onto Neerwinden but the furious assaults under the Duke of
Berwick, du Rubantel and de Montrevel drove them back to the very
edge of the village. Six Brandenburg battalions, who held the line
between Neerwinden and Laar, had also come under sustained attack.
Disaster struck in Laar. Brigadier Ramsey's garrison was driven out by
the weight of the French assault. Brigadier de Bezons, who commanded
the French horse in front of Laar, exploited the success of the infantry
and pushed through the village to form up within the Allied lines. The
right flank and rear of William's entire position were suddenly in grave
danger. Fortunately, the Allied mounted troops between Laar and the
Little Geete had resisted French pressure and the Elector of Bavaria,
who commanded the horse of the right wing, charged Bezons's left
flank, forcing him back in disorder. Ramsey seized the instant to launch
a counter-attack on Laar which restored the position on the embattled
right. William himself rallied the defenders and led them back into
Neerwinden but there were only enough men to form a single line. The
French infantry were temporarily a spent force and withdrew from
Neerwinden, the Duke of Berwick being taken prisoner by Brigadier
Charles Churchill. By the skin of their teeth and the initiative of Bavaria
and Ramsey, the Allies had weathered the opening storm.

Luxembourg had been unlucky. His scheme had asked for simultaneous attacks to be launched against Rumsdorp and Neerlanden on
the Allied left when the main assaults were made on Neerwinden and
Laar. In this manner he had hoped to pin his opponents' left to stop
them from moving troops from that sector to the centre and right.
These instructions were not executed and only when Luxembourg
reinforced his left with 7,000 fresh infantrymen and sent them forward
against Neerwinden for a second time did the supporting attacks materialise. As the columns charged forward against Laar and Neerwinden
once more to be repulsed and driven out, four regiments of French
dragoons advanced down the road into Neerlanden searching for a

weakness in the Allied left wing. In an action of over two hours' duration, Brigadier William Selwyn held onto Neerlanden. He commanded four battalions which resisted attacks by a similar number of French battalions. The street fighting with muskets, bayonets and grenades swayed to and fro and Allied success was not guaranteed until William personally intervened and reinforced Selwyn with some Danish foot. At Rumsdorp, Colonel Thomas Erle's brigade, outnumbered by five to one, was rapidly flung from the village back into the main Allied line. With Rumsdorp in enemy possession and a long battle in progress for Neerlanden, William could not move troops from his left to reinforce the centre and right around Neerwinden and Laar. Although many of his generals advised Luxembourg to abandon the battle after the failure of the second massed assault on Laar and Neerwinden, he reasoned that he was so dominant in numbers and had pushed the Allies into such an inflexible position that he must, ultimately, take the two villages. Once they fell, the whole Allied stance would automatically become untenable and they must either retreat quickly over the Little Geete or be cut to pieces. To add to their discomfort, the Allied infantry were tired having been fighting desperately for several hours under a hot sun.

Twelve thousand French guards were moved from the reserve near Overwinden to renew the attack on Neerwinden. They passed through the depleted and exhausted battalions on the French left and prepared to advance. William had originally defended the Neerwinden-Laar sector with 14,000 foot but 5,000 of these were already casualties and those who remained had no hope of relief or reinforcement and had already been in action for eight hours. The attack by the French guards, although the British, Dutch and Hanovarian infantry defended to the best of their ability, was bound to succeed and, despite the personal intervention of William, the Allies were forced from Neerwinden. The French cavalry filed through the village and formed up behind their infantry in the open country inside the Allied entrenchments. On the French right, Lieutenant-General de Feuquières had noticed the withdrawal of nine battalions from the Allied left to reinforce the defence of Neerwinden. He attacked. To his left, de Créqui, who commanded the French left-centre, also advanced to prevent the Allies shifting troops from the Neerwinden sector to face Feuquières assault on the right. Nine Allied battalions formed a hollow square to meet Feuquières. The Frenchmen ignored this act of defiance, by-passed the square and formed his cavalry into line ready to charge the open left flank of William's army. With his left turned and the hinge at Neerwinden in enemy hands, William had lost the battle and only a hasty retreat could rescue defeat from possible catastrophe. This was the time for the cavalry on the Allied right, which had seen little action, to try to protect the retreat of the infantry as they left their breastworks and fell back towards the bridges across the Little Geete. When called upon to perform this duty, both the Elector of Bavaria and his cavalrymen made a poor showing. They were charged and broken by French horse before they could come into action and the Elector left the battlefield, crossed the Little Geete and formed up a few of his surviving squadrons as a rearguard on the far bank of the river. Partial salvation was found in the horse regiments which had spent the battle lingering on the western side of the Landen Beck beyond Neerlanden. They had not fired a shot and scarcely seen a Frenchman. William led these troopers, which included six British formations, southwards and their repeated charges into the flank of the French exploitation did much to slow the enemy and gain some time for the army to scramble over the bridges. Sir Henry Bellasise and Thomas Talmash extracted the infantry from the Allied left in some sort of order under the cover of these cavalry charges and succeeded in fording the Geete. However, amongst the Allied right and centre, the French pressed hard and inflicted heavy casualties. The passage to the bridge at Eliksem was blocked by French troops and the crossing point at Overhespen was soon overrun. William protected the one remaining bridge at Neerhespen but many of his men were drowned as they tried to swim the Little Geete in full military dress, or were cut down as they attempted to negotiate its marshy banks. William came close to being captured as he supervised the last rites at Neerhespen bridge but was rescued by Lieutenant Hatton Compton and a few British horsemen.

As at Steenkirk, the nature of the Landen battlefield had meant that only half of each army was engaged. Much of the Allied cavalry did not come into action and many of the battalions lining the entrenchments of the Allied centre between Neerwinden and Rumsdorp did not meet the French until the retreat commenced. Similarly, many of the French cavalrymen did not fight until the pursuit. Landen was another battle in which the infantry bore the brunt of the fighting and the casualties. Nearly all of the cannon which had fired from the Allied centre – over sixty guns – were lost and no more than ten pieces of artillery were hauled to safety. Casualties, as always, are difficult to compute. Some reports suggest that each side lost as many as 18–20,000 men in killed, wounded and prisoners but this seems too high. The French, given the fact that they were in the open country attacking fixed positions, probably lost more men than the Allies, perhaps around 15,000. William's army suffered 12,000 casualties, twenty per cent of his strength at the beginning of the battle. Luxembourg did not pursue closely. His own army was exhausted whilst William, in falling back, would be able to gather garrisons from fortresses and call in Württemberg's corps from Flanders and Hainaut. The Frenchman thought it more prudent to retire and then use his victory to besiege an important fortress in the Sambre-Meuse.[45]

William's remnants fell back through Zoutleeuw and Louvain to rendezvous at Eppegem, between Vilvorde and Malines to the north of Brussels. His right stood at Verbrande Brug on the Antwerp Canal, known to the British as Burntbridge, and his left stretched towards Malines. Into this camp straggled the remains of William's army but he was soon cheered by the realisation that his battle losses were not as severe as he had first thought.[46] Württemberg's corps had now withdrawn from Hainaut and had come to a camp at Alost, between Ghent and Brussels, within easy supporting distance of William at Eppegem. The Allies tried to delude themselves into believing that the French had lost as many as 20,000 men at Landen, the corollary of this reasoning being that the campaign was therefore finished as Luxembourg would have neither the confidence nor the numbers to attempt anything worthwhile. To an extent, these assumptions were not baseless. Luxembourg had suffered severely. 'The Religious, both at Namur and Huy, were every day marching backwards and forwards to burials', and there were so many wounded French officers that 'every window in the town (Namur), if open, had two or three night caps at it'.[47] He required considerable reinforcements before he could consider a resumption of the campaign to remove that thorn in the French side, Charleroi. Most of Luxembourg's replacements had to trudge from a large 'standing camp' at St. Malo which had been formed under the command of 'Monsieur', the king's brother, to ward off Allied attempts to make descents on the Channel coast. Once these additional troops had arrived, along with de la Valette's corps from the Lines of the Lys and the Scheldt now released after Württemberg's withdrawal, Luxembourg felt strong enough to resume operations. He waited at Waremme for fifteen days, lulling the Allies into a false sense of security.

On 2/12 August, William adjusted his camp. He moved around to the north-west corner of Brussels and laid out his army between Zellik and Mollem with his headquarters at Wemmel, close to Württemberg at Alost. Landen brought some changes to the Allied command structure. Waldeck had died in 1692 enabling William to promote the Duke of

Holstein-Plön to be the first Field Marshal of the Dutch army. The hated Count Solms had met his end at Landen and William took the opportunity to reward the Duke of Württemberg by making him General of the Infantry over the heads of the Prince of Friesland and the Count of Nassau-Saarbruck.[48] On 5/15 August, William appointed Francisco del Castillo Taxardo, Captain-General of the Spanish artillery, to be Governor of Charleroi and he was immediately dispatched to his new command with a reinforcement of three battalions. While William made appointments, Luxembourg struck. He moved from Waremme to Boneffe on 5/15 August and onto Sombreffe on the following day. William countered by marching south of Brussels to take up a position with his right towards St. Kwintens-Lennik, his left at Tubize and his headquarters at Lembeek. This camp provided the Allies with good foraging grounds and covered Brussels. In very hot weather and with sickness rampant in both armies, Luxembourg edged westwards on 8/18 August to Bois St. Isaac, midway between William's army and Charleroi. A further movement westwards on 19/29 August brought Luxembourg to Soignies where he combined with his reinforcements from France and from the Lines of the Lys and the Scheldt. He left Soignies on 30 August/9 September to draw closer to the Sambre, taking camp at Haine St. Pierre. The next day took him closer to Charleroi, camping between Pont-à-Celles and Fontaine l'Évêque on the River Piéton. From this camp, Ximenes marched to Marchienne on the Sambre to the west of Charleroi and Guiscard marched from Namur with six battalions and a regiment of dragoons to Couillet in order to complete the investment. The noose was pulled tighter on 1/11 September and Vauban and Lieutenant-General du Rubantel brought up the main siege army of 32 battalions and 34 squadrons. The siege train was sent from Namur and Maubeuge by water.[49]

The lower Sambre flows between steep, rocky banks and was passable to a seventeenth-century army at only a few sites. Charleroi commanded one of the best. In 1666 it was no more than a village called Charnoy but in the wake of the War of Devolution, the Spaniards enlarged it, fortified it and renamed it Charleroi in honour of King Charles II of Spain. The new town lay on the south, or east bank of the Sambre but the fortifications enclosed a dominant hill on the north, or west bank which overlooked the river crossing. The fortifications, of brick and stone, included bastions, counter-guards, ravelins and a number of detached redoubts around the foot of the glacis. A large pond with a redoubt in its centre covered the defences between the Brussels Gate and the road to Fontain l'Évêque. The sluice which controlled the water supply from the Sambre into this lake was covered by a ravelin. Contemporaries did not regard the works encircling Charleroi as particularly strong although they recognised that digging trenches in the rocky soil would hinder attackers. Vauban, at whose insistence Charleroi had been chosen for assault, looked at it and muttered, 'fifteen days'.

Luxembourg positioned his covering army at Chapelle-les-Herlaimont, to the north-west of Charleroi, and handed overall command of the siege operations to Marshal Villeroi and Vauban. The French began to trace out their lines on 2/12 September and 12,000 pioneers set to with the spade on the following day. The trenches were officially opened on 5/15 September, Vauban aiming his attack towards the pond and one of the detached redoubts. Rain and fog covered the sappers and du~ing the first night the defenders threw 'firepots' beyond the glacis, large globes filled with tar and other combustible materials, which burned and illuminated considerable areas. In the light of these flares, the garrison cannon fired at the trenches. It was difficult for the French to extinguish the 'firepots' as several loaded pistol barrels had been screwed into their cases which discharged themselves at random and tended to discourage would-be firemen. Castillo and his garrison of 5,000 men clearly intended to conduct a vigorous defence.

William had no prospect of relieving Charleroi as the French had devoured all the forage between Brussels and the Sambre. They also had over 100 battalions massed around Charleroi. Instead, on 7/17 September, William detached the Elector of Bavaria with 30 battalions and 50 squadrons to Flanders to attack Furnes, as compensation for the probable loss of Charleroi. The Elector moved through rain and mud to Aaigem on 7/17 September, proceeding to cross the Scheldt at Gavere on the next afternoon. As soon as he received intelligence of Bavaria's departure, Luxembourg shifted westward to Estinnes, confident in his garrison of 5,000 men at Furnes. William perceived Luxembourg's slight alteration in stance as a direct threat to his weakened army and he hastily recalled Bavaria. The Elector rejoined the King on 12/22 September. At Charleroi, heavy fire from the French batteries had reduced the redoubt before the Brussels Gate to rubble but the attackers knew that it was mined and did not dare to risk an assault. The direction of the French trenches then switched to attack the hornwork and the redoubt in the centre of the pond. By 12/22 September, the heads of the saps had snaked past the point of the hornwork and were within ten metres of the covered way near the pond. All of his garrison guns had now been silenced although Castillo continued to launch sallies to disrupt Vauban's measured progress. Vauban arranged for six pontoons to be fastened together to form a raft sufficient to convey a force across the pond to take the redoubt. With its garrison of fifty men whittled down to twenty-five, the attack succeeded. On that same day, 14/24 September, Luxembourg returned to his original covering station at Chapelle-les-Herlaimont.

Castillo mounted sorties on three occasions between 15/25 September and 22 September/2 October, levelling portions of the siege works but he could only gain a little time. An attack was ordered for 16/26 September to take the ravelin which covered the sluice to the pond. Ten companies of grenadiers were detailed for the vanguard supported by three battalions of fusiliers. The attackers assembled in the leading parallel under orders not to advance until twelve small mortars had fired three salvoes. The third salvo would fire bombs filled with sand but containing long, ignited fuses; these were intended to keep the defenders' heads down as they waited for the explosions. During this delay and hiatus in the defending fire, the grenadiers and fusiliers would dash across the open ground before counter-mines could be sprung.

Despite these clever precautions, the operation was hazardous in the extreme. In order to arrive at the breach in the ravelin, the grenadiers had to traverse the length of the glacis whilst exposed to enfilading fire from the covered way and the main ramparts. From mid-morning the grenadiers were huddled in the place d'armes in the second parallel awaiting the expected signal. At 3.00 p.m. they were still there. A little later, orders arrived that the grenadiers were to light their fuses but there was no mention of the time of the attack. Under this increasing stress, the men grew silent and

> the more I examined them the more it seemed to me that they were no longer the same persons I had known yesterday. Their features had become changed in a most extraordinary manner; there were long, drawn-out faces, others quite twisted, others again were haggard, with flesh of a livid hue, whilst some had a wandering look about the eyes. In fact, I saw but a melancholy set of sinners under sentence of death.

Hatchets were issued at 6.00 p.m. in case the men needed to cut down palisades or other obstacles. Vauban then came along and offered some encouraging words yet the attackers continued to cower in their trenches and none had appetite for supper. Finally, at 9.00 p.m. precisely, the mortars fired. Whilst the shells from the third salvo were flying through the air, the grenadiers broke from the trenches 'like madmen' but they were hardly in the open before they came under heavy fire from the covered way. The men crowded together for protection to such an extent that our observer was carried along with his feet quite off the ground. In spite of the noise and long approach, the defenders were taken by surprise because the grenadiers and fusiliers assaulted the rear of the ravelin through the gorge rather than the faces. The garrison was driven out onto the glacis where a number were shot down by their own comrades. The French immediately set to work to build an epaulement across the gorge of the ravelin to protect themselves against fire from the covered way and the ramparts. Some of the soldiers lay flat on the ground holding their musket butts before their faces as crude shields. Many died but the epaulement was finished by dawn. The sluice was opened, the pond drained and a heavy breaching battery was built in the ravelin opposite the covered way.

An attack on the hornwork on 24 September/4 October was successful and all was ready for an assault on the covered way for the next morning. It failed, as did a second attempt on 26 September/6 October. Matters were becoming a trifle anxious for the French. The garrison of Charleroi, as befitted a corps which had operated against the French with such effect since the very beginning of the war, was putting up a spirited defence and embarrassing both Vauban and Luxembourg. Winter was fast approaching. Villeroi and Vauban launched a third attack on the covered way on 28 September/8 October which succeeded in effecting a large lodgement at the cost of over 600 casualties. Sappers zig-zagged their trenches into the ditch on the next day and made ready for a general assault as the artillery blasted the ramparts from the covered way. Villeroi invited Castillo to surrender but he refused. To make his point, the garrison then successfully resisted a heavy attack on the breach in the ramparts and obliged the French infantry to retire. Yet Castillo knew that he could not hold a second general assault and to save his town and garrison he beat the chamade at 8.00 a.m. on 1/11 October. Having inflicted over 4,000 casualties on the French and resisted for thirty-two days from the date of investment and twenty-six days from the opening of the trenches, the garrison was permitted to march out to Brussels with the full honours of war.[50] William remained to the south-west of Brussels, having shifted his camp to Ninove on 10/20 September to open new foraging grounds.[51]

It had been a humiliating and disastrous year for the Grand Alliance in the Low Countries. The loss of Charleroi and Huy gave the French the control of the Sambre and the Meuse as far north as the latter town, a solid logistical and tactical base from which to advance towards

Brussels or Maastricht. Vauban estimated that the capture of Charleroi so strengthened the French frontier that 16,000 fewer men were required in neighbouring garrisons.[52] The defeat at Landen had given Luxembourg the opportunity to capture Charleroi without interruption. Landen reinforced the impression that William was neither competent nor inspired as a general. He was also terribly unlucky. Yet, the year was not without positive aspects. The Dutch, Hanovarian and British troops had fought well at Landen and the Duke of Württemberg's expedition through the Lines of the Lys and the Scheldt had revealed the weakness of the French position in Flanders suggesting that it was possible to take the war to the French and act offensively. A campaign in which William lost two major fortresses and suffered heavy defeat in battle might have represented the nadir of his fortunes during the war but Luxembourg had not achieved the decisive victories sought by his master. It had been a bad year but there was no need to throw in the towel.

The Allies separated into winter quarters from Ninove on 5/15 October. The British were assigned billets in Flanders. Three battalions of the Guards, the Royal Fusiliers and William Selwyn's were lodged in Ghent; Bruges received the Royal Scots, the Scots Guards, Bath's, Tidcomb's, Castleton's, Leven's, Graham's, O'Farrell's and Mackay's; Churchill's, Trelawney's and Erle's found quarters in Malines in company with the Dutch Guards; Collingwood's and Stanley's went to Dendermonde; and Lauder's, Ferguson's and Argyll's came into Ostend. All of the British cavalry was stabled in Ghent except for the Life Guards who wintered on Dutch territory at Breda in readiness to protect the King. William was worried that the French might attempt another winter campaign in Flanders against the ports of Nieuport and Ostend and he sent twelve battalions from England in November to reinforce these towns. This service came as a nasty shock to soldiers who had so far enjoyed the war from the comfort of Great Britain. The three Huguenot regiments and Tiffany's battalion found themselves billeted amongst the polders between Ostend and Nieuport, 'and their quarters are strait and ill and the place very unwholesome. I am afraid many of them will fall sick.'[53] The one fact that William did not know and which might have dispelled his gloom was that the enormous efforts of the French on land during 1693 had represented their great and final attempt to force the Allies to an early peace. They were not able to muster such an offensive effort again. The worst, unknown to William, was over.

NOTES

1 John A. Lynn, 'The Growth of the French army during the seventeenth century', *Armed Forces and Society*, vi. (1979–80), pp. 569–77.
2 Mark A. Thomson, 'Louis XIV and William III, 1689–97', *EHR*, lxxvi. (1961), pp. 43–4; Symcox, *Crisis of French Sea Power*, pp. 141–6; Wolf, *Louis XIV*, pp. 472–3; François de Callières, *The Art of Diplomacy*, eds H. M. A. Keens-Soper & K. W. Schweizer (Leicester, 1983), pp. 7–8; W. T. Morgan, 'Economic Aspects of the Negotiations at Ryswick', in *Essays in Modern History*, ed. Ian R. Christie (London, 1968), pp. 173–4.
3 Thomson, 'Louis XIV and William III', pp. 40–1.
4 Symcox, *Victor Amadeus II*, pp. 112–13; Derek Mackay, *Prince Eugene of Savoy* (London, 1977), p. 36.
5 Onno Klopp, *Der Fall des Hauses Stuart* (Vienna, 1875–88), vi. 173–4.
6 Beaurain, ii. 241–2.
7 *Morrison 1st Series*, i. 106n.
8 SP 76/56, f. 160.
9 Villars, i. 154–5; BL, Stowe 444; HMC, *Denbigh MSS.*, pp. 91–2; *Colonie*, p. 26; Edward D'Auvergne, *The History of the Last Campaign in the Spanish Netherlands* (London, 1693), pp. 2–4; CMC 4/60.
10 HMC, *Denbigh MSS.*, pp. 91–2; BL, King's MSS. 228, ff. 5–42.
11 SP 77/56, ff. 166–7; HMC, *Bath MSS.*, iii. 2–3.
12 *Archives d'Orange-Nassau*, i. 307; BL, King's MSS. 228, ff. 73–6.
13 SP 77/56, ff. 170–1.
14 Ibid., ff. 172–5.
15 Ibid., f. 178.
16 *Archives d'Orange-Nassau*, i. 310; Burnet, *History*, iv. 198–200.
17 SP 77/56, ff. 179–81.
18 Ibid., ff. 185–8.
19 Ibid., ff. 187–8; HMC, *Bath MSS.*, iii. 3–4.
20 BL, Add. MSS. 9,731, f. 5.
21 SP 77/56, f. 213.
22 HMC, *Bath MSS.*, iii. 4–5; D'Auvergne, *1693*, p. 4.
23 SP 77/56, ff. 216–17.
24 HMC, *Bath MSS.*, iii. 5–6; Luttrell, *Historical Relation*, iii. 60.
25 SP 77/56, ff. 218–19; BL, Add. MSS. 9,731, f. 8.
26 BL, Stowe 444; BL, Add. MSS. 9,731, ff. 11–4; D'Auvergne, *1693*, pp. 6–7.
27 A bilander was a single-masted vessel with a trapezoidal mainsail. It was Dutch in design and much used on canals and inland waterways.
28 BL, Stowe MSS. 458, 'The Diary of Jacob Richards, 1693', ff. 2–3.
29 Beaurain, ii. 244–53; D'Auvergne, *1693*, pp. 708.
30 Walton, pp. 235–6; D'Auvergne, *1693*, pp. 16–17, 23–4.
31 BL, Stowe 458, ff. 4–7; HMC, *Le Fleming MSS.*, p. 332; LUL, MS. 12, ff. 172–5.
32 SP 77/56, ff. 220–1; Beaurain, ii. 254–5; *Saint-Simon*, xii. 36–7.
33 HMC, *Le Fleming MSS.*, p. 332; D'Auvergne, *1693*, pp. 24–7; SP 77/56, f. 222.
34 *Archives d'Orange-Nassau*, i. 322–3.
35 BL, Stowe 458, ff. 7–10; D'Auvergne, *1693*, pp. 27–8.
36 D'Auvergne, *1693*, p. 10.

37 Walton, pp. 239–40; D'Auvergne, *1693*, pp. 29–31.
38 BL, Stowe 458, ff. 12–3; D'Auvergne, *1693*, pp. 29, 32; Baxter, *William III*, p. 312; Beaurain, ii. 269–72.
39 Japikse (Welbeck), ii. 209.
40 Walton, pp. 241–6; D'Auvergne, *1693*, pp. 32–46.
41 BL, Stowe 458, ff. 12–13.
42 BL, Stowe 458, ff. 14–15; LUL, MS. 12, ff. 175–82; D'Auvergne, *1693*, pp. 49–52; *Archives d'Orange-Nassau*, i. 324; CMC 4/67 & 68; *Mérode-Wester-loo*, i. 84–5; PRO, MPH 20/Part 1; MPH 19/Part 2, f. 19.
43 D'Auvergne, *1693*, pp. 54–8. 96–7.
44 Edward D'Auvergne, *The History of the Campaign in the Spanish Netherlands, 1694* (London, 1694), p. 28.
45 The acount of the Battle of Landen is based on: *A Relation of the Battel of Landen* (London, 1693); HMC, *Hamilton (Supplementary) MSS.*, pp. 125–6; Beaurain, ii. 287–97; HMC, *Portland MSS.*, iii. 538–9; Bonneval, *Memoirs*, pp. 12–13; Berwick, i. 77–84; HMC, *Le Fleming MSS.*, pp. 333–4; Burnet, *History*, iv. 201–4; *Saint-Simon*, i. 85–97; *Colonie*, pp. 26–8; 'Remarks upon the London Gazette relating to the Straits' Fleet and the Battle of Landen in Flanders', in, *A Collection of Scarce and Valuable Tracts*, ed. Sir Walter Scott (London, 1809–15), xi. 462–71; HMC, *Downshire MSS.*, i. 425; Feuquières, ii. 77–88; Walton, pp. 250–69; Fortescue, i. 370–6; D'Auvergne, *1693*, pp. 58–95; PRO, MPH 19/Part 1; Landmann, pp. 36–44.
46 *Archives d'Orange-Nassau*, i. 325.
47 BCRO, Trumbull Add. MSS. 103; D'Auvergne, *1693*, pp. 87–8.
48 HMC, *Buch MSS.*, iii. 7; LUL, MS. 12, ff. 186–92.
49 LUL, MS. 12, ff. 192–4; D'Auvergne, *1693*, pp. 98–109; Beaurain, ii. 299–310.
50 BL, Add. MSS. 64,108, ff. 103–4; *Colonie*, pp. 28–36; HMC, *Portland MSS.*, iii. 542–3; HMC, *Downshire MSS.*, i. 434; Beaurain, ii. 310–24; D'Auvergne, *1693*, pp. 110–24.
51 LUL, MS. 12, ff. 194–201; *Archives d'Orange-Nassau*, i. 329–30.
52 Duffy, *Fortress in the Age of Vauban and Frederick the Great*, pp. 29–30; HSL, vii. 64–82.
53 D'Auvergne, *1693*, pp. 127, 132; BL, Add. MSS. 9,731, ff. 15–16.

IX

1694: THE SCHELDT AND HUY

Anxious to capitalise on Luxembourg's limited achievements, Louis started a second peace offensive in the winter of 1693–4. The French envoy, Callières, contacted Dijkveldt on 21/31 January 1694. Callières had already proposed that deputies of the King of France and of the States-General should meet in a French town or in one belonging to the United Netherlands. To this Dijkveldt had objected that such an arrangement would not be secret and instead suggested a closed conference somewhere in Brabant or Spanish Flanders. Dijkveldt had also stressed that this was only to be a preliminary discussion as 'the affair is not yet ripe for settlement'. Callières's response to these rather half-hearted replies was to refuse the Spanish Netherlands on the grounds that Frenchmen would be liable to 'insult'. However, he thought that the proposed conference ought to proceed towards the conclusion of peace as enough of the background business had been cleared away. He insisted that the representatives of the States-General should come equipped with full powers to treat for a peace settlement and be ready to sign a treaty during an open and public meeting at the termination of the conference.[1] Clearly, the disagreement was too wide to be easily bridged and the peace feelers were withdrawn during the campaigning season. In the autumn of 1694, Callières and Dijkveldt met in clandestine session at Maastricht. These talks broke down when Dijkveldt reiterated that peace could not be considered without the unconditional recognition of William as King of England. Dijkveldt was also disappointed to discover that the French envoys did not possess full powers but only expected to test the temperature of the diplomatic water. When the Allies began to spread the story that France had actually sent diplomats to contact the Grand Alliance at Maastricht, Versailles vehemently denied such scandalous inventions.[2]

This seeming volte-face between the winter and autumn of 1694 was not occasioned by any startling military successes during the summer. Not for the first time, the word had proved mightier than the sword and French diplomacy towards the Empire and Savoy had begun to show signs of a possible breakthrough. Contacts between the Duke of Savoy and General Tessé had continued whilst in Switzerland the agents of Louis XIV and Emperor Leopold I had enjoyed secret negotiations over the future position of James II's son. It looked to William, who was incensed when he found out about these undercover activities of his supposed allies, as though the Grand Alliance might fall apart into a protestant-catholic split or, at least, the Emperor and some of the German states might well be detached from the Alliance by French intrigues. The solemn reaffirmation of the Grand Alliance, which was to occur in August 1695, was a political necessity as far as William was concerned. Regardless of these glimmers of light at the end of the diplomatic tunnel, they could not compensate for the ill condition of France and her armed forces. The harvest of 1693 had been the worst since the beginning of the war and Louis had neither the food, the money nor the resources to undertake another series of offensives. Everywhere in 1694, both by land and sea, French arms would have to stand on the defensive for the first time during the Nine Years' War.[3]

Harvests were also poor in England and the Dutch Republic but they possessed the maritime power and the geographical location to make good some of their shortfall by imports of grain from the Baltic, a recourse which France found ever more difficult as the war progressed. War weariness existed in England but it took a different form to that experienced across the Channel. With France stubbornly refusing to renounce the claims of James II and insisting that William III was not the legal monarch, the English had nothing to gain from a peace during 1693 and 1694, especially as the country was not suffering from the acute shortages and starvation then current in France. Parliament was able to agree to a substantial increase in the army and navy estimates and provided their sovereign with 93,635 soldiers for 1694, of whom 68,725 were to be recruited from within the British Isles.[4] Information on the conditions in France began to filter into London and The Hague; the French garrisons were short of bread and other essentials and the whole country was filled with 'misery and desolation'.[5]

The winter weather was hard with severe frosts and heavy snows. Several hundred men from the Allied garrison of Dendermonde were given the daily task of breaking the ice to keep open the moat.[6] After their experiences during the previous winter, the Allies were apprehensive that the French would seize upon the cold spell to launch a lightning offensive but nothing materialised.[7] Instead of the anxious winter of 1693 when the Allied commanders had been unable to stem the tide of French cavalry raiding around the fringes of Brussels, the generals settled back and enjoyed a series of balls and masquerades.[8] The reasons for the French inactivity soon became clear. Travellers from France told of starvation in the streets of Paris and in the frontier garrisons of Cambrai, Mons and Valenciennes they had found French soldiers without food or pay.[9] The French commissariat was at its wit's end trying to feed the soldiers in their winter quarters; the task of building magazines ready for a summer campaign was beyond its capabilities. Without those magazines, the French would be unable to undertake offensive operations and the army would be locked into its frontier garrisons. To make matters worse, after the losses at Landen and Charleroi, the French infantry battalions were full of raw recruits and the cavalry was weak from the want of forage occasioned by the abysmal harvest. By default, the initiative would rest with the Allies.

The rich agricultural lands of Brabant were exhausted. They had been fought over for five successive summers, stripped and wasted by both the French and the Allies. The peasant farmers in the quadrilateral outlined by the Sambre-Meuse and the line between Brussels and Louvain had grown tired of producing crops for rival armies to comandeer or cut down before they were ripe in order to feed their voracious horses. They started to mow their grass early to prevent it filling the bellies of army horses or being burned by the French and 'this year they had neglected the tilling of the ground, being unwilling to work in vain'. Although he could probably garner sufficient supplies to keep the field, there was no question of Luxembourg gathering the resources to mount a major siege. Liège, the next French target on the Meuse, was unlikely to come under attack. It was expected that Luxembourg would shift his weight towards Flanders

> because the country is not so much ruined by the war on that side as 'tis everywhere else on this, and consequently they (the French) hope to find more forage there than they can expect anywhere in these parts, a great deal of the ground being perfectly waste and not having been ploughed or sowed last year, both between Louvain and Namur and this town (Brussels) and Mons.[10]

With the country in such an ill condition, both armies were also more likely to stay very close to the major river lines in order to draw supplies from magazines.

The Allies were unable to take advantage of French misfortunes. They too had suffered serious losses at Landen, Charleroi and Huy and their replacements were slow to come into the field. Both sides were late in starting their campaigns. At the end of April, Brigadier Pierre Belcastel advanced into Flanders with his brigade of four battalions, three consisting of Huguenot refugees, and scattered the French troops who were busy demolishing the fortifications of Dixmuyde. A better spirit prevailed amongst the Allies. When William reached Het Loo in mid-May he fretted to Shrewsbury in London that the political problems which had delayed him in England had prevented him from seizing the initiative in Flanders by following up Belcastel's success. William sensed, rightly, that Luxembourg was slow coming into the field and had not made his usual preparations for an offensive campaign.

> The length of the session in Parliament, which detained me in England, occasioned my losing a favourable opportunity of anticipating the movements of the enemy. This I told you before my departure and now that I am on the spot, I am more clearly convinced of its truth. God knows when we shall have so good an opportunity, the loss of which we shall have cause to regret this whole campaign.[11]

Towards the end of May and into the beginning of June, in very hot weather, the Allied army began to assemble at Meldert and Bethlehem Abbey, near Louvain, whilst Luxembourg brought his army together around Gembloux, some thirty kilometres to the south-east of William's camp. Forage was so scarce that William did not bring his cavalry into the main camp but kept them in cantonments in order to ease the supply of green fodder. If it had been possible, William wanted to attempt the recapture of Namur but the political delays which had kept him in England and the shortage of fodder and corn in Brabant obliged him to remain in the vicinity of Brussels. Luxembourg took the opportunity to establish his army between William and the Meuse, bringing William's design to a temporary conclusion.[12]

Louis XIV appointed the Comte de Lorge to command on the Rhine and Luxembourg again had charge of the Netherlands theatre. Catinat observed the Savoyard and Imperial forces in northern Italy and Noailles was entrusted with holding Catalonia. Philippe, Duke of Orléans, commanded the camp in Britanny to guard the coasts against descent and invasion. Despite the stories spreading from France of starvation and privation, Luxembourg and the French armies in the Low Countries remained considerable and threatening. At Gembloux, Luxembourg had

82 battalions and 164 squadrons, a total of 69,000 whilst Boufflers stood in a flying camp between Waremme and the Mehaigne with 12,000, 15 battalions and 25 squadrons. D'Harcourt commanded 3,600 cavalry at Chiny in Luxembourg and de la Valette controlled the Lines of the Lys and the Scheldt with 8,000 men. The French armies in the Netherlands amounted to 92,000. For the first time in the war, the Allies disposed of more men in the Low Countries. William's main army around Louvain consisted of 82,000 soldiers and a further 7,000 were stationed at Ghent under the Spanish Major-General, the Comte de Thian.[13] A further 24,000 Allied troops were positioned in Liège. This city had now become a frontier post and 'required an army for a garrison'. During the winter, Coehoorn had refortified much of the city although he was still worried by the weakness of the citadel and the Carthusian Monastery.[14]

William arrived at the army on the night of 24 May/3 June having travelled from Het Loo via Breda. Despite the ravaged fields of Brabant, it seemed as though Luxembourg intended to attack Liège. On 29 May/8 June, he advanced north from Gembloux to Jandrain, twenty kilometres south of Tirlemont, in order to interpose his army between William and Liège. The Allies responded by marching east from around Louvain to encamp at Roosbeek, six kilometres to the north-west of Tirlemont. Luxembourg's riposte was to march north on 31 May/10 June to St. Truiden, almost exactly midway between William at Roosbeek and Liège.[15] The French now occupied the ideal position from which to cover a siege of Liège but several factors militated against this course of action. In the first place, Luxembourg was numerically inferior. His main army had increased to 81,000 as garrisons were called in and Boufflers, who had concentrated at Dinant before moving to encamp at Waremme, had 12,000 men. D'Harcourt's small force of cavalry remained on the east bank of the Meuse around Chiny. Luxembourg planned to launch Boufflers and d'Harcourt against Liège enveloping the city from east and west whilst he covered William's army from around St. Truiden. Liège, with a garrison of 24,000, could not have been successfully besieged by 15,600 men and Luxembourg would have been forced to send substantial reinforcements to Boufflers from his main army. At Roosbeek, William's forces had increased to 90,000 and Luxembourg dared not emasculate his own army as his opponent was showing his customary aggression. Weight of numbers was decisive. The French weakness resulted, partly, from economic difficulties but, more particularly, from tactical over-commitment. The recent acquisition of Mons, Namur, Huy and Charleroi, as well as the constant fear of an Allied attack through the Lines in Flanders, had pulled considerable numbers of soldiers away from the field armies into the garrisons. William, on the other hand, having lost these fortresses, was encumbered by fewer garrisons and was able to commit more men to his operational corps.[16]

Liège was an extremely powerful fortress. Coehoorn reported to William on 6/16 June that his task of refortifying Liège was almost complete with just some work to finish 'on the escarpment of the mountains' and in preparing palisades. By 2/12 June, General Johan von Heiden, the commander of the Brandenburg troops, had encamped his corps at Visé, the main bridging point of the Meuse between Liège and Maastricht. From here he could both throw troops into Liège and observe the movements of d'Harcourt who had advanced to St. Vith. Brandenburg reinforcements were stationed at Eschweiler, to the east of Aachen. So favourable was the Allied position that Coehoorn complained to William about the weight of troops in and around Liège; 'in case of an attack we shall be robbed of all the glory of being attacked'.[17] Coehoorn's garrison was divided between a large entrenched camp at St. Walburge, just to the north of the city, which contained 15,000 and a corps of 9,000 within Liège itself. Not only was Liège too tough for Luxembourg to tackle but its garrison and Heiden's troops formed a substantial threat to the French right flank at St. Truiden.

A month of stalemate followed. The ground between William and Luxembourg was criss-crossed by rivers and streams making it almost impossible for one army to stage a set-piece attack upon the other. Neither commander seemed to have a clear plan of campaign. William was content that both armies should remain in Brabant and consume forage as this reduced the likelihood of the enemy staging a major operation along the Meuse. Luxembourg regarded the Allied army as better employed in Brabant, where it could achieve little, than in Flanders where it might make a more significant contribution. Both Louis and his marshal were extremely touchy about the French frontier in Flanders.

Supply continued to dominate the campaign. The first major forage from the Allied camp at Roosbeek on 9/19 June produced just enough hay for one night. Under these conditions, the horses could not be retained in the camp and they had to be 'grassed' in the neighbouring fields and meadows. With his cavalry and transport horses dispersed, William could neither march nor respond rapidly. The notion of attacking Huy, the southern bastion of Liège and a vital post if Namur was ever to be regained, was beginning to form in William's mind. Searching for forage, Luxembourg moved back to Lauw on the River Jeker, midway between Tongres and Waremme, on 11/21 July from where he continued to threaten Liège but covered Huy. It took William two days to gather together his separated army and march to Mont St. André, twenty kilometres south of Tirlemont. This pointed a lance at both Huy and Namur, causing Luxembourg to shift south-westwards to Vinalmont, seven kilometres to the north of Huy. Both sides threw up field fortifications, the Allies concentrating on strengthening their left wing towards Ramillies whose heights commanded the road to Huy. An engagement was possible across the plains between the Meuse and Mont St. André; the Allied march from Roosbeek had been made in eight columns as if expecting to meet the French and force them to battle. Luxembourg was in no position to risk an engagement. The Anglo-Dutch Fleet was still menacing the coasts of France after having attacked Brest on 8/18 June and the marshal was short of men, supplies and forage. He was further encumbered by a French offensive across the Rhine at Philippsburg, aimed at attacking the region around the Bergstrasse, which might have required reinforcement at any time. In the intense heat, Luxembourg was content to sit and watch the Allies.[18]

> We are in a very good condition and in a very good camp, and as our horses are now cantoned on the villages about, we may subsist, for ought I know, this three weeks or more and, when we have eaten up the country on this side, march by common consent, facing each other and do the same in Flanders until the end of the campaign.[19]

Life in both camps dropped into tedium. To fill in the boring hours, the Comte de Bonneval organised raids on Allied convoys and outposts largely, it seems, on his own initiative. During July, he received intelligence that a convoy of money was to be ferried from Brussels to the Allied camp. Bonneval took 200 of his own men and waited in the corn 'which was then very high' within two kilometres of the Allied lines. Half an hour before dusk, Bonneval noticed two waggons which had broken down and were struggling back to camp in the company of twenty-four infantrymen and sixty dragoons. Virtually within sight of safety, the escort had grown careless. Bonneval's men scattered them to be rewarded by one waggon containing 95,000 livres and the other full with barrels of 'strong waters'. Being a sensible man, Bonneval refused to let his soldiers loose on the drink and had the casks broken on the spot. The party then made good their escape to share out the spoils. Shortly afterwards, Bonneval organised another private expedition. Taking 400 men from his own regiment and a number of drummers from other formations, he set off to capture and ransom a market town of 2,000 people situated near Louvain on the Brussels road. During the night, the place was surrounded and the drummers were positioned at each of the three roads leading into the town centre. They were instructed to beat their several regimental marches to create the impression that the town was under attack from a number of units instead of just one. The Frenchmen closed in at dawn and although there were 500 armed men in the town, they succumbed to Bonneval's trickery and surrendered. Twenty hostages were secured to ensure that the alarm was not given to neighbouring villages and Bonneval's men then felt sufficiently secure to execute an 'orderly plunder' to the value of 40,000 livres 'without reckoning a prodigious quantity of hams'. Another pastime was horse raiding which was made especially easy by the dispersal of both the French and Allied horses into cantonments. Major-General Thian, commanding the corps of 7,000 near Ghent to observe the Lines of the Lys and the Scheldt, dispatched a large raid on 21/31 July. A detachment of 300 horse collected 1,000 infantry from the garrison of Ath and forced their way through the French Lines along the River Haine near St. Ghislain, to the west of Mons. They plundered St. Ghislain, whose garrison ran away on the approach of the Spaniards, before retiring to Ath with their booty.[20]

Both armies were finding forage extremely scarce. They had been in Brabant and the Pays de Liège for over two months, indeed the French had been there since the opening of the campaign. Luxembourg was restricted to foraging between the Jaar and the Meuse and had to send his horses across the Meuse by pontoon bridges to graze in the wooded hills of the Condroz. The only plentiful commodity was coal drawn from the numerous coal-pits and mines in the Condroz. By 1/11 August, William had consumed the country as far east as Liège and a move of camp was imperative, preferably to Flanders, but such a march might expose Liège. The only permanent method of protecting Liège was the recapture of Huy but for this to occur Luxembourg had to be prised away from Vinalmont.[21] William's camp was conveniently placed between Luxembourg and the Scheldt. If he marched for that river, then the Frenchman would be bound to follow. Not only would William enjoy a head-start but Luxembourg's pursuit would take him across the Sambre, a manoeuvre which would increase William's lead. The only danger in this projected plan was that Luxembourg might descend on Liège as the Allies marched towards the Scheldt and Flanders. However, Liège retained its garrison of 24,000 men and the barren countryside of the Pays de Liège and Brabant made virtually certain that Luxembourg would not be able to sustain an operation against the city. The march to Flanders enjoyed the additional advantage of freeing the large corps in and around Liège to join the Allied army giving William an overwhelming numerical superiority, provided that the Liège garrison did not leave prematurely but waited for Luxembourg to declare his intentions. For once, it looked as though William was close to out-manoeuvreing his opponent.

After a conference with the Elector of Bavaria and the Dutch Field Deputies, William decided to gamble on 'a race for the Scheldt' in order to force the French Lines, levy contributions from enemy territory and draw Luxembourg away from Huy and the Meuse. There was even the prospect of battle to warm William's heart. Luxembourg had anticipated William's scheme. Both generals sent their heavy baggage to the rear – the Allies' to Brussels and the French to Namur – ready for a sudden march. On 8/18 August, William moved to Sombreffe and Luxembourg marched along the Meuse to Daussoir, near Namur. William rested at Sombreffe for twenty-four hours to allow his men to recover from their gruelling march in the intense August heat, but Luxembourg wasted no time in crossing the Sambre and dividing his army into ten corps. Each corps was to march and camp separately but remain sufficiently close to concentrate if threatened. In this Napoleonic fashion, Luxembourg hoped to be able to march fast enough along all the available roads to reach the Scheldt ahead of the Allies. In addition, 3,000 dragoons were sent on to Charleroi with orders to gallop for the Lines of the Lys and the Scheldt to reinforce de la Valette's twelve battalions.

Undoubtedly, Luxembourg was aided and abetted by spies in William's camp as he seemed to possess a clear picture and adequate notice of his enemy's intentions. Security in the field was unachievable in the face of the steady trickle of merchants, clerics, peasant pioneers, bona fide travellers and deserters between the camps.[22] William marched to Nivelles on 10/20 August, onto to Soignies on the following day and into Cambron on 12/22 August.[23] Contrary to all expectations, particularly those of William, Luxembourg kept up with the Allied progress. Through the rugged and wooded terrain on the edge of the Ardennes to the south of Namur and Charleroi, across the Sambre twice and over the Mehaigne and the Scarpe, Luxembourg flogged his infantry through heat and thunder storms for over two hundred kilometres. Perhaps as many as 3,000 men were lost, some through exhaustion more from desertion, and an equal number of horses, but William was not able to gain an advantage even though his march measured one-third less distance and traversed easier country. By the standards of the times, the French forced march was a remarkable achievement and saved the campaign.

From south of the Sambre, Luxembourg had set his ten columns in motion on 12/22 August. His cavalry and dragoons were in Tournai late on 13/23 August. William crossed the River Dender on 13/23 August and sent the Elector of Bavaria ahead with 20,000 men to surprise de la Valette in the Lines. General Tettau was instructed to take a corps of 5,000 soldiers and prepare bridges over the Scheldt at Outrijve. On this day, Luxembourg's infantry and artillery were betwixt Mons and St. Ghislain. When he received the accurate news that Tettau was about to bridge the Scheldt and the false report that the Elector had actually crossed near Oudenarde, he spurred his men with bribes and threats and they struggled into Tournai on the morning of 14/24 August. As Tettau approached the banks of the Scheldt he was astonished to find not only de la Valette's twelve battalions from within the Lines but also Villeroi with 3,000 dragoons and a brigade of guards who had been force marched to Condé and then shipped down the Scheldt. William advanced during the morning of 14/24 August expecting to find Tettau's bridges spanning the river but rain poured down and his progress through the close country was slow. At midday the army reached the Scheldt only to find Tettau still on the eastern bank, no bridges and Villeroi strongly posted on the western side. In the distance, could be seen Luxembourg's main army marching up the road from Tournai and into the Lines. By evening, the whole French army was arrayed along the western bank of the Scheldt between Pont d'Espierres and Outrijve. William and the Elector had only themselves to blame. They could have marched faster and certainly took one rest day too many. They ought to have recalled the marching ability of the French army from 1691 when another forced march over the same difficult country had rescued Luxembourg from an awkward corner around Beaumont on the Hantes. In that year too, he had been helped by the indolence of William. Bavaria could have pushed on much more rapidly with the advance party of 20,000 and secured bridges but the Allied generals thought that it was impossible for Luxembourg to make up two days' march in the region to the south of the Sambre. Out of promising beginnings, William had suffered another strategic defeat.[24]

Probably in one of his frequent bad tempers, William withdrew ten kilometres to Cordes. On the next morning, 15/25 August, he pressed upto the Scheldt at Berchem and engaged in a cannonade with the left wing of Luxembourg's army. In an effort to bring on a general action in which his weight of numbers might prove decisive, William tried to seize some advantageous ground near Moregem and Petergem on the west bank of the Scheldt opposite Oudenarde. Württemberg was entrusted with this mission but he ran into a French detachment bent on the same business and both sides withdrew rather than risk an engagement.[25] William was in no position to force Luxembourg into battle. If he sensed a significant threat developing, Luxembourg could simply pull back his left wing and withdraw into the Lines of the Lys and the Scheldt. William crossed the river with his army on 17/27 August and camped at Kruishoutem, to the north-west of Oudenarde, where he waited to be joined by the garrison of Deynze and a corps of 8,000 men which Coehoorn was bringing from Liège. Heavily outnumbered, Luxembourg fell back to Courtrai and camped along the River Lys with his left at Moorsele. Luxembourg's right flank was guarded by de la Valette with 5,000 men in the Lines of the Lys and the Scheldt whilst Villeroi covered his left with 12,000 men in the Lines between the Lys and Ypres. Close at hand lay Furnes with its garrison of 15,000. The French stance was well balanced.[26] William was more than content to pin Luxembourg in Flanders by threatening Furnes and Dunkirk. With this in mind, he moved camp to Roeselare on 29 August/8 September where orders were given to the troops 'to hut', a clear indication that the camp was intended to endure for some time.[27] In an effort to distract the Allies from their dominance in Flanders, the French launched a limited offensive through the Eifel towards the Rhine. The Landgrave of Hesse-Cassel had not enough troops to oppose this movement and looked for reinforcements either from the Margrave of Baden around Philippsburg or from William in Flanders.[28]

Penned into Flanders and compelled to protect the Lines and Dunkirk, Luxembourg was powerless to prevent William from taking full advantage of his predicament to undertake a major siege. Huy was the target. The recapture of Huy was essential if the Allies were going to defend Liège and attack Namur in 1695. Huy was also important because of political problems within Liège. The Prince-Bishop had died and the Chapter was divided over the election of a successor. One faction favoured the elevation of the brother of the Elector Palatine but the stronger group wanted to elect Joseph Clement of Bavaria, the Elector of Cologne and brother of Max Emmanuel, Elector of Bavaria and Governor of the Spanish Netherlands. This was a potential embarrassment for the Grand Alliance. Louis XIV was already flattering Max Emmanuel with offers of the sovereignty of the Spanish Netherlands upon the death of Carlos II of Spain. Aware of the vulnerability of Bavarian lands to French attack and influence, the Elector was inclined to react favourably to the overtures of his powerful neighbour. The possible election of Joseph Clement to the Bishopric of Liège threatened to form a Wittelsbach family state comprising the Spanish Netherlands, Liège and Cologne. In the long run, this grouping was bound to be more friendly towards France than the Dutch Republic or the Holy Roman Empire. All that could be said in support of the election of Joseph Clement was that the Pope encouraged his candidacy and, at the moment, both the new Prince-Bishop and the Elector of Bavaria remained anti-French and within the Grand Alliance. Nevertheless, the situation was uncertain and the recapture of Huy was seen as a vital insurance in case French diplomacy removed the Wittelsbach brothers from the Grand Alliance.[29]

The Duke of Holstein-Plön rode from Woutergem alone towards Huy. General Tilly left Liège on 5/15 September with the majority of the Liège garrison and a substantial force from Maastricht. Holstein-Plön met this force close to Huy on 6/16 September and the town was blockaded on the following day. The Allies boasted forty battalions and thirty-eight squadrons, around 24,000 men, all of whom had been produced from the garrisons of Liège and Maastricht; no troops were withdrawn from the main army in Flanders. When Tilly and Holstein-Plön invested Huy on 7/17 September, the French Governor, de Regnac, found himself in a hopeless position. His garrison consisted of just 1,400 men and there was no substantial assistance within two hundred kilometres. He immediately surrendered the town to the Allies and retired into the castle, Fort Picard and Fort Rouge. Once Regnac had vacated the town, Coehoorn and Major-General Schwerin crossed the Meuse and invested Huy on its eastern side. Five batteries had been built by 11/21 September and these started to fire on the following morning. At the same time, the trenches were opened attacking towards Fort Picard. Despite their inferior numbers and cheerless prospect, the defenders kept up a steady and harassing fire but they could not affect the rapid progress of the sappers. By nightfall, the trenches had reached the counterscarp and the well had been destroyed. Breaches were made in the defences of both Fort Picard and Fort Rouge on 13/23 September and infantry assaults carried both works on the next day. The batteries switched their attention to the castle on 15/25 September blasting a breach within twenty-four hours. The gap was widened on 16/26 September and Regnac did not wait for the inevitable infantry attack on the covered way but beat the chamade on 17/27 September. The garrison marched out on the following morning. Hölstein-Plon and Tilly had captured Huy in five days, exactly the same duration as the French siege under Villeroi in 1693.[30]

William prepared to leave the army at Roeselare but waited for news from the Meuse before making his departure. The welcome announcement of the fall of Huy was received on 20/30 September and William immediately set off, via Brussels, to inspect the Meuse fortresses of Liège and Maastricht before turning north for Graves and Het Loo.[31] Roeselare had proved an excellent camp. After the privations of Brabant and the Pays de Liège, Flanders abounded in potatoes, turnips and parsnips for which the men were permitted to forage. The disadvantage of the camp site was its location in close and wooded country. Bread columns were frequently attacked by French patrols, a situation which was made worse by the sutlers who attached their waggons to the bread convoys when they went in search of provisions and stores. This made the waggon trains so long that the escorts could not adequately protect them and many men and waggons were lost. Much of the Roeselare camp was actually in a thick wood. When the army left, the vegetation had been flattened for a kilometre on all sides, the trees having been felled to make huts and provide firewood. In partial revenge for their defeat at Huy, a raiding party of 500 from the garrison of Mons attacked Tilly's flying camp and seized the unfortunate general in his bed. Holstein-Plön hurriedly arranged a ransom. On 8/18 October, the army withdrew from Roeselare to Drongen on the outskirts of Ghent and there the troops began to separate into winter quarters. The British infantry were billetted in Ghent, Bruges, Malines, Dendermonde, Ostend, Dixmuyde, Deynze, Damme, Laar and Oudenarde. The cavalry were spread further afield to Breda, The Hague, 's-Hertogenbosch, Ghent, Bruges and Gertruidenburg.[32] As in previous years, the Allied winter quarters were so arranged that a field force could be rapidly assembled in the event of any French advance across the frozen rivers and canals.[33]

William had taken the initiative in the Netherlands for the first time. He had displayed a caution and prudence in the conduct of operations contrasting with the rash and almost desperate pursuit of battle which had characterised his manoeuvres in 1691, 1692 and 1693. His one rush of blood had occurred after the loss of the 'race for the Scheldt' when, for a couple of days, he seemed anxious to engage Luxembourg and assuage his defeat through manoeuvre by success in action. This carefulness contributed greatly to the containment of Luxembourg and the recapture of Huy even if William had shown a significant lapse of concentration and control during the 'race for the Scheldt'. The renewed confidence of the Allied army and its commanders had been based on their numerical superiority. In turn, this was founded upon the generosity and co-operation of the English Parliament. To make the point more emphatically, the upturn in the Allied fortunes was matched by the decline in the effectiveness of the French army as it struggled to come to terms with shortages of supply and money. On 4/14 January 1695, William enjoyed an even greater stroke of luck: François Henri de Montmorency, Duke of Luxembourg, died at the age of sixty-seven. This great soldier, trained under Turenne and Condé, was a master of positional warfare. With uncanny precision he was able to put himself in the shoes of the opposition and work out the likely counters to his own manoeuvres. No doubt the leaky security within the Allied camp and the services of the Elector of Bavaria's secretary greatly helped in making these predictions, but Luxembourg was a wily opponent and William failed to get the better of him in four campaigns. Perhaps his most important attribute was his ability to dig himself out of a hole. On the rare occasions when he was out-manoeuvred, as before Beaumont in 1691 or during the 'race for the Scheldt' in 1694, he was capable of redeeming his mistakes. No other French marshal during the Nine Years' War came within shooting distance of Luxembourg's skill, with the possible exception of Nicolas Catinat. Now that France had lost the initiative in Flanders and no longer possessed the resources to undertake offensive warfare, Luxembourg's loss was the more keenly felt.[34]

NOTES

1 *HMC, Denbigh MSS.*, pp. 93–4.
2 Thomson, 'Louis XIV and William III', pp. 45–6; Burnet, *History*, iv. 237–8; Callières, *Diplomacy*, p. 8; Morgan, 'Ryswick', pp. 174–5.
3 Wolf, *Louis XIV*, pp. 475–7; Baxter, *William III*, pp. 316–17.
4 Childs, *British Army of William III*, p. 268.
5 Burnet, *History*, iv. 230; *HMC, Bath MSS.*, iii. 17–20.
6 *HMC, Le Fleming MSS.*, p. 333.
7 *CSPD 1695*, p. 233.
8 *HMC, Denbigh MSS.*, p. 93.
9 SP 77/56, ff. 209–10, 294; *Colonie*, p. 37.
10 D'Auvergne, *1694*, pp. 1–8; DCRO, D60/X43, 9/19 Mar. 1694, Sir John Trenchard to Sir Henry Bellasise; SP 77/56, ff. 304–5.
11 *Shrewsbury Correspondence*, pp. 32–3.
12 LUL, MS. 12, f. 206; R. L. Pomeroy, *The Regimental History from 1685 to*

1922 of the 5th Princess Charlotte of Wales' Dragoon Guards (London & Edinburgh, 1924), i. 11.

13 *CSPD 1695*, pp. 248, 253; D'Auvergne, *1694*, pp. 11–15, 33–4; Parker, *Memoirs*, p. 44n.; SP 77/56, f. 313; NLI, MS. 4166, The Diary of Brigadier Robert Stearne, 1678–1702, p. 24.

14 *CSPD 1694–5*, p. 136; Beaurain, ii. 332–3.

15 *HMC, Buccleuch (Montagu) MSS.*, ii. 70, 72; BL, Stowe MSS. 481, f. 37; NLI, MS. 4166, p. 24; LUL, MS. 12, ff. 207–10; Beaurain, ii. 345–50.

16 Walton, pp. 277–8; Beaurain, ii. 350–3.

17 *CSPD 1694–5*, pp. 164, 174–5, 187, 195; Japikse, iii. 340–1.

18 LUL, MS. 12, ff. 210–13; NLI, MS. 4166, p. 24; Parker, *Memoirs*, p. 44; *HMC, Buccleuch (Montagu) MSS.*, ii. 93, 101–4; *HMC, Bath MSS.*, iii. 25; Beaurain, ii. 361–8.

19 *HMC, Downshire MSS.*, i. 443–4, 2/12 July 1694, Roosbeek, Rev. William Hayley to Sir William Trumbull.

20 Bonneval, *Memoirs*, pp. 13–14; *HMC, Marchmont MSS*; p. 124; D'Auvergne, *1694*, p. 49.

21 D'Auvergne, *1694*, pp. 51–2.

22 *Ibid.*, p. 26.

23 LUL, MS. 12, ff. 213–19.

24 Parker, *Memoirs*, pp. 45–6; NLI, MS. 4166, pp. 25–6; Beaurain, ii. 372–6; Walton, pp. 279–82; Berwick, i. 85–6; *HMC, Marchmont MSS.*, pp. 124–5; PRO, MPH 20/Part 1.

25 LUL, MS. 12, ff. 221–2.

26 *HMC, Buccleuch (Montagu) MSS.*, ii. 117–18.

27 LUL, MS. 12, ff. 226–8; *HMC, Buccleuch (Montagu) MSS.*, ii. 126.

28 *CSPD 1694–5*, p. 303.

29 Burnet, *History*, iv. 229–30; Baxter, *William III*, pp. 317–18.

30 CMC 4/67 & 68, 'Le Siege de Huy'; *CSPD 1694*, p. 280; D'Auvergne, *1694*, pp. 82–94; Landmann, pp. 62–3.

31 *HMC, Buccleuch (Montagu) MSS.*, ii. 138–9.

32 LUL, MS. 12, ff. 230–1; D'Auvergne, *1694*, pp. 96, 104.

33 *CSPD 1695*, p. 285.

34 *Saint-Simon*, ii. 221–3.

X

1695: THE GREAT SIEGE
OF NAMUR

As early as 1/11 January 1695, it was common knowledge in London that the French would be in no condition to undertake an offensive in the Netherlands during the coming campaign. In the following month, reports reached Antonie Heinsius in The Hague that 'the heart of France' was in great misery and that this was bound to affect the performance of the army in the summer.[1] The critical state of French revenues and resources was recognised in the adoption of a defensive military strategy but it was not mirrored in the diplomatic effort. On the contrary, having succeeded in holding the Allies on all fronts in 1694 despite labouring under a numerical inferiority, Louis was confident that he could hold out for reasonable terms and wait until the economic ravages of war bit into the Dutch and English economies. There were already signs of fissures in English government finances which were to widen into the chasm of the coinage crisis in 1696 and it must have been clear to Louis that William could not fight indefinitely. Negotiations between Dijkveldt and Callières were resumed in June 1695. The Dutchman was assisted by Jacob Boreel, the burgomaster of Amsterdam, who was considered to be more conciliatory than the stern Dijkveldt.

Callières offered to accept William as the unconditional King of England as soon as a peace was signed. He said Louis was prepared to extend this concession to the possible signature of a limited peace between England, France and the United Provinces provided that the English and the Dutch then used their good offices to bring the other members of the Grand Alliance into a general treaty. Unfortunately, Callières's diplomacy was undermined by inconsistencies. A group of French clergy sent a deputation of two bishops to compliment James II and Mary of Modena at St Germain-en-Laye where they made speeches extolling the virtues of the exiled monarchs. This could hardly have occurred without Louis's knowledge and approval. Louis also thought that the Allied siege of Namur was provocative and seriously damaged the chance of reaching a peace settlement. Significantly, Boufflers surrendered Namur to the Elector of Bavaria, not to William. To add fuel to the flames, Louis allowed an extract from a dispatch by D'Avaux to be leaked; it made clear that the French government was still actively assisting James II to regain his throne. The failed peace negotiations indicated that neither side earnestly wanted a cessation of hostilities; both thought that they had something to gain from a further recourse to military decisions. The campaign of 1695 saw the Allies attempting to make advances in the field sufficient to compel the French to adopt a more amenable attitude, whilst the French remained confident that a defensive strategy would bring the Allies to the conference table as attrition wore down their resolve. The gradual revelation of the secret meetings between François de Callières, Dijkveldt and Boreel had the affect of convincing the Duke of Savoy that William was not wholly sincere and was actually trying to arrange a separate peace between England, France and the Dutch Republic without prior reference to the Empire or his German allies. Perhaps this provided some respectability for the Duke of Savoy's own course of deception.[2]

The first positive manifestation that the French had adopted a totally defensive strategy in the Low Countries occurred during the winter. Instead of raiding into Brabant and Spanish Flanders, they spent the time improving their frontier defences. They were especially concerned for the safety of Dunkirk and Flanders. The country between the Lys and Ypres was flat and open and the frontier did not run behind a convenient waterway. Indeed, there was no suitable water barrier as the land between Menin and Ypres lay along the watershed between the drainage systems of the Lys and the Ijzer. Through the experience of several campaigns, the French had found that the Lines of the Lys and the Scheldt were too long and difficult to defend, partly because the important fortress of Courtrai stood to the north of the Lines and was open to attack. At Courtrai, the distance between the Lys and the Scheldt was considerably less than the existing Lines between Menin and Pont d'Espierres. Accordingly, the French decided to build new Lines running from the St. John's Gate of Courtrai to a point on the Scheldt between Bossuit and Avelgem. At the same time, they resolved to dig field fortifications across the gap between Ypres and Comines on the Lys. In mid-March, huge numbers of peasants were summoned to rendezvous at Ypres and Courtrai by the end of the month. Boufflers, the Governor of French Flanders and based at Lille, drew out the

frontier garrisons into a camp between Wevelgem and Courtrai to cover
the work details.

The Allies were determined to interrupt the French progress. The
Elector of Bavaria and Holstein-Plön met in Brussels and agreed to
draw out 500 men from each of the garrison battalions in Flanders,
Brussels, Malines and Louvain to form a camp between Deynze and
Ghent. The Elector commanded this force which amounted to an army
of 35,000 foot and 15,000 horse, with its left at Deynze and its right
at Drongen. It was too early in the year for serious and sustained
campaigning and the Allied horses had to be supplied with dry fodder
from the magazines in Ghent. Vaudemont and Württemberg reinforced
Dixmuyde with dragoons and artillery, in case Boufflers advanced from
his position, whilst Bavaria built a bridge across the Lys below Deynze.
However, all these efforts were in vain. Boufflers was too strong and
refused to be pulled away from his task of covering the 20,000 workmen
who were labouring on the new lines. The Allies were also disinclined
to risk a battle so early in the campaign; if they lost, then the French
would be the masters for the remainder of the season.

Once the works had been completed, the French possessed strong
defences from Dinant to the North Sea. Namur closed the Sambre-
Meuse and the course of the Meuse to the south of Namur was covered
by the strong fortresses of Dinant, Givet and Charlemont. The River
Sambre protected the region between Namur and Charleroi and on the
Sambre to the south-west of Charleroi, at Thuin, the system of field
fortifications commenced. A line of trenches and redoubts stretched
from Thuin to the River Haine at Mons, covering the country between
Maubeuge and Mons. The line then followed the River Haine from
Mons to Condé from where it ran along the Scheldt to Bossuit. The
newly-dug lines protected the gap between the Scheldt and the Lys,
from Bossuit to Courtrai, and then ran southwards along the Lys to
Comines. Another new section had been excavated between Comines
and Ypres from where the lines followed the canal that flowed from
Ypres to Dunkirk, via Fort Knokke and Furnes. Although this system
of fortifications did not represent the legal frontier between France and
the Spanish Netherlands, it marked the effective extent of French military authority. In the rear of the lines, from Mons to the Channel coast,
the French had constructed a complementary system of roads. The
'Royal Ways' were designed to move troops rapidly from one section
of the Lines to another, enabling the whole system to be maintained
with a relatively small number of troops. These roads were wide enough
for a squadron of horse to march abreast and were as straight as

possible. This was achieved by 'cutting or pulling down all they met, without any regard to houses or villages, if they happened in the line of the Royal Way'. The Lines between the Lys and the Scheldt, even in their new position, still formed the central focus of the frontier defences. They were very strong with dry, wide ditches, a 'breast-work equal to standing fortifications', palisaded and stockaded redoubts and salient angles. The Marquis de la Valette had died during the winter and Maréchal de Camp the Comte de la Motte assumed command of the Lines. The new fortifications had been completed by 25 April/5 May and both armies returned to their winter quarters.[3]

With the French busy digging miles of trenches and ditches, it was the turn of the Allies to indulge in a little winter raiding. A party of 160 infantry from the garrison of Ath marched towards St. Ghislain, a key post on the Lines between Mons and Condé. Three of the bolder members of the company slithered across the ice on the River Haine, clambered over the palisades and put a torch to a magazine containing 1,000 rations of forage. At about the same time, a fire in Ypres destroyed twenty houses and a small French magazine. Extra-curricula activities petered out towards the end of April when both sides concentrated in Flanders.[4] After the armies had returned temporarily to their winter quarters, William started to plan the summer campaign. He intended to divide his forces into two armies. The first was to operate in Flanders, initially under Vaudemont but later to be commanded by William himself. The second corps, directed by Bavaria and Holstein-Plön, was to assemble in Brabant.[5] The British forces which had been quartered in Ghent, Bruges and Nieuport concentrated at Mariakerke, on the north-western edge of Ghent, on 16/26 May. They then marched to join Vaudemont's army which was coming together on the banks of the Lys with its right at Aarsele and its left at Deynze. When complete, Vaudemont's Army of Flanders was to consist of 70 battalions and 82 squadrons, a total of 53,000 men. The Elector of Bavaria and the Duke of Holstein-Plön gathered the Army of Brabant at Asse, to the north-west of Brussels. It comprised 35,650 soldiers in 32 battalions and 91 squadrons. Major-General Ellenburg commanded a detached corps of 12,500 at Dixmuyde to observe Furnes, Dunkirk and the French Lines. In the Pays de Liège, Lieutenant-General Heiden controlled 15,800 Brandenburgrs in the city of Liège where he was joined by the Liègeois army of 3,600 under Count Tilly. The total Allied forces between the Meuse and the North Sea numbered 125,000 men, a significant increase over the previous year. Few additional men had been recruited and the extra troops had become available through the recapture of Huy. This obviated the need to garrison Liège as a frontier town.[6]

As the Allies concentrated, the French put the finishing touches to their Lines. Boufflers's camp had broken up in mid-April; the cavalry went back into garrison in Menin, Courtrai and Tournai but the infantry were dispersed to garrison the Lines. It was at this point that the fatal weakness of the new system of lines was revealed. De la Motte required a garrison of 30,000 infantry and 84 pieces of artillery, a force which could only be found to the severe detriment of the operational forces.[7] Villeroi gathered the main French field army of 62,640 men in a camp with the left at Blaton and the right at Quiévrain, a position well sheltered by the Lines and the fortresses of Condé and Mons. Boufflers commanded the cavalry concentration of 9,000 at Gosselies to the north of Charleroi. The Comte de Montal guarded the coastal region of Flanders with 18 battalions, 10,800 men, based on Furnes and General Rosen commanded a small 'flying camp' to cover the Lines between Ypres and Comines. Across the Meuse around Chiny in Luxembourg, d'Harcourt hovered with 1,800 horse observing the country between the Meuse and the Moselle.[8] Villeroi directed a total of 115,000 soldiers.

William boarded his yacht at Gravesend on Sunday 11/21 May and was in The Hague three days later. William arrived to find that the French were not fully in the field whilst his own armies were enjoying the benefit of an early concentration.[9] The King heard with satisfaction of Vaudemont's assembly around Deynze and he approved the Elector of Bavaria's scheme to advance to Ninove from Asse on 18/28 May. William's intention, as relayed by Blathwayt to the Lords Justices in England, was to open the campaign 'in five several places to keep the enemy in the dark'. This enterprising plan had been agreed after a series of meetings between the Elector of Bavaria, the Elector of Brandenburg and Prince Vaudemont. The Allied troops were to be stationed in four camps: the main army was to stand at Grammont (Geraadsbergen), Ellenburg remained at Dixmuyde in Flanders, the Elector of Bavaria's army was to operate between Ninove and Halle, and the Brandenburg and Liègeois corps was to move close to Huy.[10] Naturally, these plans were only theoretical and depended upon French reactions.

William stole a few days at Het Loo before proceeding to join Vaudemont's army at Deynze on Sunday 22 May/1 June.[11] Villeroi considered that the Allied dispositions indicated an attack in West Flanders, possibly against Dunkirk, Ypres or Fort Knokke. He marched to Leuse, where he was joined by the Duke of Berwick's corps, whilst Boufflers continued at Gosselies to observe Heiden and Tilly on the Meuse between Liège and Huy. On 19/29 May, Villeroi moved forward to Cordes and then struck north-west to cross the Scheldt at Escanaffles and enter the Lines. Bavaria's march from Asse to Ninove on 18/28 May convinced Boufflers that this Allied corps constituted a greater danger than Heiden's force on the Meuse. Accordingly, Boufflers shifted from Gosselies to St. Ghislain.[12] The French were beginning to dance to the Allies' tune. William hoped to draw Villeroi's main force into Flanders and then use the Elector of Bavaria's army to besiege Namur. If the Elector moved quickly enough from Ninove, then there was a chance that the French would be unable to reinforce Namur before the investment shut tight. To facilitate this aspect of the operation, William intended to stage a demonstration in Flanders that was sufficiently convincing to persuade Villeroi to strip his garrisons along the Sambre and the Meuse in order to strengthen his own position in Flanders. All depended upon the speed and co-ordination of the Allied corps and the degree to which Villeroi could be deceived by William's commitment to Flanders. The only problem appeared to be Boufflers who stood with his detachment around Charleroi specifically observing the Meuse fortresses, and he was much closer to Namur than the Elector of Bavaria. To start the ball rolling, William had to occupy Villeroi in Flanders by undertaking a significant operation. His eye fell upon Fort Knokke, a vital post along the Lines on the Ijzer Canal between Ypres and Furnes.

On 27 May/6 June William assumed personal command of Vaudemont's army which was still encamped with its right at Aarsele and its left on the Lys at Deynze. Villeroi remained at Escanaffles. William reviewed his 53,000 men on 31 May/10 June and 'found them all well recruited and extremely fine'. The opening move was made by Boufflers who shifted his position from Gosselies north-eastwards to Fleurus, closer to Namur. The Earl of Athlone marched out of the Elector of Bavaria's camp at Ninove with a detachment of horse to keep Boufflers under close observation.[13] After the lack of security during previous years, there was an attempt to improve standards by spreading disinformation. The King wrote to Lord Shrewsbury at Whitehall stating that he hoped for an 'active' campaign and disingenuously denied that he had any specific plan in mind but would be guided by the actions of the French.[14] With all his preparations complete, William marched southwards from Aarsele on 2/12 June for five hours and came into the last year's ground at Roeselare. A three hour hike on the following day brought the army south to Beselare, opposite the Lines between Comines and Ypres. From this central location, the Allies threatened Ypres, Menin, the Lines, Furnes, Fort Knokke and Dunkirk. To add weight to the deception, the Elector of Bavaria marched from Ninove to Oudenarde as if he intended to reinforce William in Flanders. Villeroi had no option but to respond in strength. He left Escanaffles on the Scheldt, marched behind his Lines to the Lys and then camped with his right at Menin and his left at Houthem. Because the Allied army was no more than nine kilometres from his new position, Villeroi feared a sudden attack and formed his camp in line of battle. It would have been relatively simple for the Allies to have surprised the French camp as the country was extensively enclosed and 'extremely thickly planted so that you cannot see above forty yards any way at once which makes it very hazardous to stir out of the camp.'

The Beselare position was forty kilometres from Bruges and fifty from Ghent. The Allied bread convoys had to wend their way through the close and wooded country, highly vulnerable to ambush and attack despite the heavy escorts. This resulted in a shortage of supplies but the local peasants were ordered to bring provisions 'upon pain of being plundered, which they did very willingly not looking upon us as enemies but as friends, being very desirous to be freed from the French yoke under which they have been ever since the Treaty of Nijmegen.' The advanced camp at Beselare also suffered from a lack of forage. There was little arable land in the forested countryside and what there was had been left untilled on the orders of the French to deny subsistence to the Allies should they approach the Lines, William's army foraged towards the French Lines virtually every day stripping the country bare but also facilitating close reconnaissance of the enemy's stance. Ypres was only seven kilometres distant and horse patrols ventured upto the very palisades of the town. Indeed, the French feared a bombardment and began to lift the paving stones in the streets in order to eliminate potential splinters.[15]

Bavaria's march to Oudenarde on 6/16 June had pulled Boufflers away from the Sambre-Meuse. Boufflers arrived at Pont d'Espierres on the Scheldt where he received a reinforcement of 10,000 men from Villeroi. As if to confirm the French interpretation of the Allies' plans, Bavaria moved even closer to Boufflers coming upto Outrijve on the banks of the Scheldt. The Duke of Württemberg departed from the Beselare camp on 7/17 June to take command of Ellenburg's corps at Dixmuyde with the aim of besieging Fort Knokke. Major-General Charles Churchill took eight battalions, some gunners, fireworkers and engineers to join Württemberg at Dixmuyde on the following evening. They were closely observed by the Comte de Montal.[16]

The investment and capture of Fort Knokke was probably a compromise operation. In a letter to the Earl of Shrewsbury, William recounted how he had ridden ahead of his army during its march from Roeselare to Beselare to reconnoitre the French Lines with a view to launching a surprise assault. Unfortunately, his heavy artillery and much of his infantry was straggling and it was not possible to attack immediately. William had reconnoitred again on the following morning but had discovered Villeroi's army filing into position between Menin and Houthem. It was in the wake of this disappointment that William had decided to send Württemberg against Fort Knokke in an effort to unlock the French Lines in the west of Flanders. At the same time, the Elector of Bavaria was instructed to cross the Scheldt at Outrijve and attempt to pass the Lines of the Lys and the Scheldt in the face of Boufflers's corps. By aggressive movements in both the east and the west, William clearly hoped that the French line would become unhinged at some point and present a favourable opportunity for exploitation. He also requested a naval operation against Dunkirk, a move which would threaten the rear of Villeroi's left wing in Flanders. As William and Bavaria struggled to stage the major operation in Flanders which would draw in and commit Villeroi's main forces, the Allied position in Brabant and the Pays de Liège was strengthened and balanced. Count Tilly combined with the Earl of Athlone's cavalry detachment at Tirlemont on 10/20 June whilst General Heiden's Brandenburg corps remained around Huy.[17]

Württemberg had left the Beselare camp very early on the morning of 7/17 June and had arrived at Dixmuyde at 9.00 a.m. He then reviewed the 19 battalions and 10 squadrons of Ellenburg's corps before ordering them to march for Fort Knokke 'and gave the plunder of the Boors between Dixmuyde and this place (Knokke) to the soldiers, in revenge of some which they had barbarously murdered'. The Duke arrived before Knokke in the evening, it was only eight kilometres from Dixmuyde, and camped with his left on the Knokke-Dixmuyde Canal and his right on the canal that flows from Knokke to Furnes. The headquarters were positioned in Nieuwkapelle. The Allied camp was almost within musket shot of the fort. At 11.00 a.m. on 9/19 June, Churchill's reinforcement column joined Württemberg and Ellenburg. Fort Knokke was a very strong, triangular work nestled into the angle of the confluence of the Furnes-Dunkirk Canal and the Ijzerkanaal which ran from Dixmuyde to Ypres. At the very point of the confluence was a strong bastion, complete with a deep and wet ditch, covered by counter-guards on the far banks of the canals. The southern or open end of the triangle was defended by a large hornwork with a 'boggy morass' stretching from one canal to the other. Another inundation protected the side along the Ijzerkanaal towards Bruges. The most accessible front, opposite which Württemberg was encamped, lay to the west but even this was covered by counter-guards, trenches and a drawbridge. Knokke was 'a great passage into the enemy's country, it being open from this to St. Omer. Besides, it commands the communication between Ypres and Dunkirk and would secure Furnes in our hands, which consequently would make Dunkirk a frontier and expose it to a siege.' It was a daunting prospect but Württemberg possessed a plan of the fortifications of Knokke which had been obtained during a reconnaissance in March. He was further helped by the fact that the fort had only a small garrison commanded by a mere major, although Montal rapidly brought his corps of observation into a camp at the rear of the fort and received considerable reinforcements from Villeroi.[18]

Württemberg wasted no time. At 2.00 p.m. on 9/19 June, the Allies attacked some houses and small redoubts which stood on the very spot where Württemberg wished to mount his principal batteries. With the loss of five hundred men, the French were driven off by Colonel James Maitland of the Scots Guards and Colonel Zachariah Tiffin although the latter was wounded during the action. Engineers and artillerymen immediately set to work to construct gun platforms. On the same day, the Elector of Bavaria shifted his camp slightly northwards, his left resting on the Scheldt at Kerkhove and his right at Kaster. Some higher ground about Tiegemberg, topped by a windmill, overlooked the Elector's right wing and Boufflers was quick to advance and occupy this dominant position. Brigadier Fagel forced the two French battalions from this prominence and established Allied control. From The Hague, the developing campaign was watched with interest. Mathew Prior thought that the attack on Fort Knokke was intended to draw in Villeroi's main army thus enabling the Elector of Bavaria to break through the Lines of the Lys and the Scheldt.[19] Prior's reaction indicated that the campaign against Knokke looked realistic. As the defenders fired from the fort on 10/20 June, the Allied pioneers erected batteries, their work partially disrupted by a vigorous French sally on 11/21 June. Two 'young spies' were arrested and interrogated on the following day. They revealed a plan whereby a certain Monsieur La Tour, 'the famous French partizan', was supposed to burn the ammunition of the Allies as it lay in their boats on the River Ijzer. As a precaution, the ammunition ships were moved downstream towards Dixmuyde every night, a pontoon bridge was built across the river and guards were posted. In addition, two battalions were returned to Dixmuyde to guard against a surprise attack from the direction of Furnes.

Guns from the fort began to fire into the Allied camp on 13/23 June with uncanny accuracy, the shooting being directed by a miller 'who made signs from his mill'. This gentleman was dealt with very promptly. Then, to the pleasure of the French, the Allied guns were withdrawn from their batteries on 14/24 June only to be ordered back into position on the next morning. However, in the afternoon the cannon were finally towed away and prepared for the road. The pontoon train was readied for the march on 17/27 June and on the following day the whole corps returned to Beselare having lost some 600 men and inflicted double that number of casualties on their opponents.[20] Württemberg had been able to make a convincing withdrawal from before Fort Knokke through the unwitting actions of the French. Montal had opened the sluices and flooded much of the area around the fort making a siege almost impossible. Although Knokke was 'un petit fort d'une tres grande conse-quence' and could have been bombarded into submission, Montal had also reconstructed the French Lines across the rear of the position thereby committing the Allies to staging a second operation if they wanted to break into the French Lines after the fall of the fort. The attempt which Württemberg had made against Knokke was enough to persuade the French that they had thwarted a major Allied offensive.[21]

Whilst the attacks on Fort Knokke continued, William made his final preparations for the siege of Namur. In the papers of Arnoust van Keppel, 1st Earl of Albemarle, is a 'Memoire au sujet de siege' which emanated from the camp at Beselare.[22] It is clearly a planning document for the assistance of William and his senior commanders and it was probably compiled by Keppel, Portland or Huygens. It reminded William of a series of tasks which needed to be tackled and of decisions which had to be made: Athlone at Louvain and Heiden at Huy had to carry eight days supply of bread and biscuit; an officer must be appointed at Maastricht and Liège to supervise the delivery of these foodstuffs; sufficient pioneers and waggons had to be organised for the siege. William had also to make up his mind about how many troops to allocate to the siege itself and how many to the covering army and where to quarter them. These tasks were referred to subordinate generals who were reminded that it was essential to billet the engineers and the pioneers in the correct places. Three bridges were to be built, two over the Meuse and one across the Sambre; Heiden was to undertake the bridging whilst Athlone was made responsible for transporting the pontoons and bridging equipment from Huy. It was preferable to embark the heavy artillery just before the siege opened and artillery officers were instructed to supervise the water carriage of their guns. Generals had to be selected to command the assaulting forces and the Prince-Bishop of Liège was deputed to organise the preparation of the thousands of fascines that would be required. Wool-sacks would be needed for the trenches. Hospitals had to be established at Huy, Liège, Visé and Maastricht. Finally, there was the matter of arranging ambulances to convey the sick and wounded to these hospitals. Even in the seventeenth century, successful military operations revolved around efficient and competent staff-work. By 17/27 June, William was able to report to Shrewsbury that everything was ready for the projected siege. 'It is, I avow, a very great undertaking; God grant that it may succeed.'[23] William Blathwayt seemed confident. Although the attack on Fort Knokke had been cancelled because it was too difficult.

> but it has served for the amusement of the enemy while the preparations are making for the siege of Namur and the troops of Brandenburg and others have had the opportunity of posting themselves in such a manner as is necessary for carrying on that siege wherein those troops and the forces under the Elector will be chiefly concerned. Tomorrow, we march back to Roeselare, having consumed the forage in these parts.[24]

On Friday 11/21 June, a bread convoy was making its way from Ghent to William's camp at Beselare. Intelligence reached the camp that 200 French horse and 400 foot had marched through Menin with a view to intercepting this tempting target. William ordered out the Earl of Essex, a colonel of horse, with 500 dragoons to escort the waggons into the camp. They made contact at Roeselare and performed their duty satisfactorily. At the same time, William asked Portland to take 600 dragoons and 500 horse to deal with the enemy raiders. They found them at midnight in Moorsele, ten kilometres east of Beselare, with their infantry drawn up in the market place and the horse a short distance away in support. Portland's dragoons dismounted, charged into the town and routed the French, leaving 80 dead at the cost of just 17 Allied casualties.[25]

William felt sufficiently confident to tell Heinsius on 17/27 June that he intended to besiege Namur and for this purpose he would march back to Roeselare on the following morning.[26] As William's army withdrew northwards in Flanders, the Brandenburg and Liègeois troops under

Tilly, Heiden and Athlone converged on Namur but not before Boufflers had noticed what was afoot. He rapidly decamped from Pont d'Espierres and marched over the Sambre to Philippeville. On the next day he hurried across the Meuse at Dinant where he was met by d'Harcourt's detachment and then he rushed for Namur with seven regiments of dragoons. He arrived just ahead of the Allies on 20/30 June who invested Namur later on that same day. William left his army in Flanders at 4.00 a.m. on 19/29 June with a guard of 2,000 cavalry and travelled via Ghent, Brussels and Louvain to join Athlone before Namur. The Elector of Bavaria also made his way towards Namur, using the road to the south of Brussels through Halle, his freedom of action assured now that Boufflers had departed for the Meuse.[27] William committed the care of the army in Flanders to Vaudemont whose first move was to withdraw to the Aarsele position, just to the west of Deynze, on 20/30 June. Between this date and 28 June/8 July, when the formal investment of Namur was completed, Vaudemont's army was gradually reduced as more and more troops were sent across Brabant to reinforce the besieging forces at Namur and to form a covering army under William's personal command. To reinforce the Allied position in Flanders, Ellenburg remained at Dixmuyde with a corps of infantry.

On receiving the ill news that Namur had been invested, Villeroi did not panic and dash to its relief. Instead, he crossed the Scheldt and encamped at Popuelles, between Ath and Tournai, content to bide his time. One of the reasons for Villeroi's seeming indolence was the belief that Namur was impregnable. Vauban had added many new works since 1692, especially more redoubts on the Heights of Bouge, and Boufflers possessed an enormous garrison of 16,000 men. Rather than rush to its rescue, there seemed every possibility that William's forces would be tied down before Namur in an endless and ultimately unsuccessful siege leaving Villeroi free to ravage Flanders, capture fortresses and perhaps even attack Brussels. Before these glories could be realised, he had first to deal with Vaudemont at Aarsele and Ellenburg at Dixmuyde, the only significant Allied forces outside the ring around Namur. Vaudemont's camp between Wontergem and Aarsele was an excellent position as it observed the French Lines around Courtrai and so obliged the enemy to retain substantial garrisons within the Lines of the Lys and the Scheldt and between the Lys and Ypres. This threat was further reinforced by Ellenburg at Dixmuyde whose corps not only endangered the French Lines west of Ypres but was also close to Furnes and Dunkirk. The advanced Allied garrison of Ath remained vulnerable and there was concern that Villeroi might use his advantage to seize first this fort and then proceed to take Oudenarde. After the departure of the soldiers to strengthen the ring around Namur, Vaudemont was left with 50 battalions and 57 squadrons, a total of 37,000 men. Ellenburg at Dixmuyde had been reduced to 6,500 infantry and dragoons and a small force of 15 cavalry squadrons was stationed in Brussels.[28]

All was quiet on Vaudemont's front between 21 June/1 July and 25 June/5 July and the corps was well provided with information on French movements by its spies and informers. The main source of intelligence was three Capuchin friars, one of whom hung around Villeroi's headquarters. These gentlemen sent word that Villeroi was about to move from Popuelles and this was confirmed when French cavalry disturbed Vaudemont's foragers on 1/11 July. Vaudemont issued orders that on the firing of two cannon, the army was to form a line of battle before its camp and prepare to repel an attack. Villeroi left Popuelles at 10.00 p.m. on 2/12 July and arrived in Rozebeke on the left bank of the Lys on the following morning, having crossed four rivers during a remarkable night march. He was now within ten kilometres of Vaudemont's position, hoping that his speed of march had surprised Vaudemont. Thanks to his spies, Vaudemont was ready. As Villeroi advanced on the morning of 3/13 July driving in the Allied outposts and advance guards, the two signal cannon were fired and Vaudemont's army came into line of battle with its right on rising ground at Dentergem and the left at Grammene towards the River Lys. By 1.00 p.m., Vaudemont was in position with his cannon mounted. During the afternoon, the infantry entrenched their positions and the French came into view before Dentergem. At 8.00 p.m., Vaudemont ordered a partial stand-down as the French did not appear to wish for a night engagement but at 10.00 p.m. the Allied left was ordered to improve its fortifications, Vaudemont having received information that Villeroi had selected this sector for attack. Two hundred men were detached from each battalion to dig trenches and breastworks in front of the threatened flank. The battalion guns were pulled into the first line at 1.00 a.m. on 4/14 July and, three hours later, Vaudemont ordered his centre and right to excavate better defences. The French were steadily advancing from Rozebeke and Villeroi had detached Berwick with cavalry and dragoons to envelop the right of Vaudemont's line and break into the rear of his position. Despite the strength and balance of his situation, Vaudemont's predicament was serious. Villeroi, having drawn in the garrisons of Ypres, Courtrai and Menin, had over 90,000 men against the meagre 37,000 of the Allies. The nearest assistance was Ellenburg's small force at Dixmuyde.

Vaudemont's men had completed their trenches by 11.00 a.m. French cavalry observed the Allied left at Grammene and started a cannonade with their light field guns but Vaudemont's gunners responded in kind and the French kept their distance. Colonel Johan van Goor, the commander of the Dutch artillery train, ordered his carpenters to fell trees to make roadblocks on all the routes and lanes around Vaudemont's position, except for the roads to Nevele and Deynze, the latter town housing the vital bridge over the Lys. With Berwick swinging round Vaudemont's right, the routes to Deynze and Nevele were the sole avenues of escape. As soon as Goor's men had completed their obstacles and barricades, tents were struck and the baggage train began its march for Deynze. At 3.00 p.m., the artillery and the ammunition waggons withdrew. The guns from the right flank travelled along the Aarsele-Deynze road whilst the cannon from the left moved on the Deynze-Wortegem road. The artillery reassembled to the right of Deynze, in a position to cover the retreat of the main army. Villeroi brought his troops closer to Vaudemont's lines at 7.00 p.m. but the withdrawal was already well under way. Vaudemont ordered his cavalry to dismount and man the trenches and breastworks whilst the infantry disengaged and 'slinked off' towards Deynze. The retreat went according to plan except when a Brandenburg infantry brigade under Borensdorf was surprised by some French dragoons and hussars who challenged the Germans in 'high Dutch'. These Frenchmen were rather unsportingly wearing green boughs in their hats, the Allied recognition signal. Fortunately, the Brandenburgers rallied in time and realised their mistake but they lost two hundred men and a number of ammunition waggons. Villeroi failed to press Vaudemont's men closely. The abbatis and barricades on the roads severely hampered his soldiers but Vaudemont's measured and unhurried retreat behind Holstein-Plön's Dutch rearguard presented Villeroi with few opportunities for exploitation. Even so, given the strategic and tactical stranglehold he had gained over Vaudemont's force, which was only one-third the size of his own army, Villeroi could and should have been far more vigorous in his attack. Four Dutch regiments from the rearguard faced a stern action against three squadrons of French dragoons and Sir David Colyear's brigade came under fire from French cavalry but, generally, the French kept a respectful distance.

The infantry battalions detailed to escort the artillery train back towards Deynze got ahead of the guns on the road and, for a short time, the cannon were very exposed. Vaudemont spotted this danger and dispatched some dragoons to cover the artillery. By 8.00 p.m., the guns were in position outside Deynze protecting the withdrawal of the foot and horse. One of the maxims of Vaudemont's father, Duke Charles IV of Lorraine, had been that when an army was forced to retreat it had to ensure that it withdrew completely out of the enemy's reach. Vaudemont's army was past the bottleneck of Deynze at 11.00 p.m. and it marched throughout the night clearing Ghent by 6.00 a.m. on 5/15 July. One hour's march the other side of Ghent, Vaudemont drew his army into a camp astride the Antwerp road. During the night, Lieutenant-General Sir Henry Bellasise had stood as rearguard along the Bruges Canal with six British battalions. The artillery left Deynze at 2.00 a.m. and passed through Bellasise's screen to rejoin the main army. On 6/16 July, Vaudemont adjusted his camp slightly to Oostakker, to the north of Ghent on the right bank of the Scheldt, and sent his heavy artillery and baggage into Antwerp.

Having escaped from Villeroi's trap, Vaudemont looked to the defences of Flanders. On 7/17 July, Colonel Schlundt was sent with ten 3-pounders to reinforce Nieuport and on 8/18 July, the Duke of Württemberg and Sir Henry Bellasise took twelve battalions toward Nieuport and Bruges. This party left early in the morning and had great difficulty in marching back through Ghent against the tide of baggage waggons and stragglers still making their way from Deynze. Ellenburg remained at Dixmuyde, now dangerously separated from Vaudemont, and Brigadier Francis Fergus O'Farrell was left in Deynze with a small garrison. Vaudemont's new position at Oostakker enabled him to draw supplies from the magazines in Ghent and Antwerp and saw him ideally placed to interfere with anything that Villeroi might attempt in Flanders. His main task was to prevent Villeroi's massive field army from pressing too close to Namur too soon and he was assisted in this by Villeroi's belief in the invincibility of the fortress. However, whatever Villeroi chose to venture in Flanders would be a minor operation when compared with the chance that he had missed at Aarsele. What had gone wrong?

Villeroi had been anxious to close the trap on Vaudemont, both rival commanders thinking that the fate of Namur and Spanish Flanders rested on the outcome of the Aarsele action. In the first place, Villeroi tried to command from too far back and was not close enough to the front. He relied upon the observations of subordinates. Secondly, Villeroi was guilty of dithering and indecisiveness. He did not make up his mind to attack Vaudemont until 7.00 p.m. and by the time his infantry had got under way all they discovered were the Allied rearguards. This delay in launching the principal assault may have been the fault of the Duke du Maine, the commander of the French right wing.

According to Saint-Simon, Villeroi sent five or six orders to du Maine to begin the action but he wanted time to reconnoitre, time to confess himself and then lost his nerve, refusing to advance until it was far too late. Montal did eventually succeed in breaking into the Allied rear but he ran into the left flank of the retreating infantry and was held off by Sir David Colyear with two brigades of foot who fought from hedgerow to hedgerow as the army trailed back to Deynze. Berwick and the Prince de Conti could also have acted with more energy. As they commanded the French left hook around the Allied right, they could see that Vaudemont was beginning to withdraw and yet they did not seize the initiative and attack. Not until daylight did Villeroi's cavalry appear before the Ghent-Bruges Canal, the principal means of communication between Vaudemont and Bruges, Nieuport, Ostend and Dixmuyde. The canal possessed a considerable breastwork for defence along this sector and Sir Henry Ballasise's six battalions were sufficient to deter Villeroi from crossing. In relative peace, Vaudemont's army was allowed to retire through Ghent. Luxembourg would never have acted in such a pusillanimous fashion.

Part of the right wing of Vaudemont's army had retired through Nevele and not through Deynze, Colonel Goor having been instructed to leave the Aarsele-Kruisweg-Nevele-Mariakerke-Ghent road open to allow this retirement to occur. General Hendrik van Overkirk had commanded Vaudemont's right wing and he led the retreat through Nevele even though the route lay dangerously close to Berwick and Conti's outflanking corps. Again, if the French had acted more decisively then Overkirk's corps must have been destroyed on the march. The corps halted at Nevele for a while to permit stragglers to rejoin. Major-General Charles Churchill found himself outside the house which had been his billet during the previous spring when the Allies had formed a camp between Deynze and Ghent to observe Boufflers's pioneers working on the new Lines. He went in to rest in the company of Lieutenant-Colonel Sidney Godolphin of Sir Bevil Grenville's Foot, Major Francis Negus of Churchill's own battalion and Captain Leonard Lloyd, Churchill's adjutant and aide-de-camp. They left a guard of one sergeant and twelve men outside the door. They all fell asleep but in the interim the army had marched and the guard had not been recalled. The officers arose early on the following morning to find Nevele deserted and their guard party reported that a French patrol was close at hand. Churchill summoned the sergeant and six men, the remainder having deserted, into the house. The French turned out to be marauders busy plundering the countryside and, rather rashly, the British soldiers fired on the French through the windows and forced them to withdraw. Seizing the opportunity, Churchill left his fellow officers and men inside the house and tried to slip away but the Frenchmen soon recovered. Churchill was apprehended and relieved of his gold, watch, coat and cravat. Whilst they divided the spoils, Churchill was instructed to sit by a hedge. Sensing that no-one was paying him much attention, Churchill slipped under one thicket, through another and onto a road. Here he encountered a sentry who mistook the coatless, cravatless Churchill for a French officer and asked him which way the army had marched. Churchill must have given a convincing answer in a polished accent as he was permitted to walk away and rejoin Vaudemont's army at Mariakerke outside Ghent.

Lloyd, Negus and Godolphin, who had stayed inside the house, did not fare so well. The marauders returned with a drum which made the British think that the French had an officer with them. They opened the door and yielded themselves as prisoners of war, expecting good treatment. Instead the marauders poured into the house and began to strip the place bare. The officers had stored a considerable amount of baggage in the house – saddles, swords, money and horse furniture – and several good horses were in the stable. When all the booty had been seized, Godolphin, Negus and Lloyd were relieved of much of their clothing and carted off to the French camp. They were carried before Villeroi who looked somewhat sheepish and made a few lame excuses for the ill behaviour of his men. He gave the affronted officers a decent dinner and then sent them back to Vaudemont's army without charging a ransom.[29]

Whilst Vaudemont entertained Villeroi in Flanders, the siege of Namur gathered pace. There were several important differences between the French siege of 1692 and the Allied attack. In the intervening years, Vauban had supervised the construction of many new works. On the Heights of Bouge, a detached bastion had been built before the St. Nicholas Gate, complete with a bomb-proof casement. Two more detached bastions guarded the Porte de Fer. A fortified sluice by the Porte de Fer filled the wet ditch from the Brook of Verderin and a stone dyke, three metres tall, by the St. Nicholas Gate prevented the water from the ditch draining into the Meuse. All along the Heights of Bouge, a palisaded covered way had been constructed to protect both the new bastions and the existing fortifications. The French had seized the citadel in 1692 by driving trenches around the base of the Coehoorn Fort, thus cutting it off from the Terra Nova. This vulnerable gap between the Coehoorn and the Terra Nova was plugged by a strong, stone redoubt, equipped with a bomb-proof casemate, which commanded the slope towards the Sambre. A palisaded covered way, stretching from the gorge of the Coehoorn to the cliff above the Meuse, guarded the new work. An extra ravelin crowned the hornwork of the Coehoorn and the Devil's House was strengthened by the addition of a stone redoubt, La Cassotte. A second new covered way was dug from the point of the Coehoorn, across the front of La Cassotte, to the incline down to the Meuse. Vauban had completed the citadel by digging an entrenched line, supported by nine redoubts, across the entire front from the banks of the Meuse to the banks of the Sambre. An unfinished ceremonial gate ornamented the centre of this line. The Allied army before the citadel was to be faced by three, and in places four tiers of fortifications, rising one above the other. Boufflers, the Governor, and the Comte de Guiscard, the Lieutenant Governor, commanded 16,000 men, consisting of 12,000 infantry and 4,000 dragoons, miners and engineers. One hundred and twenty cannon and mortars were mounted around the town and the citadel, 500,000 lb. of powder, 80,000 grenades and 10,000 spare arms were stocked in the magazines and there were provisions for six months. Villeroi's optimism that Namur would occupy the Allies for many, many weeks was not misplaced.[30]

The Earl of Athlone invested the town of Namur to the north between the Sambre and the Meuse; the Elector of Bavaria advanced from Mazy to occupy the peninsula formed by the two rivers opposite the citadel; and the Brandenburg corps under Heiden lined the eastern bank of the Meuse before the Faubourg de Jambes and the Hill of St. Barbes. William placed his headquarters at Flawinne on the north bank of the Sambre and the Elector of Bavaria set up his staff at Malonne Abbey, opposite William's station but on the south bank. By 27 June/7 July, the soldiers and pioneers were hard at work digging lines of contravallation whilst the engineers threw pontoon bridges over the rivers to ease communication between the three separated corps. The siege artillery was shipped at Liège but the water level of the Meuse was very low necessitating the reloading of the guns into shallow draft vessels at Huy. The heavy baggage arrived before Namur on 26 June/6 July. As they had little to do during a siege, Athlone removed the Allied cavalry to Mazy to serve as a mobile covering corps. With the majority of the horses out of the way, the besieging troops did not have to bother about finding large quantities of forage.[31]

The Allies planned to attack the town of Namur from two directions. The Heights of Bouge obviously had to be overcome in order to master the main defences but there was also the prospect of attacking the

Faubourg de Jambes and the prominence of St. Barbes. On 1/11 July, the siege train containing 120 cannon and 80 mortars sailed into view and all was ready for the commencement of proceedings. Major-General Nicolaas Fagel supervised the opening of the trenches on the Heights of Bouge above the St. Nicholas Gate on 2/12 July. An immediate sally by 1,200 Frenchman announced the intention of Guiscard and Boufflers to conduct a vigorous and active defence. Lieutenant-General Julius von Tettau of the Dutch artillery and Major-General Louis du Puy, the Chief Engineer, had overall charge of the attack on the town whilst Coehoorn waited in the wings ready to step onto the stage to conduct the assault upon the citadel. Two days later, Adam de Cardonnel wrote to James Vernon that he was not over-impressed by the performance of the engineers who were both slow and lethargic. He was also critical of the King who, as usual, frequently exposed his person to danger but 'is inclined to spare the town so that all the efforts will be chiefly against the castle. This, we fear, may prolong the siege.' At this time, Athlone moved his cavalry corps to Piéton, west of Charleroi, to observe any movement by Villeroi's forces towards Namur.

By 8/18 July, the trenches were within pistol-shot of the redoubts along the Heights of Bouge and a general assault was ordered for 6.00 p.m. that evening. Major-General George Ramsey commanded five battalions on the right and nine in the centre, whilst Major-General Salust led eight Dutch battalions on the left. Ramsey placed his two Dutch battalions in support on the right and spearheaded his attack with the 1st battalion of the 1st Food Guards, the 1st battalion of the Coldstream Guards and the 1st battalion of the Scots Guards. The 2nd battalion of the 1st Foot Guards and a battalion of the Dutch Blue Guards led the centre attack, with the remaining seven battalions in reserve. In front of each of the two formations stood 120 fusiliers carrying fascines, supported by 120 grenadiers and 100 pioneers to help level ditches and palisades. Ramsey's men had first to seize a fortified country house that stood in advance of the French fortifications. Once this straightforward task had been performed satisfactorily, the fusiliers marched up to the palisades of the redoubts, threw their fascines into the ditches, crossed and then fired into the works. Close behind, the grenadiers lobbed their bombs into the redoubts. This was too much for the defenders who withdrew into a large place d'armes on the other side of the counterscarp from where they returned fire. Ramsey then brought up the two supporting battalions on the right and Lord Cutts led forward Collingwood's, Tidcomb's and Stanley's battalions to sustain the assault in the centre. The additional pressure forced the French out of the place d'armes, down the slope to the edge of the Verderin Brook, 'part into the water and the rest where they could best escape'. Lord George Hamilton then led forward his own battalion together with Ingoldsby's, Saunderson's, Lauder's and Maitland's to relieve the Dutch Guards and form a reserve in the event of a counter-attack. Ramsey instructed his pikemen to fetch more fascines and set his pioneers digging a musket-proof retrenchment across the rear of the redoubts. Ingoldsby's, Saunderson's, Lauder's and Maitland's battalions manned this retrenchment and the rest of Ramsey's force withdrew to the main camp at Temploux. Both the French and the Allies lost some 2,000 men during this short but vicious action. The British lost 2 officers and 308 men killed and 9 officers and 604 men wounded.[32] On the same evening, Boufflers abandoned the Faubourg de Jambes and burned it to the ground. Earlier, a battalion of Brandenburg infantry had been severely mauled during a French sally as they began to dig trenches close to the simple covered way that protected the suburb. Now that the Heights of Bouge were safely in their hands, the Allies concentrated on attacking the main defences of Namur between the Brussels Gate and the St. Nicholas Gate. Vaudemont had stripped heavy artillery from the garrisons of Ghent and Bruges and these additional guns arrived at Namur in time to take part in the attack on the town.[33]

Ramsey's success brought the besiegers close enough to begin the serious business of breaching the ramparts. Eleven batteries were soon in operation pounding the bastions on either side of the St. Nicholas Gate. Opposite the citadel, the Elector of Bavaria had opened his trenches on 4/14 July and a battery of mortars had been brought into action even though no serious attack was to be mounted until the town had fallen. Athlone's cavalry marched north to Pont-à-Celles after the forage had been consumed around Piéton. On 17/27 July, sufficient damage had been done to the bastions by the St. Nicholas Gate to risk an infantry assault against the covered way. The selected target was a counter-guard before a ravelin which, in turn, protected the enceinte between the demi-bastion St. Roch and the Bastion St. Nicholas. Between the counter-guard and the ravelin ran the Verderin Brook and between the ravelin and the bastions flowed the wet ditch. Major-General Ramsey again commanded eight British battalions in the successful attack on the counter-guard. The batteries were then advanced and significant breaches had been effected in the Bastion St. Nicholas by 23 July/2 August. Opposite the citadel, the Elector of Bavaria took the opportunity presented by the attacks on the town to capture the Grand Entrenchment which Vauban had constructed as the first line of defence across the peninsula between the Sambre and the Meuse. With a major bastion breached and Dutch miners digging beneath the stone dam which held back the waters of the wet ditch, Namur surrendered after a defence of fourteen days. Boufflers hoped to repeat the arrangements of 1692 whereby the attackers had agreed not to assault the citadel from the town side but he found William most unco-operative. The French retired into the citadel expecting to be fired on from all sides. William was delighted, especially with the performance of the British Foot Guards during the attacks on the Heights of Bouge and on the counter-guard. He wrote ecstatically to Lieutenant-General Lord Sydney, the Colonel of the 1st Foot Guards.

> Je suis si satisfait de ces battaillons de mon régiment des gardes que vous commandes, que j'ay esté bien aise de vous l'escrire moy-mesme. Il se sont comporté avec une très grande valeur en un attaque très rigoreuse que nous avons fait la semaine passée. Il y a eu beaucoup de brave gens de tués et blessés, mais cela ne se peut pas autrement en de tels occasions, et qui y ont bien fait.[34]

As operations at Namur progressed with unanticipated speed, considerable activity had been taking place in Flanders. Following his failure to ensnare Vaudemont at Aarsele, Villeroi tried to tempt him away from the safety of Ghent by threatening to inflict massive damage on the Allied garrisons. If Villeroi reduced the Allied outposts in Flanders, Vaudemont would have two choices: to come out and fight, or break up his field army and throw the troops into garrison in Bruges, Ghent, Nieuport and Ostend. Either of these outcomes might be sufficient to draw William away from Namur. From his camp at Rozebeke, Villeroi eyed the exposed and vulnerable post at Dixmuyde. Even after Vaudemont had sent Württemberg and Bellasise to reinforce Bruges and Nieuport and stand behind the Nieuport-Bruges Canal, Ellenburg's position at Dixmuyde, where the fortifications were but 'indifferent', was unenviable.[35] From Rozebeke, Villeroi ordered Montal to besiege Dixmuyde with 13,000 men and he completed his investment on 8/18 July. Twenty kilometres to the west at Nieuport stood Bellasise and Württemberg with 14,600 infantry and 2,000 dragoons. Provided that Ellenburg made a reasonable defence, Vaudemont's dispositions were such that the Dixmuyde position could be either reinforced or relieved. If neither occurred, then a stout resistance would gain time for the reduction of Namur. Major-General Johan Anton Ellenburg had been born in Hesse in 1637, supposedly the son of a shoemaker. He had entered the Danish army rising from the ranks to become a colonel and brigadier by 1690. In that year he had commanded a brigade of the Danish corps in Ireland and was promoted to Major-General when the Danes were transferred to Flanders in 1691. All sorts of stories circulated about Ellenburg, most of them appearing after his execution. He was said to be on bad terms with the Duke of Württemberg, the commander of the Danish corps in both Ireland and Flanders, although Ellenburg's advancement from Brigadier to Major-General occurred whilst Württemberg was his corps commander. Reputedly, he had made several loud comments about the ill usage which the Danish troops had received at the hands of the British in Ireland and how this hindered the recruitment of reinforcements in Denmark. How much of this was true and how much was invented *ex post facto* is impossible to untangle. Most of it was probably exaggerated and unfair. The facts state that Ellenburg had served competently in Ireland and at Steenkirk he had commanded his brigade effectively and took a prominent part in the rearguard action which covered the withdrawal of the Allied infantry.[36]

Upon Montal's investment, Ellenburg opened the sluices and inundated the southern side of the town. At Nieuport, Bellasise broke the dykes and flooded the country between Dixmuyde and the sea. These inundations reduced the perimeter which Ellenburg had to defend by over one half. The only direction from which Montal could attack was from the east, opposite the Roeselare Gate. Unfortunately, this was the weakest sector of the defences, dominated by rising ground. The French also made some approaches from the other side of the Fort Knokke-Nieuport Canal, where the ravelin guarding the bridge into Dixmuyde offered a tempting target. Ellenburg's situation was regarded as serious but not desperate. His garrison consisted of eight infantry battalions and one regiment of dragoons. Four of the foot regiments were British – Brewer's, Lesley's, Graham's and Lorne's – two were Danish and two were Dutch. The dragoon regiment was the Queen's Dragoons, commanded in the absence of Colonel William Lloyd who 'had a dangerous fall last Spring', by Major Thomas Brereton. Lord Lorne's was under the command of Major Robert Duncanson, Lieutenant-Colonel Patrick Hume having been wounded at Namur.

For a week, nothing happened. By 15/25 July, Montal's cannon were in place and his trenches were opened before the ravelin guarding the bridge. During the night of 15/25 July – 16/26 July, Montal's trenches advanced 'incredibly' quickly and, in the morning, eight cannon and three mortars began to fire upon the Roeselare Gate but did little damage. Ellenburg contemplated launching a sally but he decided against it; incredibly, the Allied gunners had no orders to return the fire of the besiegers. During the night of 16/26 July – 17/27 July, the trenches were driven within musket-shot of the palisades of the ravelin by the bridge and a small new work before the Roeselare Gate was in danger of being cut-off. The Governor finally decided to sally but discovered that he could not approach the siege works because of the inundations. When he noticed a third battery being erected opposite the ravelin and bridge, Ellenburg summoned a council of war. On the morning of 17/27 July, the Governor met with his field officers. The trenches, he pointed out, were very close to the glacis, especially near the uncompleted redoubt before the Roeselare Gate, and the enemy was rapidly approaching the ravelin before the bridge. Ellenburg stressed that the inundations were insufficiently deep, despite the sluices at Nieuport being fully open. As a final coup de théâtre, Ellenburg stated that the French were preparing for a general assault and the town could fall within four hours. To avoid the horrors of a storm, Ellenburg advised surrender. Feebly, his engineers agreed. Some of his braver officers argued that Ellenburg had no orders for this course of action and that he ought to wait for possible relief from Württemberg and Bellasise. These points made no visible impact upon Ellenburg and he sent Colonel Sir Charles Graham to negotiate with Montal. Contrary to the rules of war, Montal continued to work on his trenches and batteries during the haggling. Graham returned to Dixmuyde with the grim tidings that the French demanded hostages and surrender at discretion. He went back to Montal with hostages and asked for a stay of decision until the following morning. During the night of 17/27 July – 18/28 July, Montal secured a lodgement on the covered way and positioned a battery so close to the glacis by the Roeselare Gate that it would have torn the ramparts to shreds in a few hours. With these shots in his locker, Montal confidently renewed his demand for the garrison to surrender themselves as prisoners-of-war. Ellenburg met his officers again on the following morning of 18/28 July. He was advised to send an express to Württemberg asking for assistance or orders but Ellenburg over-ruled this counsel and decided to accept capitulation on the French terms: the soldiers were to be made prisoners-of-war, forfeit their weapons and be pillaged of all they possessed. Ellenburg and six of the seven battalion commanders signed the instrument of surrender, including the commanding officers of the battalions of Richard Brewer, Sir James Lesley and Sir Charles Graham. The exception was Major Robert Duncanson, commanding Lord Lorne's battalion, who flatly refused to put his name to the ignoble document. Major Thomas Brereton of the Queen's Dragoons not only would not sign but demanded to be allowed to cut his way out of Dixmuyde. This was denied and the entire garrison of eight battalions and one dragoon regiment marched off to Ypres and captivity.[37]

Having disposed of Dixmuyde in next to no time, Villeroi turned his attention to Deynze. The capture of this town would have placed the forces of Bellasise and Württemberg around Nieuport in jeopardy and removed one of the bastions of Vaudemont's position at Ghent. Deynze was a very poorly defended town. Its fortifications consisted of 'a good retrenchment palisaded, which was double towards Aarsele, one within another, this being the weak side of the town, the rest being a morass caused by the neighbourhood of the Lys.' A good musket shot outside the retrenchment was a star-shaped fort upon the road to Aarsele and Tielt. Eight small cannon were available to bolster both the town and the fort. Apart from its sizeable magazines of hay and possession of an important bridge over the Lys, Deynze was not a militarily significant town. Appointed to the governorship was Brigadier Francis Fergus O'Farrell who commanded his own infantry battalion and the battalion of Scheltinga from Friesland.[38] O'Farrell was an old soldier who had trained in the Spanish and Dutch armies before entering the English establishment in 1689. Villeroi sent Feuquières to deal with Deynze. At the head of a small division, he marched upto Deynze on 19/29 July and summoned O'Farrell to surrender. The Governor tried to gain honourable terms but Feuquières insisted that the garrison give themselves up as prisoners-of-war, the French being desperate to deprive William's armies of troops. On the following day, without having fired a single shot, O'Farrell consented. He had more excuse than Ellenburg for it was well recognised that Deynze was no more than a fortified village 'hardly sufficient to keep out a partizan party'.

William was furious. He found the 'joke' of the loss of Dixmuyde and Deynze and some 7,000 men highly unamusing. 'You may easily conceive my mortification, not at the loss of these two trifling posts, on which I had calculated, but for the dastardly and precipitate manner in which they surrendered, and their not having employed the enemy so long as they ought to have done.'[39] The last point was crucial. The crime of Ellenburg and O'Farrell was that they had not fought their commands to their expected potentials. In turn, this resulted in 'dishonourable surrenders' in which the garrisons were incarcerated as prisoners-of-war instead of being returned to the army. Ellenburg should have defended more stoutly through sallies and retrenchments and O'Farrell had been expected to retire towards Vaudemont at Ghent rather than collapse in abject capitulation. He might, at least, have discharged a musket. Initially, in the wake of the disgrace, it was rumoured that Ellenburg and O'Farrell had sold their garrisons for money but at their courts-martial it soon became apparent that lack of judgement and panic were to blame. Holding independent commands and under severe pressure without recourse to superiors for guidance and instruction, both officers simply took wrong decisions. Blathwayt described O'Farrell as an 'old fool' and that seems an adequate summary. In short, neither was upto the job. The punishments were dire. After a spell of imprisonment in France,[40] O'Farrell, Ellenburg and the regimental commanders were court-martialled in Ghent before a tribunal chaired by Sir Henry Bellasise. Ellenburg was sentenced to death by decapitation and O'Farrell was cashiered with infamy. Three other colonels were dismissed and the remainder suspended. O'Farrell was disciplined 'pour encourager les autres' but the Allied army was short of experienced officers in the latter stages of the war and all of the cashiered and suspended commanders found their ways back into employment before many months had elapsed. O'Farrell regained his commission as brigadier in 1696. Only poor Ellenburg, an officer 'de réputation et de crédit', paid a lasting penalty.[41]

Logically, with Dixmuyde and Deynze under his belt, Villeroi should have turned on Württemberg and Bellasise at Nieuport and then tackled Oudenarde and Ath before he dealt with Vaudemont's weakened army at Oostakker. Bruges and Ghent would then have fallen into his lap like ripe plums and the whole of West Flanders would have come under French control. In terms of the Nine Years' War, this would have represented a massive territorial gain. Villeroi did not pursue this strategy because he had begun to incubate grave doubts about the impregnability of Namur and its citadel. The key to Villeroi's thinking was that the town should have resisted for considerably longer than fourteen days. Reluctantly, he abandoned his successful campaign in Flanders and turned eastwards towards Namur. Leaving Montal with 6,000 men to watch the Lines and de la Motte with a strong detachment to guard Dunkirk, Villeroi took the main army to Avelgem on the Scheldt on 25 July/4 August. On the next day, the army trailed through Renaix to Enghien. Still well informed of all that occurred in Villeroi's camp through his network of spies, Vaudemont struck his tents at Oostakker on 25 July/4 August and marched to cross the Scheldt at Appels before encamping at Baasrode near Dendermonde. Here he waited for twenty-four hours until he had definite news of Villeroi's move to Enghien before marching to Willebroek on 27 July/6 August and via Vilvorde to Diegem on 28 July/7 August. On the next morning, 29 July/8 August, Vaudemont marched through the streets of Brussels and encamped close to the Anderlecht Gate. Expecting a movement by Villeroi towards Brussels, Vaudemont ordered his men to entrench the camp and he also opened the sluices on the River Senne and flooded the south-western approaches to the city. Hurrying from around Nieuport, the Duke of Württemberg brought twelve battalions into the Anderlecht camp on 31 July/10 August.[42]

Villeroi advanced from Enghien to Halle on 1/11 August and immediately sent patrols towards Brussels. He was less than delighted to receive their intelligence that his attempt to surprise Brussels had been forestalled and Vaudemont blocked his path at Anderlecht. The appearance of the French caused a minor exodus from the city, many of the inhabitants seeking shelter for both themselves and their livestock on the eastern bank of the Brussels-Vilvorde Canal. Vaudemont rendered some assistance by sending cavalry back through the streets of Brussels to guard the line of the canal and prevent marauding French horse from crossing and enjoying themselves amongst the crowd of refugees. Villeroi's march to Brussels also caused something of a panic in the Allied siege lines around Namur. Athlone was ordered north from Pont-à-Celles to Waterloo where he was joined by William himself on 31 July/10 August. Ten battalions were then sent from Waterloo to Anderlecht and on the afternoon of 2/12 August, Vaudemont rode to Waterloo to confer with the King. Happy with the arrangements, William returned to Namur later that afternoon. Villeroi advanced cautiously from Halle and encamped on some high ground about two kilometres from Vaudemont's position, the two camps separated by the inundations.

Villeroi's intention was always to bombard Brussels rather than attempt a formal siege. In keeping with the thin veneer of politeness which characterised seventeenth century warfare, Villeroi sent a letter to the Governor of Brussels, the Prince de Berghes, in which he stated that Louis XIV had given orders for the bombardment of the city in retaliation for the Allied naval raid on Dunkirk which had taken place on 22 July/1 August. A column of 400 waggons loaded with bombs trundled into his camp from Mons and on 2/12 August he had ready a battery of ten cannon. Twenty-two mortars had been mounted by the next morning.[43] At 6.00 p.m. on 3/13 August, the French guns opened fire and continued for thirty-six hours, not ceasing until the morning of 5/15 August. Three thousand shells and 1,200 red-hot shot fell into Brussels starting a host of fires which were rapidly fanned by a strong wind. Over 2,000 houses, 17 churches, a number of palaces, two town houses, the town hall and a monastery were destroyed. There were not many casualties as much of the population had evacuated the city but the unfortunate Electress of Bavaria was shocked into miscarrying. From the military point-of-view, the bombardment was of little consequence. No magazines or stores were burned and no attempt was made to attack the city's fortifications. It was purely a terror raid of the kind which had become one of Louis XIV's hallmarks since the bombardment of Genoa in 1684. Leaving the southern quarter of Brussels wreathed in smoke and flame, Villeroi limbered-up his cannon and marched back to his old camp at Enghien.[44]

After the surrender of the town of Namur on 24 July/3 August at 2.00 p.m., the articles were finally agreed at 10.00 a.m. on 25 July/4 August. The French were given two days in which to evacuate the town and retire into the citadel. Boufflers could have resisted another attack but he had already lost too many men and needed to preserve his strength for the defence of the citadel.[45] It was well appreciated in the Allied camp that the town had fallen relatively quickly but the siege of the citadel would be an altogether tougher proposition. In the first place, its dominant location on a rocky outcrop in the apex of the peninsula formed by the confluence of the Sambre and the Meuse meant that although the citadel could be bombarded from all three sides, a land assault could only be mounted from within the peninsula itself. The garrison could thus concentrate its defensive efforts on a very restricted front. Secondly, the breaching cannon had to fire at a high elevation which reduced their effectiveness; mortars and howitzers were to be at a premium before Namur. Thirdly, being built on rock, all the barracks, storehouses and magazines had been placed in natural caves against which contemporary cannon, mortars and muskets could achieve little. Equipped with these advantages, the success of the defence would depend very much upon how the nerves and morale of the garrison withstood the incessant gunfire and stress of battle. However, Namur suffered from one identifiable weakness. 'My only hope is that which is common to all rocky castles, that their shooting spoils or diverts their water, by shaking some earth into the veins of water and stopping them or spoiling the fountain. And therefore I have heard the French have a design of fetching water by pipes from the river.'[46]

Vaudemont's corps continued to observe Villeroi. The French marshal had received direct orders from Louis XIV to do all that he could to relieve Namur. After his terror raid on Brussels, Villeroi had retired to Enghien before advancing to Soignies and then onto Nivelles where he stood within reach of Namur, well supported by his magazines at Mons and Charleroi. Villeroi reached Nivelles on 5/15 August. Until the arrival of Villeroi in the vicinity of Namur, the Allies had not needed to maintain a covering army, sufficing with Athlone's small cavalry corps of observation at Pont-à-Celles. Fortunately, the requirement for a covering army coincided with the fall of Namur town which released a considerable number of troops from duty in the trenches enabling a field corps to be formed. Vaudemont marched from Brussels to Waterloo on 7/17 August and combined with Athlone's horse. This corps then travelled to Sombreffe and St. Amand on 9/19 August, placing itself directly between Villeroi and Namur. On the following day, 10/20 August, Athlone and Vaudemont withdrew to rendezvous with William's covering corps of 30 battalions and 40 squadrons which was coming together at Mazy, two hours march from Namur. The Mazy position was very strong situated on the same ground which had been occupied by Luxembourg's covering army during the French siege of Namur in 1692. The camp lay in two lines describing a long crescent with the left resting on the River Sambre and the centre packed with artillery. Villeroi advanced eastwards from Nivelles on 5/15 August coming into a camp stretching from Fleurus to Marbaix. On arrival, he fired five signal cannon to inform Boufflers that possible relief was at hand.[47] With Brussels safe from attack and preparations well under way for the assault on the citadel, William took command of the covering army from Vaudemont leaving the Elector of Bavaria in charge of the siege. As Villeroi edged closer to the Mazy position, William withdrew five kilometres to a camp centred on the village of St. Denis to the north of Namur. This camp had its right protected by the headwaters of the River Mehaigne and its left and centre guarded by thick woods.

Villeroi manoeuvred north-east to Gembloux on 18/28 August. On the same day, his men crept silently forward towards William's position and camped across the front of the woods which now separated the rival armies. As he began to patrol and reconnoitre towards the Allied lines, he discovered an impossibly strong camp and an unexpectedly large number of men. Having persuaded himself that he ought to try to relieve Namur, Villeroi had not hurried in his march from Flanders. On the contrary, he had allowed himself time to mutilate Brussels *en route*. Villeroi clearly believed that so many Allied soldiers were falling before Namur that he had only to appear late in the day to deliver the coup de grâce to William's covering army. The Paris Gazettes exuded exaggerated reports of the Allied losses in front of the fearful citadel.

William had received ample intelligence of Villeroi's marches on 16/26 August and had set his army to entrenching the left and centre of the St. Denis camp that same day. The three most obvious passages through the woods were barricaded, strewn with abbatis and enfiladed by massed batteries. All the artillery officers had temporarily transferred to St. Denis from Namur on 17/27 August to take charge of the field guns. Villeroi approached the Allied camp at midnight on 17/27 August and fired signal cannon to inform Boufflers that succour had finally arrived. Serious probing and reconnoitring of the Allied right occurred on the morning of 18/28 August but William was already in receipt of information that Villeroi planned to outflank the Allied right wing and cross the Mehaigne. Accordingly, he extended his right and entrenched. Throughout 19/29 August and 20/30 August, the Allied covering army of 90,000 stood to arms expecting an attack from Villeroi's 120,000 but, at the crucial moment, 12,000 Hessian cavalry rode into William's camp after thirty days of marching. Despite this, some French horse did cross the Mehaigne on 21/31 August, beating back the Allied out-guards. Reinforcements were rushed forward to seal-off the penetration and then throw the insurgents back across the river. Two negligent captains were subsequently cashiered. The speed with which the Allies reacted to his probing attacks caused Villeroi to remark that the Prince of Orange's army 'had wings'. Wings or not, Villeroi could find no sure method by which to attack the covering army and he was obliged to relax the pressure and draw off to the north of the Mehaigne and camp between Perwez and Grand-Rosières in pursuit of an alternative tactical objective.

The French occupation of the Perwez position was highly incon-venient for William's soldiers who were 'now shut up in a kind of line of circumvallation, where forage was very scarce'. Villeroi had cut their communications with Brussels and Louvain, the major bases, and he also commanded the left bank of the Meuse between Liège and Namur. As the forage was consumed between the Meuse and the Mehaigne, William's army had to search for fodder and supplies in the Marlagne and the Condroz towards Dinant, 'very difficult country'. Although the French dominated the Meuse's western shore, the Allies were still able to run vessels southwards from Maastricht, Liège and Huy but it was a tenuous and vulnerable lifeline. If Villeroi had come into the Perwez position earlier and not wasted time by dallying and bombarding Brussels, he might have seriously embarrassed the progress of the siege. Villeroi's position was further improved by the arrival of the Duc de

Tallard with 15,000 men from the Comte de Lorge's army in the Rhineland.[48]

Before retiring with his depleted garrison into the citadel, Boufflers broke down all the connecting bridges across the Sambre. Nearly 1,500 sick and wounded were left in the town and the Allies discovered over five hundred deserters, skulking in cellars, having avoided service in the citadel. Perhaps Boufflers had lost half his original force of 16,000 men. In contrast, William was awash with troops, so much so that a regular system of reliefs was established from 13/23 August, with battalions in the trenches before Namur circulating with rested formations from the covering army. All but four of the British battalions left Namur to join the army at St. Denis. William shifted his headquarters to the Abbey of Malonne and the Elector of Bavaria moved to the Carmelite Convent.[49]

The trenches were opened before the citadel on 2/12 August, Vauban's long entrenchment forming an ideal base. On the right towards the Meuse, trenches zig-zagged from parallel to parallel to attack the Cassotte. On the left, where the British regiments were engaged, the trenches aimed at the hornwork of the Coehoorn Fort. By 8/18 August, the trenches were close to 'the foot of the mountain' and batteries of fifty heavy guns and mortars were positioned in the town to fire into the rear of the Terra Nova. Thirty-two 24 pounders arrived by water from Maastricht on the same day. On average, the trenches advanced some 200 metres every night and the garrison's sallies grew fewer and fewer as the ground became more difficult, casualties took their toll and morale sagged. Also, the Allies had so many men packed into the peninsula that the French sallies were almost bound to fail. Across the Meuse in the Jambes sector, Brandenburg batteries hammered the flanks of the Cassotte and the Terra Nova; on 8/18 August, over 150 cannon and mortars were blasting away at the citadel and it was becoming difficult for the garrison to find shelter from the fire.[50] Communications between the two Allied attacks were established on 9/19 August and the narrowing of the peninsula allowed the left and right trenches to merge into a general frontal assault on the Cassotte and the Coehoorn. Seventy cannon and forty heavy mortars opened fire from the town on 11/21 August to which the garrison replied with five mortars and a few heavy guns. Pouring rain added to everyone's enjoyment.

Boufflers sallied with 200 dismounted dragoons and 500 grenadiers at 11.00 p.m.on 8/18 August, but Lord Cutts and the Count de Rivera, Master of the Horse to the Elector of Bavaria, contained the attack until some Spanish and Bavarian cavalry counter-charged and drove the party back into the Terra Nova. Desertion from the garrison steadily increased and Boufflers dared not risk any more sallies for fear that his men would seize the opportunity to slip away. Bombs and solid shot hailed down on the Coehoorn, the Cassotte and the Terra Nova from three sides at once. The meat store was destroyed as well as one of the magazines of hay and the garrison was reduced to eating the horses of the redundant dragoons and cavalry.[51] Masonry was beginning to crumble on the counterscarp of the hornwork of the Coehoorn on 13/23 August and it was estimated that it would be breached and ready for assault within seven days. A small, stone redoubt, the Redoubt de la Sambre, on the right front of the Coehoorn was surrounded on 15/25 August and its garrison of a lieutenant and fifteen men surrendered. Six big breaches were visible on 19/29 August. One was in the apex of the Terra Nova at the Gronis Gate; another was in the demi-bastion on the right of the Terra Nova; three were in the right flank of the Coehoorn; and the Cassotte had also been pierced.[52] By this stage, Portland wrote to Shrewsbury confident that the citadel would soon fall and its only hope lay in Villeroi forcing the covering army to battle. There was one potentially awkward scenario. It was quite possible for Villeroi to by-pass William's covering army and march to attack a vital Allied fortress – Louvain, Liège or even Maastricht – all of which were defended by skeletal garrisons. Fortunately Villeroi had neither the orders nor the imagination for such a move.[53]

Content with the situation on the Mehaigne and satisfied that the breaches were of sufficient size, William ordered a general assault. Twenty thousand Allied troops were packed into the trenches, indeed the lines were so over-crowded that the Royal Irish and one other battalion had to form up at Salsine Abbey, one kilometre behind the start-line. Between noon and 1.00 p.m. on 20/30 August, the explosion of two barrels of powder signalled the attack. Lord Cutts led the British grenadiers and four other battalions against the breach in the demi-bastion on the right flank of the Terra Nova; the Bavarians under Rivera attacked the breaches in the Coehoorn; the Dutch, led by Schwerin, headed for the Cassotte; and 2,000 Brandenburgers, Hanoverians and Hessians under Prince Walrad von Nassau-Saarbruck assaulted the point of the Coehoorn. A simultaneous but subsidiary attack against the 'basse ville' below the castle on the banks of the Meuse was made by 1,000 Dutch infantry. Cutts's foot soldiers had to cross nearly a kilometre of open ground before they came to the breach in the Terra Nova. William watched the show from the heights above Salsine Abbey. He saw Cutts's men advance from their trenches with drums beating and colours flying. Fifteen grenadiers and a sergeant led the van, followed by a lieutenant with fifty more grenadiers, then a company of cadets and finally the four battalions in line. These battalions – Courthope's, Buchan's, Hamilton's and Mackay's – were amongst the greenest and worst in the British army, only Hamilton's having seen action before. The troops lost all formation as they galloped over the open ground and into the breach only to discover an untouched retrenchment blocking their path. Above them, from the ramparts of the Terra Nova, the French poured down a 'shower of stones', musketry and grenades until the untried battalions took to their heels and ran. There were virtually no officers left to rally them. Colonel John Courthope had been shot in the groin, Lieutenant-Colonel Sir Mathew Bridges's shoulder was shattered and Lord Cutts had received a slight head wound and was *hors de combat* until it had been dressed. His head swathed in bandages, Cutts led three supporting battalions, including the Royal Irish, back into the attack. Some soldiers managed to gain the counterscarp but the weight of defensive fire was too heavy and the assault was called off. Cutts's force had lost 1,349 men killed and wounded. Fortunately for the Allied cause, the Bavarians, Brandenburgers and Dutch fared much better and their attacks all secured lodgements on the counterscarps of the Coehoorn and the Cassotte.[54] By 5.00 p.m. the fighting was over and Allies were lodged within the citadel.

On 21/31 August, Boufflers signalled to Villeroi from the top of the Terra Nova. Villeroi replied that he could not force the Allied positions and Boufflers must make the best terms that he could. Boufflers and Guiscard informed William on the next day that they were prepared to surrender the Coehoorn and retire into the Terra Nova; ideally, they wanted to gain ten days' grace in which to await relief. These suggestions were instantly refused and on the same day at 4.00 p.m., Boufflers offered to surrender the entire citadel. Terms were agreed at 3.00 a.m. on 23 August/2 September.[55] There was a massive sense of relief on both sides, especially the French who had been demoralised not by the Allied infantry assaults but by the noise and blast of the incessant drumfire from cannon and mortar. The garrison had been bombarded into surrender. As soon as the defenders beat their drums for a parley on the afternoon of 22 August/1 September,

> then all the besiegers in the trenches and the besieged in their works stood up and discoursed and became so familiar that several officers went in and out. This occasioned an apprehension in the Governor that too many of us should get into the works, which made him fire a cannon

at our trenches, upon which everyone retired to his own post and as
soon as that was done they received a salvo from all our batteries which
did them no small damage. Then, immediately, the chamade was beaten
again.[56]

As soon as the surrender had been agreed and signed, the Elector of
Bavaria went forward to inspect the citadel. He was impressed with the
improvements to the fortifications which the French had made since
1692, particularly the double and triple palisades. He also appreciated
the extent of the shell-shock suffered by the garrison whilst locked in
their underground caves, casemates and barracks. On the surface, 'the
ground of the Coehoorn is perfectly ploughed over with our bombs'.[57]
    The garrison marched out of the citadel on 26 August/5 September;
there were just 5,000 men left from the original 16,000. 'That proud
and haughty man' Boufflers, was arrested and retained as a hostage
until Louis XIV released the remnants of the Allied garrisons from
Dixmuyde and Deynze but his short imprisonment in Maastricht was
one of 'great civility'. William instructed the Lords Justices in England
to organise a day of public rejoicing to celebrate the recapture of
Namur. The fortress yielded considerable stores of war to the Allies:
69 cannon, 8 mortars, 281,000 lb. of powder and over 40,000 grenades.[58] As soon as he heard that Namur had surrendered, Villeroi drew
away from William's army and marched to stand nearer to Mons and
Charleroi, two posts which he thought might be in some danger. He
reinforced Dinant with 2,000 men and retired within his Lines between
Mons and Tournai. Under the terms of the capitulation, William's
covering army moved back to Mazy before marching into Flanders in
readiness for separation into winter quarters. No-one expected any
more significant action in 1695. A sizeable garrison of Brandenburgers,
Hessians, Lüneburgers and three British battalions was left in Namur
to level the siege works and repair the fortifications. On 29 August/8
September, the main army marched to Sombreffe, through Bois St.
Isaac and into a camp between Halle and Lembeek on 31 August/10
September. William spent two days reviewing his troops before leaving
for Het Loo, heeding the advice of the Earl of Shrewsbury.

I cannot but wish that if success attends the attempt upon the Castle of
Namur, you would not too long delay your returning home, but make
use of the reputation that success will give your affairs, immediately to
summon a new parliament. If the campaign should continue, with your
Majesty at the head of the army, for any time after the siege, great

expectations would be raised; and if nothing considerable more should be done, the glory of the last action would be dead and forgot.[59]

Prima facie, Namur was a spectacular achievement. In an age when diplomacy and warfare were viewed in terms of personal prestige expressed through the capture and loss of major towns and fortresses, Namur was a great and cheering victory. The impregnable fortress, lost in 1692, had been regained in spite of Vauban's improvements. The French grip on the Meuse was broken at its critical junction with the Sambre; should the war continue, then the French hold over Charleroi and Mons might also be loosened. Yet there were sceptics. That acerbic observer Richard Hill, Paymaster of the British forces in the Low Countries, was not easily deceived.

> His Majesty is a fair gamester. . . . He is resolved to have the Castle (of Namur) at any price and the enemies seem resolved to succour it at any price. We have abandoned all Flanders and Brabant, which we sacrifice to Namur: but the French are not so blind as not to see our blots, and had rather attempt the succour of a cursed heap of rubbish than spoil and plunder all the towns in these countries.
>   I have had an ill summer. . . . I was bombarded in Brussels. . . . I borrowed about Fl 300,000 amongst those poor, frightened people, but stayed so long about it that the house I lay in was beaten down about an hour of so after I got out of it. I reckon one-sixth part of the town is beaten down, and they reckon the loss of 30 millions of florins, or £3,000,000 sterling. Namur is worth that to the States since Brussels, not Amsterdam, pays it.[60]

Conventional thinking had resulted in conventional war but what chances the French had missed! Whilst the Allies were occupied before Namur, Villeroi could have inflicted enormous damage on the Allied frontier in Flanders; Brussels, Ghent, Bruges, Ostend and Nieuport were all at their mercy. Both sides could have burgled each other's houses. Instead, the French took the minor posts of Deynze and Dixmuyde and executed an annoying but ultimately pointless bombardment of Brussels, seeming to be intent on the raising of the siege of Namur. Why? Because 'it was the darling of the French King's Conquests, the finest scene of his history, and therefore a place not to be taken from the arms of France and Lewis the 14th in person'. The recapture of Namur did not assist the cause of peace. Before the opening of the siege, Dijkveldt and Callières were probably on the road towards a

settlement but Namur, the detention of the garrisons of Dixmuyde and
Deynze, the bombardment of Brussels, the arrest of Boufflers and some
supposed ill treatment of French wounded by William in the wake of
the siege pushed all talk of peace to one side and ensured that the war
dragged on for at least one more campaign. There was little prospect
of a monarch like Louis XIV signing a peace treaty after he had just
suffered a major defeat; he would only countenance an end to the war
if he was in the ascendant.[61] Although it was the first victory, apart
from the Boyne, which William had secured during the Nine Years'
War and the first major success in the Low Countries, it did not much
benefit Allied interests.

William reached Breda on 6/16 September having left the Elector of
Bavaria in charge of the field army at Lembeek and Halle. Villeroi
manoeuvred onto the Plains of Cambron close to Ath. Continual heavy
rain hampered both armies and threatened to bring the campaign to an
end. Villeroi began to organise his forces ready for winter quarters.
D'Harcourt observed Namur from a position within the Sambre-Meuse
and Précontal was dispatched with 3,000 horse to Bastogne to watch
the movements of the Hessians and the Brandenburgers as well as to
secure communications with the Moselle. Following a minor raid by
the garrison of Ath on 10/20 September, the Elector of Bavaria led the
army to St. Kwintens-Lennik on 12/22 September and issued orders for
the soldiers 'to hut'. From this camp to the west of Brussels, the Elector
could observe Villeroi on the Plains of Cambron. Any major initiatives
were out of the question on account of the rain and the mud. By 18/28
September, Villeroi had shifted westward to Leuse in search of forage,
d'Harcourt had taken station close to Philippeville and Précontal had
been reinforced to 9,000 men at Bastogne. With the Hessian, Brandenburger and Lüneburger troops already on their way to the Rhine, having
crossed the Meuse at Visé, the Elector started to break up the main
army on 19/29 September. The heavy guns and 150 waggons went to
Alost ready to be shipped down the Dender and the Scheldt to the
artillery base at Ghent. The field artillery had departed for Ghent four
days earlier. The British regiments marched out of the camp to take up
billets in Bruges, Ghent, Ostend, Nieuport and in the villages along the
banks of the Bruges-Ghent Canal to serve as a screen to deter French
raids into East Flanders. Satisfied that the Allies had concluded their
campaign, Villeroi ordered d'Harcourt and Précontal to return their
men to winter quarters whilst he broke up the field army. A sudden
concentration of French troops near Nieuport caused the Duke of Württemberg to assemble a force from amongst the British soldiers in Fland-

ers but it was soon discovered that the Frenchmen were simply improving their Lines and had no offensive intentions.[62]

William sailed for England on 9/19 October to receive the plaudits of the City of London who had, at last, seen some results for their money. Villeroi set his men to work to dig Lines between the Sambre and the Meuse to create a new defensive front after the loss of Namur. The fortifications of Charleroi were marked down as in need of modernisation and plans were drawn up to build Lines between that city and Mons. The French were gripped by a defensive fever.

NOTES

1 *CSPD 1695*, p. 303; Heim, ii. 96–7.
2 Thomson, 'Louis XIV and William III', pp. 46–9; Morgan, 'Ryswick', pp. 175–7; *Lexington Papers*, pp. 104–5, 107; Callières, *Diplomacy*, pp. 8–9.
3 D'Auvergne, *1695*, pp. 2–7, 26; Japikse, iii. 351–2; CMC 4/69, 'Line from Courtrai to the Scheldt, 1695'; CMC 4/46, *Théâtre de la Guerre dans les Pays-Bas* (Paris, 1744).
4 *CSPD 1695*, p. 313; HMC, *Frankland-Russell-Astley MSS.*, p. 85.
5 D'Auvergne, *1695*, p. 8.
6 BL, Add. MSS. 18,776, 'A Journal of the Marches and most remarkable actions of the Confederate armies against France in the Low Countries during the campaign of 1695'; LUL, MS. 12, f. 237; D'Auvergne, *1695*, pp. 11–18; Japikse, iii. 350–1.
7 *Lexington Papers*, pp. 79–80; HMC, *Hastings MSS.*, ii. 248.
8 LG, nos. 3078, 3079; Walton, pp. 288–9; D'Auvergne, *1695*, pp. 18–23.
9 SP 87/1, f. 3; BL, Add. MSS. 9,722, f. 34; HMC, *Downshire MSS.*, i. 469.
10 SP 87/1, f. 5, 17/27 May 1695.
11 BL, Add. MSS. 9,722, f. 38; SP 87/1, f. 9.
12 Heim, ii. pp. lii–liii; D'Auvergne, *1695*, pp. 25–6.
13 LUL, MS. 12, ff. 238–40; SP 87/1, ff. 11, 29.
14 *Shrewsbury Correspondence*, p. 85.
15 SP 87/1, ff. 21, 35; BL, Add. MSS. 18,776; LUL, MS. 12, ff. 240–5; Heim, ii. pp. lii–liii; D'Auvergne, *1695*, pp. 26–34.
16 BCRO, Trumbull Add. MSS. 103; SP 87/1, f. 19; BL, Add. MSS. 18,776.
17 *Shrewsbury Correspondence*, pp. 86–7; HMC, *Bath MSS.*, iii. 55.
18 LG, no. 3089; D'Auvergne, *1695*, pp. 3, 30–1; Guerlac, 'Vauban', p. 81; CMC 4/46.
19 SP 87/1, f. 33; Trumbull Add. MSS. 103; HMC, *Bath MSS.*, iii. 55.
20 BL, Add. MSS. 18,776.
21 Trumbull Add. MSS. 103; SP 87/1, ff. 37, 39.
22 BL, Add. MSS. 63,629, ff. 24–9, 12/22 June 1695.
23 *Shrewsbury Correspondence*, p. 90.
24 SP 87/1, f. 41.
25 LG, no. 3092.
26 *Archives d'Orange-Nassau*, i. 396.

27 Heim, ii. pp. lii–lvii; BL, Add. MSS. 18,776; LUL, MS. 12, ff 246–8; SP 87/1, f. 43; Japikse, iii. 353.

28 Japikse, iii. 354, 355; Heim, ii. 99.

29 BL, Add. MSS. 18,776; Heim, ii. pp. lii–lvii; Parker, *Memoirs*, pp. 46–54; NLI, MS. 4166. pp. 28–9; HMC, *Downshire MSS.*, i. 494–5; CMC 4/70, J. Harrewyn, *Plan du Camp. . . . à Woutergem et à Arsele* (Brussels, 1695); *Saint-Simon*, i. 261–3.

30 BL, Add. MSS. 64,108, ff. 105–10. See the plan of Namur, 'comme il est en 1695', in *Atlas Portatif: Ou Théâtre de la Guerre en Europe* (Amsterdam, 1702); CMC 4/76a-d, Nicolas Vischer, *Plan de la Ville et du Château de Namur* (Amsterdam); CMC 4/75, Étienne Foulque, *Plan Général des Attaques faites devant la ville et le Château de Namur* (The Hague). D'Auvergne, *1695*, pp. 41–4; *An Exact Account of the Siege of Namur, with a Perfect Diary of the Campagne in Flanders, by a Gentleman attending his Majesty during the whole Campagne* (London, 1695); Kane, *Campaigns*, p.110.

31 SP 87/1, f. 55.

32 BL, Add. MSS. 9,722, f. 73; SP 87/1, f. 57; *Shrewsbury Correspondence*, p. 92; *CSPD 1695*, p. 17.

33 SP 87/1, ff. 47, 51; HMC, *Le Fleming MSS.*, p. 336; *Archives d'Orange-Nassau*, i. 396–7; *Shrewsbury Correspondence*, p. 91.

34 HMC, *Downshire MSS.*, i. 511–12, 526; HMC, *Le Fleming MSS.*, p. 336; *Shrewsbury Correspondence*, pp. 94–5; BL, Add. MSS. 9,722, ff. 82, 84, 86; Japikse, iii. 358, 359; Landmann, pp. 72–6.

35 Kane, *Campaigns*, pp. 21–2; Trumbull Add. MSS. 103.

36 K. Danaher & J. G. Simms, *The Danish Force in Ireland, 1690–1691* (Dublin, 1962) pp. 142–3; Kane, *Campaigns*, p. 21; Parker, *Memoirs*, pp. 58–9; HMC, *Finch, MSS.*, iii. 36; *Shrewsbury Correspondence*, p. 99.

37 BL, Add. MSS. 63,629, ff. 30–1; HMC, *Downshire MSS.*, i. 512–13; D'Auvergne, *1695*, pp. 74–9; SP 87/1, ff. 162–4.

38 Heim, ii. 101.

39 *Archives d'Orange-Nassau*, i. 397; *Shrewsbury Correspondence*, pp. 97–8; Kane, *Campaigns*, pp. 21–2; Lediard, iii. 461; D'Auvergne, *1695*, pp. 80–4; John Davis, *History of the Second Queen's Royal Regiment* (London, 1887–95), ii. 241; Japikse, iii. 359.

40 See pp. 40–1.

41 Trumbull Add. MSS. 103; *LG*, no. 3135; SP 87/1, f. 78.

42 BL, Add. MSS. 18,776; Japikse, iii. 357–8.

43 SP 87/1, ff. 95–7; *Shrewsbury Correspondence*, p. 100; BL, Add. MSS. 18,776; Trumbull Add. MSS. 103; Symcox, *Crisis of French Sea Power*, p. 160; HMC, *Downshire MSS.*, i. 526.

44 *LG*, no. 3105; Dangeau, p. 287; SP 87/1, f. 97; *Archives d'Orange-Nassau*, i. 398; Heim, ii. 101–2; HMC, *Downshire MSS.*, i. 525; Berwick, i. 86–92; *Blackader*, pp. 132–3; A. Wauters, *Le Bombardement de Bruxelles en 1695* (Brussels, 1849).

45 *Archives d'Orange-Nassau*, i. 397; BL, Add. MSS. 9,722, f. 97; D'Auvergne, *1695*, p. 103.

46 HMC, *Downshire MSS.*, i. 502–4, 12/22 July 1695, Hill to Trumbull.

47 BL, Add. MSS. 18,776; Heim, ii. pp. lii–lvii; SP 87/1, f. 114; Japikse, iii. 360, 364.

48 BL, Add. MSS. 18,776; *Morrison 1st Series*, vi. 421, 6/16 Aug. 1695, William

to Vaudemont; D'Auvergne, *1695*, pp. 159–60; *Lexington Papers*, pp. 102–3; *HMC, Downshire MSS.*, i. 532, 539.

49 *HMC, Le Fleming MSS.*, p. 337.

50 SP 87/1, f. 99.

51 Trumbull Add. MSS. 103; SP 87/1, ff. 105, 110.

52 Walton, p. 306; Kane, *Campaigns*, p. 110.

53 *Shrewsbury Correspondence*, p. 101; *Lexington Papers*, pp. 110–12.

54 NLI, MS. 4166, pp. 33–5; Kane *Campaigns*, pp. 23–4; *Lexington Papers*, pp. 114–17; Churchill College, Cambridge, Erle-Drax MSS. 4/18, f. 4; Gretton, *Royal Irish Regiment*, p. 22; SP 87/1, f. 122; *Colonie*, pp. 39–44.

55 BL, Add. MSS. 9,722, ff. 104, 106; BL, Add. MSS. 18,776; Trumbull Add MSS. 103; *An Account of the Surrending (sic) of the Castle of Namur to the Confederates* (London, 1695, postscript to *Post Boy*, no. 48).

56 *HMC, Portland MSS.*, iii. 565–6.

57 Trumbull Add. MSS. 114; *Blackader*, p. 136; D'Auvergne, *1695*, p. 161.

58 *Lexington Papers*, pp. 119–21; BL, Add. MSS. 9,722, f. 107; Trumbull Add. MSS. 103, 114.

59 SP 87/1, f. 148; LUL, MS. 12, ff. 250–4; BL, Add. MSS. 18,776; *Shrewsbury Correspondence*, pp. 99–100, 30 July/9 Aug. 1695, Shrewsbury to William.

60 *HMC, Downshire MSS.*, i. 537–8, 21/31 Aug. 1695, Richard Hill to Trumbull.

61 *Lexington Papers*, pp. 120–5; D'Auvergne, *1695*, p. 172.

62 BL, Add. MSS. 18,776; LUL, MS. 12, ff. 254–67; *CSPD 1695*, pp. 347, 349.

XI

1696: PLANNING FOR STALEMATE

Before departing for England in September 1695, William supervised a post-mortem on the previous campaign and initiated a conference to plan for the next. Vaudemont, the Elector of Bavaria, the Prince of Anhalt-Dessau and the Prince of Nassau participated in the sessions at The Hague and the final resolutions and papers were produced one month later by the standing congress.

The first task was to analyse the events of 1695. Three Allied armies had been in operation, two in the Low Countries and one on the Rhine, comprising a total of 190 battalions and 330 squadrons. This had permitted 90,000 infantry and 27,600 horse to serve in the Netherlands and 24,000 foot and 12,000 cavalry to fight in Germany. Villeroi had enjoyed access to a field army of 100 battalions and 200 squadrons, around 84,000 men, but his inferiority in numbers had been compensated by interior lines and the considerable bodies of troops manning the frontier garrisons. The method chosen for overcoming the geographical and strategic advantages of the French position and for rendering effective the Allies' numerical superiority had been the splitting of the French field forces by pretending to hold and attack in Flanders whilst simultaneously striking on the Meuse. Throughout the season, the French had not been expected to try anything substantial on the Rhine and so both Villeroi and William had spent much of the campaign wondering how and when the French soldiers in the Rhineland would march to reinforce their comrades in Flanders. The solution to the puzzle was that Choiseul and Tallard arrived in the Low Countries far too late to affect the issue. The basic Allied scheme had been for one army to capture Namur whilst the other stood between Dixmuyde and Deynze both to distract the French and cover the siege from long distance. Success had attended the operation, Vaudemont's small army sufficiently checking Villeroi to prevent him from intervening at Namur until Boufflers was *in extremis*.

However, the 'Memoire au sujet de la prochaine Campagne' was a self-congratulatory document rather than a rigorous analysis. It failed to recognise that the Allied achievement had rested upon Villeroi being his own worst enemy. If he had ignored Vaudemont's corps and rushed straight for Namur the moment that William had declared his intention, he might well have caught the investing army short of numbers and off balance. Either the siege would have become untenable or Villeroi would have stood a good chance of defeating the Allies in battle. There were many reasons why the French general did not follow this course of action but chose instead to dither in Flanders and then wander across Brabant by way of Brussels to appear close to Namur long after the Allies had concentrated all their troops and occupied a dominant covering position. First, Villeroi had placed unwarranted emphasis on the reputations of Boufflers and Namur. As a matter of honour, marshals of France did not surrender and, with Vauban's improvements added to Coehoorn's designs, Namur could not be taken. In making the latter assumption, Villeroi overlooked the golden rule of siege warfare: fortresses were built to endure a specified length of investment, none were impregnable. Fortresses were intended either to defend territory by delaying an enemy or to give a friendly army the opportunity to operate elsewhere. Villeroi did neither. His manoeuvres in Flanders and around Brussels were insufficient to pull William away from the Meuse and failed to produce a *quid pro quo* for the loss of Namur. Secondly, Villeroi was no Luxembourg. He was a decent general and a competent commissary but he was inclined to be timorous and conventional. He could have trapped Vaudemont at Aarsele but he commanded from the distant rear rather than the front and his subordinates let him down. Thirdly, the 'Memoire' suggests that Villeroi was daily expecting reinforcements from Germany. His meanderings through Flanders and Brabant filled in time whilst he collected all available garrisons and gathered troops from the Rhineland. These additions did indeed bring his army to parity with the enemy but he was then unable to force the covering position on the Upper Mehaigne. There was no excuse for this. Villeroi had been a lieutenant-general during the 1692 campaign in and around Namur and knew the strength of the post on the Plain of Fleury behind the Mehaigne, the same ground on which William had been unable to pass Luxembourg. Villeroi's gratuitous raid on Brussels was viewed by the authors of the 'Memoire' as an attempt to entice the Allies from Namur.

In the light of these experiences and analyses, the Allied generals set about drafting their plans for 1696. Basically, the tactics of 1695 in holding with one hand and hitting with the other were to be extended throughout the Netherlandish and German theatres. It was assumed that the French would have to maintain an army on the Moselle, based on Mont Royal, Luxembourg City and Dionville, to protect this 'gate' from the menace of the corps of Louis of Baden and the Landgrave of Hesse-Cassel. A force on the Moselle was also necessary to guard the southern flank of the French positions in Brabant. For the Allies, the victory of 1695 brought difficulties for 1696. The French had locked twenty battalions and twenty-four squadrons inside Namur in 1695; in this year, the Allies would have to find a similar garrison whilst the French could add an equivalent number of men to their marching armies. In fact, the Allies would be seriously short of men for their field corps having to garrison Namur, Huy, Liège, Ath, Oudenarde and Nieuport. The paper solution was to form four armies, all closely linked. There was to be an Army of Flanders, an Army of the Meuse and the Sambre based at Namur, an Army of the Moselle centred on Coblenz and an Army of the Upper Rhine. This arrangement surrounded the eastern frontiers of France, threatening the major invasion channels through Flanders, along the Meuse and via the Moselle. By entering the field ahead of their opponents, the Allies intended to seize the initiative and force the French onto the defensive thus negating their numerical inequality. The planners took note of the depleted and war-weary French economy. Initially, the Armies of the Upper Rhine and the Moselle were to combine whilst the Army of Flanders was entrusted with observing the French to prevent reinforcements leaving Flanders for Germany. The Army of the Meuse and the Sambre was to operate in conjunction with either the Army of Flanders or the Army of the Moselle, depending upon developments. The task of the Army of the Upper Rhine was to watch the French but to adopt a defensive stance and send whatever troops it could spare to the Army of the Moselle if the latter attempted a siege. Should the Army of the Meuse undertake a siege, then the Army of the Moselle would cover whilst the Armies of Flanders and the Upper Rhine occupied the French on their fronts. Should the Army of Flanders attempt a siege, the Army of the Meuse and Sambre would act as the covering corps reinforced from the Army of Flanders with any troops not required in the trenches.

After reciting this list of hypothetical operations, the planners stated the obvious – all armies were to liaise closely. If the French entered the campaign with numbers equal to or less than those of the Allies, then they were to be attacked on one or more fronts. Should the French appear definitely superior in strength, then the Allies might strive to form a fifth army or open another front. There remained unsolved the slight problem that the scheme to deploy four Allied armies depended upon the production of a further twenty battalions and thirty squadrons at a time when all the participants were scraping the bottom of the barrel marked 'human resources'. Finally, in order to secure its projected operations, the Army of the Upper Rhine needed to capture a major fortress on the Rhine to serve as a forward base.[1]

To anyone acquainted with the practicalities of military planning, the 'Memoire' is conjectural, lacking detail and an accurate intelligence appreciation of enemy intentions and capabilities. No precise operations are described and it is really no more than an elaborate contingency plan. Why was it prepared? In the first place, it did something to impose a common purpose on the members of the Grand Alliance when their cohesion was under severe pressure from French diplomacy. In some ways, the 'Memoire' was a restatement of the aims of the Alliance and a plea for corporate effort. Secondly, the principal axes of the next year's operations had to be outlined during the previous autumn so that the huge magazines of grain and fodder could be assembled over the winter. Although this compromised secrecy in the face of a vigilant enemy, it was the only way in which the stores could be accumulated in the correct locations. Unfortunately, the demand for early planning gave the staffs little opportunity to take into account diplomatic developments during the winter. Some slight adjustments could be made in the spring but once the magazines were stocked strategic flexibility disappeared. A similar timetable must have functioned in most years of the war: a preliminary statement of aims and methods in the late autumn and early winter followed by more detailed operational plans towards the spring. Whereas maps seem to have been little used during the campaigns themselves, officers relying heavily on guides and their own knowledge of the topography, there is every indication that they were employed extensively for planning.[2]

None of the schemes came to fruition. The campaign of 1696 was dominated not by military considerations but by a monetary crisis in England. A currency weakened by years of 'clipping', £5,000,000 of government loans issued against an inadequate revenue and a slipping exchange rate against the Dutch Guilder and the Flemish Shilling wrecked the Allied military effort. William could not acquire enough hard cash to pay his British troops and the foreign contingents funded by the English Treasury nor could he meet the demands of the various bread, waggon and forage contractors.[3]

The King could not undertake any major operations in the Low Countries without money for pay, ammunition, transport, food and contingencies. As Britain paid the bills, either directly or indirectly, of almost two-thirds of the troops in the Allied armies in the Low Countries, the collapse of confidence in the British monetary system during 1696 emasculated William's martial ambitions. With the armies in the Netherlands restricted to defensive and unambitious operations, it was scarcely conceivable that the German and Imperial forces along the Rhine would launch independent offensives. At the best of times, the Germanic members of the Grand Alliance had been less than whole-hearted and convincing in translating rhetoric into military action. There was no prospect of the Armies of the Moselle and the Upper Rhine even stirring into the field if the French were not to be distracted by considerable Allied movements in Flanders and Brabant.

Sensing that their opponents were also entering the quagmire of economic difficulties, the French peace initiatives during 1696 were desultory. Callières resumed negotiations with Dijkveldt and Boreel in May. All summer they haggled, Dijkveldt and Boreel insisting that William did not need Louis's recognition of his status as King of England and that the English and the Dutch would not desert the Grand Alliance by concluding a separate peace. Eventually, although not until December, the negotiators agreed that Louis would recognise William after the signature of a general peace. To this end, a peace conference would be summoned in 1697 at which Sweden would act as mediator.[4] The French had good reason to tread slowly in their talks with the Dutchmen. On 23 November 1695, General Tessé had resumed his clandestine discussions with Duke Victor Amadeus II of Savoy. Victor Amadeus agreed to desert the Grand Alliance and join with France provided that the key fortress of Pinerolo was ceded to his duchy. At first Louis was reluctant but he came to realise that this was an ideal instrument with which to split the Grand Alliance and force its members to come to a series of separate treaties with France. A final version of the agreement between France and Savoy was signed on 19/29 June 1696 and ratified by Louis one week later. In return for Pinerolo and all the Savoyard territory seized by France during the war, Victor Amadeus joined his army to that of Louis XIV in order to persuade the Spanish and Imperial forces in Northern Italy to evacuate Italian territory and render the region a neutral zone. On 27 September/7 October 1696, the Allies were obliged to sue for peace in Italy and a truce was proclaimed for all of Northern Italy at Vigevano. Italy was declared to be neutral and the Allied armies agreed to depart within two months.[5] Louis had divided the Grand Alliance and had freed the whole of Nicolas Catinat's army for deployment in the Low Countries or along the Rhine in 1697. A second scheme to winkle England out of the Grand Alliance and into a separate peace involved the resuscitation of the Jacobite card.

After the humiliating loss of Namur, the French grew very sensitive about the possibility of Allied incursions into the Marlagne between the Sambre and the Meuse. As many small towns and ancient castles as possible were provided with garrisons and pioneers laboured to improve the fortifications of Dinant, Philippeville and Fort Charlemont and to dig new Lines across the Marlagne in the rear of Namur.[6] The winter of 1695–6 continued the run of cold, hard seasons which characterised the decade of the 1690s. Sir William Trumbull received information of 'frost and snow' in the Low Countries on 20/30 December 1695. Ninety French troops from Mons took advantage of the frozen ground to raid two villages within a short distance of Brussels. The cold snap ended in a sudden thaw which caused flooding only to be followed by another severe spell of weather in January during which the River Thames nearly froze from bank to bank. Warmer conditions did not appear until the middle of April.[7] The Allies used the winter months to improve the defences of Brussels. New works were constructed outside the Anderlecht Gate on the site from which Villeroi's batteries had smashed the city during the previous summer. Patrols from the Allied garrison of Ath clashed with French cavalry which ventured north of their Lines during the middle of January. In addition to bolstering their Lines, the French strained every nerve to recruit more soldiers from the 'conquered territories' in the southern sections of the Spanish Netherlands and the Duchy of Luxembourg. They aimed to raise a further thirty battalions and were only partially constrained by the shortage of trained and suitable officers. The Allies, on the other hand, were finding it increasingly difficult to produce enough soldiers. England and the United Provinces could not afford to augment their own, national armies and had no money to spare to hire extra troops from Germany whilst the Holy Roman Emperor was deploying ever larger bodies of troops to chase the Turks out of Hungary. This was a far more congenial and profitable occupation than messing about on the Rhine.

Sir William Trumbull received intelligence of the French plan of campaign from an agent in The Hague, Monsieur de Chenailles, late in

January. Chenailles recounted how the French intended to sail their ships from Toulon past Admiral Russell's weak Anglo-Dutch Fleet, which had wintered at Cadiz, and link-up with the Brest Squadron in order to challenge Allied naval superiority in the English Channel. After augmenting their army in the Netherlands, it was to be divided into three corps under the command of Conti, Villeroi and Boufflers. With the benefit of an early start to the campaign, these generals intended to launch a surprise operation, seize an important target and then assume the defensive for the remainder of the summer. Just as Mathew Prior had feared, the French wanted to make their army on the Rhine under the Comte de Lorge, or the Duke de Vendôme, a powerful formation in order to prevent the Allies in the Low Countries from being reinforced from Germany.[8] Considering that this was second-hand information from a remote source, it was a remarkably accurate resumé of French operational intentions. In the meantime, the small war of patrols and digging continued. The Allies built some new works on the St. Barbes Hill at Namur and the French began the construction of Lines between Charleroi and Walcourt. A boat carrying baggage along the Bruges-Nieuport Canal was ambushed by a French patrol. On 10/20 February, the Allies commenced preparations to turn Ath into a forward base and ordered the contractors to lay in rations and 'necessaries' to sustain 40,000 men for three weeks.[9]

On 8/18 February, Chenailles wrote again to Trumbull giving the latest news from Paris and Versailles. The French, he said, would make one last military effort in 1696 in order to be able to dictate peace to the Allies. If the gamble failed, they were mentally prepared to make peace in 1697 by ceding a few towns here and there. The offensive would occur in Flanders whilst the French stood on the defensive in Germany and Piedmont. Although the French were having difficulty in raising fresh troops, the army in Flanders would be augmented by the troops who had been stationed in Normandy to guard the Channel coast against Allied descents. Then came the real news: the Toulon Fleet was to sail to Brest from where the combined force of over 100 ships would convey James II to Ireland with 40,000 men. The French court and its military advisers had been encouraged into this project by the hope that Russell's fleet would consequently be drawn away from Cádiz into the English Channel. This would permit Marshal Noailles, whose campaign in Catalonia had been hamstrung by Russell's presence in the Mediterranean, to resume his progress towards Barcelona. Naturally, the French expected Russell not to return to his home waters until the combined Toulon and Brest Squadrons had safely convoyed James II into Ireland or England.[10]

To give every credit to Sir William Trumbull, the Secretary of State for the Northern Department, he acted on this intelligence. Lieutenant-General Nicolaas Fagel seized the French post of Oost-Duinkerke, three kilometres south of Nieuport, in early February in order to secure this vital port ready for the transference of troops from Flanders to the British Isles. Until harder intelligence was received, nothing more could be done. Still abiding by the outline of the 'Mémoire', William and Vaudemont discussed the establishment of a corps of 40,000 men around Namur and began to think in terms of using the Army of the Moselle to attack Mont Royal. To balance this development, the French began to assemble troops in the Marlagne but neither side could press on with any great speed. In particular, the Allied magazines were in a poor condition through the shortage of money and because the very bad winter weather had rendered the roads, rivers, and canals impassable to the contractors' carts and boats.[11]

Trumbull received more intelligence of the projected French invasion on 14/24 February and, two days later, a letter from Strasbourg told him that the invasion plan was 'common talk in France'.[12] 'Unsigned intelligence' from Paris, dated 21 February/2 March, landed on Trumbull's desk giving a list of all the general officers who were to command the expedition of 12,000 men. Lieutenant-General d'Harcourt was in overall charge. Trumbull remained to be entirely convinced harbouring the suspicion that the reported twenty French men-of-war at Dunkirk might have been intended for the bombardment of Ostend or Flushing, a move which the Dutch had feared since the beginning of the year.[13]

Completely reliable information was not sent to England until 23 February/4 March, when Robert Wolseley wrote from Brussels to the Duke of Shrewsbury, the Secretary of State for the Southern Department, telling him that Vaudemont had received intelligence that James II was at Calais with between 12,000 and 30,000 men ready to invade England. Boufflers had been placed in command of the expedition. To take this force to England, nineteen men-of-war, one bomb vessel and eighty transports were riding at anchor off Dunkirk. On his own initiative, Vaudemont had already set up postal relays along the road from Brussels to Ostend and had ordered sections of the British garrisons in Bruges and Ghent to be ready to march to Ostend to embark for England. Transport ships were instructed to stand-by at Ostend and Nieuport whilst an emergency council of war convened in Brussels from which emerged orders for the Duke of Württemberg to take twenty British battalions immediately across the North Sea.

> I have scarce shut my eyes since I wrote my last to you. I have got shipping here and provisions for twelve battalions and money in their pockets. I have provisions at Ghent for 8 battalions more, which are going to Zealand, and now I think I shall go to sleep quietly, since the treason is discovered in England and we are as ready to sail as the enemy.[14]

Admiral Russell ran close to Calais on 28 February/9 March and counted over 300 small craft, undoubtedly intended to serve as troop transports, but only seventeen men-of-war for escort duty. A bomb vessel, lamented Russell, would have been very handy.[15] However, the danger had already passed. The plot to assassinate William III, upon the success of which the invasion depended, was uncovered on 21 February/2 March and publicly revealed to the Privy Council on the following day. This effectively ended French interest in an invasion of England. Boufflers and d'Harcourt's men were sent back to their army corps. Württemberg brought his twenty battalions into the Downs but the troops did not land and spent a few highly uncomfortable days bobbing around before being dispatched back to the Spanish Netherlands.[16] The Jacobites in England had been caught in their customary impasse. Their supporters would not rise without manifest evidence of a French invasion and the French would not invade until a Jacobite insurrection had occurred. If the invasion had gone ahead, Louis would have reaped more than the political advantages of replacing William III with a pliant James II. If it had been deprived of English economic muscle, the Army of the Grand Alliance in the Low Countries would have collapsed.[17]

The discovery of the plot allowed the Allied generals to turn their attention from sideshows to the real war. The first substantial Allied movement of the campaign was the raid on the major French magazine at Givet, on the Meuse south of Dinant. By Allied standards, this was a truly audacious operation involving a march of some forty-five kilometres from Namur deep into enemy territory. Athlone and Coehoorn left Namur with 30 battalions, 18 cannon and 6 mortars, attended by a small force of cavalry. Athlone and 14,000 infantry sealed off Dinant whilst Coehoorn took 4,000 foot and the artillery further south to attack Givet. The principal defence of Givet was the Fort de Charlemont on the west bank of the Meuse. To avoid Charlemont, Coehoorn remained on the eastern side of the river, a stance which also secured his communications with Athlone at Dinant. The guns opened at 7.00 a.m. on 6/16 March, the cannon shooting red-hot shot and the mortars lobbing explosive bombs. Within three hours, much of the town was ablaze and by 4.00 p.m. most of the magazines had been destroyed, a total of between three and four million rations. The only store to escape the inferno was the magazine of oats situated on the west bank of the Meuse; Coehoorn did not dare to cross from the east bank as he would have surrendered his line of retreat. His task completed, Coehoorn withdrew to Dinant to rejoin Athlone and the combined party then fell back along the Meuse, the rearguard holding a weak sally by the garrison of Dinant. The Duke of Holstein-Plön marched additional troops to the south of Namur to sustain the retirement. Some reports told of how many of the citizens of Dinant, on hearing of the advance of Coehoorn and Athlone, has assumed that their town was the target. In haste, they removed their belongings to Givet only to see them burned before their eyes. It is possible that the magazine at Givet had been assembled to support an operation to recapture Namur and this was certainly the Allied interpretation. It is more likely that Givet was to have served as a base for the French troops which were massing in the Marlagne to garrison the new lines. Whatever the intention, the loss to the French was huge and ruled out all thoughts of launching an offensive during 1696. Indeed, Givet was a major factor in persuading Louis that French economic salvation lay in the economic penetration of the Spanish Empire. Pointis's expedition of 1697 to tap the riches of the Americas had its progeny in the raid on Givet. As a military achievement, Givet ranked second only to Namur; in its contribution to the coming of peace, Givet was the greatest strategic blow delivered by the Allies. The governor of Givet was the unfortunate Comte de Guiscard, who had been deputy to Boufflers at Namur in the previous year. He turned his garrison cannon onto Athlone's men but had done little damage. A feature of the operation had been the way in which Athlone had feinted towards Charleroi and Nivelles at the beginning of the march from Namur to throw the enemy off the scent.[18]

William was anxious to secure an early entry into the field in order to take the initiative. Orders were issued on 18/28 April for the troops to begin their concentration but, as Richard Hill noted, 'we want nothing but clothes, arms, tents, waggon-money, hospitals and two months subsistence'.[19] The war returned to patrolling and raiding. On 20/30 March, Guiscard advanced from Dinant to inspect the new fortifications which Coehoorn, with the help of 6,000 men, was building at Namur. Guiscard, escorted by 1,000 cavalry, reconnoitred the new fort

and trenches on the St. Barbes Hill and then quietly retired. No sooner
had he disappeared, than Coehoorn rushed out his pioneers and started
to throw up a new fort on the very spot from which Guiscard had cast
his eye over the defences. The Dutchman feared that Guiscard, who
was not unacquainted with the intricacies of Namur, had discovered a
weak spot from where he might be able to gain his revenge and bombard
the town with red-hot shot. As an additional precaution, 16,000 infantry were sent to reinforce the garrison of Namur, a corps which had
been intended as the basis of the projected Army of the Meuse.[20] To
cover this development, Guiscard formed a camp of 16,000 men
between Dinant and Givet.

The French divided their forces in Flanders into two armies and four
flying columns. Villeroi commanded the main army in the Lines of the
Lys and the Scheldt whilst Boufflers collected a second major corps
around the River Orneau before marching forward to encamp at
Fleurus. De la Motte and Montal directed two of the flying columns
in Flanders, based on Dunkirk; d'Harcourt controlled a column in
Luxembourg in the region of Chiny to watch the Moselle and obstruct
any German reinforcements moving towards the Meuse; and Guiscard
commanded his column between Givet and Dinant. In total, the French
forces in the theatre numbered 120,000 men.[21] Allied councils of war
were held in Vaudemont's house in Brussels and at the Elector of
Bavaria's court to co-ordinate operational plans. By 29 March/8 April,
all was ready for an early entry into the field and tents had been
distributed to the troops. Württemberg returned to Ostend at the end
of March with the twenty battalions which he had taken across the
North Sea to combat the invasion scare. To encourage the Allies, an
accidental fire broke out in Charleroi which destroyed much of the
upper town although later intelligence indicated that the French magazines had escaped. During April, the Elector of Bavaria concentrated one
corps of the projected Army of the Meuse at Namur and Vaudemont
assembled the Army of Flanders at Mariakerke, just outside the walls
of Ghent on the north-western side.[22]

Vaudemont was of the opinion that the French would make one, last,
major effort during 1696 in order to win a more favourable peace. He
became convinced of this when he noticed the French reinforcing their
army in Flanders with troops from the Rhine and Savoy. The Prince
urged William and Heinsius to spur the Germans into action along the
Rhine to create a diversion sufficient to take the pressure off the Allies
in the Spanish Netherlands.[23] On 3/13 May, William boarded his yacht
at Margate and arrived in The Hague on the evening of Thursday 7/17

May. Orders were promptly sent out for the Army of the Meuse, now to be the principal army under William's personal command, to gather about Wavre, to the south of Louvain. Taking a leaf from Louis XIV's book, William instructed peasant pioneers to drive a road south from Wavre in case the Army of the Meuse had to march rapidly to support its advanced corps of 16,000 at Namur. Allied concern about a French expedition to recapture their new prize remained strong. More serious was the fact that the British-paid portions of the Allied army were already three months in arrears of pay.

Villeroi marched northwards from Pont d'Espierres on 9/19 May and camped across the width of the land between the Lys and the Scheldt with his left at Deynze, a mere fifteen kilometres from Ghent. The French march caught Vaudemont by surprise. His first inkling of the enemy advance came when local peasants started to carry their belongings into their churches and drove their cattle north over the Ghent-Bruges Canal. Vaudemont hurried his corps into the field to block the crossing places on both the Ghent-Bruges Canal and the Bruges-Nieuport Canal. Major-General Ramsey with seventeen battalions guarded the vulnerable ford at Bellem closely supported by twenty-five battalions under Noyelles. Fagel covered Nieuport with ten battalions. In between these major positions, infantry formed guard posts and watches along the canal banks reinforced by breastworks, some light field guns and 'swans' feathers'.[24] Vaudemont's dragoons remained in billets under orders to march at very short notice. William rode from Breda to inspect Vaudemont's dispositions and he was so satisfied that he felt able to detach 18 battalions and 8 regiments of horse from the Army of Flanders to reinforce the Army of the Meuse at Wavre. Taking the road through Brussels, William rode into the camp at Wavre where he was greeted by the cavalry, drawn up 'sword in hand', and the whole of the first line of the infantry arrayed in battalia with their arms presented.[25] This might have brought a little cheer to the King's heart but much else was gloomy. Villeroi stood at Deynze, threatening Flanders and preventing William from uniting Vaudemont's corps with his own. Boufflers hovered around Gosselies, to the north of Charleroi, with his right stretching towards Fleurus. Latest reports indicated that he was assiduously destroying the countryside to deter the Allies from operating in that direction. Money was needed everywhere and the Brandenburg troops were so short of cash that they could not be induced to undertake any long marches. Villeroi's next move was difficult to predict. He might attack Ghent or Bruges or he might decide to consume the forage and damage the country to prevent Vaudemont's army from deploying towards the French Lines. Intelligence reports told of a French camp marked out at Blaton, south of Leuse, which suggested that Villeroi would withdraw southwards either to threaten Ath or combine with Boufflers. However, he had also laid two bridges across the Lys which hinted that he might march to Roeselare. Vaudemont's pessimistic prediction had been correct. The only hope for the Allies in the Low Countries lay in a vigorous German offensive on the Rhine which would force Villeroi and Boufflers to cede troops to reinforce their comrades in the Rhineland.[26]

Boufflers drew in the garrisons from between the Meuse and the Sambre bringing his corps at Gosselies upto a total of 25,000 men supported by fifty-five cannon. A detachment of 3,000 separated from Villeroi's army and advanced towards the Scheldt. *En route*, thirty brave volunteers swam the river and set fire to the Allied hay magazine at Oudenarde. Luckily, the governor received some short notice of the enemy's approach and had sufficient men on hand to douse the flames. Four days later, Boufflers's soldiers blew up the sluice on the Sambre at Grignon Mill, lowering the water level sufficiently to render navigation hazardous. If the Allies had their eyes on Charleroi, they would no longer be able to supply the operation by water from their base at Namur. Boufflers then fortified his camp at Gosselies disposing his artillery to enfilade all possible approaches. In addition to the main Army of the Meuse at Wavre, the Allies had Fagel at Nieuport observing Montal's flying columns near Dunkirk, Vaudemont at Ghent watching Villeroi but with half his troops spread along the Ghent-Bruges Canal and a corps at Namur covering Guiscard at Dinant. In Luxembourg, d'Harcourt still waited for any movement by German forces from the Rhine towards the Meuse.[27] Richard Hill, that most acerbic yet realistic of commentators, had already dismissed the entire campaign as pointless. From Vaudemont's camp at Ghent he wrote that 'we are sending a detachment hence to him (William) of 15 battalions and 4 regiments of horse, to do nothing'. He added that during his visit to the Army of Flanders, William had created 'a great many general officers and left many more very much disquieted at their not being preferred'.[28] What to do, apart from fiddle, was indeed the question. On 4/14 June, fourteen battalions from the corps at Namur marched to join William and the Elector of Bavaria at Wavre. The King was in a quandry.

I am also very much vexed that I can give you no hopes of undertaking anything considerable this campaign, the enemy being in too great force to admit of my attempting a siege without too much risk, which, in my opinion, is not at this time advisable unless, by the movements I am now making, the enemy should give me a favourable opportunity. I am very apprehensive this campaign will pass very peacably, which to me will be no small mortification.[29]

William and the Elector left Wavre on 9/19 June and marched in four columns to Orbais. With their 60,000 men, the two generals probably intended to attack Boufflers's 40,000 in the fortified camp north of Charleroi. However, if the Allies approached too close there was the risk that Boufflers would fall back over the Sambre to a position around Gerpinnes from where he could continue to cover any move against Charleroi. All hope of success against Boufflers depended upon Vaudemont being able to prevent Villeroi from marching to his colleague's assistance. In addition to Charleroi, Boufflers was also worried about the vulnerability of Dinant and reinforced its garrison with five regiments of dragoons. If he did withdraw to Gerpinnes, it was a position from which he could easily guard both Charleroi and Dinant. Whilst these considerations were being weighed in the minds of the opposing commanders, a certain Captain Thibault marched 200 dragoons out of the Forest of Soignes and raided into France as far as Le Quesnoy and Bavay.[30] Predictably, as soon as the Allies reached Orbais they received the news that Boufflers had retired across the Sambre and had taken up a camp between Gerpinnes and St. Gérard. On 11/21 June, Boufflers shifted his main weight to the right towards St. Gérard where he combined with d'Harcourt's detachment which had ridden from Luxembourg. A force was left at Gerpinnes and patrols and listening posts were disposed along the banks of the Sambre. This screen soon came into contact with probing reconnaissance parties from the Allied army. Boufflers's retreat brought another exasperated sigh from Richard Hill – 'we must be allowed here, my Lord, a peace since all our sinews of war are shrunk'.[31] Villeroi, whose foragers regularly came within two kilometres of Vaudemont's camp at Mariakerke, made a small forward movement on 6/16 June and a section of his army caught some British battalions half asleep on the Ghent-Bruges Canal. The French forced a crossing near Bruges but the patrols and posts along the banks of the Canal soon rallied and forced the Frenchmen to retire. Vaudemont arrested the English officers of the guard for negligence.[32]

After Portland had reconnoitred the ground with 2,000 cavalry, William moved his army southward to Gembloux in six columns on 24 June/4 July.[33] As the Allied cavalry continued to test his screen along the Sambre, Boufflers fretted that from his retarded position south of the Sambre he might not be able to prevent a sudden rush by William and the Elector towards the Lines of the Lys and the Scheldt or to invest Mons. Either of these marches would have placed Villeroi's army in the gravest peril. Boufflers well remembered the 'race for the Scheldt' in 1694 and William's rapid march from Flanders to the Meuse in 1695. Although his corps, now increased to 50,000 men with the arrival of d'Harcourt, was in a good position to cover Givet, Dinant and Charleroi, Boufflers was in the midst of hilly and difficult country and would have been hard pressed to march quickly if the Allies had made an abrupt movement. All he could do was hope, patrol heavily and entrench the ford over the Sambre at Montignies to secure himself a passage towards Mons and the Lines of the Lys and the Scheldt. Fortunately, the desperate state of British finances ruled out any siege operations but Boufflers was not in possession of this priceless information. At Gembloux, William awaited the arrival of the Landgrave of Hesse-Cassel with a corps of sixteen battalions and forty-three squadrons of Hessians, Hanoverians, Holsteiners and Münsterians. This detachment had left the Rhine early in June and crossed the Meuse at Visé on 11/21 June. In an effort to give himself an even greater numerical superiority over Boufflers, William summoned the Duke of Württemberg from Flanders with a detachment from Vaudemont's army. Boufflers's incessant cavalry patrols, both around Orbais and Gembloux, were a constant irritant to William and he convinced himself that their activities contravened the laws of war. He ordered his troops to show no quarter to captured French horsemen. On the Rhine, the Duke de Choiseul fortified the region about Metz and went over to the defensive before dispatching four regiments of dragoons and 2,000 'choice' foot to reinforce Boufflers on the Sambre. When he heard of this development, William recognised the ghost of a chance that Louis of Baden might risk an offensive on the Rhine which would help to unlock the stalemate in the Low Countries.[34]

The situation in the Netherlands was too well balanced. Richard Hill thought that William's initial intention for 1696 had been to attempt nothing in the Low Countries except to launch a series of feints to pull the French first one way and then the other. Louis of Baden was supposed to take advantage of this series of manoeuvres to undertake the siege of Philippsburg. Instead, after losing the initiative in the early stages of the campaign, William found by the middle of June that although several options were available – besieging Charleroi or Dinant, bombarding Dunkirk and forcing the Lines in Flanders – Boufflers's stance at St. Gérard ruled out the first two and Villeroi was too strong for him to attempt anything in Flanders. Although he had nothing much for his men to do, William's Army of the Meuse grew ever larger; the Elector of Cologne marched into Gembloux with the Liègeois forces on 16/26 June. So great was William's army that he could even contemplate sending the Landgrave of Hesse-Cassel to the Moselle to assist Louis of Baden in the projected siege of Philippsburg. The campaign, though, was not entirely moribund. On 13/23 June, Vaudemont's intelligence service detected that 4,000 French cavalry under d'Artagnan had formed a flying camp between Ath and Lessines. Vaudemont dispatched Overkirk and all his mounted troops to surprise them. Orders to the 4,500 horsemen who were to take part in the operation were given out at 10.00 p.m. and, one hour later, all the men were ready and mounted, 'not one man wanting'. The effort was in vain. Overkirk found the French to be too strongly posted and returned to Mariakerke with his tail between his legs.[35]

On 26 June/6 July, the Duke of Württemberg trudged into the Gembloux camp with his detachment from Vaudemont's army and the Landgrave of Hesse-Cassel arrived in Huy. 'The King is very busy on this side of the Sambre and we are as busy here on the Canal of Bruges to amuse the enemy at both ends, as if we would besiege Dinant or Furnes or bombard Dunkirk or Charleroi but our enemies are too strong to suffer us to do anything, I fear, in any place.' From Huy, the Landgrave of Hesse-Cassel departed for the Moselle to operate in the region of the Southern Eifel around Mont Royal. This was a scheme that Vaudemont had first mentioned in February. It was intended to draw French troops away from the Rhine by interfering with the navigation and control of the Moselle Valley, one of the main channels of communication between France and Germany. This, it was fondly hoped, would both encourage and assist Louis of Baden to invest Philippsburg.[36]

William's continued presence at Gembloux caused Boufflers to worry about the safety of Mons. He sent Lieutenant-General Ximenes, the commander of the corps of 12,000 at Gerpinnes, to La Buissière on the Sambre with orders to construct four pontoon bridges. He planned to leave St. Gérard and join Ximenes, putting a garrison of 15,000 into Mons. Charleroi was already protected by a garrison of 6,000 men. Boufflers had 50,000 to oppose the 72,000 men of the Army of the Meuse, whilst the Army of Flanders consisted of 42,000 to observe Villeroi's 25,000. Wiliam's mind was turning once more towards his pet project, the one which he always favoured when he could think of nothing else to do – the bombardment of Dunkirk. Allied engineers stole southwards to inspect the ground about Dunkirk. They discovered two redoubts which would keep the bombardment artillery at a distance sufficient to make its shells fall short of the town, a shortage of wood for fascines, a lack of firm foundations for siege batteries and no fresh water within eight or nine kilometres. In addition, the enemy privateers and frigates in Dunkirk harbour might make life very awkward for the Allied land forces unless a naval operation was timed to coincide with the bombardment. These potential difficulties seemed to worry everyone except William.[37]

Faute de mieux, the Allies began to put in train preparations for a major operation in Flanders, either a siege of Furnes or a bombardment of Dunkirk. Vaudemont sent Noyelles with fourteen battalions to occupy Bellem, midway between Bruges and Ghent on the Canal, and to throw four bridges over the waterway to enable the Army of Flanders to march south to Roeselare. Another ten battalions escorted fifty-two vessels conveying the siege train from Ghent to Bruges. Vaudemont ordered peasants to be conscripted as pioneers and assembled at Passendale. William had taken no decision about which alternative to favour when Richard Hill brought him the grim, but not unexpected news that the finances of the army and the English government were so straitened that he would be lucky to survive in the field for the remainder of the campaign let alone conduct a major siege or bombardment.[38] William and his generals vacillated and dithered. In the meantime, the French reinforced their position on the Sambre and took steps to counter Vaudemont's movements in Flanders. Boufflers, reinforced by Tallard's detachment from Choiseul's army in Germany, Ximenes, d'Harcourt and the garrison of Maubeuge, now had a total of 70,000 men with which to hold the line of the Sambre. Allied operations towards Mons and Charleroi had become impossible. On hearing of Vaudemont's motions on the Bruges-Ghent Canal, Villeroi sent ten battalions to Furnes, and put sixteen battalions into Dunkirk along with a company of bombardiers and a company of miners. Realising that he needed more men with whom to oppose Boufflers, William halted the Landgrave of Hesse-Cassel on his march to the Moselle and recalled him to Namur, which he reached on 15/25 July. William continued to probe Boufflers's front searching for openings but he found no weak spots.[39]

Stalemate had come to the campaign not just through fiscal exhaustion and the seeming propinquity of a peace settlement. The war had reached an effective strategic end well before its political termination. From Dunkirk to Charleroi and then down the Meuse to Givet, the French possessed and had fortified a linear frontier with few salients or other points of weakness. All the major fortresses were either incorporated into this system or stood in its rear. The lines of trenches, breastworks, ditches and redoubts had been connected by straight, military roads enabling defenders to concentrate rapidly at any threatened sector. The Allied frontier stretched from Nieuport to Ostend, through Bruges, and along the canal to Ghent. It then assumed the line of the Scheldt to Dendermonde before striking to Brussels. From Brussels the Allies did not control a line but inhabited a sphere of influence across Brabant and into the Pays de Liège – via Louvain, to Tirlemont and then to the south to meet the Meuse at Namur. The wide river protected the Allied front northwards through Huy, Liège and Maastricht to the borders of the United Provinces. Although the Allies were vulnerable to raids in the Dendermonde-Brussels gap and between Brussels and Louvain, the broad no-man's land which divided the two fortified frontiers no longer contained any worthwhile military targets. Towns like Alost, Furnes, Deynze, Dixmuyde, Oudenarde and even Ath were not worth the human and financial cost of capture. Should they be taken then they merely upset the balance of the existing frontier necessitating large garrisons, constant guarding and a realignment of the frontier to protect them from counter-attack. As neither side really wanted to seize these types of targets, they possessed little or no value to the diplomats. William would dearly have loved to have regained Mons and Charleroi, but they were extremely difficult to attack having been included within the French Lines. The French, fighting a politically defensive war, would have liked to retake Namur and Huy and cast greedy eyes on Liège but their continuous system of defences from Dunkirk to Dinant left insufficient troops to mount major offensives. William's capture of Namur in 1695 had effectively ended the war. The only remotely attractive targets were Ath and Brussels. Ath was the forward bastion of the latter city lying in the open, well beyond the Allied frontier. If Ath could have been secured then it could easily have been incorporated within the French Lines. Indeed, it would have greatly strengthened the sector between Mons and Tournai.[40]

William's design to bombard Dunkirk was no more than the application to war of Parkinson's Law – operations expand and increase in number to fill the time available. As Shrewsbury pointed out, the bombardment of Dunkirk was really a waste of time for even if the town was burned to ashes and knocked to pieces what mattered were the docks and naval installations. A bombardment would have left these untouched. By 1696, the huge, lumbering armies of William and Vaudemont, Villeroi and Boufflers, locked within the confined theatre of the Spanish Netherlands, had been reduced to strategic and tactical impotence. They were too big, too slow, too blunt, too expensive. In addition, the landscape in which they functioned was devastated.[41]

Having exhausted the forage, William's staff drew up orders for the army to leave Gembloux. In four columns on 15/25 July, the troops marched to Sombreffe. The next day, 16/26 July, the army marched in one, long column to Nivelles and, after a rest day, resumed its journey to Soignies on 18/28 July. Finally, the Army of the Meuse came to rest at Attre, three kilometres to the south-east of Ath.[42] William had abandoned his attempt to break into Boufflers's cordon along the Sambre and had moved to cover Ath against a possible French attack. At the same time, his march to Ath brought him closer to Vaudemont in order to support the projected operation against Dunkirk. He also came into fresh foraging grounds which had not been used that summer and had escaped depredation by Boufflers when he had been encamped on the Plains of Fleury at the opening of the campaigning season.

Vaudemont had lost all enthusiasm for the Dunkirk operation. He told William that Villeroi would occupy his present position at Ghent within twelve hours if he marched off towards Dunkirk. Although this was granting unwarranted compliments to Villeroi's imagination and initiative, William's advance to Ath was partially designed to pin Villeroi in his camp between the Lys and the Scheldt. Seemingly unnoticed by William, Boufflers, no doubt delighted to be away from the difficult country to the south of the Sambre, had marched westwards on a parallel course and had come into camp at St. Ghislain, covering Mons. Apart from desperation and frustration, it is hard to find a concrete reason for William's insistence on the Dunkirk operation. Perhaps he felt piqued at seeing himself stronger than the French in Flanders and yet unable to attempt anything of significance. Perhaps he thought that the French could be brought to an early peace by a limited offensive against a sensitive and prestigious target. Perhaps he had decided to try anything, anywhere whilst he still had an army. Unless money could be found, the army would disintegrate. 'But we have had the misfortune to come late into the field this year and instead of sums to carry on a mighty enterprise we have scarce money to keep our army from starving. Never were such wants.'[43] To add to the royal woes, William was blamed by Louis of Baden for not releasing the Landgrave of Hesse-Cassel's corps earlier in the campaign. The lack of a diversion on the Moselle around Mont Royal had led to Baden 'losing' his campaign on the Rhine. Yet this was a minor concern when compared with the shortage of cash. William could not pay his German auxiliaries nor his bread and transport contractors; he had no money and the Lords Justices in Westminster could send him none. The Bank of England's credit had collapsed and the Dutch authorities no longer gave assurances that they would meet the Bank's bills of exchange. 'At present I see no resource which can prevent the army from mutiny or total desertion, for it is more impossible to find here than in England, money for their subsistence.'[44] In desperation, William sent Portland to England. He succeeded in raising two loans from the Bank, the first proceeds of which reached Richard Hill in Antwerp towards the end of October.[45] The news that the Duke of Savoy had deserted the Grand Alliance and joined the French was the last straw. William did not eat for forty-eight hours.

With Vaudemont pouring cold water on his schemes and bad news on all fronts, William abandoned his designs in Flanders. The Landgrave of Hesse-Cassel was released from Namur and ordered to the Moselle to operate in conjunction with Louis of Baden. Major-General Berensdorff took twelve battalions from Vaudemont's army to replace the Landgrave's men in the garrison of Namur. It was, of course, far too late in the season for the cautious Baden to attempt any operations on the Rhine and certainly not the siege of Philippsburg. William had bungled. As his own army was hamstrung by lack of funds, he should have reinforced Baden much earlier and allowed him some freedom of action in the Rhineland. He dallied too long and nothing was achieved in either theatre. On 27 July/6 August, Richard Hill informed Shrewsbury that William had pawned his jewels for 300,000 florins and Schulemburg had secured a further 100,000. This would pay the army for another fortnight.[46] The armies sat in their camps and foraged. The Landgrave of Hesse-Cassel crossed the Meuse and the River Rur, covered by d'Harcourt who left Dinant to observe the Landgrave's march.[47]

Having been in his camp by Deynze since the opening of the season, Villeroi shifted westwards to Tielt on 10/20 August. This brought him into a more direct communication with Dunkirk but it also threatened Vaudemont's perimeter along the Ghent-Bruges and Bruges-Nieuport Canals. Villeroi considered the feasibility of a bombardment of Bruges. He advanced with all his cavalry to seize a suitable battery site at the Abbey of St. André on 30 August/9 September but Vaudemont's intelligence system was working with its customary efficiency and he was able to occupy the chosen ground in strength before the French horse arrived. Villeroi then probed the Canal defences but, finding no weakness, he fell back to Wynendale on 1/11 September. William prepared to leave his army and return to Het Loo. The Elector of Bavaria assumed command and ordered the quartermasters to mark out a camp at Grimminge, between Grammont and Ninove. In two columns, the army marched back to Grimminge on 14/24 August. Before he departed from the army, William sweetened the Elector of Cologne by returning the town of Huy to his jurisdiction as a reward for his zeal towards the Allied cause. As an additional mark of respect, William did not charge him one penny towards the cost of the siege which had recaptured Huy from the French in 1694.[48]

Hesse-Cassel marched rapidly through Aachen to the Rhine where his men took boats and came to Coblenz on 15/25 August before continuing down the river to rendezvous with Louis of Baden at Mainz. There was still time, according to the armchair generals in Brussels and The Hague, for Baden to attack Philippsburg or, at the very least, take winter quarters on French territory. Baden did not concur and the campaign was over. The Elector of Bavaria's army, which had begun the campaign under the grandiose title of the Army of the Meuse, marched from Grimminge to Halle on 19/29 September and then onto Bois St. Isaac on the following day. Here the army split into corps and dispersed into winter quarters between 26 September/6 October and 28 September/8 October. The winter was cold and dry. Life during the winter of a war was not unpleasant for the officers and officials. Brussels resounded to music, comedies, plays and grand balls almost every night and the daylight hours were given over to idling and nursing hangovers. There was a slight apprehension in the air that the French might try a surprise offensive early in the new year before the Allies were in the field, perhaps another siege of Namur. However, most people were of the opinion that 1696 had been the final campaign and that peace would be concluded during the winter.[49]

NOTES

1 ARA, Raad van State, 1902/1, 12/22 Oct. 1695, 'Mémoire au sujet de la prochaine Campagne, fait a La Haye'; HSL, vii. 94–127.

2 Japikse, iii. 253–4; Van Creveld, *Supplying War*, p. 26; see, Peter Barber, 'British Cartography', in, *The Age of William III and Mary II*, eds. Maccubbin & Hamilton-Phillips, pp. 95–104; Dirk de Vries, 'Dutch Cartography', in, *ibid.*, pp. 105–11.

3 Jones, *War and Economy*, pp. 20–6; Childs, *British Army of William III*, pp. 149–53.

4 Thomson, 'Louis XIV and William III', p. 49; Callières, *Diplomacy*, p. 9.

5 Symcox, *Victor Amadeus II*, pp. 116–17; *Lexington Papers*, pp. 201–2, pp. 207–8; Morgan, 'Ryswick', pp. 177–82.

6 *HMC, Bath MSS.*, iii. 68; Japikse, iii. 375.
7 *Portledge Papers*, p. 192; Trumbull Add. MSS. 103; *LG*, no. 3141.
8 *HMC, Bath MSS.*, iii. 70; *HMC, Downshire MSS.*, i. 614–15.
9 ARA, Raad van State, 489, p. 37; Japikse, iii. 375.
10 *HMC, Downshire MSS.*, i. 619–20; J. S. Corbett, *England in the Mediterranean* (London, 1917), ii. 454–5.
11 BL, Add. MSS. 9,730, f. 35; Japikse, iii. 376.
12 *HMC, Downshire MSS.*, i. 621.
13 SP 77/57, ff. 11–12; Trumbull Add. MSS. 103.
14 SP 77/57, f. 6; *HMC, Downshire MSS.*, i. 626–7; BL, Add. MSS. 9,730, f. 41, 25 Feb./6 March 1696, Ostend, Richard Hill to Blathwayt; Japikse, iii. 378–82.
15 *HMC, Downshire MSS.*, i. 628–9, 635.
16 Jane Garrett, *The Triumphs of Providence: The Assassination Plot, 1696*, (Cambridge, 1980), pp. 138–9; Childs, *British Army of William III*, p. 176.
17 SP 77/57, f. 13.
18 Japikse, iii. 379; SP 77/57, ff. 20–1; *Locke Correspondence*, v. 562–3; CMC 4/72; *LG*, no. 3166; BL, Add. MSS. 34,504, ff. 216–17; W. T. Morgan, 'The Expedition of Baron de Pointis against Cartagena', *American Historical Review*, xxxvii. (1931–2), p. 239.
19 BL, Add. MSS. 9,730, f. 56.
20 SP 77/57, f. 35.
21 Walton, p. 316; *Lexington Papers*, pp. 194–5; SP 77/57, ff. 54–5.
22 SP 77/57, ff. 36, 38.
23 *Archives d'Orange-Nassau*, i. 439.
24 Walton, pp. 316–17.
25 ARA, Raad van State, 1896/2, 'Journal Graaf van Slippenbach', p. 4.
26 *Shrewsbury Correspondence*, pp. 114–15; SP 77/57, ff. 58, 59; *Seafield Correspondence from 1685 to 1708*, ed. James Grant (Edinburgh, Scottish History Society, 1912), pp. 199–201.
27 SP 77/57, ff. 61, 66, 69, 73.
28 Ibid., f. 74.
29 *Shrewsbury Correspondence*, p. 127.
30 Japikse, iii. 388, 394; SP 77/57, f. 76; SP 87/1, f. 367.
31 *HMC, Buccleuch (Montagu) MSS.*, ii. 349, 11/21 June 1696, Ghent, Richard Hill to Shrewsbury.
32 SP 77/57, f. 79; *Seafield Correspondence*, p. 201.
33 BL, King's MSS. 229, pp. 12–15, 'Marches fait par les Armées de sa Majesté de la Grande Bretagne, les Campagnes de l'Années 1696 et 1697'.
34 SP 87/1, ff. 183, 189–90; Japikse, iii. 391, 395; *HMC, Hastings MSS.*, ii. 264–5.
35 *HMC, Buccleuch (Montagu) MSS.*, ii. 351, 355–6; Trumbull Add. MSS. 103; SP 77/57, f. 85.
36 SP 77/57, f. 86; Japikse, iii. 375, 376.
37 *HMC, Buccleuch (Montagu) MSS.*, ii. 360; SP 77/57, ff. 88–9.
38 SP 77/57, ff. 91, 95–6; *HMC, Buccleuch (Montagu) MSS.*, ii. 366.
39 SP 87/1, f. 192; *HMC, Hastings MSS.*, ii. 264–5; *Shrewsbury Correspondence*, p. 127; CSPD 1696, p. 270; Japikse, iii. 401.
40 Walton, p. 318.
41 *HMC, Buccleuch (Montagu) MSS.*, ii. 368.
42 BL, King's MSS. 229, pp. 15–27.
43 SP 87/1, ff. 197–8; *HMC, Buccleuch (Montagu) MSS.*, ii. 369–70.

44 *Shrewsbury Correspondence*, pp. 129–30, 20/30 July 1696, William to Shrewsbury.

45 Jones, *War and Economy*, pp. 25–6.

46 SP 87/1, ff. 201–2; *HMC, Buccleuch (Montagu) MSS.*, ii. 373–4; ARA, Raad van State, 1896/2, pp. 10–11.

47 Japikse (Welbeck), i. 192; SP 87/1, f. 207; SP 77/57, f. 104.

48 Walton, p. 318; BL, King's MSS. 229, pp. 27–31; CMC 4/87; SP 77/57, ff. 111, 112.

49 NLI, MS. 4166, pp. 37–9; Parker, *Memoirs*, pp. 62–3; *HMC, Buccleuch (Montagu) MSS.*, ii. 442; BL, King's MSS. 229, pp. 31–45.

XII

1697: ATH, BRUSSELS AND PEACE

The Allies did not want another campaign. England and the United Provinces were financially exhausted and peace had seemed within reach until the defection of Savoy wrecked their expectations. The peace between France and Savoy not only neutralised Northern Italy but allowed all of Catinat's troops to be redeployed in other theatres. The military balance of power was seriously altered at a time when the Grand Alliance was at its most fragile. Catinat himself, one of the ablest of the French marshals, was given employment in the Low Countries and his 40,000 troops were used to reinforce the armies in Catalonia and the Spanish Netherlands. In contrast, the Grand Alliance lost troops. The 17 squadrons and 13 battalions of the Savoyard army were forfeited and the Spanish corps of 31 battalions and 16 squadrons which had fought in Piedmont remained in Northern Italy to police the truce. Spare troops available to bolster the Allied armies in Germany and the Netherlands amounted to only 6 Imperial battalions, 6 British battalions, all composed of Huguenot refugees, 4 Brandenburg battalions and 2 from Bavaria. None of these 18 battalions, totalling 12,000 men, found their way into the Spanish Netherlands. The Brandenburg and Bavarian formations were sent to reinforce Louis of Baden's army on the Rhine and the six British Huguenot battalions were taken into the pay of the Circles of Swabia and Franconia. The Austrian battalions were withdrawn to fight with the Imperial forces against the Turks in Hungary.[1] The augmentation of French forces put Spain under considerable pressure. France offered a pact to neutralise Catalonia, inspired by the transparent intention of freeing yet more of her forces for one last effort in the Low Countries. Spain was slow to decide whether to accept the truce and would have done so, sinking the Grand Alliance in the process, had not the British come forward with the present of a naval expedition to the Mediterranean to help save Barcelona. If Spain had taken up the French offer, then the neutrality might have spread to include the Spanish Netherlands.

All the French diplomatic schemes were aimed at securing an over-whelming superiority in the Low Countries for the campaign of 1697. With Catinat's troops, France would be able to put 150,000 men into the Spanish Netherlands whilst the Allies, still struggling under England's currency crisis, would have difficulty in raising two-thirds of this number. Peace was also delayed because Emperor Leopold I wanted the war to continue; he was fearful that the end of the French war would allow the princes of the Empire to gather strength behind his back while he was busy with the Turk. It was for this reason that Leopold had been duplicitous about the defection of Savoy. Sweden, the appointed mediator, was in no hurry to mobilise the process of peace and reconciliation desiring her new-found importance to last as long as possible. Louis XIV, with every prospect of conducting a major and important campaign in the Low Countries in 1697, was likewise reticent to conclude a peace and rather looked forward to having his armies rampage through the Spanish Netherlands and the Pays de Liège as the plenipotentiaries deliberated at The Hague. What better way could be envisaged in which to conduct negotiations from manifest strength. Only one consideration caused Louis to hesitate. The health of King Carlos II of Spain gave grave cause for international concern raising the whole issue of who was to inherit the Spanish Empire. Louis, whose eyes were firmly fixed upon the acquisition of Spain's vast territories for himself and his dynasty, needed a settlement in Europe before he turned to deal with this question. There was certainly no chance of a French succession to the crown of Spain finding favour in Madrid if the two countries were at war. It was this factor more than any other which curtailed French ambitions in 1697.

Although the campaign of 1697 can be dismissed as the last huffing and puffing whilst the envoys at The Hague sorted out the minutiae of the inevitable peace, it does form a compact and informative example of the methods and purpose of late seventeenth century strategy. In the first place, the operations were closely linked to the progress, or lack of it, of the negotiators in The Hague. In the second place, its mathematical formalism encapsulated the unimaginative and conventional approach of contemporary military minds. Into this atmosphere, Marlborough was to burst like a ray of bright light in the spring of 1702.

The year began on an ill note. Intelligence reached England that Admiral de Pointis at Brest had accumulated a battle squadron and a number of troop transports. It looked as though Louis was about to launch another invasion attempt using his redundant troops from Savoy and William promptly ordered fifteen battalions to be shipped back to the British Isles from Flanders. The panic soon subsided; Pointis embarked 1,500 men and crossed the Atlantic to capture Cartagena on 4/14 May.[2] The winter months were otherwise quiet but tense. The combination of cold weather and Catinat's men massing into the Spanish Netherlands meant that heavy raiding and limited operations might commence at any time. All the Allied troops quartered in Ghent, Bruges, Ostend and Nieuport, including the majority of the British battalions, were under constant orders to be ready to march upon any alarm. Those quartered along the Ghent-Bruges and Bruges-Nieuport Canals had standing instructions to concentrate at the first signal of danger. Every guard post lining the banks of the two canals was equipped with a beacon, or 'firepot', which could be ignited and then hoisted to the top of a tall pole. When an enemy advance was detected, the nearest firepot was to be lit and elevated; the posts which possessed cannon were to discharge them and those with only infantry in attendance were to fire volleys of musketry. Guns were to be fired in the larger garrisons and a chain of beacons in church steeples and towers was also arranged. This system was the brain-child of the Dutch Quartermaster-General and it was highly effective in the flat and featureless polderland of Flanders. The system was tested one night and the alarm reached Nieuport and Ghent, both some 60 kilometres from the initiation of the signal, in less than one hour. The network was extended eastwards from Ghent, through Dendermonde and Willebroek, and then along the canal to Brussels, a distance of 100 kilometres. The signal reached Brussels from Ghent in two hours. The Lines which Vaudemont's army had dug during their long stay at Mariakerke near Ghent during 1696 did not sufficiently cover the city of Ghent, despite the flooding of the meadows at Drongen. There remained a narrow passage by which a French force between the Lys and the Scheldt might attack the town or at least bombard it from before the Gates of Courtrai or St. Pierre. To block this approach, the sluices on the Lys and the Scheldt were closed at Ghent causing the two rivers to flood. A short system of field fortifications, capable of defence by a small garrison, was built to connect the inundations.

The other potential danger spot was Namur. According to the Allies, the reconquest of Namur had been the principal French objective in 1696 and only Athlone and Coehoorn's highly successful raid on the magazines at Givet had nipped this in the bud. Namur remained a sensitive spot, isolated by the plains of Brabant from the Allied frontier

and tenuously supported by the navigation of the Meuse and the small
garrison at Huy. During the winter, the Meuse froze hard and the
regular water convoys to Namur from Maastricht and Liège could not
break through. Overland waggon trains replaced them, guarded by
escorts from the garrisons of Louvain, St. Truiden and Liège. Suffering
little interference, this scheme worked efficiently until the water route
was restored during the thaw which began in March. Guiscard, still
commanding at Dinant, tried to intercept the first boats to sail to Namur
after the breaking of the ice but missed his target.[3]

Because they knew that the French would be heavily superior in the
Netherlands in 1697, William and his generals decided that it would
be best to gather as large a field army as possible in one sector and not
to split their forces into an army in Flanders and another in Brabant as
had been the pattern in the two previous years. Vaudemont, Württemberg, Richard Hill, General Prince Charles de Commercy from Vienna
and Field-Marshal the Marquis de Bedmar met in Antwerp on 1/11
March to discuss William's intentions and arrange the marches and
quarters to enable the British and Dutch forces presently in Flanders to
travel to Brabant. Another conference on the following day, presided
over by the Elector of Bavaria, gave further attention to these questions.
On 6/16 March, the British forces began their series of marches to effect
the redeployment. Major-General Charles Churchill led four battalions
from Ghent to Louvain; Brigadier Zachariah Tiffin took three battalions
from Ostend to Malines; and Brigadier Thomas Fairfax conducted a
further three battalions from Bruges to Brussels. The British marches
had been completed by 17/27 March. Every effort was made to cover
Flanders with an adequate defence yet one that employed the fewest
possible number of troops. All of the battalions which departed from
Flanders for Brabant, left one or two companies in their previous quarters to undertake garrison duties during the summer. Although this
weakened the field battalions, it did not tie down whole regiments to
sterile garrison service yet still provided a minimum cover for Flanders.
The defensive line behind the Ghent-Bruges and Bruges-Nieuport Canals
was strengthened by further inundations at Bruges, Nieuport and
Ostend. With luck, it was hoped, the combination of extensive water
defences and a thin garrison could hold the French at bay. Confidence
soon waned. A further planning conference in Brussels decided to form
a corps in Flanders specifically to support and reinforce the Canal Line.
By 7/17 April, the Elector of Bavaria had assembled a corps of thirty-
eight battalions outside Deynze. The scene of O'Farrell's infamous
capitulation was glorified with some temporary, hexagonal fortifi-

cations; permanent works would have breached the articles of surrender which had been signed in 1695. As an additional precaution, the ground before the Elector's camp was flooded.[4]

Richard Hill gloomily predicted that the French would beat the Allies into the field and live off the countryside which they knew they would have to surrender to its previous owners at the coming peace settlement.[5] For once, Hill was wrong. Towards the end of April, the Allied forces began to drift towards a concentration in Brabant and orders were issued on 23 April/3 May for a rendezvous at Bois St. Isaac. This movement was completed by 28 April/8 May.[6] For William, who usually brought his Brabant army together to the east of Brussels around Louvain, the selection of Bois St. Isaac represented a very forward concentration some 25 kilometres to the south of Brussels. It placed his army conveniently close to both Ath and Namur, the two most probable victims of French aggression. More importantly, his army stood clear and to the south of the great expanse of the Forest de Soignes, on the south-eastern edge of Brussels, which would have seriously hampered a march from Louvain towards Ath. William boarded the *William and Mary* yacht in Margate Road on the morning of 26 April/6 May and was in The Hague by 9.00 p.m. that same evening.[7] No sooner had William left England than Lord Romney informed the Lords Justices how the king had confided to him his intention of beginning the campaign with the siege of Ypres or Dunkirk.[8] Knowing from past experience how open mouths in London could be, this must have been a deliberate piece of false information. The concentration at Bois St. Isaac was incorrect for the prosecution of either operation. The campaign had not properly opened when the peace plenipotentiaries sat down in the Palace of Rijswijk on the outskirts of The Hague on Thursday 26 April/6 May.[9]

The army at Bois St. Isaac, under the command of Vaudemont until the arrival of William, numbered 58,400 men in 70 battalions and 151 squadrons. The Elector of Bavaria commanded 38,000 at Deynze and Major-General Fagel had 10 battalions, 6,000 infantry, at Nieuport. In total, the Allies disposed 102,400 troops. Although William was acutely aware of the vulnerability of Ath, there was little that he could do to protect the fortress as it lay close to the enemy frontier and France already possessed the adjacent towns of Courtrai, Mons and Charleroi. The best that William and Vaudemont could manage was to guard Brussels and Namur. Vaudemont sent detached corps to Waterloo and Ukkel to cover Brussels more closely and instructed the Brandenburg troops, cantoned around Aarschot and Diest, to be ready to assist the garrisons of Louvain, Maastricht and Liège in the support of Namur. The French had based their initial planning on the assumption that they would be the first into the field. Catinat travelled to the Moselle to take command of an army which was to operate between the Lower Rhine, the Moselle and the Meuse. Catinat's presence alarmed the Germans into assuming that a major offensive towards the Rhine was intended. The Circles of Swabia and Franconia raised 60,000 men and retained the six British Huguenot battalions returning from Savoy. New Lines were built to guard the gap between the confluence of the Rhine and the Neckar and the northern edge of the Black Forest. The Imperial forces also fortified the principal crossings of the Rhine at Bonn and Cologne. Despite this frantic activity, it was always more likely that Catinat's army on the Moselle was designed to cover and support an attack on Namur. Boufflers would have conducted the siege from the Sambre-Meuse with Catinat covering from the area of the Moselle. Villeroi would have observed the Allied armies in Flanders and Brabant.

When the Allies entered the field ahead of the French, these schemes were scrapped. Namur was too well masked by William at Bois St. Isaac, the Meuse garrisons and the Brandenburg corps in Brabant. Ath had to be selected as a less important, compromise target. Villeroi brought 78 battalions and 106 squadrons together at Tournai, a total of 55,620 men; Boufflers assembled 55,740 soldiers, 78 battalions and 107 squadrons, in the Sambre-Meuse; and Catinat commanded a smaller army, 33,430 men in 49 squadrons and 50 battalions, at Courtrai.[10] Ath and Oudenarde could have been siezed by the French in any campaign after the capture of Mons in 1691 but they had no need or occasion to do so. The taking of either, or both would have brought no further regions of the Spanish Netherlands under contribution but would simply have eaten up more troops in garrison. Oudenarde was stronger than Ath and so the latter was chosen 'to make a noise' during the peace negotiations. The town, or rather fortress as it was very small, stood at the confluence of two small rivers, the Dender and the Irchonwelz, whose junction occurred in its very centre. France had captured Ath in 1667 and it was legally ceded to her by the Treaty of Aix-la-Chapelle in 1668. The Peace of Nijmegen restored Ath to Spain. In the intervening ten years, Vauban had transformed the fortifications. He had created a regular heptagon, except for one longer face between the Bastion de Luxembourg and the Bastion de Flandres, defended by eight bastions. Ravelins protected the enceinte between each bastion with tenailles in the ditch in the rear of each ravelin. There was a hornwork on the north-western corner of the town where the River

Dender made its exit. All the major works were faced with stone and along the ramparts were ornate stone sentry boxes decorated with *fleurs de lys*. Four rows of elm and lime trees grew on the ramparts to shelter the buildings of the town from overshooting cannon and mortar fire. Despite Vauban's fine work, which had included transforming the old castle on the western face into a small citadel, Ath was not a naturally strong position. It was commanded by a hill, Mont Férron, between the Brussels Gate and the Mons Gate which sloped down to the foot of the glacis. During the period between 1668 and 1672, serious efforts had been made by hordes of conscripted peasants to 'level' this inconvenient feature but nature had triumphed over the human spade and in 1697 it was possible to look down into the very streets of Ath from this higher ground. The only remedy available to Vauban had been to mount cavaliers on each of the bastions. The Comte de Fariaux commanded a garrison of 3,500 men, a mixture of three Dutch, one Spanish and three Milanese battalions, a Spanish cavalry regiment and one of dragoons. It was a relatively small garrison for such large and capacious works.[11]

Catinat laid bridges across the Scheldt at Helkijn on 30 April/10 May, having ordered Montrevel to garrison the Lines of the Lys and the Scheldt with 8,000 men to observe the Elector of Brandenburg's army camped at Nevele, between Ghent and Deynze. As a waggon-train of siege stores and ammunition drove into Tournai on 5/15 May, the French armies converged on Ath. Two cavalry detachments, one from Leuse under Prince Camille de Lorraine and the other commanded by Lieutenant-General de Gassion, rode towards Ath on 5/15 May, completing the investment in the early hours of the following morning. In the wake of the cavalry, Catinat set out from Helkijn on 6/16 May, traversed his prepared bridges across the Scheldt and came into camp at Frasnes-lez-Buissenal, ten kilometres from Ath. From here, Catinat detached Créqui with a small detachment to Celles to ensure that the garrison of Oudenarde did not interfere in the siege or try to attack French convoys in the region between the Scheldt and Ath. Should the Elector of Bavaria demonstrate any aggressive intentions from Nevele, Créqui could march to the Lines to reinforce Montrevel. On 7/17 May, Catinat advanced westwards and encamped about Ath. Boufflers had crossed the Sambre at La Buissière on 4/14 May and had camped at Fontaine l'Évêque. He moved westwards to Binche on 6/16 May. In the meantime, Villeroi had marched from Tournai to camp between Leuse and Ligne, directly covering Catinat's army around Ath and watching the Elector of Bavaria at Nevele. The French were now well balanced:

Catinat was ensconced at Ath, Villeroi observed the Elector and Boufflers was watching William and Vaudemont at Bois St. Isaac.

Twenty four battalions and fifteen squadrons were sent from Villeroi's army to Catinat's besieging corps before Villeroi advanced to the
north of Ath on 10/20 May and camped at Ostiches. At the same time,
Boufflers marched north of the Sambre and took station at Soignies.
The Elector of Bavaria devised a scheme for attacking the Lines of the
Lys and the Scheldt as a diversion to distract the French from the siege,
but Montrevel was very well posted with his garrison of 8,000 men
and he could have been rapidly reinforced by Créqui from Celles or
from Villeroi's main army at Ostiches. The plan was dropped and Ath
had no hope of relief unless William and Bavaria combined their armies
but, in that event, Villeroi and Boufflers would also come together.
William decided to sit tight. With peace negotiations progressing at The
Hague, he was unwilling to risk the strategic balance in the Low Countries by rushing to the relief of Ath.[12]

The rules of civility still governed warfare. No sooner had Gassion's
men advanced from Mons to Ath than a number of carriages left the
invested town carrying the Governor's wife and several other ladies, all
permitted by Catinat to leave. The Marshal's first task was to link the
sections of his circular camp by building bridges over the Dender and
the River Irchonwelz. Within six days, his 16,000 civilian pioneers had
completed the Lines of Circumvallation. Vauban decided to attack the
Bastion de Namur and the Bastion de Limbourg, on either side of the
Brussels Gate on the east of the town, in order to take advantage of
the high ground. This direction of attack also allowed him direct access
to the dam that held back the waters of the ditch. A more malicious
writer suggested that Vauban chose this sector because it was relatively
strong and therefore his handiwork would endure a more protracted
siege. The trenches were opened on 12/22 May and during the first
night the pioneers excavated over 1,000 metres in the soft ground. In
the morning, they completed a parallel which linked the two attacks.
The trenches advanced to within 400 metres of the glacis on 13/23
May, a second parallel was dug on 14/24 May and the trenches reached
the foot of the glacis on 15/25 May. The garrison made virtually no
resistance. Upto this point, apart from a few harassing shots, Vauban
had not mounted his siege batteries. The ground had prevented him
from doing so. On this side of Ath, the high ground overlooked the
town rendering the bastions and ravelins 'sunken' and invulnerable to
cannon fire until the guns were sited at the base of the glacis. During

the 16/26 May and 17/27 May there was an unnatural hush around Ath as the French built five heavy batteries before the Third Parallel.

As soon as he received intelligence of Boufflers's march to Soignies, Vaudemont sent a brigade of foot to secure Braine-le-Château in case he should choose to march closer to the Elector of Bavaria via Halle. Through the travelling services of Major-General Daniel Dopff, the Governor of Maastricht, Vaudemont and the Elector conferred and agreed that they should combine before advancing to relieve Ath. William, who had reached Breda on his way to the army, was also consulted and concurred. Leaving Fagel to defend Nieuport, Bavaria left Nevele on 13/23 May, crossed the Scheldt and encamped to the north-west of Brussels with his right at Merchtem and his left at Asse on 14/24 May. General Heiden came into Brussels with 21 squadrons of Brandenburg horse on 13/23 May and General Tilly conducted the Liègeois and Cologne cavalry to Brussels on the next day. The Brandenburg and Liègeois infantry remained on the Meuse to observe the detachment of d'Harcourt which hovered between the Meuse and the Moselle. Vaudemont quitted Bois St. Isaac on 14/24 May and he was joined on his march to Halle by William and the troops of Generals Heiden and Tilly. On the next day, William and the Elector of Bavaria linked their armies at St. Kwintens Lennik, the whole army stretching in a huge camp from Asse on the right almost to Halle on the left. In this position, the Allies covered Brussels, retained communications with both the Meuse and Flanders and were concentrated ready for an advance towards Ath.[13] As predicted, a combination of the Allied armies resulted in a similar concentration of the French covering forces. Now that the Elector had vacated Flanders, Montrevel left the Lines of the Lys and the Scheldt and moved to Celles whilst Créqui's corps from Celles marched to reinforce Villeroi. Boufflers advanced to the north-west to encamp around Silly and Ghislenghien, close to the right flank of Villeroi's army at Ostiches and Lessines. Bridges were thrown over the Dender to open communications between the two armies.[14]

Vauban's heavy batteries opened fire on 17/27 May and continued all day, the noise of the guns carrying clearly to Vaudemont, William and the Elector at St. Kwintens Lennik. A council of war decided to send Major-General Dopff and Quartermaster-General Ivoy forward to reconnoitre towards Enghien in the hope that the army could march to the relief of Ath. Despite a brush with a French cavalry patrol near Enghien, the reports were favourable and further discussions agreed to advance the army to the right and left of Marcq, next to Enghien, on

18/28 May but before the pioneers could prepare the roads, the wind rose, the rain lashed down and the march had to be postponed.

Vauban's thirty-six breaching cannon were arranged in five batteries in such a way that the whole front under attack was doused with enfilading cannon fire. He ordered the guns to be fired on high elevation with reduced charges, so that the shot were lobbed into the bastions, ravelins and tenailles, bouncing and ricocheting leaving no corners safe for the garrison. Three mortar batteries came into action on 18/28 May, one aimed specifically at the stone dam which retained the waters of the ditch. The 'ricochet fire' cleared the ramparts of defenders and dismounted the garrison cannon in less than twenty-four hours and all was ready for an attack on the counterscarp by the evening of 19/29 May. Suffering slight casualties, the French made three lodgements on the counterscarp of the Namur Bastion, the Limbourg Bastion and the Barbançon Ravelin which covered the Brussels Gate. Silence fell over Ath once more as the French gunners spent the 20/30 May shifting their pieces forward, ready to begin breaching the bastions themselves. At St. Kwintens Lennik the Allies wondered if Ath had fallen but the reassuring sound of gunfire returned on 21/31 May. In clearing weather, the pioneers were instructed to repair roads ready for the projected advance to Marcq and Enghien. However, William had already decided to leave Ath to its fate. Villeroi and Boufflers were so close together that they effectively formed one army which heavily outnumbered the Allies. If William advanced, fought and lost, the repercussions at Rijswijk would be unthinkable. Also, forage was running short and the army would have to move from St. Kwintens Lennik. After the fall of Ath, the French would be free to advance into undefended Flanders; it was essential for the Allies to divide the army and return one corps to protect Flanders whilst the other guarded Brussels and Namur. Accordingly, the Elector of Bavaria marched back to the Nevele camp, arriving on 22 May/1 June, and William took the main army through Halle to camp around Promelles within two kilometres of Genappe. The French responded by breaking up their own concentration. Montrevel returned to the Lines to watch Bavaria; Créqui went back to Celles; and Boufflers dropped southwards from Ghislenghien to Thieusies, between Mons and Soignies.

The incessant bombing of the dam produced sufficient damage to lower the water level in the ditch by one metre on 20/30 May and, on the following day, out of the original depth of three metres the ditch contained just one. The French sapped down the counterscarp towards the breach in the Barbançon Ravelin and built a bridge of fascines across the floor of the ditch. On the evening of 22 May/1 June, grenadiers made a lodgement on the point of the ravelin and forced the garrison of a captain and 60 men back into the tenaille in the rear of the ravelin. Two hours later, the defenders gathered on the ramparts and bastion flanks behind the ravelin and tried to drive the French out by sustained musketry but salvoes from the ricochet batteries dispersed them. During 23 May/2 June, the French secured their lodgements on the ravelin and constructed two batteries, each of twenty cannon, on the covered way before the Namur and Limbourg Bastions. Mortars played on the bridge between the Barbançon tenaille and the town. The batteries opened fire on 24 May/3 June and 'before night' the face of the Namur Bastion had fallen 'to the waist the length of about twenty fathoms' and the bridge between the tenaille and the town had collapsed into the ditch. The garrison of a captain and 53 men marooned in the tenaille surrendered. On the next day, 25 May/4 June, the right face of the Limbourg Bastion was reduced to rubble and French mortars fired bombs into the bastions to prevent the defenders from digging retrenchments. During the night, the sappers put the finishing touches to the fascine bridges across the ditch towards the two semi-demolished bastions. The morning of 26 May/5 June dawned with the breach in the Namur Bastion wide enough for thirty men to advance in line abreast whilst that in the Limbourg could have accommodated twenty-five. The ditch was partially filled by the fascines and the shattered remains of the bastions. Catinat and Vauban ordered a general assault for later in the day. At 2.00 p.m., the defenders beat the chamade, exchanged hostages and the capitulation was signed that same evening. The defence had been uninspired. Out of their garrison of 3,500 men, the defenders suffered only 250 casualties whilst the French lost just 53 dead and 106 wounded. Vauban had conducted a most economical and efficient siege. Even the town had escaped relatively unscathed on account of the barrier of lime trees and Catinat's instructions not to overshoot the fortifications deliberately. Catinat set his men to work, levelling the trenches and siege works and repairing the damaged ravelin and bastions.[15]

William was now in a poor position. Fagel brought his ten battalions from Nieuport to reinforce the Elector of Bavaria at Nevele and Tilly marched the Liègeois cavalry and dragoons from Nevele to Brussels. Yet William remained critically short of men. Villeroi and Boufflers could now combine and march against either Brussels or Namur whilst Catinat's army was free to occupy the Elector in Flanders. D'Harcourt, having sent 10 battalions and 9 squadrons to reinforce Choiseul on the

Rhine, marched with 6 battalions and 8 squadrons from Mont Royal, through Luxembourg to the Marlagne. This pinned the thin Allied garrisons along the Meuse and posed a threat to Namur. At Promelles, William was neither adequately protecting Brussels nor Namur. He would have liked to have formed a third army especially to guard Brussels but the troops were not available. Instead, General Tilly posted himself at the Fort of Monterey in front of the Halle Gate, and Coehoorn rode into Brussels on 3/13 June to trace out a line of trenches and redoubts from Anderlecht to the Willebroek Canal. However, this remained simply a tracing without the troops either to excavate it or provide a garrison. One of the reasons for the Allied shortage of troops was their continuing financial plight. Eight battalions were late in sailing from England and seventeen battalions from Lüneburg, Münster and Hesse had yet to cross the Rhine, all held back for want of money. A little of this deficiency was rectified when five British battalions came ashore at Willemstadt on 5/15 June and eight battalions and twelve squadrons from Lüneburg crossed the Meuse at Visé on 6/16 June and marched to camp at Tongres. However, these reinforcements only partially solved some of the Allies' problems. With three armies opposing two, the French were able to secure the foraging grounds around Alost whilst the Elector of Bavaria had run so short of forage at Nevele that he was compelled to purchase 'dry fodder' from the regions north of the Ghent-Bruges Canal. In addition, Catinat's army at Grammont made communications between William and the Elector exceedingly tenuous and they had to use the long route to the north of Brussels through Dendermonde.

The French generals held a conference at which they considered their strategic options. Villeroi and Catinat might combine and attack Nieuport or Ostend but this was not favoured as the Allied defences behind the Flanders canals were strong and well manned. Besides, much of the land around Nieuport was flooded. Villeroi and Catinat could simply eat up the forage in the Pays d'Alost. Alternatively, Villeroi could march to Alost and Boufflers could move to Piéton, obliging the Allies to find the troops to cover both Brussels and Namur whilst Catinat continued to engage the Elector of Bavaria in Flanders. Next, they considered the idea of Villeroi besieging Oudenarde with Catinat watching Bavaria and Boufflers observing William. This was not a real possibility as Oudenarde was safe behind a ring of inundations and possessed a good garrison. Finally, they raised the concept of Villeroi and Boufflers linking their armies for a march on Brussels, again leaving Catinat to entertain the Elector. This looked attractive. If Boufflers could steal a march on William and reach the Anderlecht position without interference, he could stage another bombardment of Brussels which would strike a massive blow for French interests at the Rijswijk Conference and boost French prestige. William was separated from Brussels by a march of 30 kilometres through the 'close defiles' of the Forest of Soignes, whereas Villeroi and Boufflers would be able to advance through open country and along reasonable roads.[16]

Catinat shifted from his camp at Grammont on 9/19 June, marching southwards to Ligne. On 15/25 June, he crossed the Scheldt and encamped at St. Eloois-Vijve, a few kilometres north of Courtrai, with his left resting on the Lys. In response, the Elector of Bavaria built bridges across the Lys to secure his communications with Ghent and Dendermonde. He had already been reinforced by the arrival of Fagel's ten battalions from Nieuport. Catinat adjusted his position slightly northwards to Zulte on 17/27 June, again securing his left flank on the banks of the Lys. His closer posture made it more difficult for the Elector to throw out detachments, either to reinforce William or to attack a target in Flanders, perhaps Furnes or Fort Knokke. The Elector was effectively trapped at Nevele, his only possible movement being northward over the Ghent-Bruges Canal. With the situation sealed in Flanders, the way was open for Villeroi and Boufflers to execute their 'race for Brussels'. Villeroi edged across the Dender to Gammerages on 12/22 June and Boufflers simultaneously advanced to Enghien. From these positions, the Frenchmen intended to dash for Brussels, seize the Anderlecht position and subject Brussels to attack or bombardment, confident that they would be able to parry William's spearheads as he struggled northwards through the Forest of Soignes. At midday on 12/22 June, William's intelligence service brought him notice of the French marches. An immediate council of war decided that the army must make a forced march for Brussels that very evening. It was raining and the roads were muddy but if William delayed until the following morning, there was every chance that the French would beat him to Brussels. Fortunately, the road through the Forest of Soignes was a good, stone causeway which enabled the Allies to march relatively quickly whereas the French were slowed by earthern tracks which the rains turned into quagmires. The artillery and baggage left the Promelles camp at 5.00 p.m. and the main army marched at 10.00 p.m. It was a very dark, wet night and the infantry marched well ahead of the cavalry to avoid being trampled under hoof. William and Vaudemont departed in their carriages around midnight 'having a great many flambeaux to light them', and the Brigade of Guards left at dawn. As the head of the foot entered Waterloo at daybreak, the cavalry began to file out of the camp onto the road. The army was stretched out in a single column over twenty kilometres in length. Orders were also sent to Tilly in Brussels to quit the Monterey Fort on the road to Halle, march back through Brussels and occupy the traced lines beyond the Anderlecht Gate. By morning, Tilly was in position and had sent out patrols to observe the approach of Villeroi and Boufflers.

William and Vaudemont managed to enter Brussels early on 13/23 June and went immediately to the Anderlecht position to inspect the ground between Anderlecht and the Willebroek Canal. By 10.00 a.m., the head of the infantry column had reached the suburb of Ixelles outside the Namur Gate and here the troops waited until the proposed camp had been marked out. The infantry resumed their march at 1.00 p.m., passing through the Namur Gate, along the southern streets of Brussels, and out of the Flanders Gate into a camp between the Flanders and Anderlecht Gates. The camp covered the whole of the western half of Brussels. Its right was at Laeken on the Willebroek Canal and the left was in the Valley of the River Senne outside the Anderlecht Gate. The camp curved between these two points with its apex at Berchem and the headquarters at Koekelberg. Just as the vanguard under Major-General Dopff came into sight of the camping ground, 4,000 French cavalry appeared in the distance. Dopff, a good administrator but a weak and timid field commander, was about to withdraw in the face of a superior enemy when Vaudemont arrived on the scene and took control. Within a short while, it was the French horse who retired leaving the Allies to occupy the Koekelberg Camp.[17]

Villeroi had marched through the Wood of Lessines on 12/22 June to encamp at Kestergat but wet weather and muddy roads caused him to halt for the whole of 13/23 June. Conditions were slightly better to the south and Boufflers moved forward from Enghien to Halle on 13/23 June sending out patrols to discover if the Allies had marched from Promelles. It was one of these detachments which encountered Dopff occupying the Koekelberg position. Disappointed, Villeroi advanced to encamp at St. Kwintens Lennik, his right within four kilometres of Boufflers's left; the two French armies occupied a camp fifteen kilo-metres in length from the banks of the Senne to the Dender. Reconnaissance reports indicated that the Allied camp was extremely strong and daily becoming more so as Coehoorn supervised entrenchments and field fortifications. Attack was out of the question. The Allies' right wing was protected by a stream, the Brook of Zellik, whose narrow valley was damned to form a series of fish ponds. Beyond the stream stretched a number of wooded defiles. The valley of the River Senne guarded the left and here also a number of ponds gave additional protection. Six thousand soldiers and pioneers were labouring at the camp's defences by 14/24 June. The ring of villages and suburbs around the western side of Brussels was fortified and formed into a network of defensive posts – Berchem, Jette, Ganshoren, Laeken, Dilbeek Abbey and Neerpede. All was complete by 19/29 June.[18]

Gradually, the campaign wound down. Catinat, finding it impossible to forage under the close attentions of the Elector of Bavaria, withdrew through Harelbeke to Courtrai where he entered the Lines on 24 June/4 July. Again in search of forage, the Elector came forward to Roeselare on 4/14 August. Villeroi and Boufflers fell back from their position opposite the Koekelberg Camp and camped between Alost and Ninove, behind the line of the Dender.[19] Once the Allies had settled into the Koekelberg position and the French had camped between Ninove and Alost, neither side wanted to jeopardise the developments at the peace conference by risking a general action. This was particularly the case for the Allies. With their inferior numbers, they would probably have lost any engagement thereby uncovering Brussels rendering the French negotiators even more awkward. Also, the pay and provisions of the Allied army were in such short supply that it was questionable if all the troops would actually have fought, if put to the test.[20] It behoved the Allies to be extremely cautious on all fronts. Tilly led fifty squadrons of Liègeois and German cavalry out of the camp on 24 June/4 July to camp at Mazy, covering Namur and Huy. This also saved forage at Koekelberg. All major forages were heavily guarded. A French forage on 27 June/7 July put the Allied camp into a state of alarm as it was feared that Villeroi and Boufflers were advancing in search of battle. William drew out his dragoons and had the army stand-to but the French gathered their forage and departed.[21] Gradually, tension eased and a degree of live and let live permeated the relations between the armies. On 26 June/6 July, the French foraged to the east of their camp whilst the Allies foraged to the west, as if by mutual agreement. Observers distant from the armies thought that the French dispositions indicated aggressive intent but there was no reflection of this in the field. Almost the last action of the war in Flanders was an attempt by fifty Frenchmen to steal grazing horses belonging to the Allies. The marauders were surrounded and captured. A shift in the French camp towards Alost was only to find better foraging grounds but William covered the move by marching an infantry brigade to Verbrande Brug on the Willebroek Canal. He also ordered cavalry and dragoons in

Diegem to rendezvous with Belcastel's men and sent ten cannon from Koekelberg.

The peace negotiations at Rijswijk had not been proceeding too smoothly. The Spanish envoy, Don Bernardo de Quiros, disobeyed his instructions from Madrid to conclude a peace at almost any price as he, personally, wanted the war to continue. William and Louis still did not trust one another, and the French would not talk directly to the English but would only operate indirectly through the agency of the Dutch. Another problem was that Louis sought an amnesty for Jacobites in France and wanted William to provide a pension for Mary of Modena, James II's queen. In turn, William required Louis to repudiate James II's claim to the throne of England. The fall of Ath made the French plenipotentiaries even more arrogant and obstinate but William's successful defence of Brussels did much to deflate them and raise William's credit amongst the Spanish and the Dutch.[22] A method was needed to circumvent the conference. To break the deadlock, William asked Portland to open direct talks with Boufflers. The two men had got to know each other when Boufflers had been Portland's prisoner after the surrender of Namur in 1695. Portland's brief was to discover from Boufflers whether Louis really did want peace and to invent a formula whereby Louis could accept William as King of England without losing face.[23] Initially, William regarded these talks as a means by which to shift the log-jam at Rijswijk but they were to lead to the end of the war in their right.

Boufflers met Portland in the village of Brucom, near Halle, on 28 June/8 July, a point roughly equidistant between the two armies. Protected by formal guards, the two generals conversed inside a summer house in an orchard and they soon realised that all William wanted was formal French recognition of his position in England and for Louis to renounce his support for James II. This appeared to be the only substantial sticking point. It took a further eight meetings to overcome this problem.[24] Tension remained high. The French were poised to seize Oudenarde the moment that either of the sets of peace talks looked like failing. However, Boufflers and Portland brought matters to a head. Portland let it be known that William would be happy to agree to a peace between England, the United Provinces and France. In other words, William was prepared to split the Grand Alliance in order to gain a settlement regardless of the fate of Spain or the Holy Roman Empire. In reality, as Louis well knew, the Emperor did not have the strength to make war against France on the Rhine and pursue the Turks through Hungary simultaneously, unless he had Anglo-Dutch assistance in the west. As soon as England and the United Provinces signed a peace with France, the Empire would have no option but to follow suit. The same applied to Spain. Although William had protected Brussels from France, Spain could not have done so on her own. Indeed, without the British and the Dutch in the Netherlands and the Anglo-Dutch Fleet in the Mediterranean, Spain was virtually powerless to help herself.

The Peace of Rijswijk represented a substantial victory for the Grand Alliance.[25] William was recognised as King of England and Louis XIV undertook not to support the candidature of James II's son to the throne of England after the death of his father. Nothing was said about the Jacobites being asked to leave French soil. The majority of the territories which France had 'reunified' between 1678 and 1684 were restored to their previous owners, with the important exception of Strasbourg. As if to rub French noses in the mud, Leopold I concluded the Peace of Carlowitz with the Turk in 1699, a treaty which placed all of Hungary and Transylvania under Habsburg suzerainty. Not only had Louis XIV suffered his first military and diplomatic setback, but the balance of power in Europe had taken a decisive shift away from Paris.

On 21 September/1 October, Vaudemont wrote orders for the army to disperse from Koekelberg and go home. The exodus from the Spanish Netherlands began on the following day.[26] The bulk of the British forces were marched from Brussels to Ostend, Ghent, Bruges and Nieuport and shipped across the North Sea between the end of October 1697 and the middle of February 1698. Most of the infantry were ferried from the quayside of Ostend and Nieuport in a variety of small craft out to the anchored transports and men-of-war. The majority of the cavalry and their mounts were shipped from Rotterdam and Willemstadt, an operation which had to be halted temporarily in mid-December when ice closed the ports. Sir Henry Bellasise supervised the evacuation with efficiency and attention to detail. Irish and Scottish regiments sailed directly to their home ports, usually Cork and Leith, whilst the English troops came ashore at Hull, Newcastle upon Tyne, Harwich, Ipswich, Deal, Dover, Gravesend and Dartford. They returned to face a general disbandment which, within the space of two years, had reduced the army to little more than a cadre.[27]

'Welcome tidings of the peace', noted John Evelyn. The Mayor and Aldermen of Oxford were a little more enthusiastic and decided to 'meet in their scarlet at the bench at six o'clock this evening and have a bonfire with the bells ringing and the City music playing as is usual on such a joyful occasion'.[28]

NOTES

1 Edward D'Auvergne, *The History of the Campaign in Flanders for the year 1697* (London, 1698), pp. 11–12.
2 Japikse, iii. 417–18; *Archives d'Orange-Nassau*, i. 511; Morgan, 'The Expedition of Baron de Pointis against Cartagena', pp. 242–54.
3 D'Auvergne, *1697*, pp. 12–13, 17–18.
4 *Ibid.*, pp. 13–18, 23–4; Japikse, iii. 431–2.
5 *HMC, Buccleuch (Montagu) MSS.*, ii. 457.
6 BL, King's MSS. 229, pp. 50–6.
7 Trumbull Add. MSS. 103; Japikse, iii. 421–2.
8 *Letters illustrative of the Reign of William III from 1696 to 1708, addressed to the Duke of Shrewsbury by James Vernon, Esq.*, ed. G. P. R. James (London, 1841), i. 226.
9 Baxter, *William III*, p. 353; *HMC, Buccleuch (Montagu) MSS.*, ii. 464.
10 D'Auvergne, *1697*, pp. 24–5, 35–42, 52–9; *HMC, Bath MSS.*, iii. 108.
11 Wright, *Fortifications*, pp. 16–18; *Atlas Portatif*, p. 51; *Journal of the Late Motions*, pp. 20–1; D'Auvergne, *1697*, pp. 31–2; D'Auvergne, *1694*, pp. 59–61; Sonnino, *Origins of the Dutch War*, pp. 110, 127, 151. On the building of the fortress of Ath see, Roland Mousnier, *The Institutions of France under the Absolute Monarchy, 1598–1789* (Chicago & London, 1979), i. 723–9.
12 D'Auvergne, *1697*, pp. 32–46; *HMC, Downshire MSS.*, i. 741; Japikse, iii. 440; WO 78/2648, three plans of the Siege of Ath, 1697.
13 BL, King's MSS. 229, pp. 59–61; Sevin de Quincy, *Mémoires du Chevalier de Quincy* (Paris, 1898), i. 33–44.
14 D'Auvergne, *1697*, pp. 48–60.
15 Quincy, i. 45; *Colonie*, pp. 50–1; D'Auvergne, *1697*, pp. 69–73; Walton, p. 322; BL, King's MSS. 229, pp. 61–5; Landmann, pp. 95–8.
16 D'Auvergne, *1697*, pp. 75–81; Quincy, i. 55.
17 Trumbull Add. MSS. 103; BL, King's MSS. 229, pp. 65–6.
18 ARA, Raad van State, 1896/2, pp. 11–12; CMC 4/89, 4/90.
19 BL, Add. MSS. 9,726, ff. 22–3; Quincy, i. 55–6; NLI, MS. 4166, pp. 39–40; Parker, *Memoirs*, pp. 63–5; Burnet, *History*, iv. 353–4.
20 *HMC, Downshire MSS.*, i. 748–9.
21 *CSPD 1697*, p. 216.
22 *Shrewsbury Correspondence*, p. 342; Callières, *Diplomacy*, pp. 10–11.
23 Thomson, 'Louis XIV and William III', pp. 51–3.
24 *Letters of William III and Louis XIV and of their Ministers, 1697–1700*, ed. Paul Grimblot (London, 1848), i. 9–10; Morgan, 'Ryswick', pp. 183–95; *HMC, Buccleuch (Montagu) MSS*; ii. 486–547.
25 Baxter, *William III*, pp. 355–8; Wolf, *Louis XIV*, pp. 485–8; Liverpool, *Treaties*, i. 299–305. The Peace of Rijswijk was signed on 10/20 September 1697.
26 BL, King's MSS. 229, pp. 66–92.
27 Childs, *British Army of William III*, pp. 203–4.
28 *The Diary of John Evelyn*, ed. E. S. de Beer (Oxford, 1955), v. 267; *Oxford Council Acts, 1665–1701*, ed. M. G. Hobson (Oxford, Oxford Historical Society, 1939), p. 313.

Dramatis personae

AALFELDT: *see* AHLEFELDT

AHLEFELDT, Frederik (1662–1708)
Danish. Colonel of Prince George of Denmark's foot in Danish army, 1689; served in Danish corps in Ireland, 1690; brigadier, 1692; major-general, 1695; lieutenant-general, 1701.

ALBEMARLE, Arnoust van Keppel, 1st Earl of (1669–1718)
Dutch. Favourite of William III. Major-general, 1697; lieutenant-general, 1701; governor of Tournai, 1709.

ANGUS, James Douglas, 13th Earl of (1669–1692)
Scottish. Colonel of the Cameronians, 1689; killed at Steenkirk, 1692.

ANHALT-DESSAU, Johann George, Duke of
Swedish major-general who transferred into the Brandenburg army as a full general. Colonel of a Brandenburg infantry regiment, 1676–94.

ARCO, Jean Baptiste, Count d' (d. 1715)
Piedmontese. Entered Bavarian army; general, 1694; general of cavalry, 1697; president of Bavarian council of war and a field marshal, 1702; defended the Schellenberg against Marlborough, 1704; commanded the French left wing at Ramillies, 1706. Arco acted as chief of staff and principal military adviser to Elector Maximilian Emmanuel of Bavaria.

ARGYLL, Archibald Campbell, 10th Earl & 1st Duke of (d. 1703)
Scottish. Colonel of an infantry battalion, 1689–94; resigned his commission to his son, Lord Lorne, 1694.

ARTAGNAN, Pierre de Montesquiou, d' (1645–1725)
French. Sous-lieutenant, 1670; lieutenant, 1673; served at Maastricht, 1673, and Seneffe, 1674; brevet major-general, 1683; brigadier, 1688; major-general, 1691; lieutenant-general, 1707; marshal of France, 1709.

ASFELD, Alexis Bidal, Baron d' (1648–89)
Of a Swedish family settled in France. Commander of the French garrison during the siege of Bonn, 1689.

ASFELD, Claude-François Bidal, Chevalier d' (1667–1743)
Younger brother of Alexis. Lieutenant, 1683; captain, 1684; brigadier, 1694; maréchal de camp, 1702; lieutenant-general, 1704; marshal of France, 1734.

ATHLONE: *see* GINKEL

AUGER, Guy d' (d. 1691)
French. Lieutenant-general, 1688; killed at Leuse, 1692.

AVAUX, Jean-Antoine des Mesmes, Comte d' (1640–1709)

French diplomat. Ambassador at The Hague, 1679–88; Louis XIV's representative with James II in Ireland, 1689–90; ambassador to Stockholm, 1692.

AYLVA, Hans Willem, Baron van (d. 1691)
Dutch. Major-general, 1668; lieutenant-general, 1672; lieutenant-admiral of Friesland.

BADEN, Ludwig Wilhelm, Margrave of (1655–1707)
German. Served at siege of Vienna, 1683; commanded Imperial armies on the Upper Rhine, 1689–97; fought in a total of 26 campaigns.

BARBANÇON, Octavius de Ligne, Prince de (1640–93)
Walloon. Major-general in the army of the Spanish Netherlands, 1671; mestre de camp general; governor of Namur, 1692; died of wounds suffered at Landen, 1693.

BARFUS, Albert de
Dutchman in Brandenburg-Prussian service. Major-general of foot, 1692.

BATH, John Granville, 1st Earl of (1628–1701)
English. Governor of Pendennis Castle and Scilly Isles, 1689; colonel of an infantry battalion, 1688–93; governor of Plymouth, 1693.

BAVARIA, Maximilian-Emmanuel von Wittelsbach, Elector of (1662–1736)
Succeeded as Elector of Bavaria, 1679; appointed governor of the Spanish Netherlands in 1691 as a reward for his alliance with the Holy Roman Emperor against France. In 1702 he allied with France but his lands were confiscated after the defeat at Blenheim in 1704. He was restored to his electorate in 1714.

BEDMAR, Don Isodoro de la Cucoa y Benevides, Marquis de (1652–1733)
Spanish. Sergeant-major de batailles and governor of Brussels, 1681; general of the artillery of the Spanish Netherlands, 1682; mestre de camp general, 1692; promoted to general after Landen, 1693; field marshal of the Spanish armies in the Netherlands, 1700; governor of the Spanish Netherlands, 1701–4; retired because of ill health, 1704.

BELLASISE, Sir Henry (d. 1717)
English. Served in the Anglo-Dutch Brigade in the United Provinces upto 1688; brigadier in the English army, 1689; major-general, 1692; lieutenant-general, 1694; second-in-command of the Cádiz expedition, 1702.

BERGHES, Philippe François de Glimes, Prince de (1650–1704)
Walloon. Mestre de camp general in the army of the Spanish Netherlands, 1676; general, 1684; governor of Hainaut, 1690; governor of Brussels, 1695.

BERKELEY, John, 3rd Baron Berkeley of Stretton (1663–97)
English. Rear-admiral, 1688; vice-admiral, 1689; admiral, 1693.

BERLO, Albert Ferdinand van (d. 1690)
Dutch. Colonel, 1676; brigadier, 1688.

BERWICK, James Fitzjames, Duke of (1670–1733)
Bastard son of James II of England. Fought in Ireland, 1689–91; joined French army, 1691; marshal of France, 1706.

BEZONS, Jacques Bazin, Marquis de (c. 1646–1733)
French. Brigadier in French army, 1691; marshal of France, 1709.

BIRKENFELD, Christian II von Wittelsbach, Prince de (1637–1717)

Bavarian. Lieutenant-general in Bavarian army, 1688; transferred into French army, 1702.

BLACKADER, John (1664–1729)
Scottish. Of Glencairn, Dumfries. Lieutenant in the Cameronians, 1689; captain, 1693; major, 1705; lieutenant-colonel, 1709; deputy governor of Stirling Castle, 1717.

BLATHWAYT, William (1649–1717)
English. Secretary-at-war 1683–1704; secretary of state, 1691–7; commissioner of trade, 1696–1706.

BOREEL, Jacob (1630–97)
Dutch. Burgomaster of Amsterdam; envoy of the States-General to the peace negotiations at Rijswijk, 1697.

BOUFFLERS, Louis-François, Duc de (1644–1711)
French. Cadet in Africa, 1662; sous-lieutenant, 1666; major, 1670; served in Holland, 1672; brigadier of dragoons, 1675; maréchal de camp, 1677; colonel-general of dragoons, 1678; lieutenant-general, 1681; marshal of France, 1693.

BOUTEVILLE, Charles de Béon, Marquis de (d. 1725)
French. Son of the Duke of Luxembourg. Maréchal de camp.

BRERETON, Thomas
Irish. Quartermaster of the Earl of Meath's foot, 1692; captain, 1695.

BRESSÉ, Jean-Claude de Bressy de Belfry, Comte de (d. 1704)
French. In Spanish service as an engineer until 1691 when he entered the French army; maréchal de camp, 1692; lieutenant-general, 1696.

BRIDGES, Sir Mathew (d. c. 1703)
Irish. Lieutenant-colonel of Solomon Richards's infantry battalion, 1688; colonel, 1695; severely wounded at Namur, 1695.

CALLIÈRES, François de (1645–1717)
French diplomat. Envoy at Rijswijk, 1697.

CALVO, Jean-Sauveur de (1625–93)
Born in Andorra. Initially entered the Spanish army but joined the French in 1641. Captain of horse, 1647; maréchal de camp, 1651; fought at the Battle of St. Gotthard in Hungary, 1664; lieutenant-general, 1676; died at Deynze, 1693.

CASTAÑAGA, Francisco Antonio Agurto, Marquis de (d. 1702)
Spanish. Governor of the Spanish Netherlands, 1678–92; viceroy of Catalonia, 1694–6.

CASTILLO: *see* CASTILLO-TAXARDO

CASTILLO-TAXARDO, Don Francisco de, Marquis de Villadarias
Spanish. Captain-general of the Spanish artillery; returned to Spain, 1693; commanded siege of Gibraltar, 1704–5; retired from field command, 1710.

CASTLETON, George Saunderson, 5th Viscount (d. 1714)
Irish. Colonel of an infantry battalion, 1689–94.

CATINAT, Nicolas (1637–1712)
French, Lieutenant-general, 1689; marshal of France, 1693.

CHAMLAY, Jules-Louis, Marquis de Bolé (1650–1719)
French. Maréchal Général des Logis aux Campes et Armées du Roi, effectively chief of staff to Louvois and Louis XIV.

CHOISEUL, Claude de, Comte de (1632–1711)
French. Marshal of France, 1693; retired, 1697.

CHURCHILL, Charles (1656–1714)
English. Brother of Marlborough. Ensign in Duke of York's foot, 1674; lieutenant-colonel, 1682; major-general, 1694; lieutenant-general, 1702; general, 1707.

CHURCHILL, George (1654–1710)
English. Brother of Marlborough. Captain, Royal Navy, 1678–88; commissioner of the Admiralty, 1699–1702; admiral, 1702.

CHURCHILL, John: *see* MARLBOROUGH

CODRINGTON, Christopher the Elder (1640–98)
English. Governor-general of the Leeward Islands, 1689–98.

COEHOORN, Menno, Baron van (1634–1704)
Dutch. Served at the siege of Maastricht, 1673; engineer at the siege of Bonn, 1689; brigadier, 1690; lieutenant-general, 1695, following the capture of Namur; engineer-general of the fortifications, 1695; master-general of the Dutch artillery, 1697.

COLYEAR, Sir David (1656–1730)
Scottish. Lieutenant-colonel in the Anglo-Dutch Brigade, 1683; colonel of foot on Scottish establishment, 1688; brigadier, 1693; major-general, 1696; lieutenant-general, 1702; general, 1710; created Baron Portmore, 1699; Earl of Portmore, 1703.

CONTI, François-Louis de Bourbon (1644–1709)
French. Served in Germany, 1689; maréchal de camp, 1690; lieutenant-general, 1692; left the army, 1695.

COURTHOPE, John (d. 1695)
English. Captain in 1st Foot Guards, 1689; colonel of an infantry battalion, 1694; killed at Namur, 1695.

CRÉQUI, François Joseph de Blanchefort de (1659–1718)
French. Son of Marshal de Créqui. A.d.c. to his father at Freiburg and Kehl, 1677; colonel, 1679; maréchal de camp in Piedmont, 1691; commanded French Lines from the Lys to the North Sea, 1692; lieutenant-general, 1696; director-general of French infantry, 1702.

CUTTS, John, Baron Cutts of Gowran (1661–1707)
English. Captain in the Anglo-Dutch Brigade, 1688; colonel of foot, 1689; brigadier, 1693; major-general, 1696; lieutenant-general, 1702; commander-in-chief in Ireland, 1705.

DOPFF, Daniel Wolff van (1655–1718)
Dutch. Client of Waldeck. Lieutenant-quartermaster-general, 1676; quartermaster-general of the cavalry, 1687; quartermaster-general of the Dutch army, 1694; governor of Maastricht; major-general, 1694; lieutenant-general, 1701.

DOUGLAS, James (d. 1691)

Scottish. Colonel of Scottish Foot Guards, 1684; brigadier, 1685; commander of the Brigade of Guards in Flanders, 1691; died of fever, 1691.

DOUGLAS, Sir Robert, 3rd Bt. (d. 1692)
Scottish. Colonel of the Royal Scots, 1689–92.

DUNCANSON, Robert (d. 1705)
Scottish. Lieutenant of foot, 1689; major of Earl of Argyll's battalion, 1690; lieutenant-colonel, 1695; colonel, 1703; killed at Valencia de Alcantara, 1705.

DURAS, Jacques-Henri, Duc de (1625–1704)
French. Nephew of Turenne. Abjured his protestant faith in 1665. Marshal of France, 1675; seized Philippsburg and Mannheim in 1688.

DYCKVELDT, Everard van Weede, Heer van
Dutch diplomat and confidant of William III.

ELLENBURG, Johan Anton (1637–95)
Hessian. Served in Danish army; brigadier, 1690; major-general, 1691; executed in 1695 for the surrender of Dixmuyde.

ERLE, Thomas (1650–1720)
English. Colonel of foot, 1689; brigadier, 1693; major-general, 1696; lieutenant-general, 1703; general, 1711.

EUGENE OF SAVOY, Prince (1663–1736)
French citizen of Italian parentage. Volunteer at siege of Vienna, 1683; colonel in Imperial army, 1683; major-general, 1685; lieutenant-general, 1687; general of the Imperial cavalry in Italy, 1690–3; Imperial commander-in-chief in Italy, 1694; victorious over the Turks at Zenta, 1697; Imperial commander-in-chief in Italy, 1701–2; president of the Imperial war council, 1703; combined with Marlborough at Blenheim, 1704, Oudenarde, 1708, and Malplaquet, 1709; fought in Turkish War, 1715–18; commanded Imperial armies in War of the Polish Succession, 1733–5.

FAGEL, Francis Nicolaas, Baron (1655–1718)
Dutch. Major-general, 1694; lieutenant-general, 1701.

FAIRFAX, Thomas (1657–1710)
English. 2nd son of Sir William Fairfax of Steeton, West Yorkshire. Captain in 1st Foot Guards, 1676; lieutenant-colonel of Lord Castleton's foot, 1689; brevet colonel, 1689; colonel of foot, 1694; brigadier, 1697; dismissed from colonelcy, 1703; major-general and governor of Limerick at his death in 1710.

FITZPATRICK, Edward (d. 1696)
English. Captain in Holland Regiment, 1678; colonel of foot, 1689; brigadier, 1695; drowned whilst crossing North Sea, 1696.

FLEMING, Heinrich (1632–1706)
Prussian. Served in Prussian army before transferring to the army of Electoral Saxony in the rank of general; senior officer of the Saxon army after the disgrace of Schöning in 1692.

FLODROFF, Count Adriaan van (d. 1690)
Dutch. Entered Dutch army in 1671; major-general of cavalry, 1683; killed at Fleurus, 1690.

FOREST: *see* SUZANNET

FOULKES, John (d. 1693)
English. Captain in Anglo-Dutch Brigade, 1685; fought for Monmouth at Sedge-moor, 1685; cashiered from Anglo-Dutch Brigade but remained in the Dutch Republic until 1688; lieutenant-colonel of Sir John Guise's foot in England, 1688; colonel, 1689; commander-in-chief of land forces in expedition to the West Indies, 1692; died in West Indies, 1693.

FREKE, Robert (d. 1709)
English. Of Upway, Dorset. Lieutenant-colonel of Thomas Erle's foot, 1689; brevet colonel, 1694; deputy-governor of Plymouth, 1696.

FRIESLAND, Hendrik Casimir II van Nassau-Dietz, Prince of (d. 1696)
Dutch. Cousin of William III. Stadholder of Friesland and Groningen; 3rd field marshal in Dutch army, 1689; resigned, 1692.

FULLERTON, John (d. 1692)
Scottish. Captain in Lord Leven's foot, 1689; lieutenant-colonel of Earl of Angus's foot, 1692; killed at Steenkirk, 1692.

GALWAY: *see* RUVIGNY

GASSION, Jean de (1636–1713)
French. Cornet, 1667; with Turenne in Germany, 1672–4; major, 1675; brigadier, 1688; maréchal de camp, 1692; lieutenant-general, 1696.

GASTAÑAGA: *see* CASTAÑAGA

GIBSON, Sir John (1636–1717)
English. Served in the Anglo-Dutch Brigade before 1688 reaching the rank of captain by 1687; lieutenant-colonel of Sir Robert Peyton's foot in England, 1689; lieutenant-governor of Portsmouth, 1689; colonel of foot, 1694; commander of land forces in expedition to Newfoundland, 1697; knighted, 1705.

GINKEL, Godart van, 1st Earl of Athlone (1630–1703)
Dutch. Born and died in Utrecht. Major-general, 1675; lieutenant-general, 1683; general, 1692; field marshal, 1702. Commander-in-chief in Ireland, 1691; victor at Aughrim, 1691; created Earl of Athlone, 1692; commanded Dutch cavalry in Flanders, 1692–7.

GODOLPHIN, Sidney (1652–1732)
English. Cousin of Sidney, 1st Earl Godolphin, Lord Treasurer of England. Captain in Earl of Bath's foot, 1685; lieutenant-governor of Scilly Isles, 1690; lieutenant-colonel of Bath's, 1694–6; major of Queen's foot, 1700–2; governor of Scilly Isles, 1700–32.

GOOR, Johan van
Dutch. Lieutenant-colonel, 1690; colonel, 1695; major-general, 1701. Commander of the Dutch artillery train in England, 1688, and in Flanders after 1690.

GOURNAY, Jean-Christophe de (1639–1693)
French. Maréchal de camp, 1685; lieutenant-general, 1689; killed at Landen, 1693.

GRAHAM, Charles
Scottish. Captain in the Anglo-Dutch Brigade, 1675; brigade-major of the Scottish Brigade in the Dutch army in Flanders, 1691; wounded at Steenkirk, 1692; still serving, 1697.

GRAVENMOER, Adam van der Duyn, Heer van 's- (1639–1693)

Dutch. Colonel, 1668; quartermaster of Dutch cavalry, 1674; quartermaster-general of the Dutch army, 1687; major-general, 1683; governor of Bergen-op-Zoom, 1690; lieutenant-general, 1692.

GUISCARD, Louis de (1651–1721)
French. Served in the Dutch Republic and Germany with Turenne, 1672–4; colonel of Régiment de Normandie, 1674; brigadier, 1689; maréchal de camp, 1690; lieutenant-general, 1693; ambassador to Sweden, 1698.

HALES, John (d. 1726)
English. Captain in Anglo-Dutch Brigade, 1676; lieutenant-colonel, 1688; colonel of foot in England, 1688; dismissed because of suspected Jacobitism, 1692; governor of Chelsea Hospital, 1702.

HAMILTON, Lord George: *see* ORKNEY

HANOVER, George Ludwig, Duke of Brunswick-Lüneburg (1660–1727)
German. Electoral Prince of Hanover, 1692; King of Great Britain, 1714–27.

HARCOURT, Henri d' (1654–1718)
French. Served under Turenne in Alsace and Germany, 1672–5; colonel of Régiment du Picardie, 1677; inspector-general of infantry, 1682; maréchal de camp, 1688; lieutenant-general, 1693; ambassador to Madrid, 1697; marshal of France, 1703.

HEIDEN, Johann Sigismund von
German. Lieutenant-colonel in the Brandenburg army before 1688; colonel 1688; major-general by 1695.

HESSE-CASSEL, Karl, Landgrave of (1654–1730)
Hessian. Landgrave, 1670–1730.

HILL, Richard (1655–1727)
English. Deputy-paymaster in Flanders, 1692–9; envoy to the Elector of Bavaria in Brussels, 1696; ambassador to The Hague, 1699; lord of the Treasury, 1699; envoy to Savoy, 1703–6.

HODGES, Robert (d. 1692)
Scottish. Captain-lieutenant of Sir John Talbot's dragoons, 1678; captain in the Royal Scots, c. 1680; served in Tangier, 1680–3; lieutenant-colonel of the Royal Scots, 1688; colonel of foot, 1688; killed at Steenkirk, 1692.

HOLSTEIN-PLÖN, Jan Adolf, Duke of (1634–1704)
German. Fought at Seneffe with his own regiment, 1674; governor of Maastricht, 1693; 1st field marshal of the Dutch army, 1693; captured Huy, 1694.

HOLT, Henry
English. Lieutenant in the Holland Regiment, 1685; brevet colonel, 1689; lieutenant-colonel of Duke of Bolton's battalion in West Indies, 1693; colonel of Bolton's in West Indies, 1694; colonel of marines, 1702; major-general, 1707; lieutenant-general, 1710.

HORNES, Willem Adriaan, Graaf van (d. 1694)
Dutch. Master-general of the Dutch artillery, 1672–94. A member of William III's small circle of trusted advisers.

HUME, Hon. Patrick (d. 1709)
Scottish. Eldest son of Patrick Hume, Baron Polwarth and Earl of Marchmont.

Captain-lieutenant of Lord Cardross's dragoons, 1689; major, 1695; lieutenant-colonel, 1697; brevet colonel, 1704; colonel of foot, 1707.

HUMIÈRES, Louis de Crevant, Duc d' (1628–94)
French. A childhood friend of Louis XIV. Governor of Compiègne, 1646; maréchal de camp, 1650; lieutenant-general, 1656; marshal of France, 1668.

HUYBERT, Johann d' (d. 1701)
Dutch. Major-general, 1694; lieutenant-general, 1697.

IVOY, Frederik Thomas van Hangest-Genlis, d' (1663–1727)
Dutch. Colonel, 1699; quartermaster-general of the Dutch army, 1701.

JOYEUSE, Jean-Armand de (1631–1710)
French. Marshal of France, 1693; retired, 1697.

KERR, Daniel (d. 1692)
Scottish. Captain in the Cameronians, 1689; major by 1692; killed at Steenkirk, 1692.

KRUSEMARCH(K), Adam von
German. Colonel in Brandenburg army, 1688.

LANIER, Sir John (d. 1692)
English. Served in the British Brigade in France, 1672–8; lieutenant-colonel of horse in England, 1678; colonel of horse, 1685; lieutenant-general, 1688; killed at Steenkirk, 1692.

LEINSTER, Meinhard von Schomberg, 1st Duke of (1641–1719)
German. 1st son of Herman von Schomberg. Served with the British Brigade in Portugal, 1662–8; fought in Hungary, 1686; general of horse in England, 1690; created Duke of Leinster, 1692; commander-in-chief in England, 1692–7; commander-in-chief of allied forces in Iberia, 1703–4.

LEVEN, David Melville, 2nd Earl of (d. 1728)
Scottish. Colonel of foot, 1689; fought at Killiecrankie, 1689, and Steenkirk, 1692; resigned commission, 1694; commander-in-chief in Scotland, 1706.

LILLINGSTONE, Luke (d. 1713)
English. Of Ferriby, East Yorkshire. Ensign in Earl of Mulgrave's foot, 1673; joined Anglo-Dutch Brigade, 1674; captain by 1688; fought in Ireland, 1689–91; lieutenant-colonel of John Foulkes's foot in West Indies, 1692–3; colonel in succession to Foulkes, 1693; half-pay, 1697–1705; colonel of foot, 1705; brigadier, 1708; buried in North Ferriby church.

LIPPE, Frederik Adolf, Graf van der (d. 1718)
German. Colonel in Dutch army, 1689; ruling prince of Lippe, 1697–1718.

LLOYD, Leonard
English. Lieutenant and adjutant to Princess Anne of Denmark's foot, 1691; captain-lieutenant, 1696; captain, 1702; wounded at Blenheim, 1704; still serving, 1709.

LLOYD, William
English. Captain-lieutenant of Princess Anne of Denmark's dragoons, 1691; lieutenant-colonel, 1693; colonel, 1695; brigadier, 1702; major-general, 1704; served in Iberia after 1702.

LORGE, Guy Alphonse de Durfort, Duc de (1630–1702)
French. Nephew of Turenne and father-in-law of the Duc de Saint-Simon. Abjured his protestant faith in 1668. Marshal of France, 1676.

LORRAINE, Prince Camille de (1666–1715)
French. Maréchal de camp; served at Philippsburg, 1688, and in Germany.

LORRAINE, Duke Charles V of (1643–90)
Born in Vienna, an exile from his duchy. Entered the Imperial army; general of cavalry, 1672; commander-in-chief of Imperial armies, 1676; commanded at the relief of Vienna, 1683; commanded in Hungary, 1683–9; died at Linz, 1690.

LOUVOIS, François Michel le Tellier, Marquis de (1641–91)
French. Secretary of state and war in conjunction with his father, Michel le Tellier, 1666; effectively sole secretary of state for war after 1677. Louvois and his father were the organisers and administrators of Louis XIV's armed forces.

LUXEMBOURG, François-Henri de Montmorency, Duc de (1628–95)
French. First campaigned under Condé in Catalonia, 1647; lieutenant-general, 1672; marshal of France, 1675; commander-in-chief of French armies in the Low Countries, 1677–8, and 1690–5.

MAINE, Louis Auguste de Bourbon, Duc de (1670–1736)
French. Son of Louis XIV and Madame de Montespan.

MAITLAND, James (d. 1716)
Scottish. Captain in Scots Guards, 1679; major, 1687; lieutenant-colonel, 1689; brevet colonel, 1691; brigadier, 1692; colonel of the Cameronians, 1694; lieutenant-general under Queen Anne.

MARLBOROUGH, John Churchill, 1st Duke of (1650–1722)
English. Served in British Brigade in France, 1672–7; colonel of foot, 1678; created Baron Churchill, 1682; colonel of Royal Dragoons, 1683; major-general, 1685; created Earl of Marlborough, 1689, for services rendered during the Glorious Revolution; lieutenant-general, 1690; dismissed for suspected Jacobitism and treachery, 1692; governor of Duke of Gloucester, 1698–1700; master-general of the Ordnance, 1702–11; commander-in-chief of Anglo-Dutch forces in Low Countries, 1701–11; created Duke of Marlborough, 1702.

MONSIEUR: *see* ORLÉANS

MONTAL, Charles de Montsaulnin, Comte de (1621–96)
French. Lieutenant-general, 1676. A veteran who had lost an ear and was covered in wound scars. Fought with distinction at Steenkirk and Landen even though he was over seventy years of age.

MONTBRUN, François, Comte de (1632–1708)
French. Lieutenant-general, 1688; governor of Cambrai.

MONTCLAIR, Joseph de Pons de Guimera, Baron de (d. 1690)
French. Lieutenant-general, 1677.

MONTREVEL, Nicolas-Auguste de la Baume, Marquis de (1645–1716)
French. Served at siege of Lille, 1667; served under Turenne in Germany, 1672–5; maréchal de camp, 1688; lieutenant-general, 1693; marshal of France, 1703.

MOTTE, Louis Jacques du Fosse, Comte de la (1643–1728)

French. Maréchal de camp, 1688; lieutenant-general, 1702.

NASSAU-SAARBRUCK, Walrad, Count van
Dutch. Cousin of William III. 2nd field marshal of the Dutch army, 1689; 1st field marshal, 1696.

NEGUS, Francis
English. Captain in Prince George of Denmark's foot, 1691; major, 1694; brevet lieutenant-colonel, 1703.

NOAILLES, Ann-Jules, Duc de (1650–1708)
French. A.d.c. to Louis XIV, 1672; governor of Rousillon, 1678; governor of Languedoc, 1682; marshal of France, 1693.

NORRIS, Sir John (c. 1660–1749)
English. Commander, Royal Navy, 1690; captain, 1693; rear-admiral, 1707; admiral, 1709.

NOTTINGHAM, Daniel Finch, 2nd Earl of (1647–1730)
English. Secretary of State, 1689–93, and 1702–4.

NOYELLES, Jacques Louis, Graaf van
From Picardy but served in the Dutch army. Major-general, 1691; lieutenant-general, 1694.

O'FARRELL, Francis Fergus
Irish. Served in Dutch army reaching rank of lieutenant-colonel by 1688; colonel of Royal Fusiliers in England, 1689; brigadier, 1694; cashiered for the surrender of Deynze, 1695; reinstated, 1696; brigadier in Portugal, 1703; major-general, 1706.

O'HARA, Charles, 1st Baron Tyrawley (1640–1724)
Irish. Client of 2nd Duke of Ormonde. Captain in 1st Foot Guards, 1686; lieutenant-colonel, 1689; knighted, 1689; brigadier, 1695; colonel of Royal Fusiliers, 1696; major-general, 1702; served in Iberia, 1702–7; lieutenant-general, 1704; general, 1714; commander-in-chief in Ireland, 1714–21.

OPDAM, Jacob van Wassenaer, Heer van (1635–1714)
Dutch. Major-general, 1683; lieutenant-general, 1691; general, 1702; retired after his defeat at Eckeren, 1703.

ORKNEY, Lord George Hamilton, 1st Earl of (1666–1737)
Scottish. 5th son of Duke of Hamilton. Captain in Royal Scots, 1684; served in Ireland, 1689–91; commanded Royal Fusiliers at Steenkirk, 1692; wounded at Namur, 1695; brigadier, 1695; created Earl of Orkney, 1696; major-general, 1702; lieutenant-general, 1704; general, 1711; field marshal, 1736.

ORLÉANS, Philippe de Bourbon, Duc d' (1640–1701)
French. Younger brother of Louis XIV, known as 'Monsieur'.

ORMONDE, James Butler, 2nd Duke of (1665–1745)
Irish. Captain of 2nd troop of English Life Guards, 1689; fought at the Boyne, Steenkirk and Landen; lieutenant-general, 1694; commander-in-chief of expedition to Vigo Bay, 1702; captain-general, 1711–12; impeached for Jacobitism, 1715, and retired to France.

OVERKIRK, Hendrik van Nassau, Heer van (1640–1708)

Dutch. Cousin of William III. Major-general, 1683; lieutenant-general in English army, 1689; lieutenant-general in Dutch army, 1691; general, 1701; master of the horse to William III.

POINTIS, Jean-Bernard Louis Desjean, Baron de (1645–1707)
French. Captain in French navy, 1685; commissaire général de l'artillerie de la marine, 1687; chef d'escadre, 1699.

PORTLAND, Hans Willem Bentinck, 1st Earl of (1649–1709)
Dutch. Friend and confidant of William III; first gentleman of the bedchamber; privy councillor. Major-general in the Dutch army, 1683; lieutenant-general, 1691.

PRACOMTAL, Armand, Marquis de (d. 1703)
French. Maréchal de camp, 1696; lieutenant-general, 1697.

PRÉCOMTAL: *see* PRACOMTAL

PRIOR, Mathew (1664–1721)
English. Poet and diplomat. After service as secretary to the English embassy in The Hague, Prior became secretary to the English negotiators at Rijswijk, 1697; chief British negotiator of the Treaty of Utrecht, 1711–12; envoy to Paris, 1712–14.

PUY, Louis Charles du (d. 1695)
Dutch. Director-general of Dutch fortifications, 1692–5.

PUY, François du (d. 1692)
Dutch. Director-general of Dutch fortifications, 1688–92.

RAMSAY, George (c. 1625–1705)
Scottish. 3rd son of George Ramsay, 2nd Earl of Dalhousie. Captain in British Brigade in France, 1674–5; joined Anglo-Dutch Brigade, 1676; major, 1685; lieutenant-colonel, 1687; colonel, 1688; brigadier, 1690; colonel of the Scots Guards, 1691; major-general, 1694; commander-in-chief in Scotland, 1700; lieutenant-general, 1702.

RAMSEY: *see* RAMSAY

RANELAGH, Richard Jones, 1st Earl of (c. 1636–1712)
Irish. Paymaster to the English army, 1686–1702.

ROSEN, Conrad von (1628–1715)
Livonian. Spent career in French army. Lieutenant-general, 1688; maréchal d'Irlande, 1689; marshal of France, 1703.

RUBANTEL, Denis Louis de (1627–1705)
French. Lieutenant-general, 1688; lieutenant-colonel of Régiment des Gardes, 1688; dismissed, 1696.

RUSSELL, Edward, 1st Earl of Orford (1653–1727)
English. Lieutenant, Royal Navy, 1671; captain, 1672; admiral of the blue, 1689; admiral, 1690; victor at La Hogue, 1692; took Anglo-Dutch fleet into the Mediterranean, 1694–5; first lord of the Admiralty, 1694–9, 1709–10, 1714–17; created Earl of Orford, 1697.

RUVIGNY, Henri de, Earl of Galway (1648–1720)
French Huguenot. Served under Turenne, 1672–5; left French army and came to England, 1688; major-general in English army, 1691; commander-in-chief in Ireland and created Viscount Galway, 1692; commander-in-chief of allied forces in Pied-

mont, 1694; created Earl of Galway, 1697; served in Iberia, 1702–10; commander-in-chief of allied forces in Portugal, 1704–10; defeated at Almanza, 1707.

SALISCH, Ernst Willem van
Dutch. Major General, 1694; lieutenant-general, 1697; general, 1705.

SAXONY, John George III, Elector of
Elector of Saxony, 1641–91.

SAXONY, John George IV, Elector of
Elector of Saxony, 1691–4.

SCHOMBERG, Herman von, 1st Duke of (1615–90)
German protestant, born in Heidelberg. Entered Dutch army, 1633; Swedish army, 1634; French army, 1635; Dutch army, 1639–50; maréchal de camp in French army, 1652; lieutenant-general, 1655; commander of the French and British forces in Portugal, 1661–8; commander of British forces for the attack on Walcheren, 1673; created duke and commander of French forces in Rousillon, 1673–4; marshal of France, 1675; left France at Revocation of Edict of Nantes, 1685; entered Brandenburg army, 1687; second-in-command of William III's invasion of England, 1688; commanded British corps in Ireland, 1689; killed at the Boyne, 1690.

SCHOMBERG, 3rd Duke of: *see* LEINSTER

SCHÖNING, Hans Adam von (1641–96)
Prussian. Entered Saxon employ after service in Brandenburg army. Senior military adviser to Elector John George IV of Saxony although secretly in league with France and in receipt of French pension. Arrested and imprisoned in Brno, 1692.

SCHWERIN, Otto von (1645–1705)
Brandenburg diplomat.

SELWYN, William (d. 1702)
English. Client of Marlborough. Captain in 1st Foot Guards, 1681; colonel of Queen's foot, 1691; brigadier, 1695; major-general, 1702; governor of Jamaica, 1701; died in Jamaica, 1702.

SHREWSBURY, Charles Talbot, 12th Earl and 1st Duke of (1660–1718)
English. Secretary of State, 1689–90, 1693–5; lord lieutenant of Ireland, 1713.

SLANGENBURG, Frederick van Baer van (d. 1713)
Dutch. Major-general, 1683; lieutenant-general, 1692.

SOLMS, Hendrik Trajectinus, Graaf van (d. 1693)
Dutch. Lieutenant-general, 1683; general, 1691; killed at Landen, 1693.

SOURDIS, François d'Escoubleau, Marquis de (d. 1707)
French. Lieutenant-general, 1692; governor of Orléans.

SPAEN, Alexander von (1619–92)
Brandenburger. General in Brandenburg army. Served as liaison at The Hague between the Elector of Brandenburg and William III, 1688–9.

STANLEY, James, 10th Earl of Derby (1664–1736)
English. Served in Anglo-Dutch Brigade, 1686–8; captain in 1st Foot Guards, 1689; colonel of foot, 1692–1705; succeeded as 10th Earl of Derby, 1702; major-general, 1704.

STEWART, William (d. 1726)

English. Captain in Sir Charles Wheeler's foot, 1678; captain in 1st Foot Guards, 1685; colonel of foot, 1689; brigadier, 1694; major-general, 1696; lieutenant-general, 1703; general, 1711; commander-in-chief in Ireland, 1712.

SUZANNET, Frédéric Henri, Marquis de la Forest (d. 1701)
French Huguenot and a friend of Schomberg. Initially served in French army but left to join the Danish. Colonel by 1683; major-general, 1688; major-general of horse in the Danish corps in Ireland, 1690; colonel of 1st regiment of Danish cavalry, 1691; lieutenant-general in Allied army in Low Countries, 1694; lieutenant-general in Danish army, 1697; commanded 8,000 Saxon cavalry in Danish army, 1699.

SYDNEY, Henry, 1st Earl of Romney (1641–1704)
English. Titular commander of the Anglo-Dutch Brigade, 1681–5; privy councillor and created Viscount Sydney, 1689; secretary of state, 1690–2; colonel of the 1st Foot Guards, 1689–90, 1693–1704; master-general of the Ordnance, 1693–1702; created Earl of Romney, 1694.

TALLARD, Camille d'Hostun, Comte de (1652–1728)
French. Lieutenant-general, 1693; envoy to England to negotiate the Partition Treaties, 1697–1700; marshal of France, 1703; defeated at Blenheim, 1704, and a prisoner in England until 1711; member of the council of regency, 1717; minister of state, 1726.

TALMASH, Thomas (1651–94)
English. Captain in Coldstream Guards, 1678; lieutenant-colonel of Royal Fusiliers, 1685–6; joined Anglo-Dutch Brigade, 1686; colonel by 1688; colonel of Coldstream Guards, 1689; major-general, 1690; lieutenant-general, 1693; killed whilst in command of the raid on Brest, 1694.

TESSÉ, René III de Froulay, Comte de (1651–1725)
French. Lieutenant-general, 1692; marshal of France, 1703; commanded at siege of Gibraltar, 1705; defended Toulon, 1707.

TETTAU, Julius Ernst von (1644–1711)
East Prussian. Entered Dutch army as a cadet, 1657; transferred to French army in 1660 and served under Turenne studying fortification and military engineering; entered Brandenburg army as an engineer, 1666; tutor to Crown Prince Frederick, later King Frederick I; joined Danish army as a colonel, 1676; major-general, 1684; served on the Duke of Württemberg's staff in Ireland, 1690; colonel of the Zealand regiment, 1690; left Danish service for the Dutch army at the request of William III; lieutenant-general in Dutch army, 1696; retired to his estates in Prussia, 1697.

THIAN: *see* THIANGE

THIANGE, Claude Philibert Damas, Marquis de (1663–1707)
French. Nephew of Madame de Montespan. Brigadier, 1693; lieutenant-general, 1704.

TIFFIN, Zachariah
English. Lieutenant in Duke of Monmouth's foot, 1678; captain, 1679; captain in Tangier, 1680–4; major, 1684; colonel of foot, 1689; brigadier, 1696.

TILLIARDET, J. B. de Cassagnet (d. 1692)
French. Lieutenant-general; governor of Arras; wounded at Steenkirk, 1692, and died of his injuries at Mons, 20 August 1692.

TILLY, Albert-Octave, Comte T'Serclaes de (1646–1715)
Walloon. Grandson of Comte de Tilly, the Imperial general of the Thirty Years' War. Volunteer in the army of the Spanish Netherlands, 1665; lieutenant-colonel, 1670; major-general, 1685; commander of the army of Liège, 1689–97, in the rank of a Dutch lieutenant-general.

TILLY, Claude Frédéric, Comte T'Serclaes de (1651–1723)
Walloon. Younger brother of Albert-Octave. Volunteer in army of the Spanish Netherlands, 1672; major in Dutch army, 1675; colonel of horse, 1680; major-general, 1691; lieutenant-general of horse, 1695.

TIRIMONT, Comte de
Walloon. Conseilleur des Finances in the Spanish Netherlands.

TRUMBULL, Sir William (1639–1716)
English. Secretary of state, 1695–7; clerk of the signet, 1683–1716.

VALETTE, Louis Félix de Nogaret, Marquis de la (d. 1694)
French. Lieutenant-general in 1693.

VALSASSINE, François Sigismund de Tour et Taxis, Comte de
French. Maréchal de camp; lieutenant-general, 1714.

VAUBAN, Sebastien le Prestre de (1633–1707)
French. Foremost military engineer of the 17th and 18th centuries. Engineer to the King, 1653; commissary-general of the fortifications, 1654; used his system of 'three parallels' at Maastricht, 1673; brigadier, 1674; lieutenant-general, 1688, as a reward for the capture of Philippsburg; marshal of France, 1703; retired, 1704. He built or redesigned 160 fortresses.

VAUDEMONT, Charles Henri de Lorraine, Prince de (1649–1723)
Lorrainer. Illegitimate son of Duke Charles IV of Lorraine. Entered army of the Spanish Netherlands; commanded rearguard at Seneffe, 1674; commander of Spanish cavalry in the Netherlands, 1688–91; commander-in-chief of army of the Spanish Netherlands, 1691–7; governor of Milan, 1698; fought for Spain in Italy during War of the Spanish Succession. Confidant and trusted subordinate of William III.

VENDÔME, Louis Joseph, Duc de (1654–1712)
French. Served under Turenne in Germany and Alsace, 1672–5; brigadier, 1677; maréchal de camp, 1678; lieutenant-general, 1688; fought at Leuse, Steenkirk and in Italy under Catinat; marshal of France, 1695; commanded French forces in Catalonia, 1695–7; commanded French army in Italy, 1702; commander of French armies in Flanders, 1706; defeated at Oudenarde, 1708; commander in Spain, 1710.

VERTILLAC, Nicholas de la Brousse, Comte de (d. 1693)
French. General by 1692; governor of Mons, 1691–3; killed whilst commanding a convoy escort.

VILLADARIAS: see CASTILLO-TAXARDO

VILLARS, Claude Louis Hector, Duc de (1653–1734)
French. Served at Maastricht, 1673, and Seneffe, 1674; colonel of cavalry, 1674; volunteer in Imperial army in Hungary, 1683–8; promotion in the French army was slow as he was not a favourite of Louvois; brigadier, 1688; maréchal de camp, 1689; lieutenant-general, 1693; ambassador to Vienna, 1697–9; marshal of France,

1702, after victory at Friedlingen; crushed Camisard Revolt, 1704; created duke, 1705; commander on Upper Rhine, 1704–8; commanded French armies in Low Countries after 1709 beating Eugene at Denain, 1712; severely wounded in the knee at Malplaquet, 1709; member of council of regency, 1715–18; marshal-general of the French armies in Italy during War of the Polish Succession, 1733–4; died in Turin, 1734.

VILLEROI, François de Neufville, Duc de (1644–1730)
French. Favourite of Louis XIV. Lieutenant-general, 1677; marshal of France, 1693; commanded French armies in Low Countries, 1695–7; commanded in Italy, 1702, but was captured at Cremona; commanded French armies in Low Countries, 1703–6; dismissed after defeat at Ramillies, 1706.

WALDECK, Georg Friedrich, Graf von (1620–92)
German. After service in the armies of Brandenburg and Brunswick he entered Dutch employ in 1672; served at defence of the 'Water Line', 1672, and was promoted 1st field marshal of Dutch army; commanded a Franconian contingent during the relief of Vienna, 1683; Imperial field marshal in Hungary, 1683–5; marshal-general of the Dutch armies, 1688; commander of Anglo-Dutch forces in Low Countries, 1688–90. Responsible for training both William III and the Dutch armed forces.

WEI(J)BNOM, Johann Theobald van (1610–91)
Dutch. Major-general, 1675; lieutenant-general, 1683.

WIJNBERGEN, Ditmar van (d. 1696)
Dutch. Colonel, 1678; major-general, 1691; governor of Bergen-op-Zoom, 1694.

WÜRTTEMBERG-NEÚSTADT, Ferdinand Wilhelm, Duke of (1659–1701)
German. Member of cadet branch of the ruling family of Württemberg. Entered Württemberg army, 1675, but soon transferred to Danish establishment; lieutenant-general, 1682; volunteer at relief of Vienna, 1683; served in Imperial armies in Hungary, 1683–6; recalled to Denmark, 1686; commander-in-chief of Danish corps in Ireland, 1690–1; commanded Danish corps in Allied army in Low Countries, 1691–7; governor of Dutch Flanders, 1697; commanded Saxon and Polish armies against the Turks, 1698; commanded Danish forces in Holstein against the Swedes, 1700; died in his governorship in Flanders after complications from a head wound which he had received in 1685. Württemberg was a thorough professional; in 1697 he was one of the few Allied officers disappointed to hear of the Peace of Rijswijk.

WYMBERG: *see* **WIJNBERGEN**

XIMENES, Joseph, Duc de (d. 1706)
Of a Spanish family which settled in France in 1641. Colonel of the Régiment de Royal-Rousillon; lieutenant-general.

ZUYLESTEIN, Willem van Nassau, Heer van (1649–1718)
Dutch. Cousin of William III. Major-general in Dutch army, 1691; lieutenant-general in English army, 1690; master of the robes to William III; created Earl of Rochford, 1695.

Index